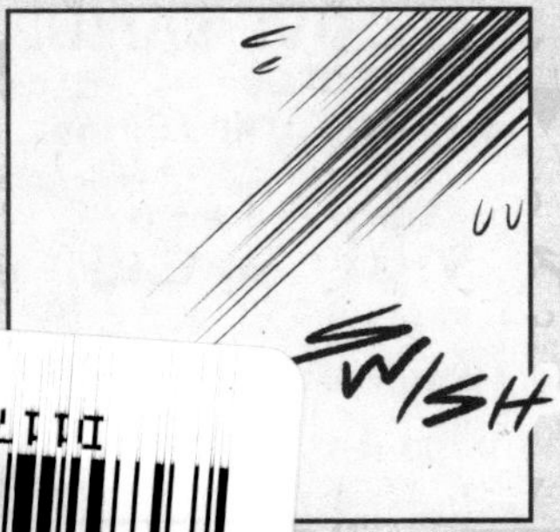
SWISH

Yusei Matsui

When I was a boy, I was good at dodging in dodgeball. I would always be the last player remaining, so I felt like a hero.

The boy in this story is a historical personage who re-creates that feeling for me. If readers find a little-known period in Japanese history to be thrilling through the unique perspective he provides, both the boy from 30 years ago and the boy from 700 years ago would be proud.

Yusei Matsui was born on the last day of January in Saitama Prefecture, Japan. He has been drawing manga since elementary school. Some of his favorite manga series are *Bobobo-bo Bo-bobo*, *JoJo's Bizarre Adventure*, and *Ultimate Muscle*. Matsui learned his trade working as an assistant to manga artist Yoshio Sawai, creator of *Bobobo-bo Bo-bobo*. In 2005, Matsui debuted his original manga *Neuro: Supernatural Detective* in *Weekly Shonen Jump*. In 2007, *Neuro* was adapted into an anime. In 2012, *Assassination Classroom* began serialization in *Weekly Shonen Jump*.

THE ELUSIVE SAMURAI
VOLUME 1
SHONEN JUMP Edition

Story and Art by
Yusei Matsui

Translation & English Adaptation John Werry
Touch-Up Art & Lettering John Hunt
Designer Jimmy Presler
Editor Mike Montesa

NIGEJOZU NO WAKAGIMI © 2021 by Yusei Matsui
All rights reserved.
First published in Japan in 2021 by SHUEISHA Inc., Tokyo.
English translation rights arranged by SHUEISHA Inc.

The stories, characters, and incidents mentioned
in this publication are entirely fictional.

Printed in Canada

Published by VIZ Media, LLC
P.O. Box 77010
San Francisco, CA 94107

10 9 8 7 6 5 4 3 2 1
First printing, July 2022

PARENTAL ADVISORY
THE ELUSIVE SAMURAI is rated T for Teen and is
recommended for ages 13 and up. This volume
contains realistic and fantasy violence.

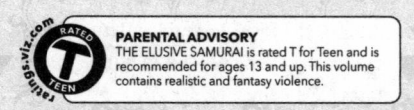

viz.com

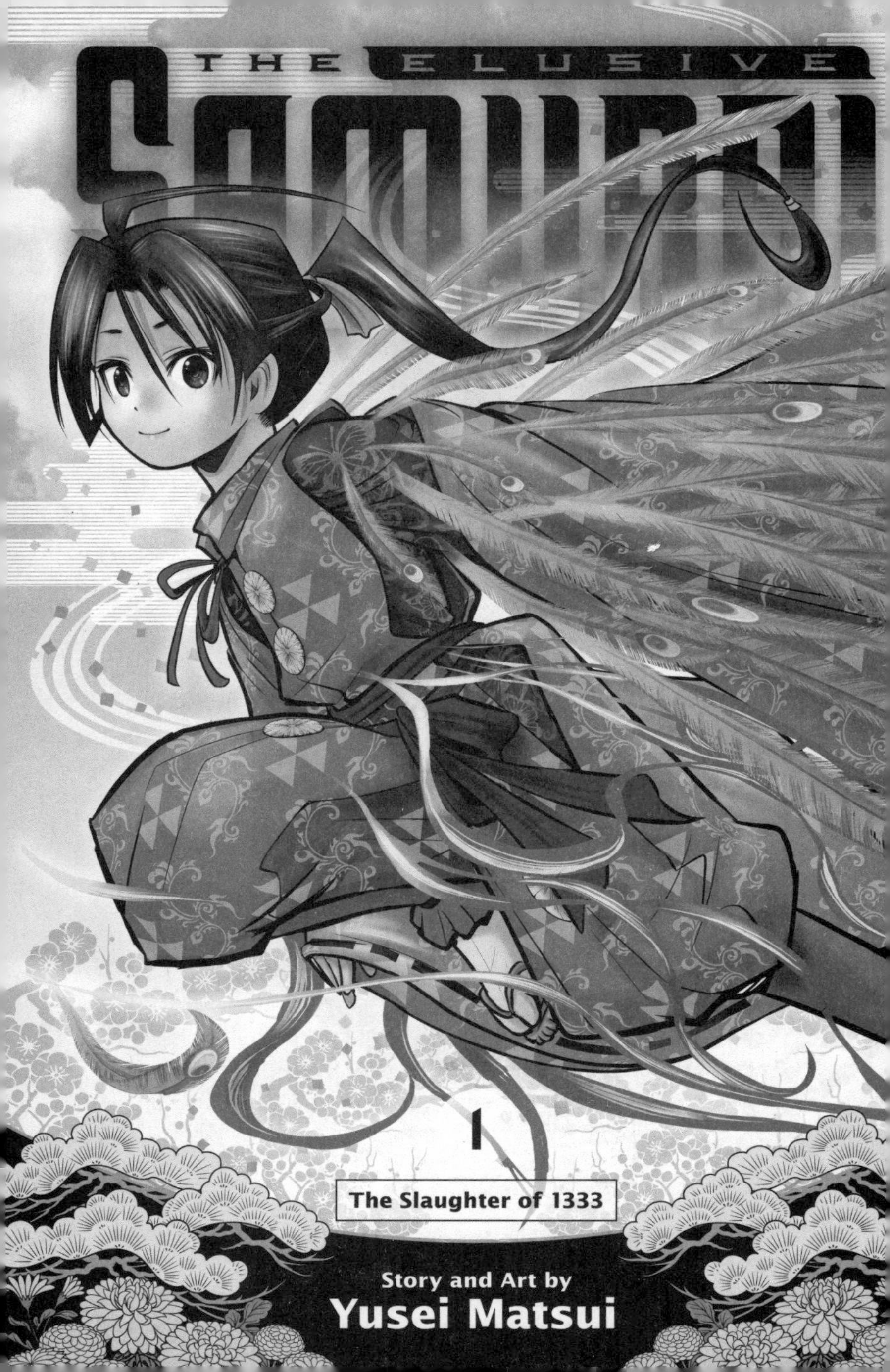
THE ELUSIVE
SAMURAI
1
The Slaughter of 1333
Story and Art by
Yusei Matsui

THE ELUSIVE SAMURAI

① 1

CONTENTS

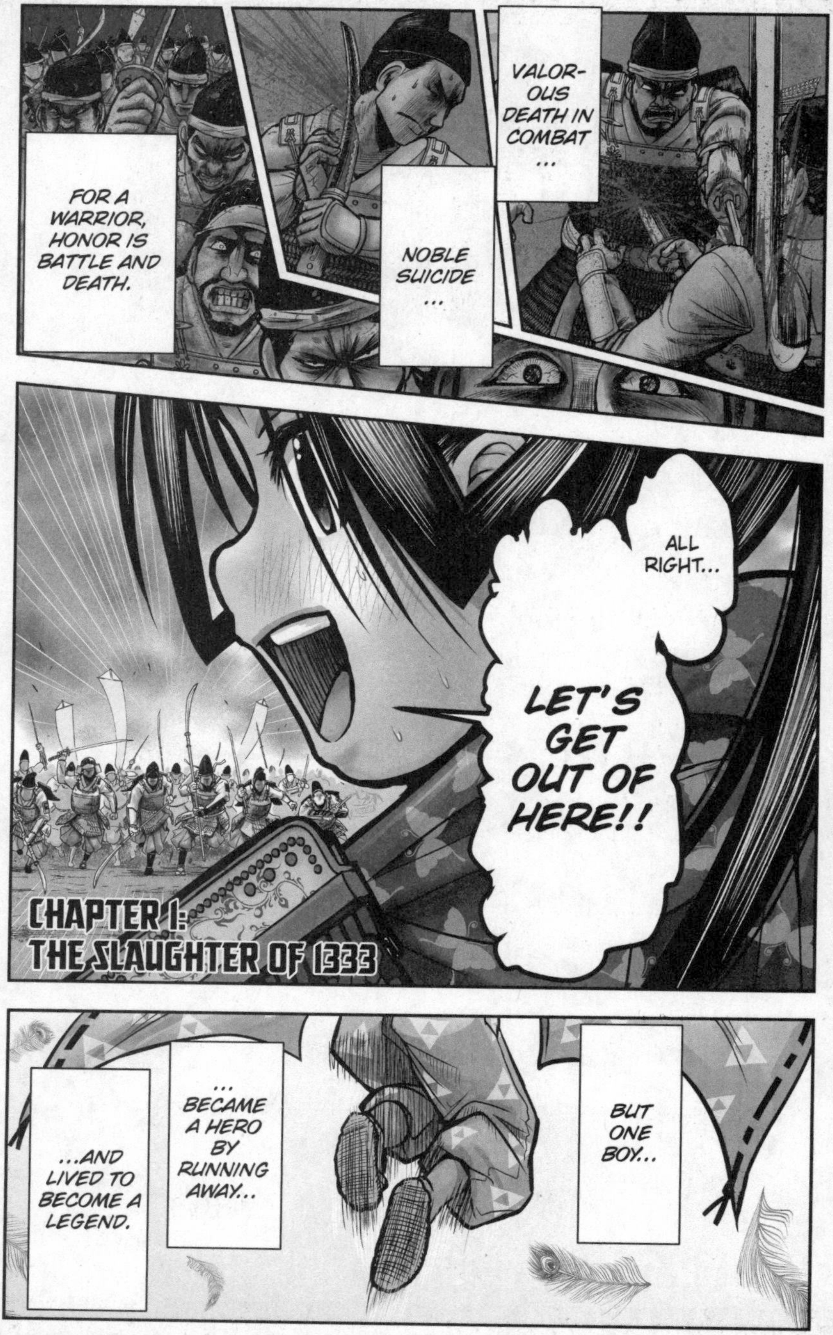
VALOR-OUS DEATH IN COMBAT ...
NOBLE SUICIDE ...
FOR A WARRIOR, HONOR IS BATTLE AND DEATH.
ALL RIGHT...
LET'S GET OUT OF HERE!!
CHAPTER 1: THE SLAUGHTER OF 1333
BUT ONE BOY...
... BECAME A HERO BY RUNNING AWAY...
...AND LIVED TO BECOME A LEGEND.

CHAPTER 1: THE SLAUGHTER OF 1333

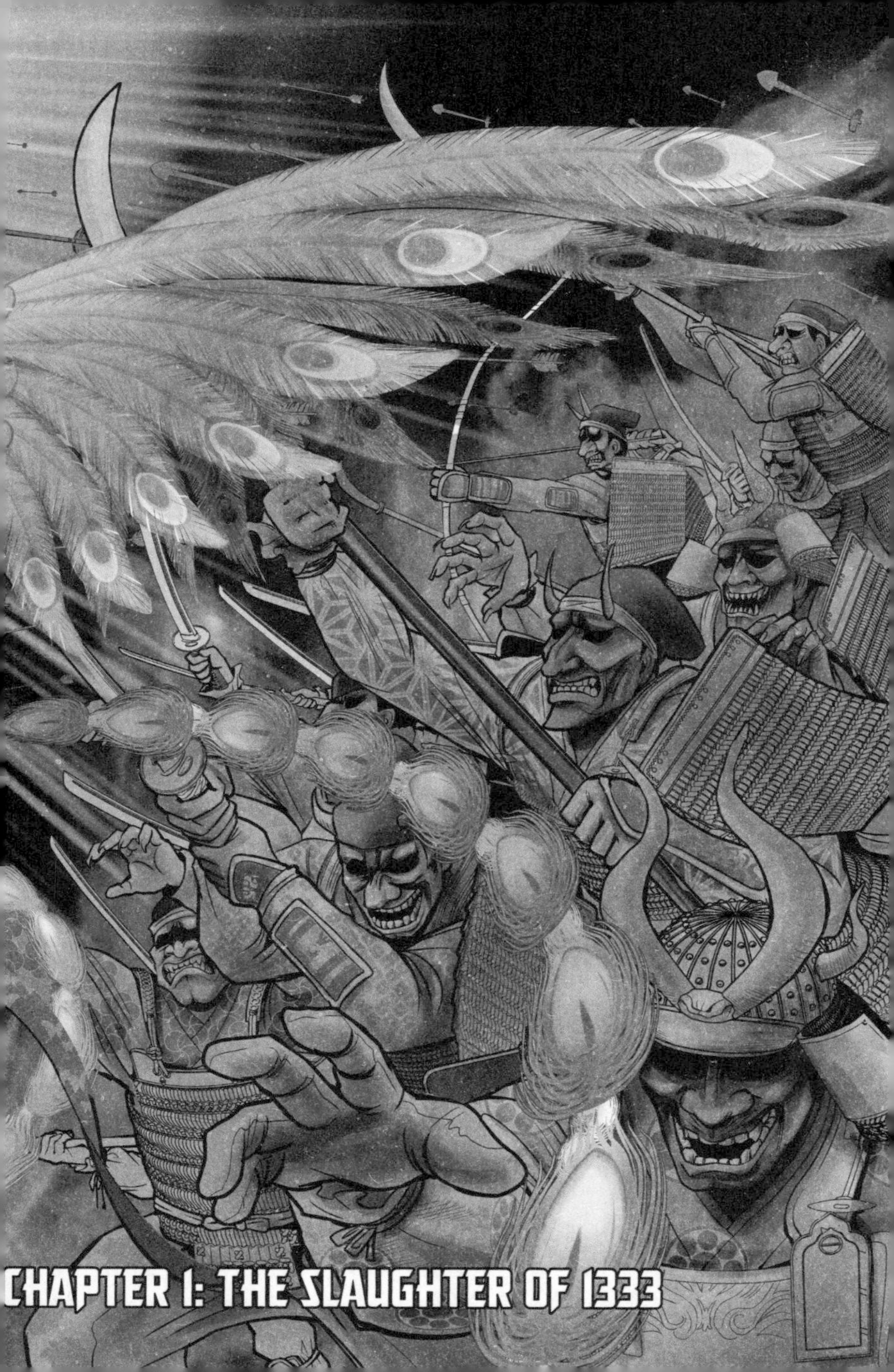

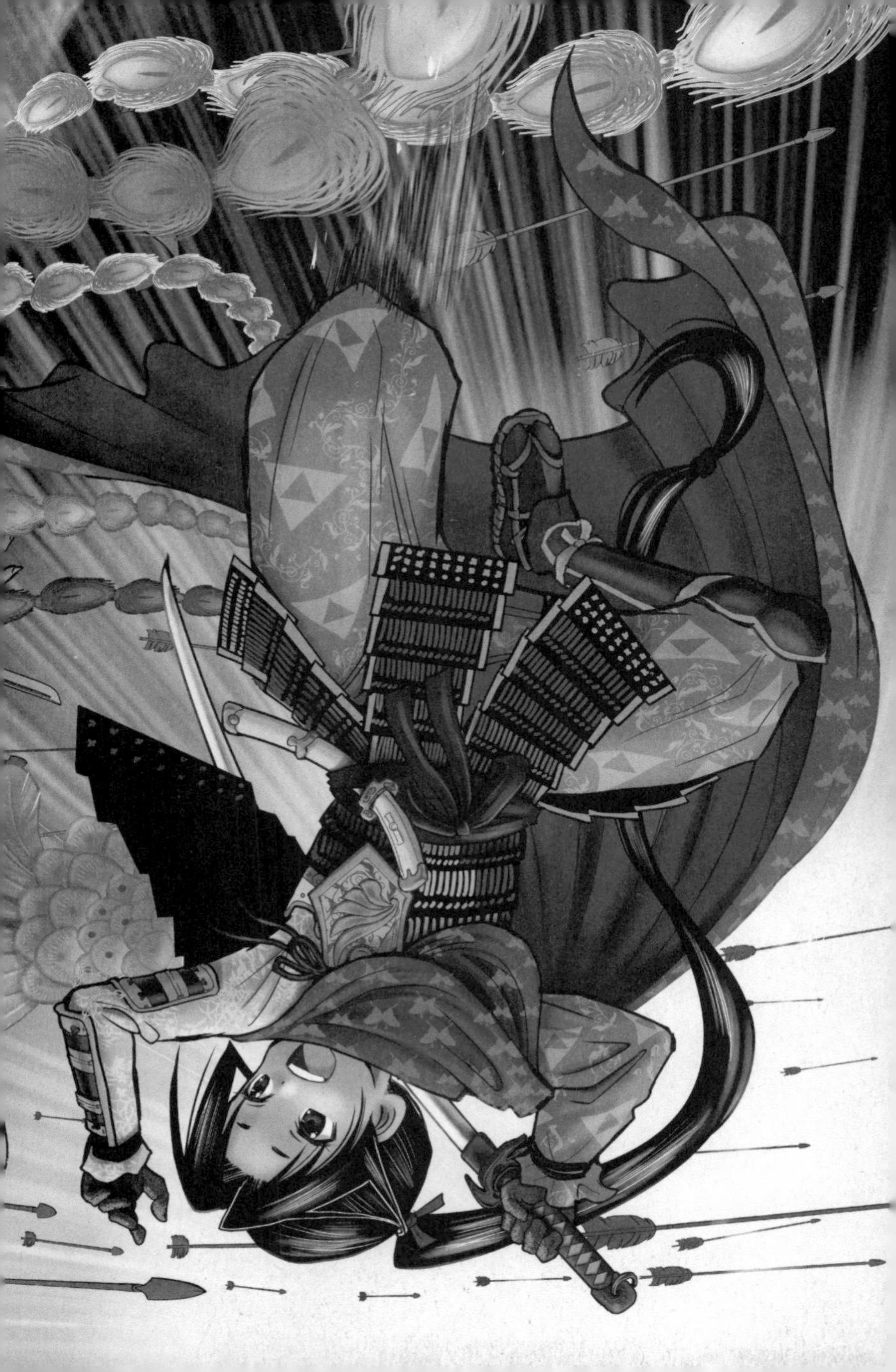

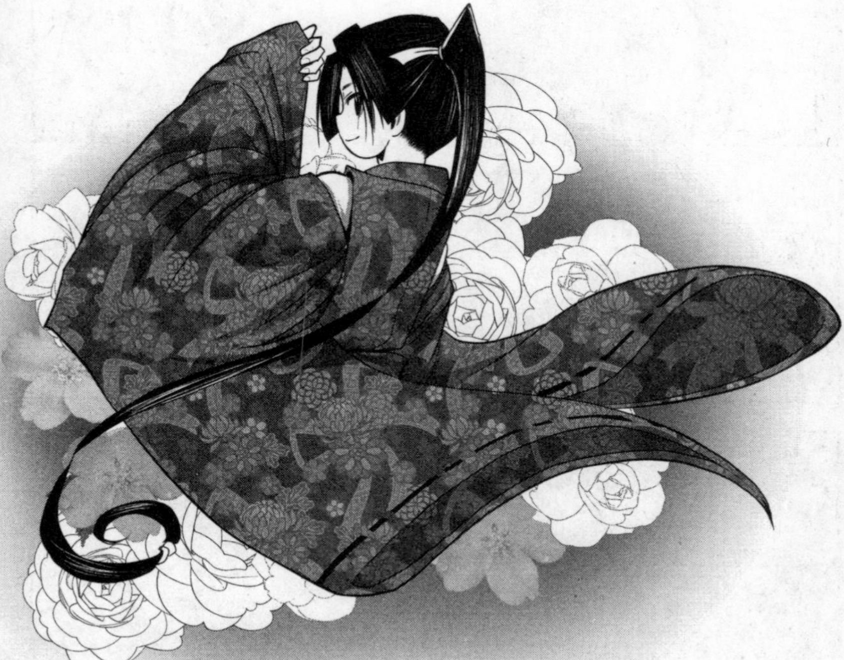

THE ELUSIVE SAMURAI

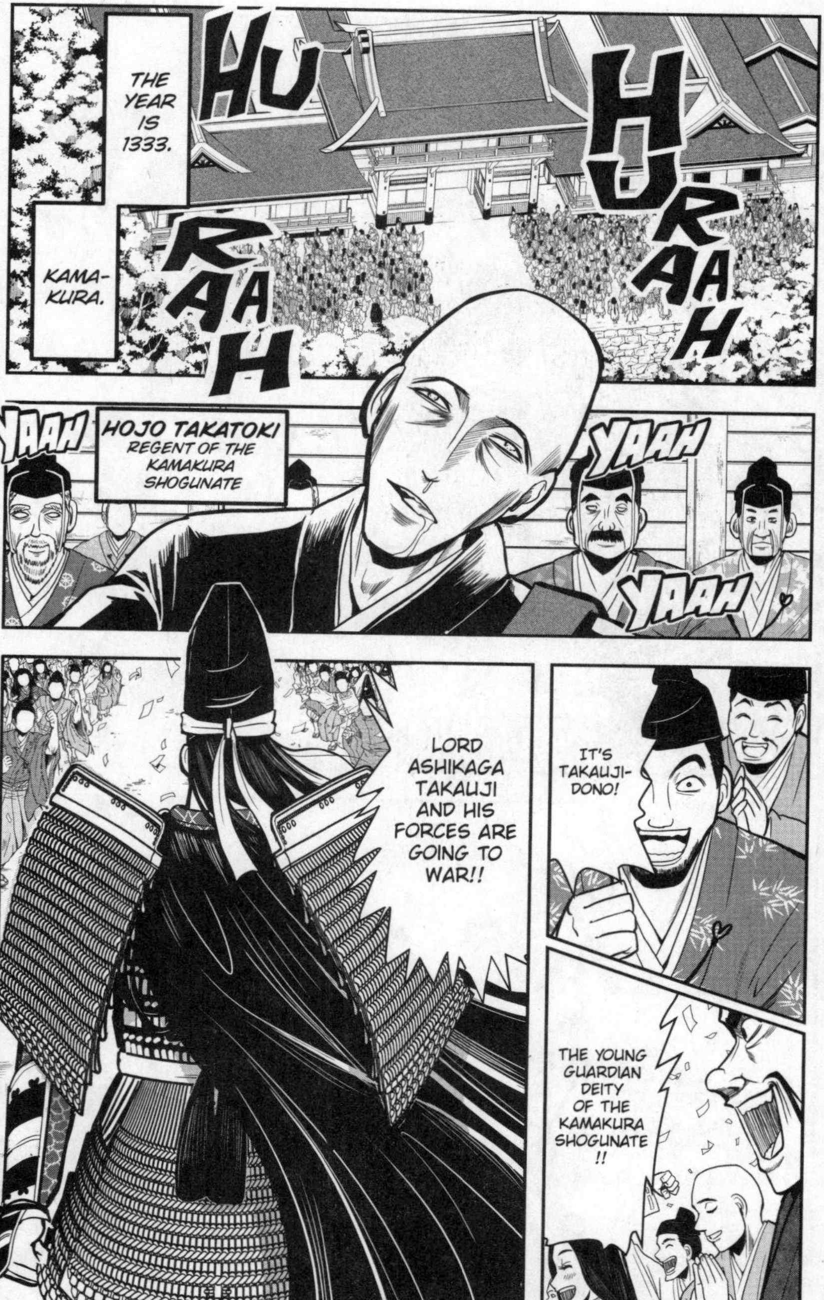
HURAAH
THE YEAR IS 1333.
HU
KAMA-KURA.
RAAH
YAAH
YAAH
HOJO TAKATOKI
REGENT OF THE KAMAKURA SHOGUNATE
YAAH
IT'S TAKAUJI-DONO!
THE YOUNG GUARDIAN DEITY OF THE KAMAKURA SHOGUNATE!!
LORD ASHIKAGA TAKAUJI AND HIS FORCES ARE GOING TO WAR!!

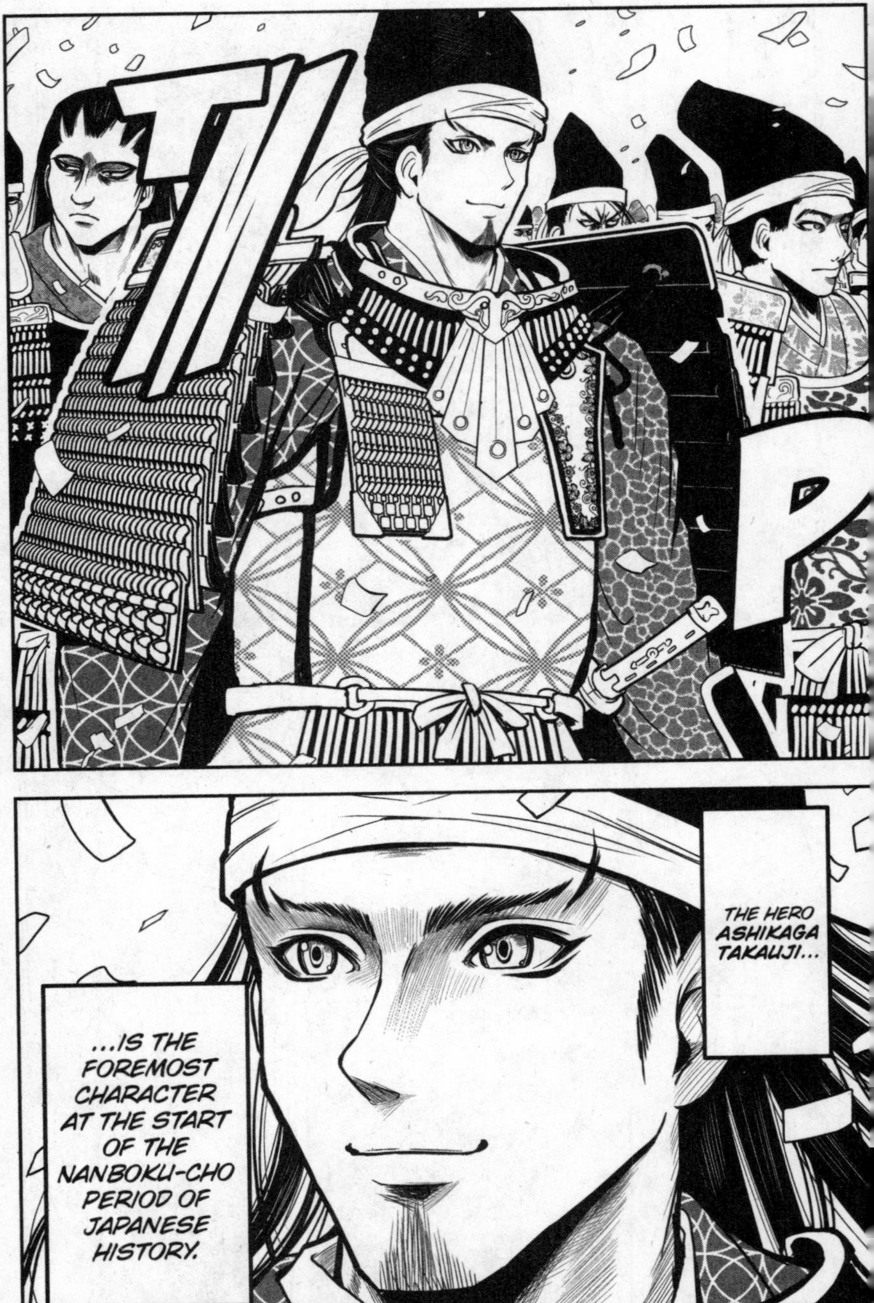

THE HERO ASHIKAGA TAKAUJI...
...IS THE FOREMOST CHARACTER AT THE START OF THE NANBOKU-CHO PERIOD OF JAPANESE HISTORY.

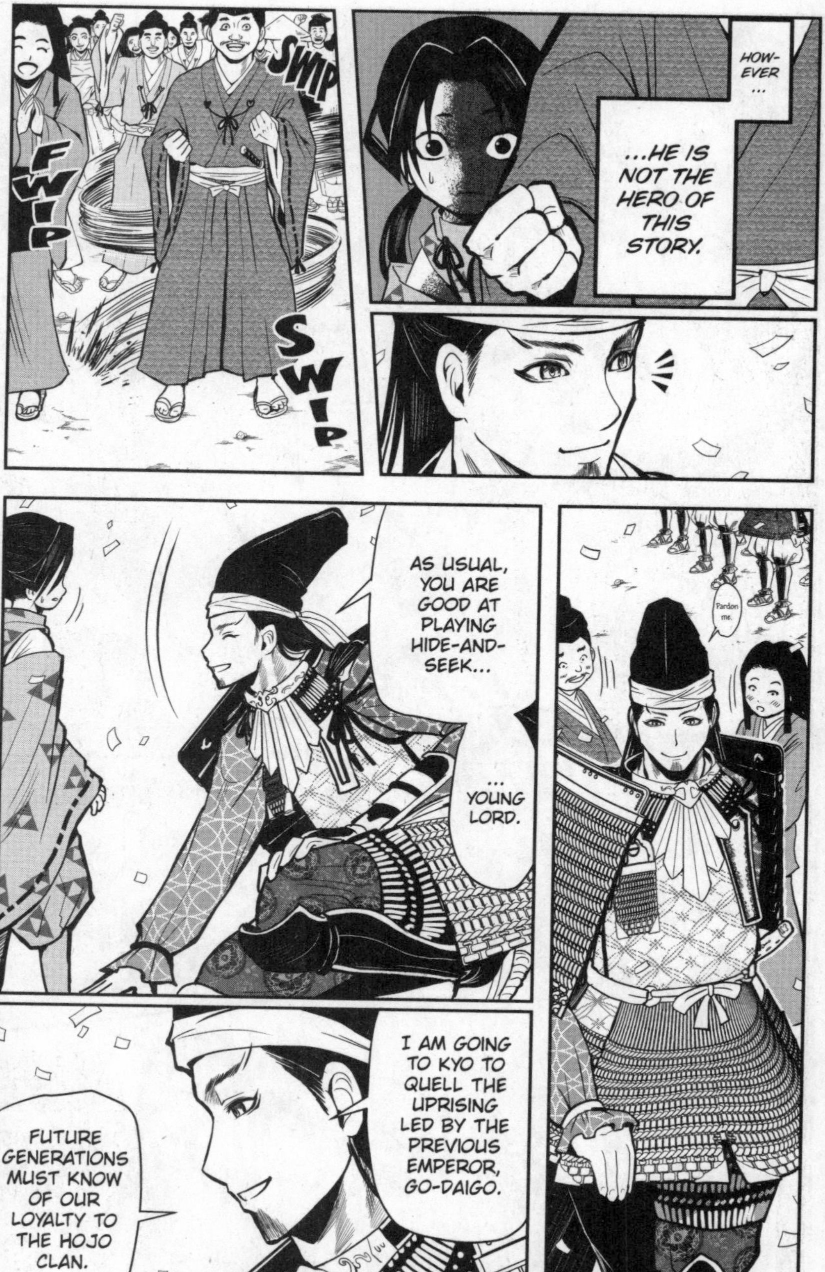
HOW-EVER...
...HE IS NOT THE HERO OF THIS STORY.
SWIP
FWIP
SWIP
Pardon me.
AS USUAL, YOU ARE GOOD AT PLAYING HIDE-AND-SEEK...
...YOUNG LORD.
I AM GOING TO KYO TO QUELL THE UPRISING LED BY THE PREVIOUS EMPEROR, GO-DAIGO.
FUTURE GENERATIONS MUST KNOW OF OUR LOYALTY TO THE HOJO CLAN.

*KYO: MODERN KYOTO

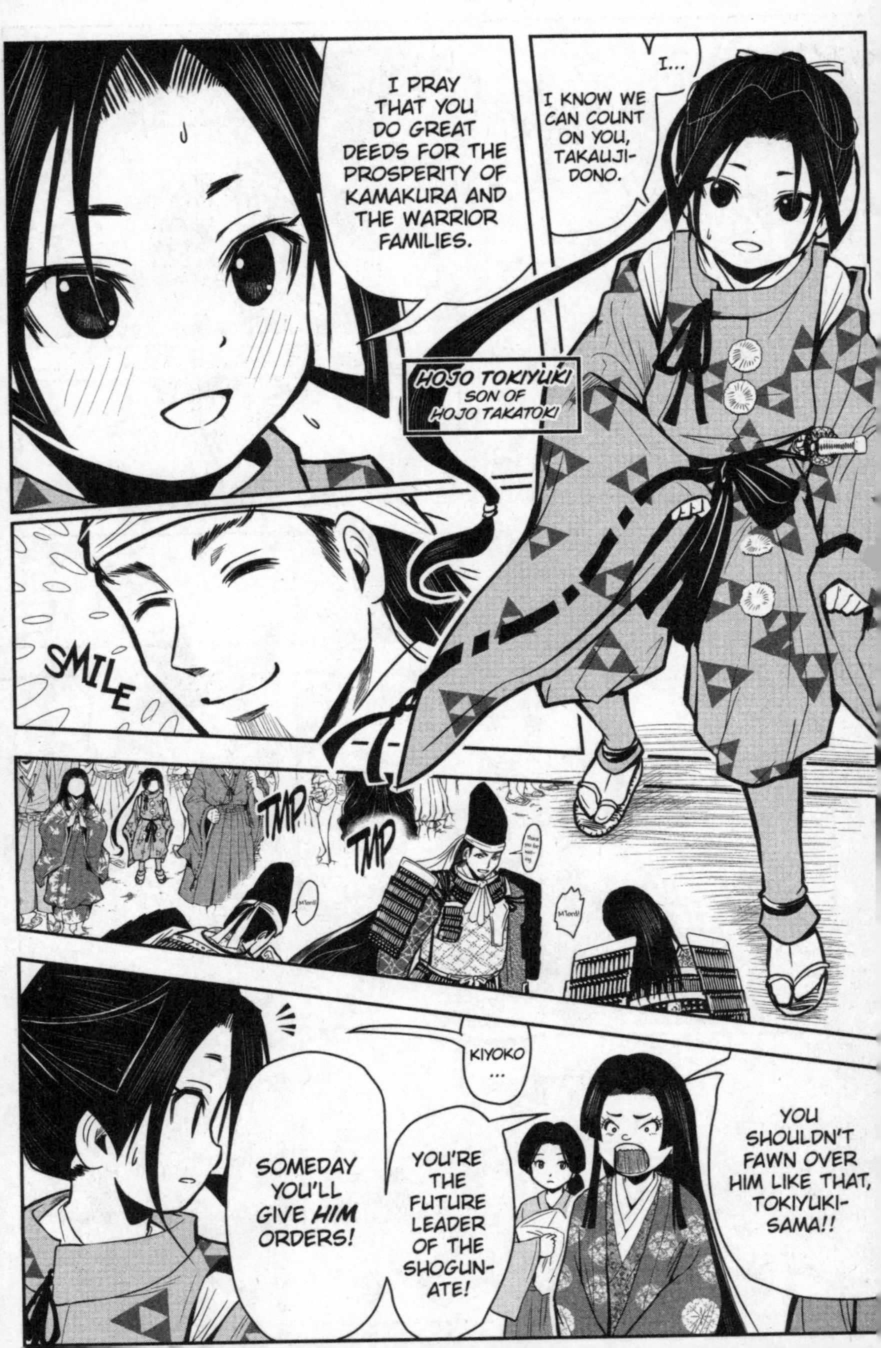
I...
I KNOW WE CAN COUNT ON YOU, TAKAUJI-DONO.
I PRAY THAT YOU DO GREAT DEEDS FOR THE PROSPERITY OF KAMAKURA AND THE WARRIOR FAMILIES.
HOJO TOKIYUKI SON OF HOJO TAKATOKI
SMILE
M'lord!
Thank you for wait-ing.
TMP
TMP
M'lord!
YOU SHOULDN'T FAWN OVER HIM LIKE THAT, TOKIYUKI-SAMA!!
KIYOKO ...
YOU'RE THE FUTURE LEADER OF THE SHOGUN-ATE!
SOMEDAY YOU'LL GIVE *HIM* ORDERS!

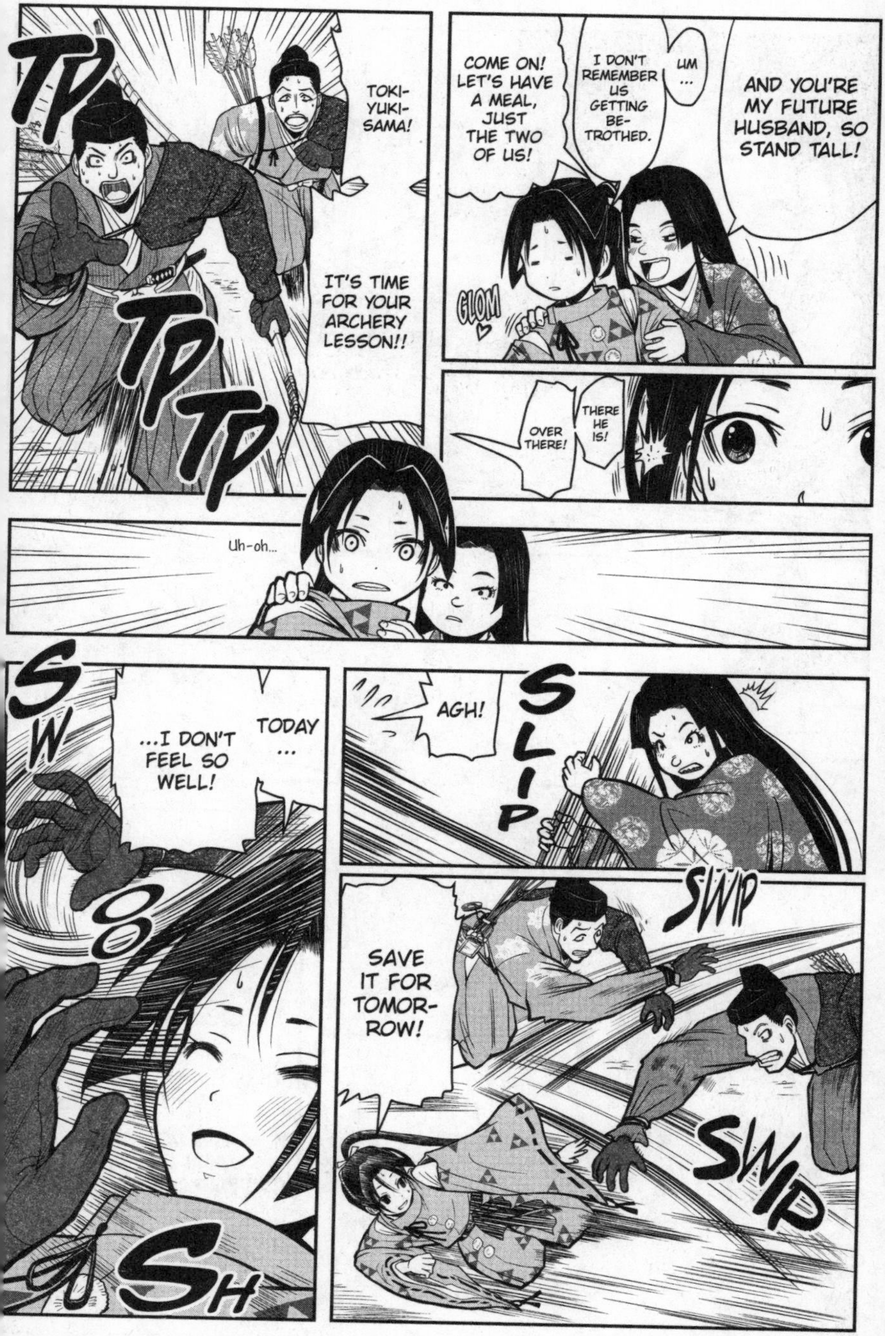
AND YOU'RE MY FUTURE HUSBAND, SO STAND TALL!
UM ...
I DON'T REMEMBER US GETTING BE-TROTHED.
COME ON! LET'S HAVE A MEAL, JUST THE TWO OF US!
GLOM
THERE HE IS!
OVER THERE!
TOKI-YUKI-SAMA!
IT'S TIME FOR YOUR ARCHERY LESSON!!
TP
TP TP TP
Uh-oh...
AGH!
SLIP
SWIP
SAVE IT FOR TOMOR-ROW!
SWIP
TODAY ...
...I DON'T FEEL SO WELL!
SWOOSH

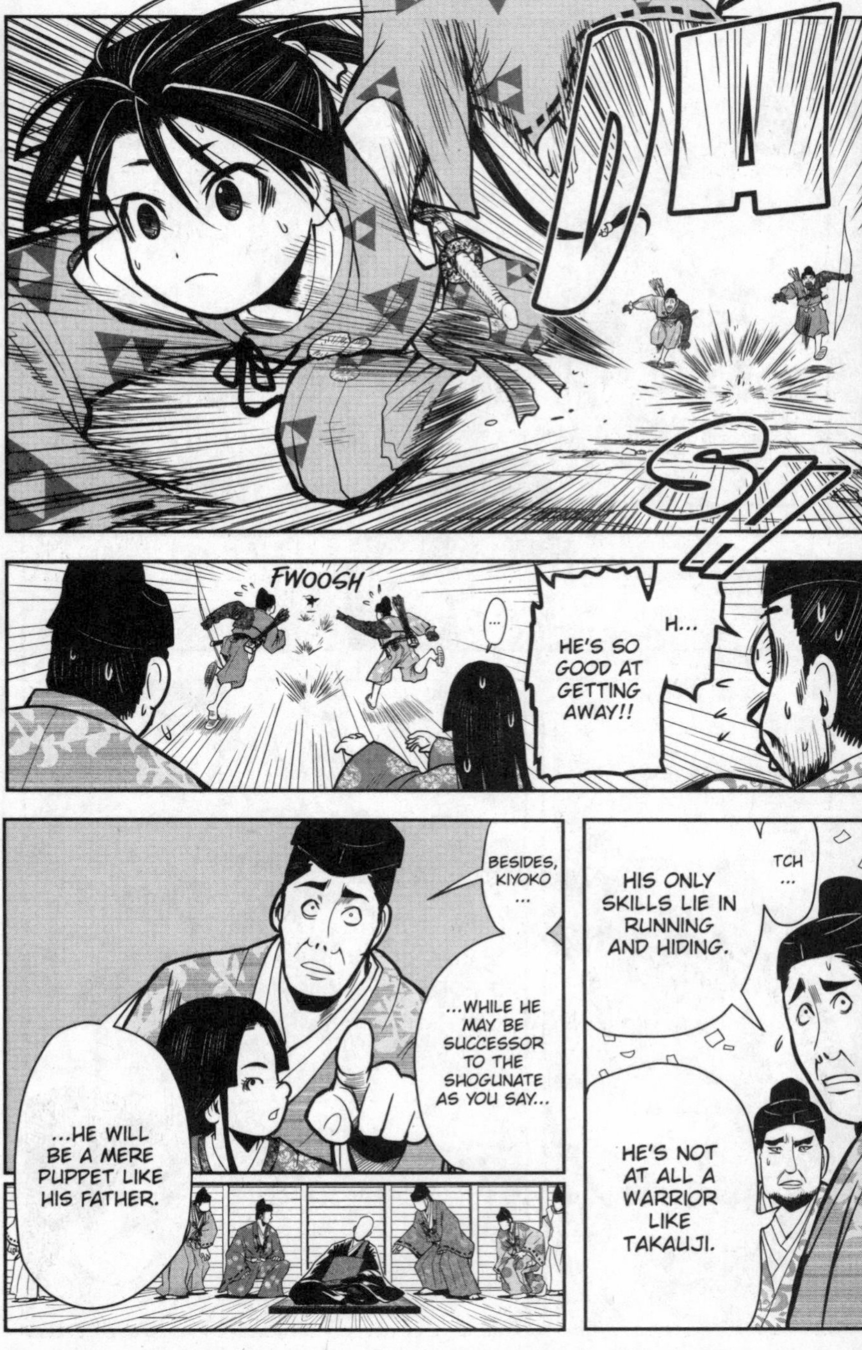
DASH
FWOOSH
...
H...
HE'S SO GOOD AT GETTING AWAY!!
TCH ...
HIS ONLY SKILLS LIE IN RUNNING AND HIDING.
HE'S NOT AT ALL A WARRIOR LIKE TAKAUJI.
BESIDES, KIYOKO ...
...WHILE HE MAY BE SUCCESSOR TO THE SHOGUNATE AS YOU SAY...
...HE WILL BE A MERE PUPPET LIKE HIS FATHER.

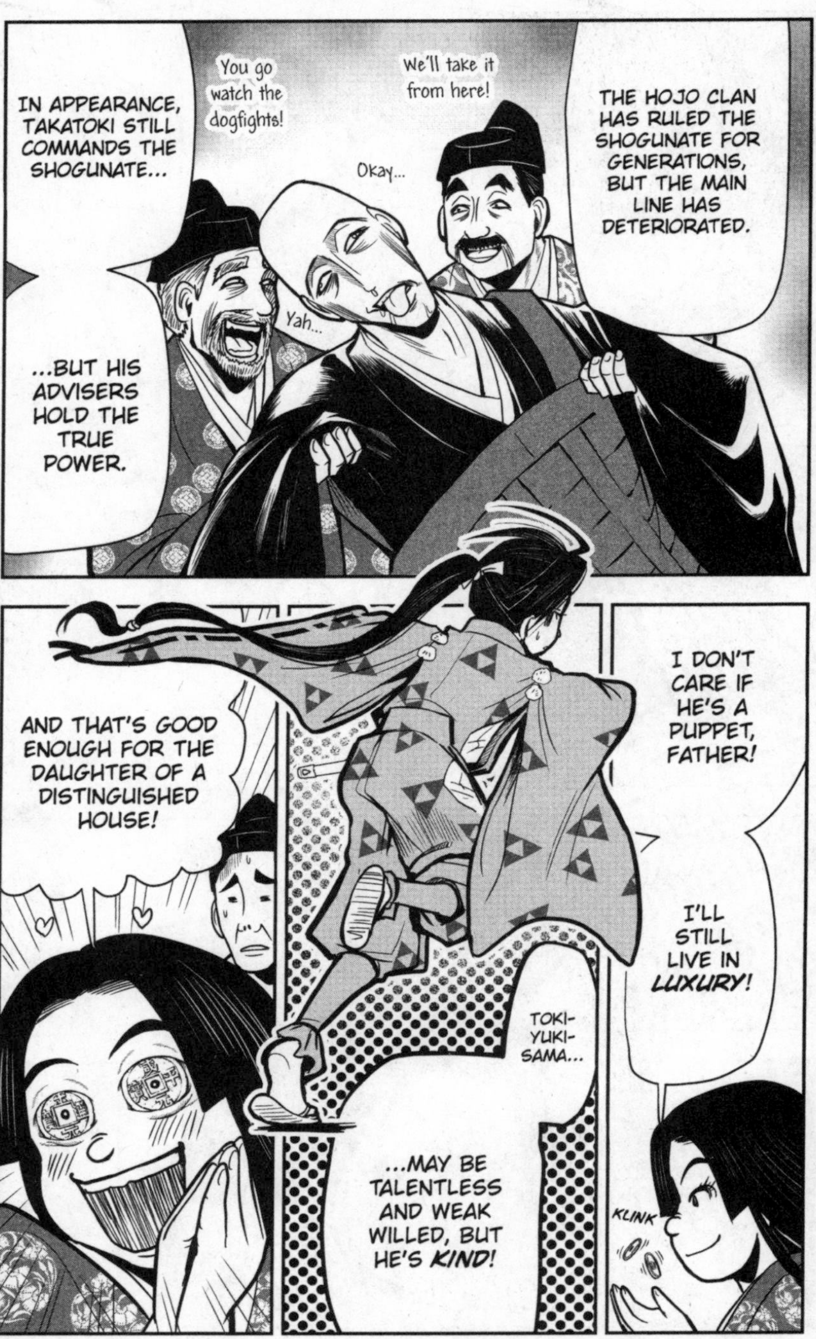
THE HOJO CLAN HAS RULED THE SHOGUNATE FOR GENERATIONS, BUT THE MAIN LINE HAS DETERIORATED.
We'll take it from here!
You go watch the dogfights!
Okay...
IN APPEARANCE, TAKATOKI STILL COMMANDS THE SHOGUNATE...
Yah...
...BUT HIS ADVISERS HOLD THE TRUE POWER.
I DON'T CARE IF HE'S A PUPPET, FATHER!
I'LL STILL LIVE IN LUXURY!
KLINK
TOKI-YUKI-SAMA...
...MAY BE TALENTLESS AND WEAK WILLED, BUT HE'S KIND!
AND THAT'S GOOD ENOUGH FOR THE DAUGHTER OF A DISTINGUISHED HOUSE!

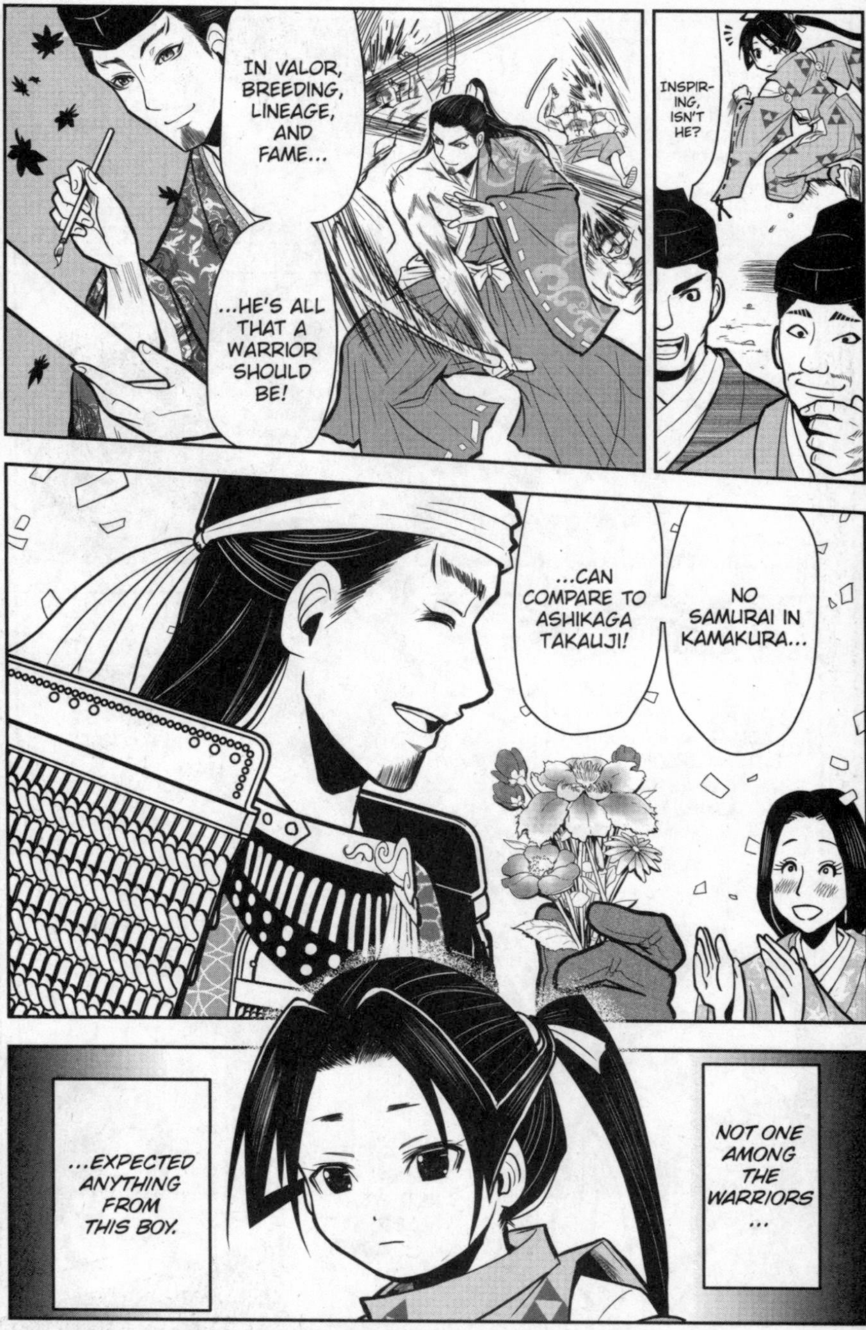
INSPIRING, ISN'T HE?
IN VALOR, BREEDING, LINEAGE, AND FAME...
...HE'S ALL THAT A WARRIOR SHOULD BE!
NO SAMURAI IN KAMAKURA...
...CAN COMPARE TO ASHIKAGA TAKAUJI!
NOT ONE AMONG THE WARRIORS...
...EXPECTED ANYTHING FROM THIS BOY.

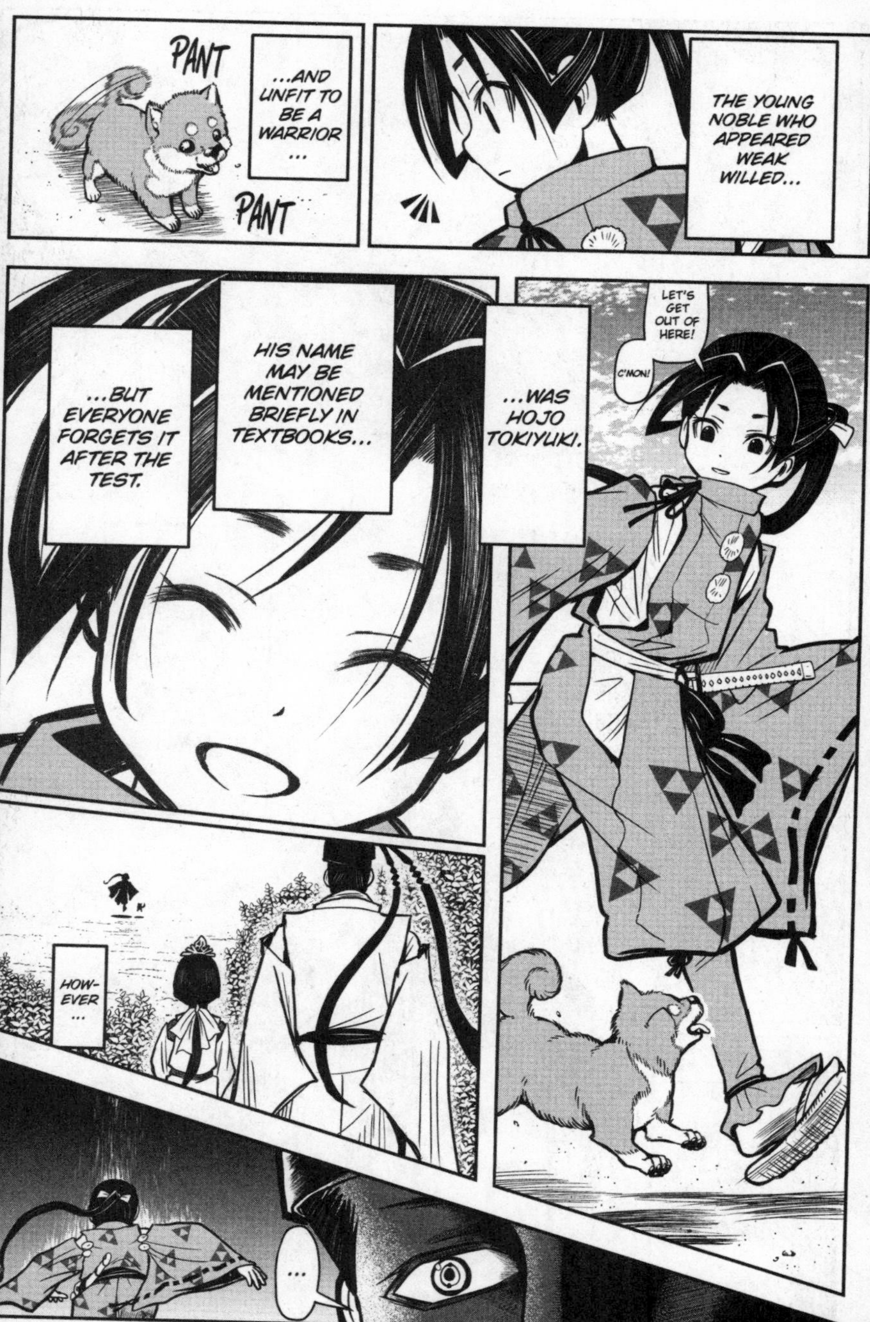
THE YOUNG NOBLE WHO APPEARED WEAK WILLED...
...AND UNFIT TO BE A WARRIOR ...
PANT
PANT
LET'S GET OUT OF HERE!
C'MON!
...WAS HOJO TOKIYUKI.
HIS NAME MAY BE MENTIONED BRIEFLY IN TEXTBOOKS...
...BUT EVERYONE FORGETS IT AFTER THE TEST.
HOW-EVER ...
...

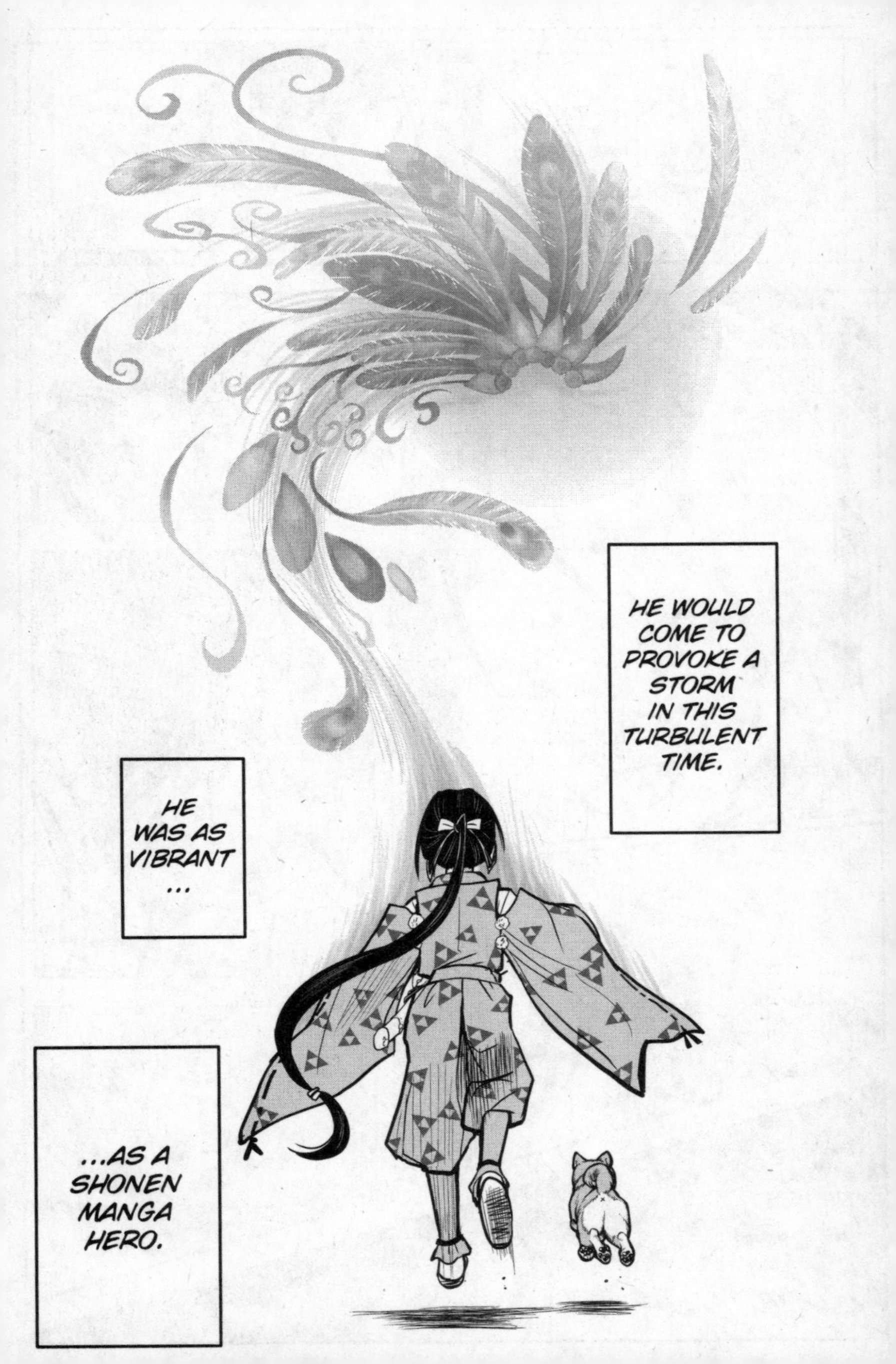
HE WOULD COME TO PROVOKE A STORM IN THIS TURBULENT TIME.
HE WAS AS VIBRANT ...
...AS A SHONEN MANGA HERO.

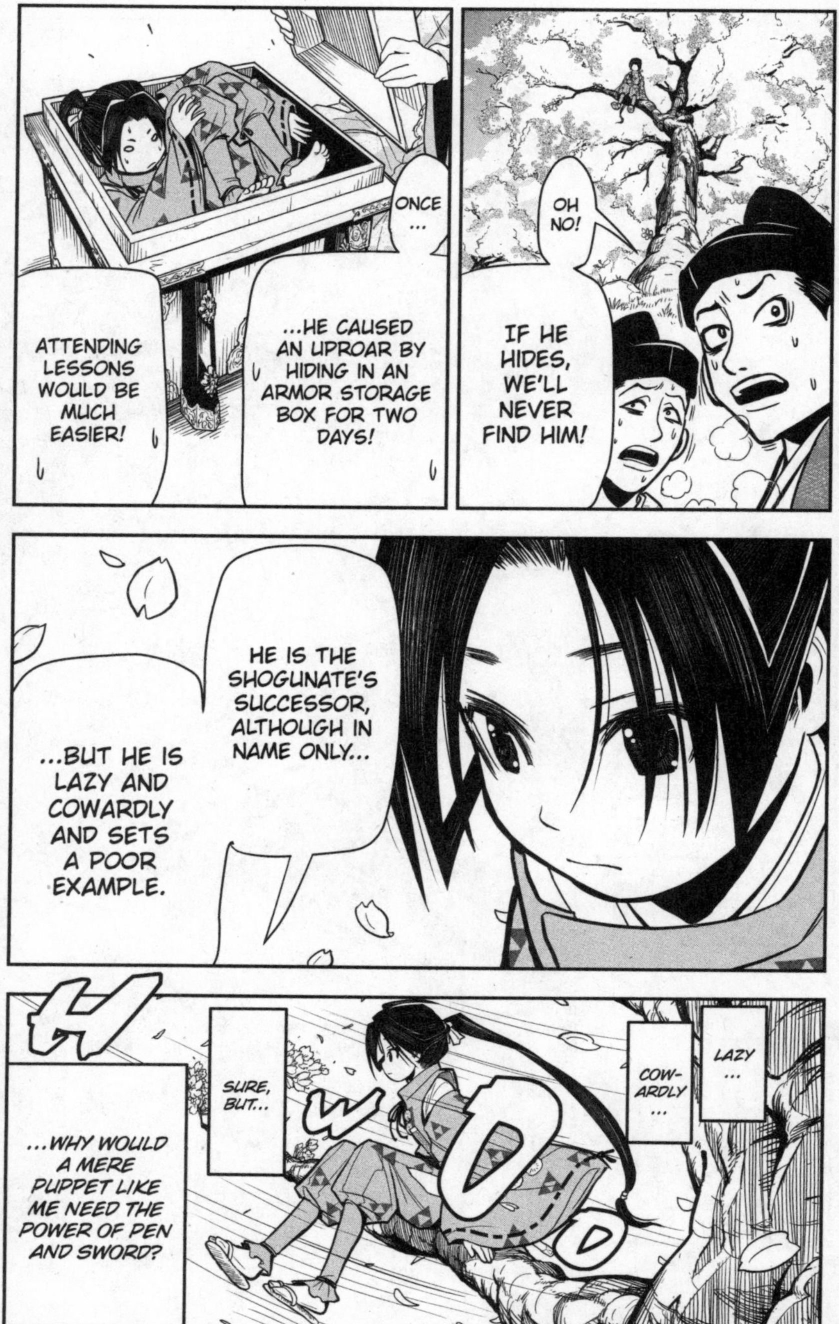
OH NO!
IF HE HIDES, WE'LL NEVER FIND HIM!
ONCE ...
...HE CAUSED AN UPROAR BY HIDING IN AN ARMOR STORAGE BOX FOR TWO DAYS!
ATTENDING LESSONS WOULD BE MUCH EASIER!
HE IS THE SHOGUNATE'S SUCCESSOR, ALTHOUGH IN NAME ONLY...
...BUT HE IS LAZY AND COWARDLY AND SETS A POOR EXAMPLE.
LAZY ...
COW-ARDLY ...
WOOSH
SURE, BUT...
...WHY WOULD A MERE PUPPET LIKE ME NEED THE POWER OF PEN AND SWORD?

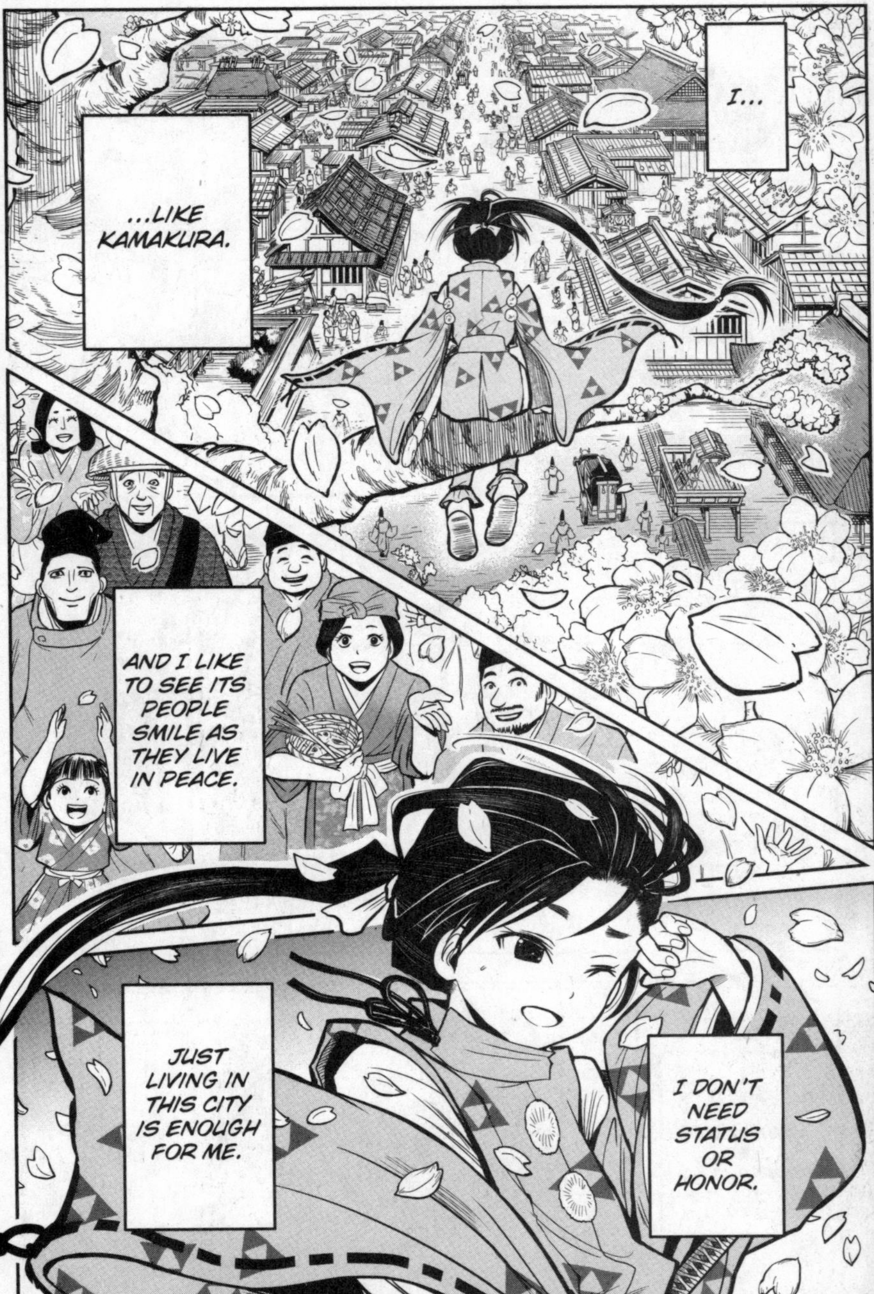
I...
...LIKE KAMAKURA.
AND I LIKE TO SEE ITS PEOPLE SMILE AS THEY LIVE IN PEACE.
I DON'T NEED STATUS OR HONOR.
JUST LIVING IN THIS CITY IS ENOUGH FOR ME.

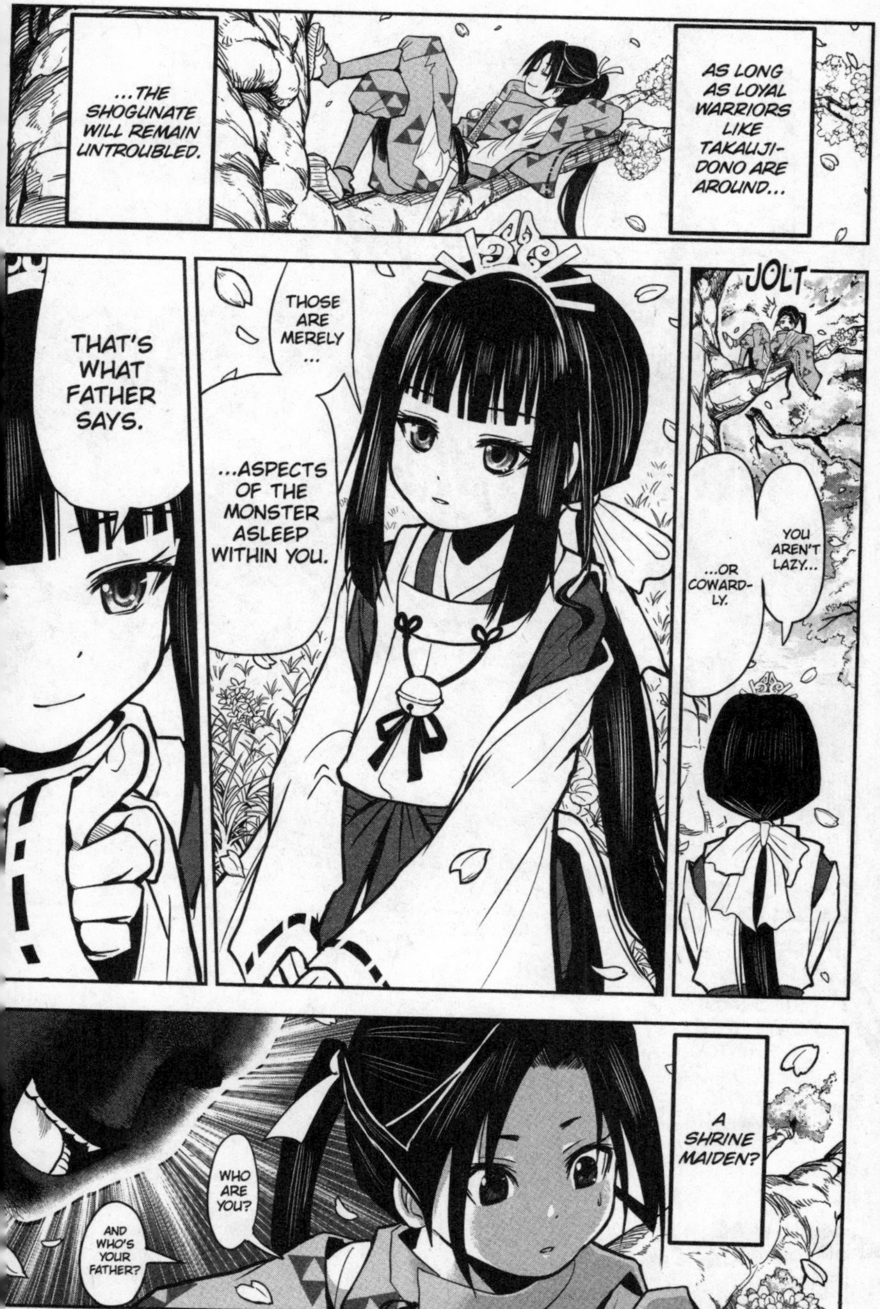
AS LONG AS LOYAL WARRIORS LIKE TAKAUJI-DONO ARE AROUND...
...THE SHOGUNATE WILL REMAIN UNTROUBLED.
JOLT
YOU AREN'T LAZY...
...OR COWARDLY.
THOSE ARE MERELY...
...ASPECTS OF THE MONSTER ASLEEP WITHIN YOU.
THAT'S WHAT FATHER SAYS.
A SHRINE MAIDEN?
WHO ARE YOU?
AND WHO'S YOUR FATHER?

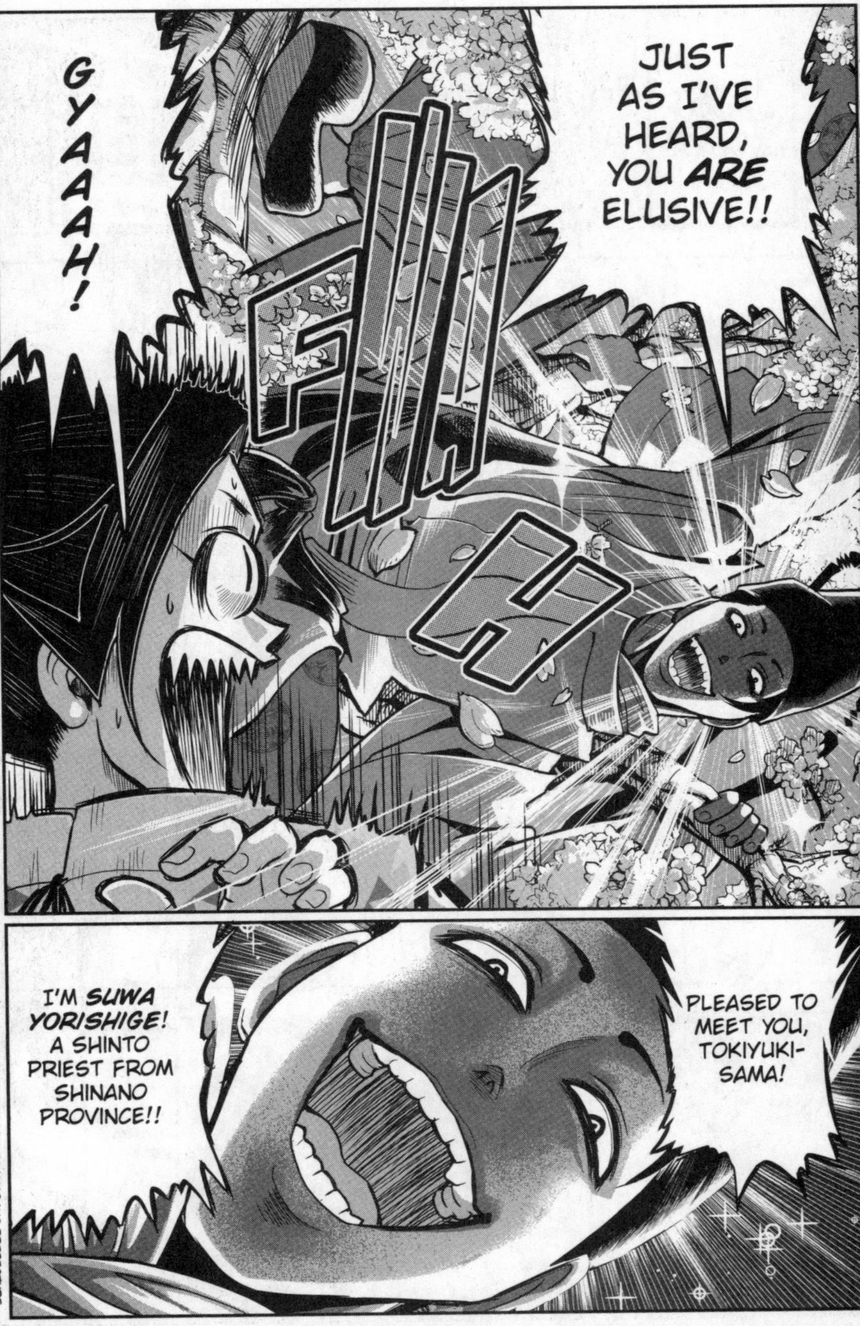
JUST AS I'VE HEARD, YOU ARE ELUSIVE!!
GYAAAAH!
PLEASED TO MEET YOU, TOKIYUKI-SAMA!
I'M SUWA YORISHIGE! A SHINTO PRIEST FROM SHINANO PROVINCE!!

*SHINANO PROVINCE: NEAR MODERN-DAY NAGANO PREFECTURE

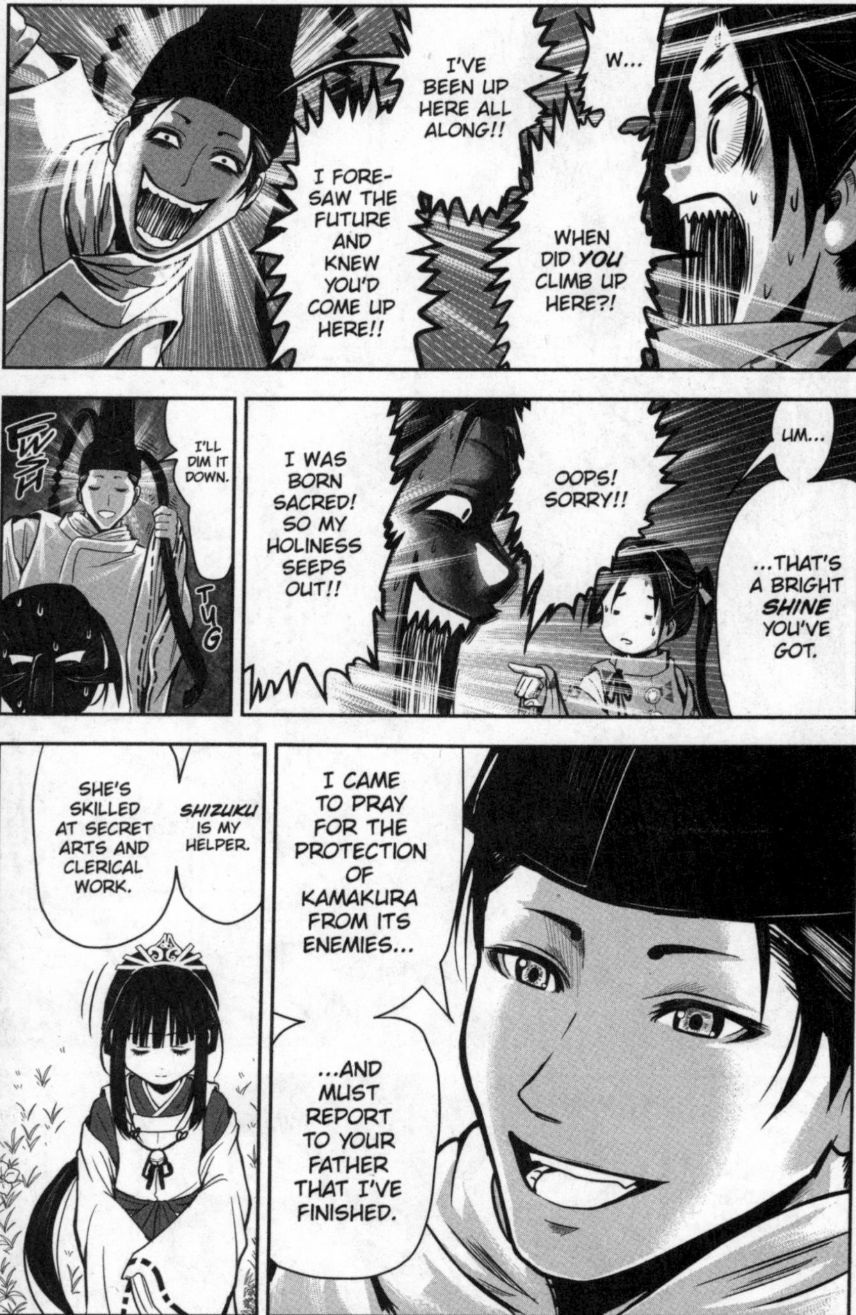
W...
WHEN DID YOU CLIMB UP HERE?!
I'VE BEEN UP HERE ALL ALONG!!
I FORE-SAW THE FUTURE AND KNEW YOU'D COME UP HERE!!
UM...
...THAT'S A BRIGHT SHINE YOU'VE GOT.
OOPS! SORRY!!
I WAS BORN SACRED! SO MY HOLINESS SEEPS OUT!!
I'LL DIM IT DOWN.
FWSH
TUG
I CAME TO PRAY FOR THE PROTECTION OF KAMAKURA FROM ITS ENEMIES...
...AND MUST REPORT TO YOUR FATHER THAT I'VE FINISHED.
SHIZUKU IS MY HELPER.
SHE'S SKILLED AT SECRET ARTS AND CLERICAL WORK.

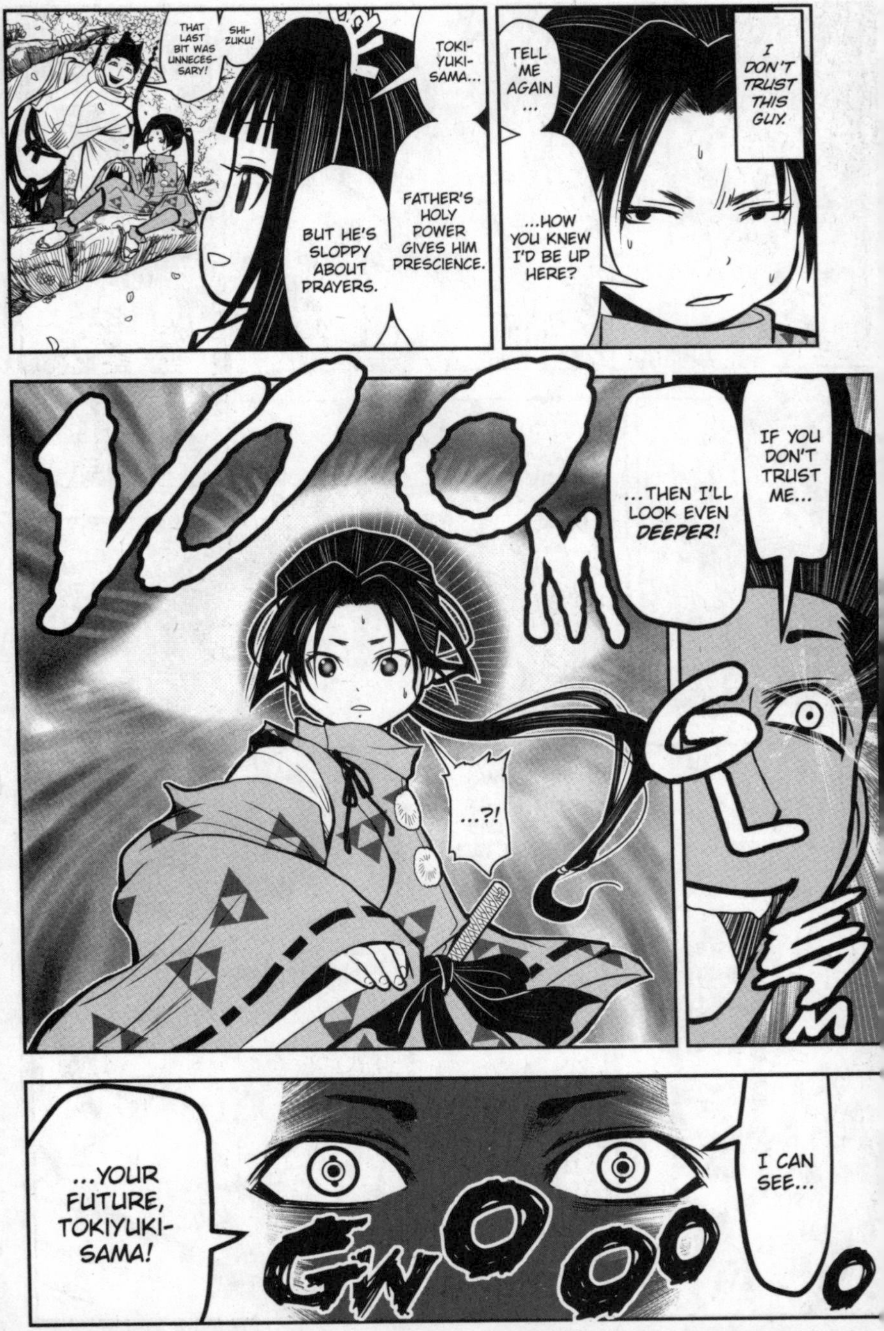
I DON'T TRUST THIS GUY.
TELL ME AGAIN ...
...HOW YOU KNEW I'D BE UP HERE?
TOKI-YUKI-SAMA...
FATHER'S HOLY POWER GIVES HIM PRESCIENCE.
BUT HE'S SLOPPY ABOUT PRAYERS.
SHI-ZUKU!
THAT LAST BIT WAS UNNECES-SARY!
IF YOU DON'T TRUST ME...
...THEN I'LL LOOK EVEN DEEPER!
GLM
VOOM
...?!
I CAN SEE...
...YOUR FUTURE, TOKIYUKI-SAMA!
GWOOOOO

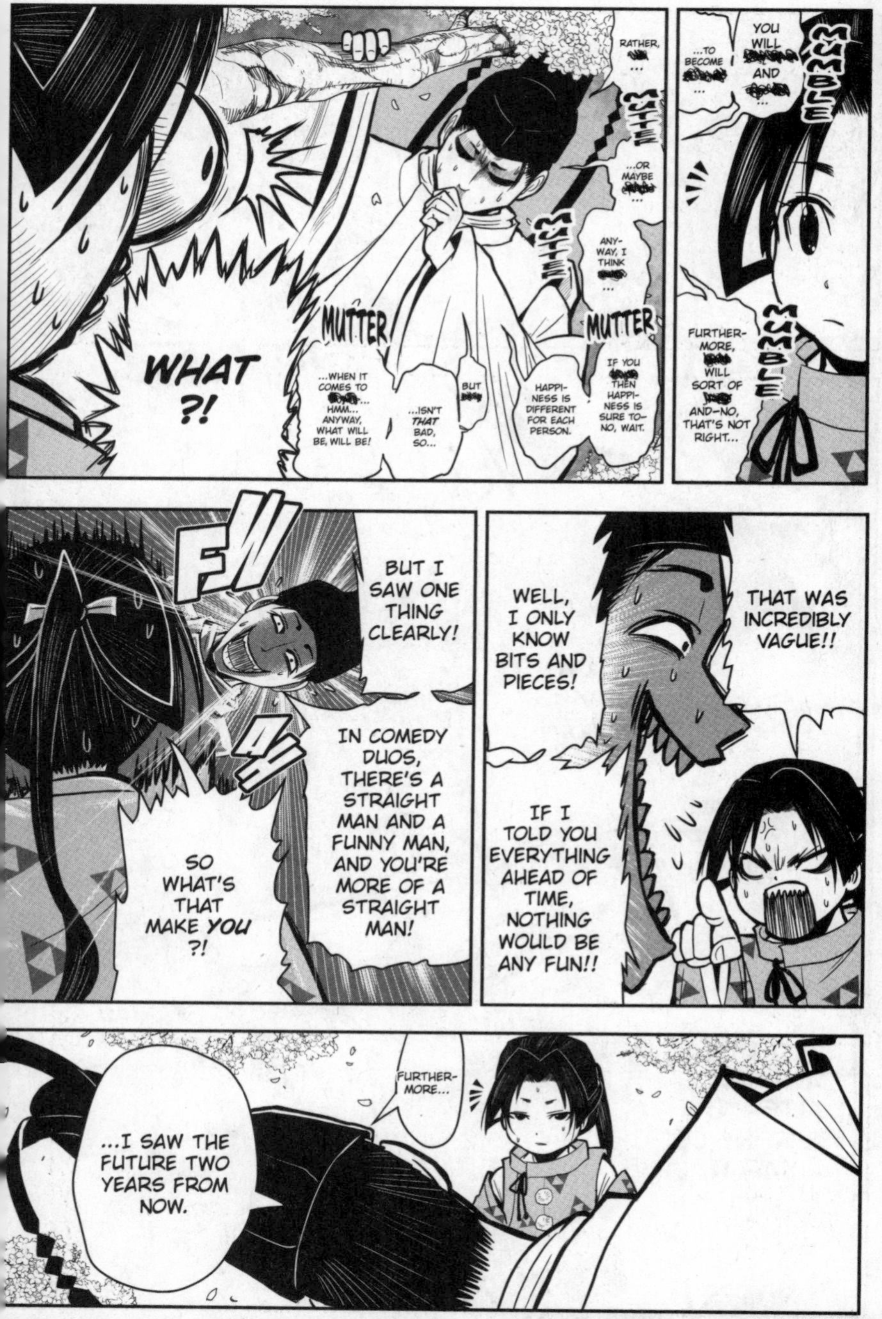
MUMBLE
YOU WILL [redacted] AND [redacted]...
...TO BECOME [redacted]...
FURTHERMORE, [redacted] WILL SORT OF [redacted] AND—NO, THAT'S NOT RIGHT...
MUMBLE
RATHER, [redacted]...
MUTTER
...OR MAYBE [redacted]...
MUTTER
ANYWAY, I THINK [redacted]...
MUTTER
IF YOU [redacted] THEN HAPPINESS IS SURE TO—NO, WAIT.
HAPPINESS IS DIFFERENT FOR EACH PERSON.
BUT [redacted]
...ISN'T THAT BAD, SO...
MUTTER
...WHEN IT COMES TO [redacted]... HMM... ANYWAY, WHAT WILL BE, WILL BE!
WHAT ?!
THAT WAS INCREDIBLY VAGUE!!
WELL, I ONLY KNOW BITS AND PIECES!
IF I TOLD YOU EVERYTHING AHEAD OF TIME, NOTHING WOULD BE ANY FUN!!
BUT I SAW ONE THING CLEARLY!
IN COMEDY DUOS, THERE'S A STRAIGHT MAN AND A FUNNY MAN, AND YOU'RE MORE OF A STRAIGHT MAN!
SO WHAT'S THAT MAKE YOU ?!
FURTHERMORE...
...I SAW THE FUTURE TWO YEARS FROM NOW.

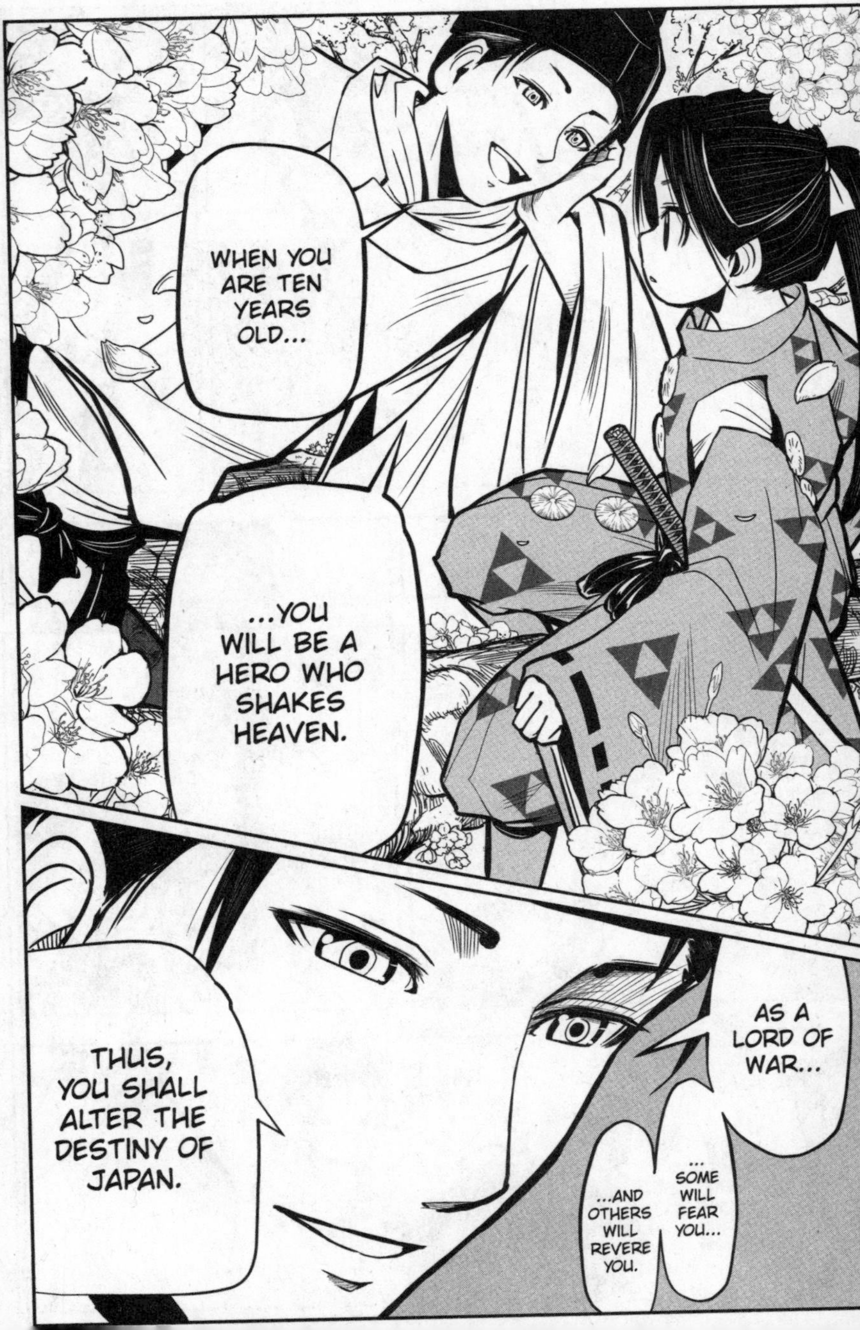
WHEN YOU ARE TEN YEARS OLD...
...YOU WILL BE A HERO WHO SHAKES HEAVEN.
AS A LORD OF WAR...
...SOME WILL FEAR YOU...
...AND OTHERS WILL REVERE YOU.
THUS, YOU SHALL ALTER THE DESTINY OF JAPAN.

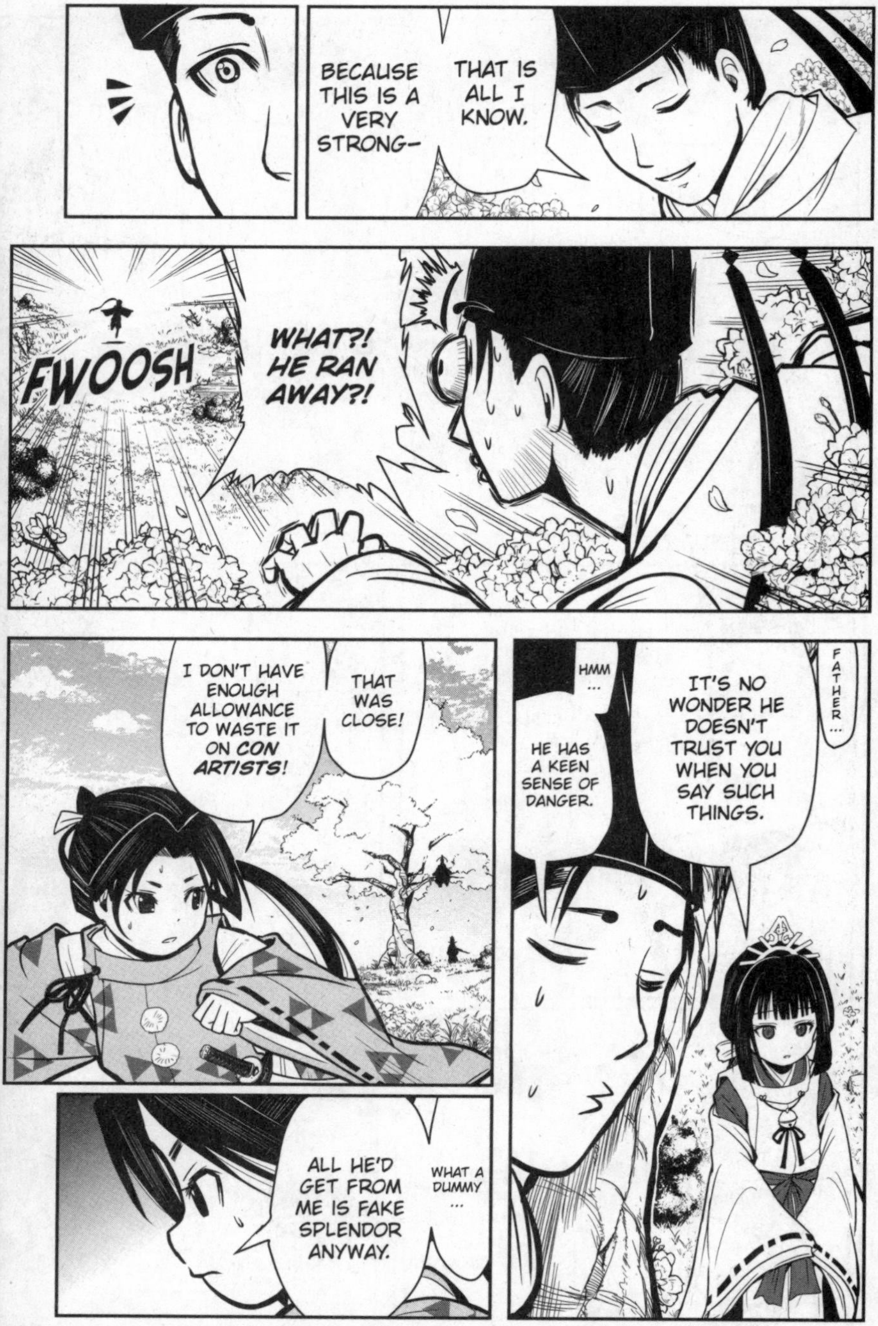
THAT IS ALL I KNOW.
BECAUSE THIS IS A VERY STRONG-
WHAT?! HE RAN AWAY?!
FWOOSH
FATHER...
IT'S NO WONDER HE DOESN'T TRUST YOU WHEN YOU SAY SUCH THINGS.
HMM...
HE HAS A KEEN SENSE OF DANGER.
THAT WAS CLOSE!
I DON'T HAVE ENOUGH ALLOWANCE TO WASTE IT ON CON ARTISTS!
WHAT A DUMMY...
ALL HE'D GET FROM ME IS FAKE SPLENDOR ANYWAY.

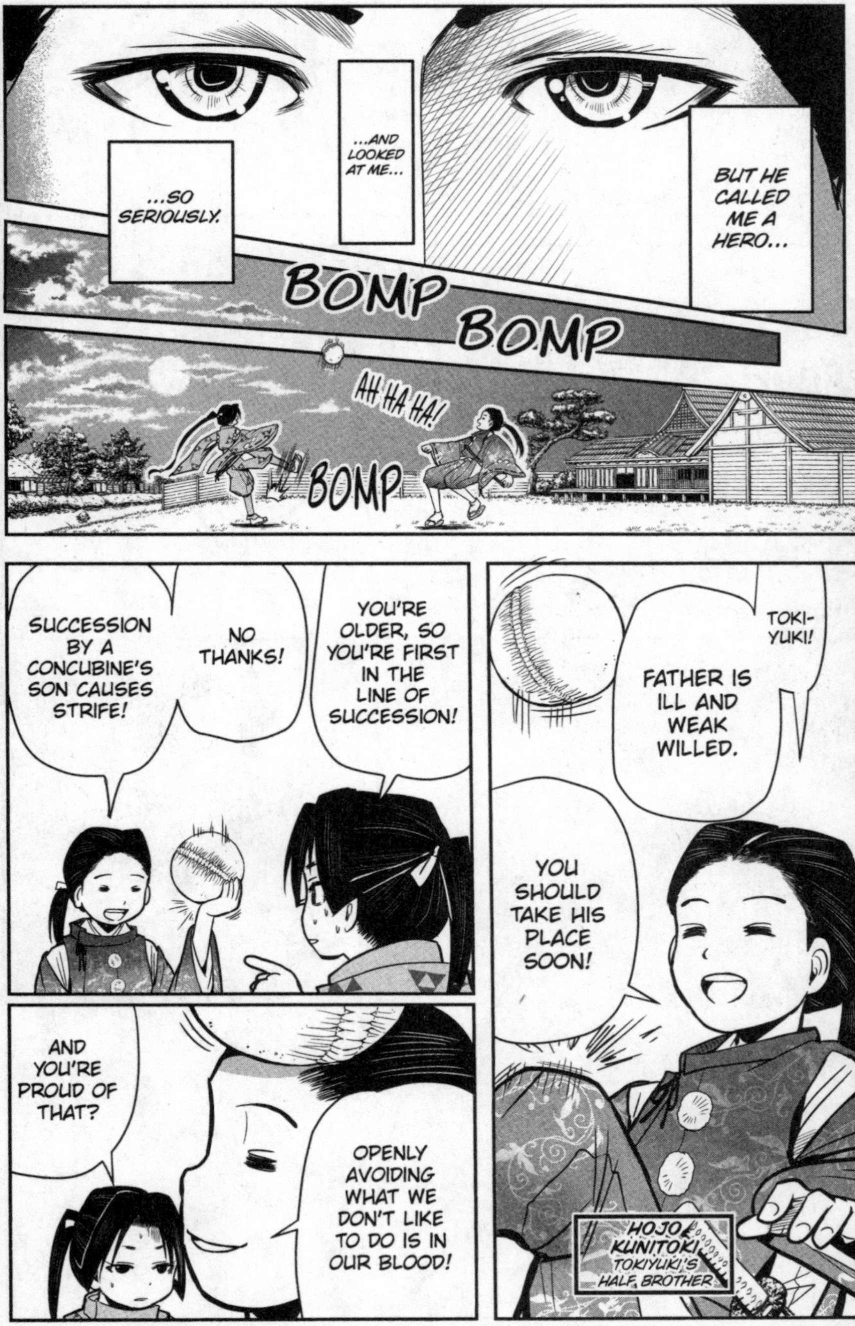
BUT HE CALLED ME A HERO...
...AND LOOKED AT ME...
...SO SERIOUSLY.
BOMP
BOMP
AH HA HA!
BOMP
TOKI-YUKI!
FATHER IS ILL AND WEAK WILLED.
YOU SHOULD TAKE HIS PLACE SOON!
HOJO KUNITOKI TOKIYUKI'S HALF BROTHER
YOU'RE OLDER, SO YOU'RE FIRST IN THE LINE OF SUCCESSION!
NO THANKS!
SUCCESSION BY A CONCUBINE'S SON CAUSES STRIFE!
OPENLY AVOIDING WHAT WE DON'T LIKE TO DO IS IN OUR BLOOD!
AND YOU'RE PROUD OF THAT?

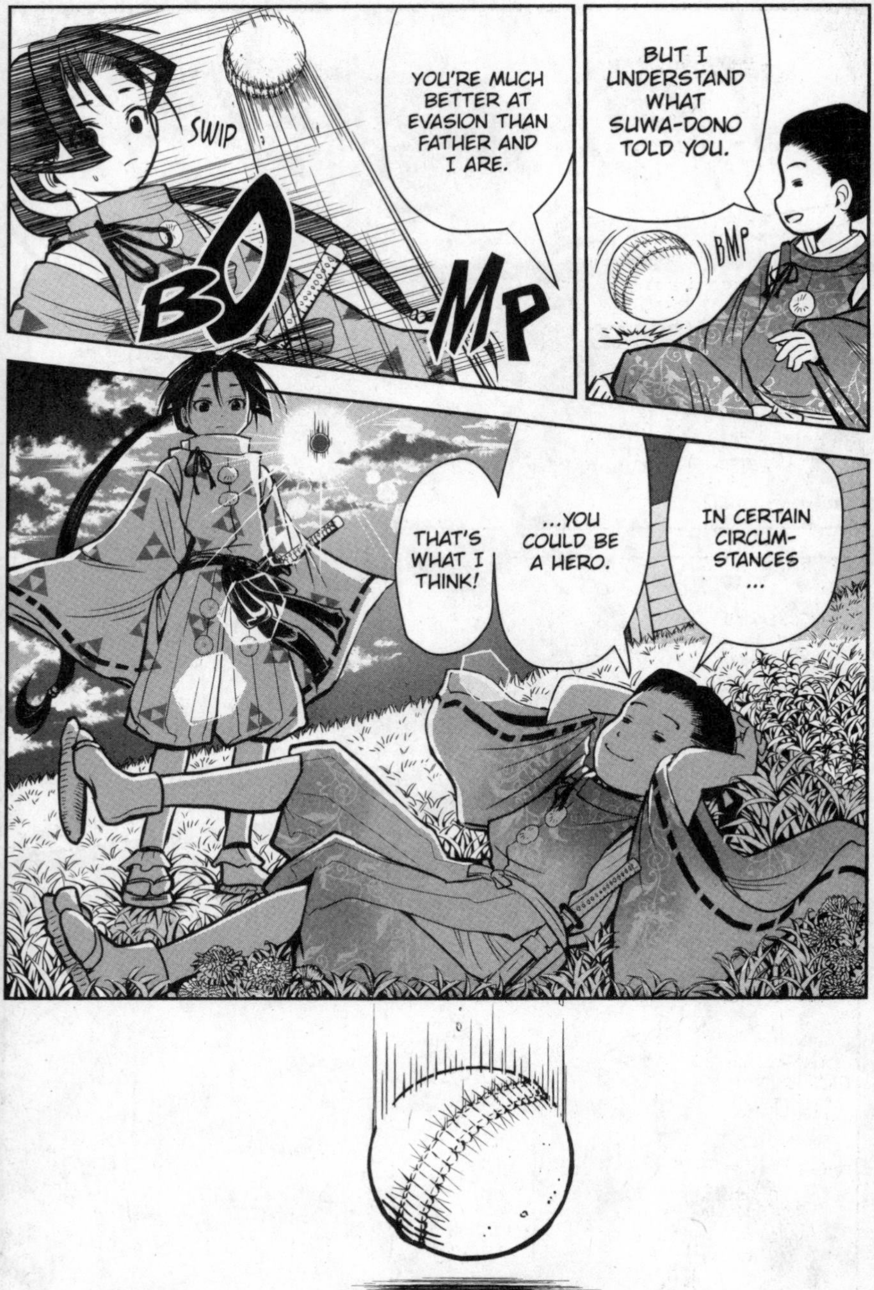
BUT I UNDERSTAND WHAT SUWA-DONO TOLD YOU.
BMP
YOU'RE MUCH BETTER AT EVASION THAN FATHER AND I ARE.
SWIP
BOMP
IN CERTAIN CIRCUM- STANCES ...
...YOU COULD BE A HERO.
THAT'S WHAT I THINK!

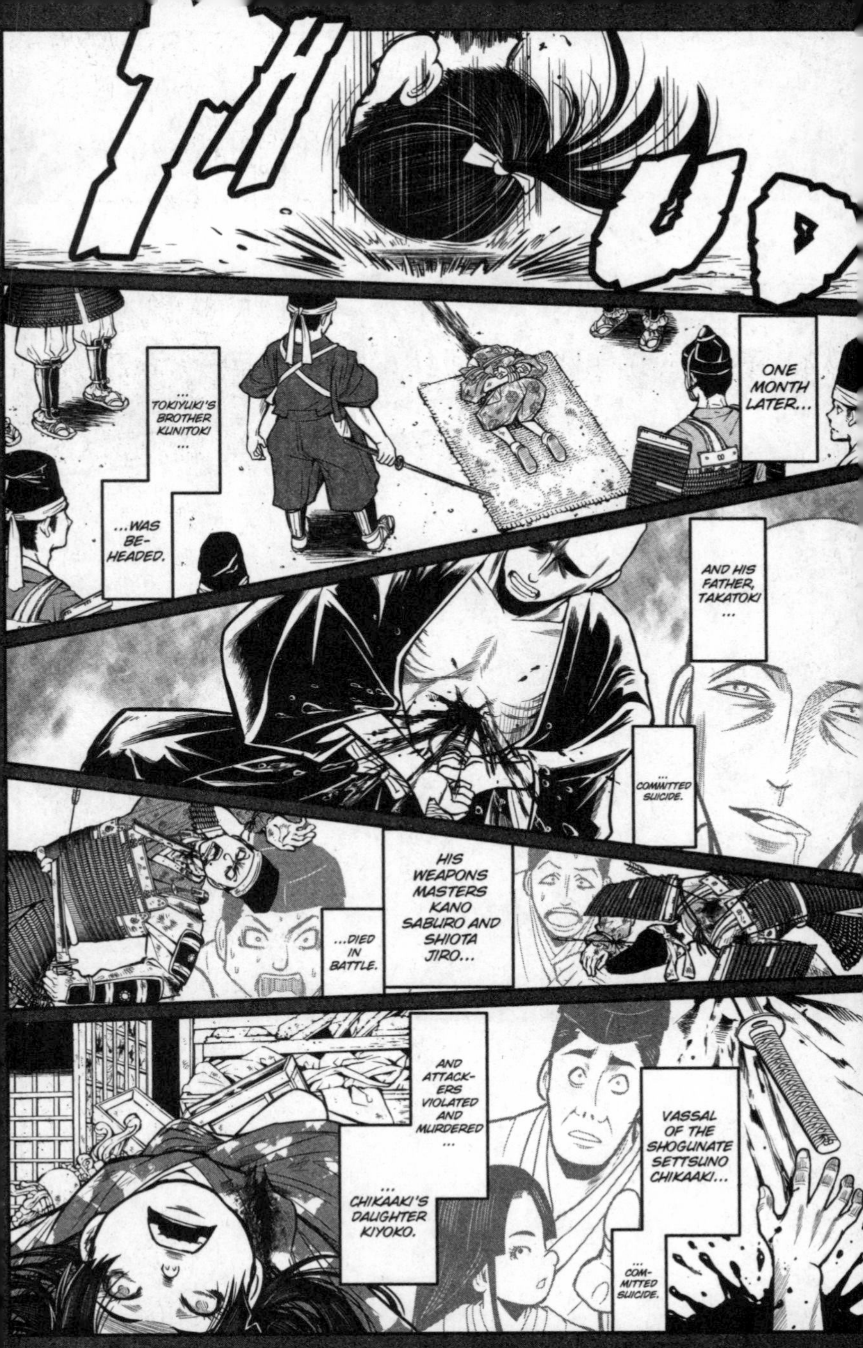
THUD
ONE MONTH LATER...
...TOKIYUKI'S BROTHER KUNITOKI ...
...WAS BE-HEADED.
AND HIS FATHER, TAKATOKI ...
...COMMITTED SUICIDE.
HIS WEAPONS MASTERS KANO SABURO AND SHIOTA JIRO...
...DIED IN BATTLE.
VASSAL OF THE SHOGUNATE SETTSUNO CHIKAAKI...
...COM-MITTED SUICIDE.
AND ATTACK-ERS VIOLATED AND MURDERED ...
...CHIKAAKI'S DAUGHTER KIYOKO.

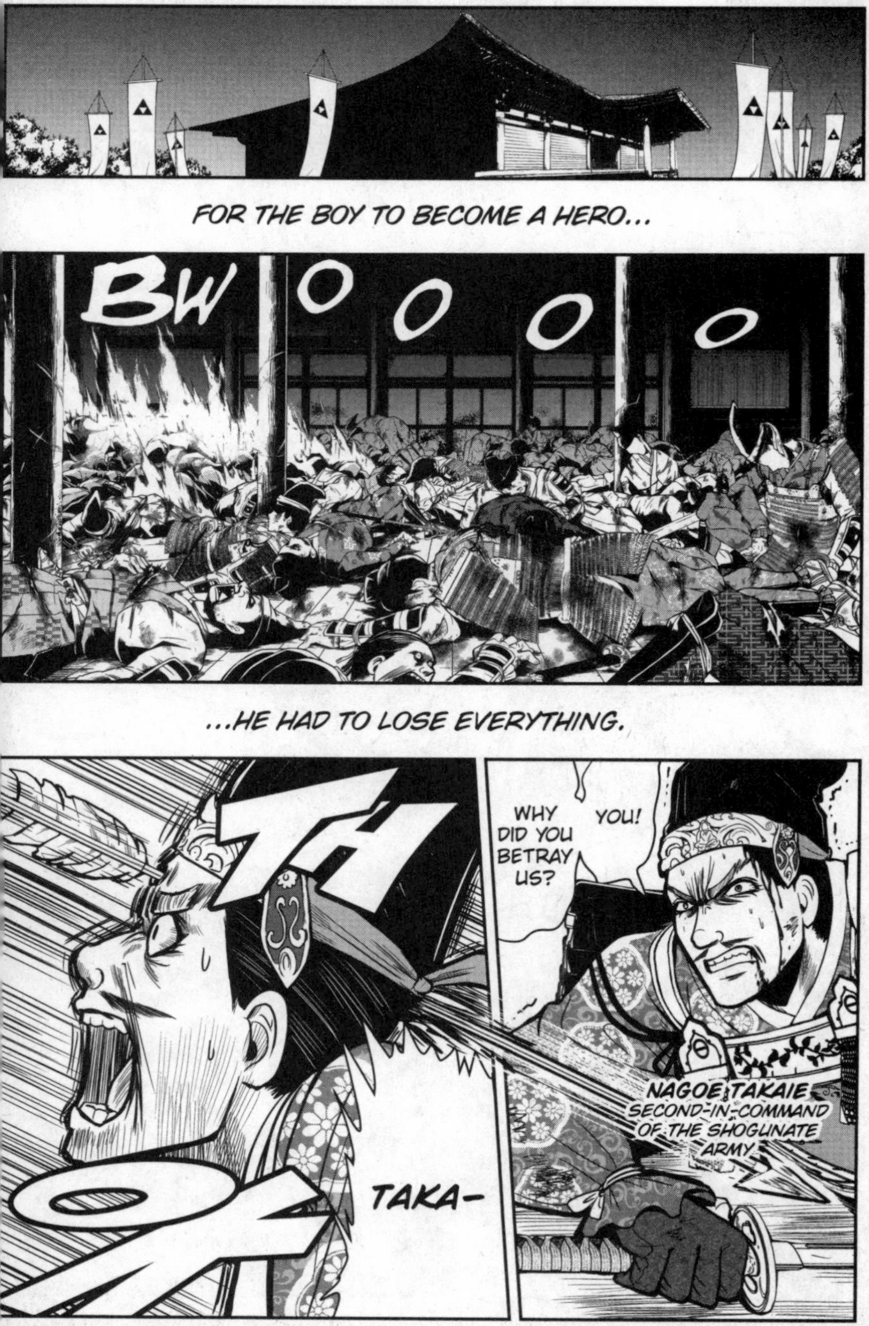
FOR THE BOY TO BECOME A HERO...
BWOOOO
...HE HAD TO LOSE EVERYTHING.
YOU!
WHY DID YOU BETRAY US?
NAGOE TAKAIE
SECOND-IN-COMMAND OF THE SHOGUNATE ARMY
THUNK
TAKA-

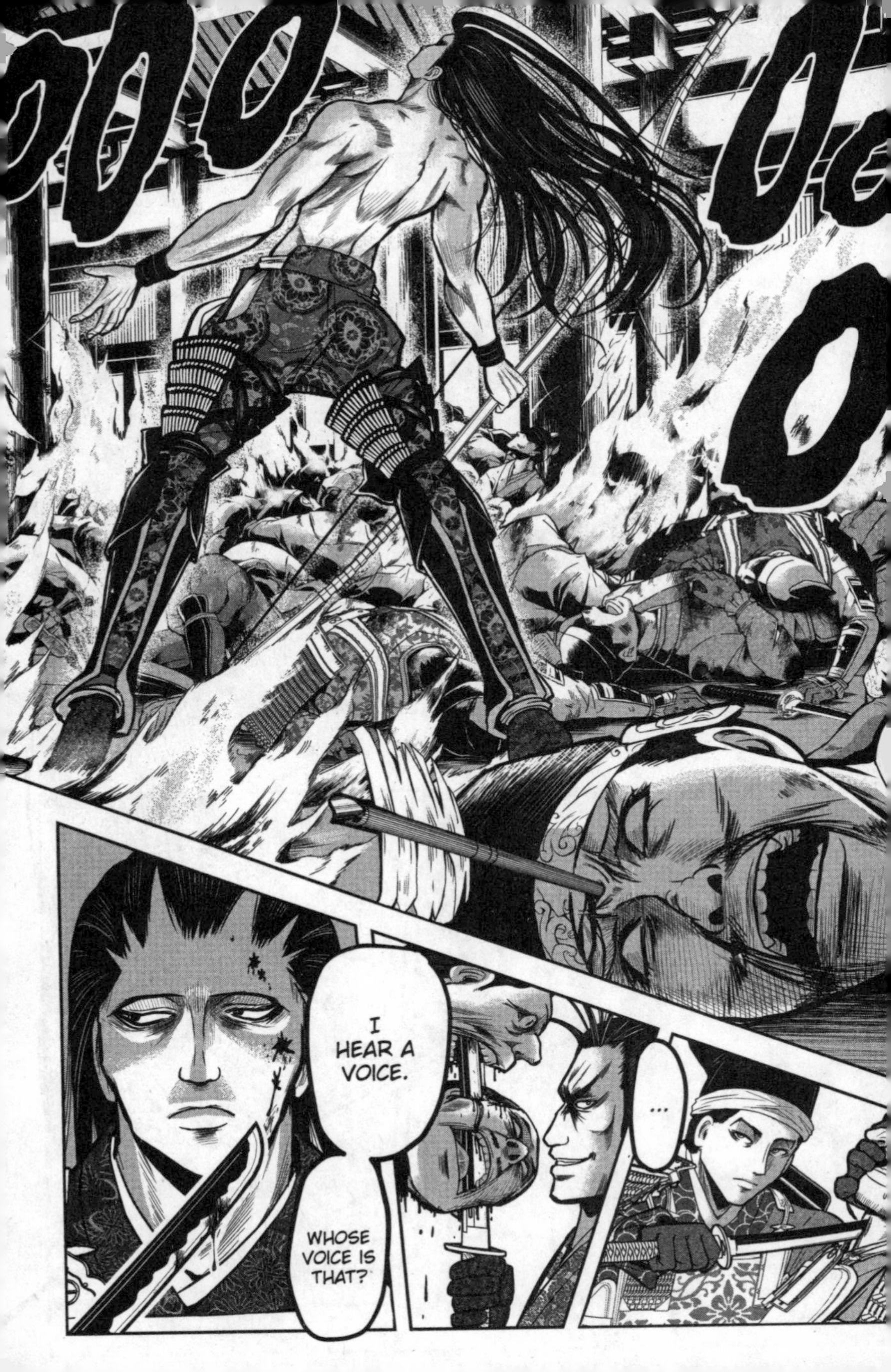
...
I HEAR A VOICE.
WHOSE VOICE IS THAT?

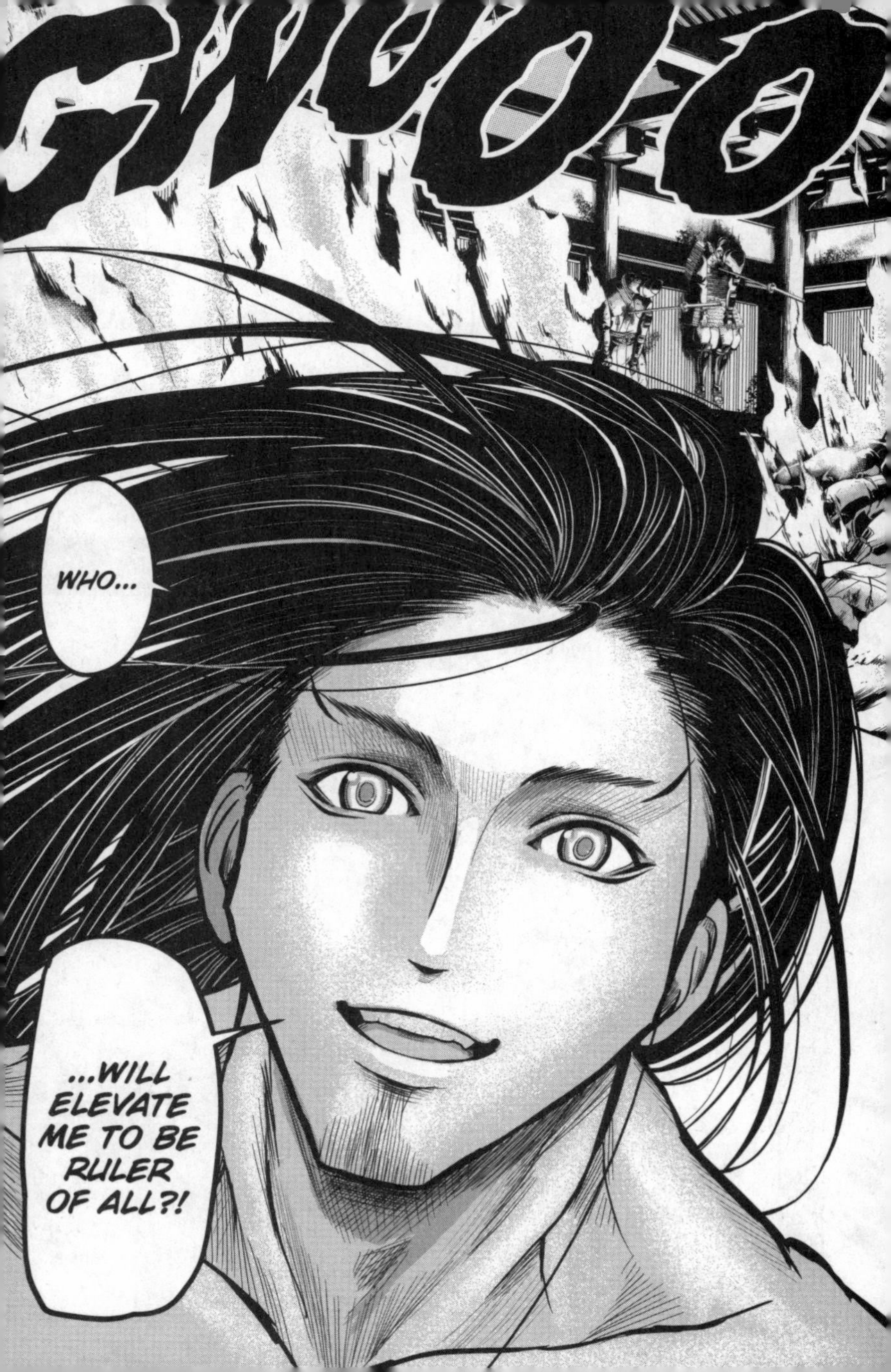
GWOOO
WHO...
...WILL ELEVATE ME TO BE RULER OF ALL?!

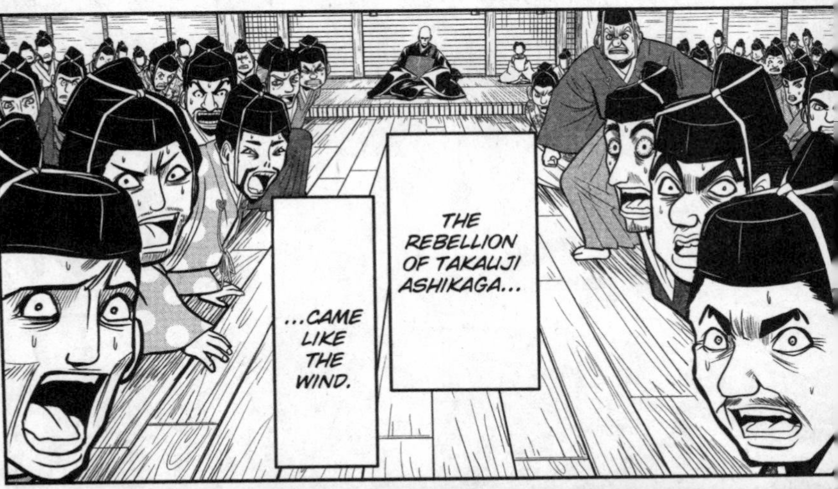
THE REBELLION OF TAKAUJI ASHIKAGA...
...CAME LIKE THE WIND.
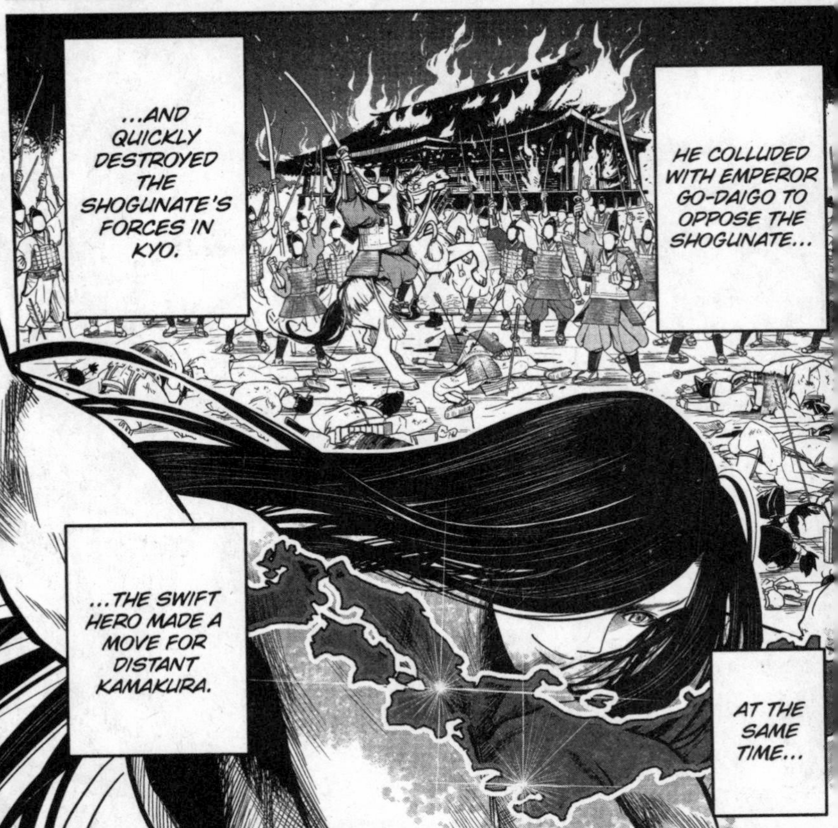
HE COLLUDED WITH EMPEROR GO-DAIGO TO OPPOSE THE SHOGUNATE...
...AND QUICKLY DESTROYED THE SHOGUNATE'S FORCES IN KYO.
AT THE SAME TIME...
...THE SWIFT HERO MADE A MOVE FOR DISTANT KAMAKURA.

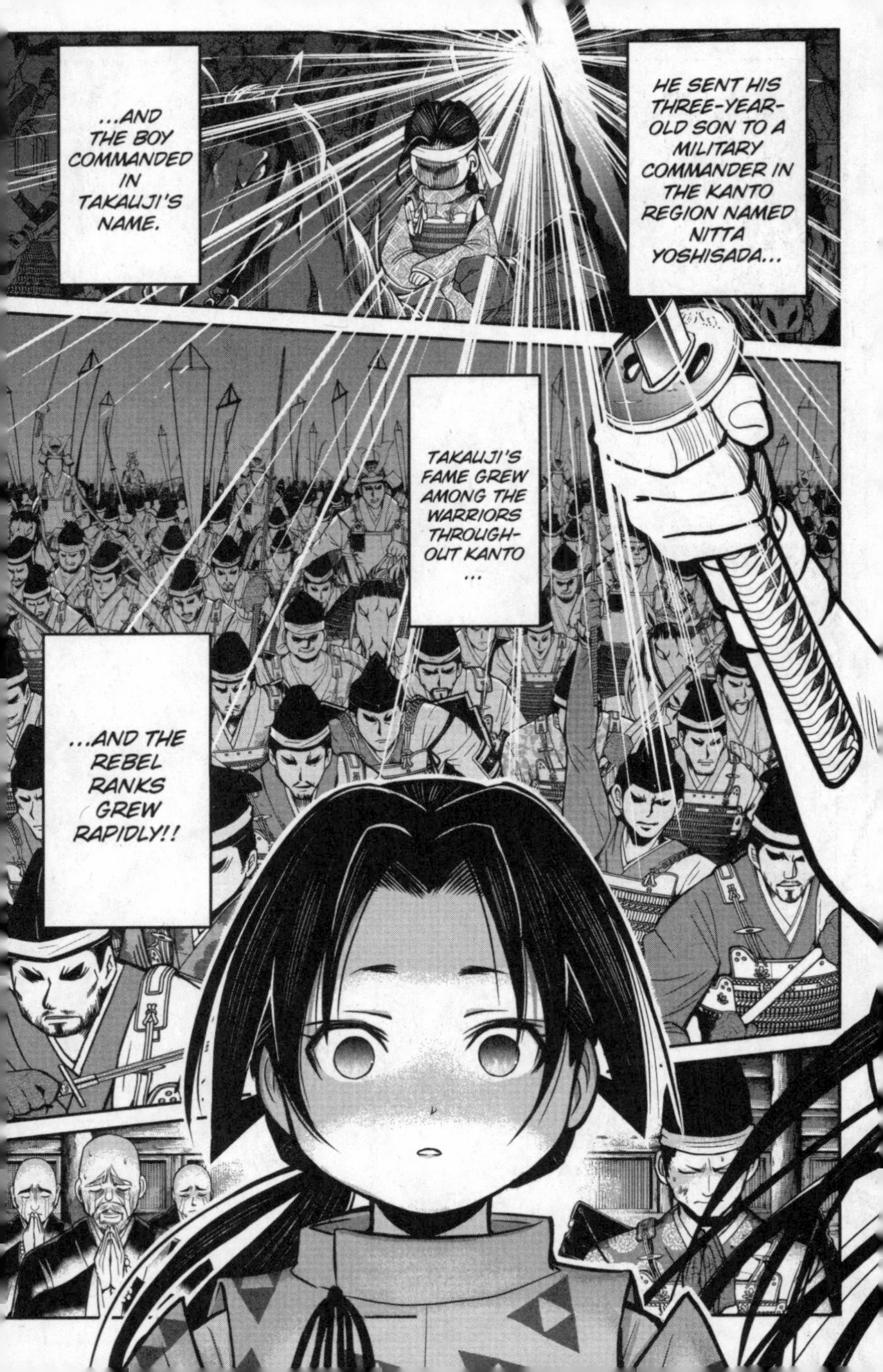
HE SENT HIS THREE-YEAR-OLD SON TO A MILITARY COMMANDER IN THE KANTO REGION NAMED NITTA YOSHISADA...
...AND THE BOY COMMANDED IN TAKAUJI'S NAME.
TAKAUJI'S FAME GREW AMONG THE WARRIORS THROUGH-OUT KANTO ...
...AND THE REBEL RANKS GREW RAPIDLY!!

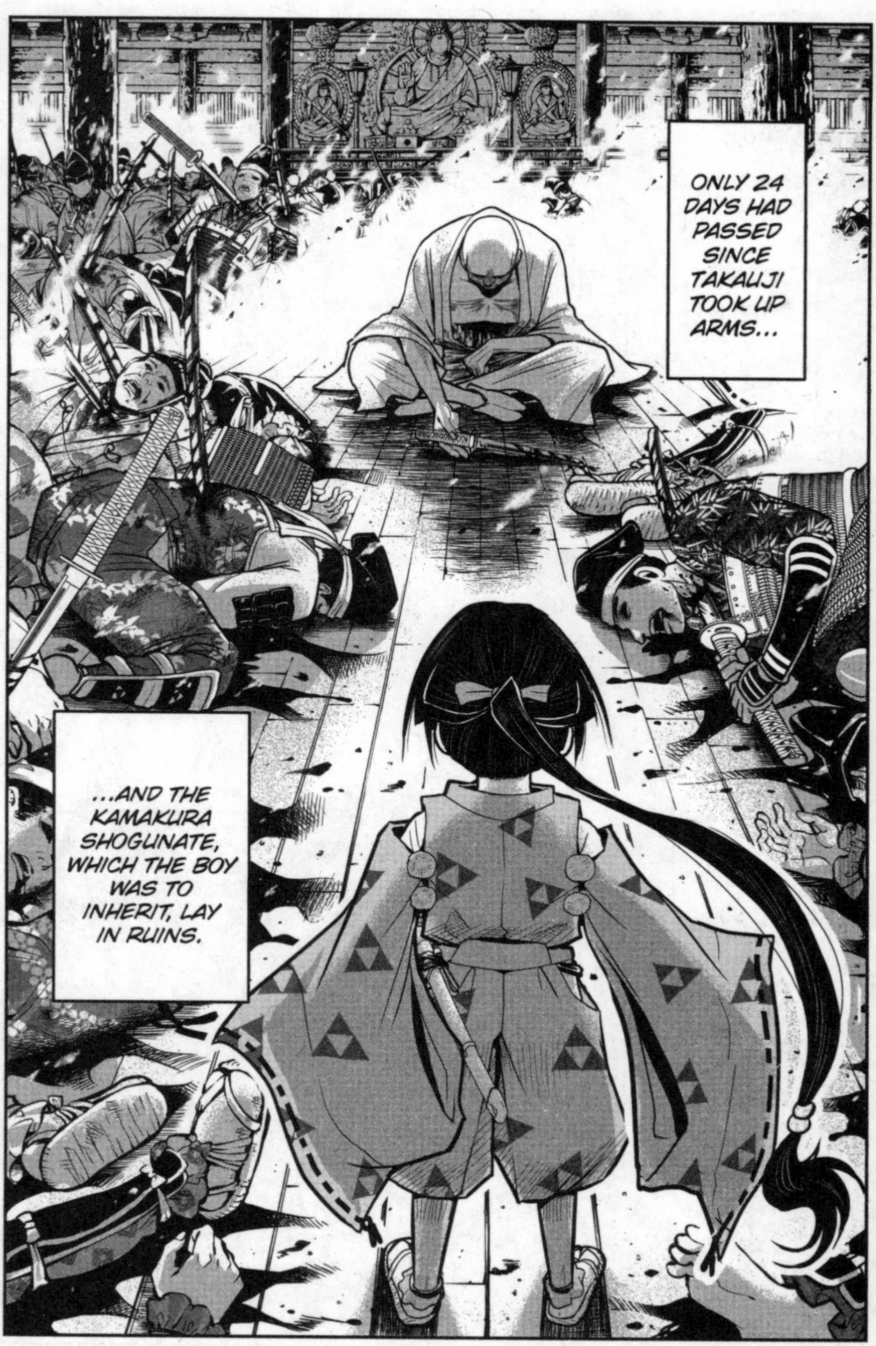
ONLY 24 DAYS HAD PASSED SINCE TAKAUJI TOOK UP ARMS...
...AND THE KAMAKURA SHOGUNATE, WHICH THE BOY WAS TO INHERIT, LAY IN RUINS.

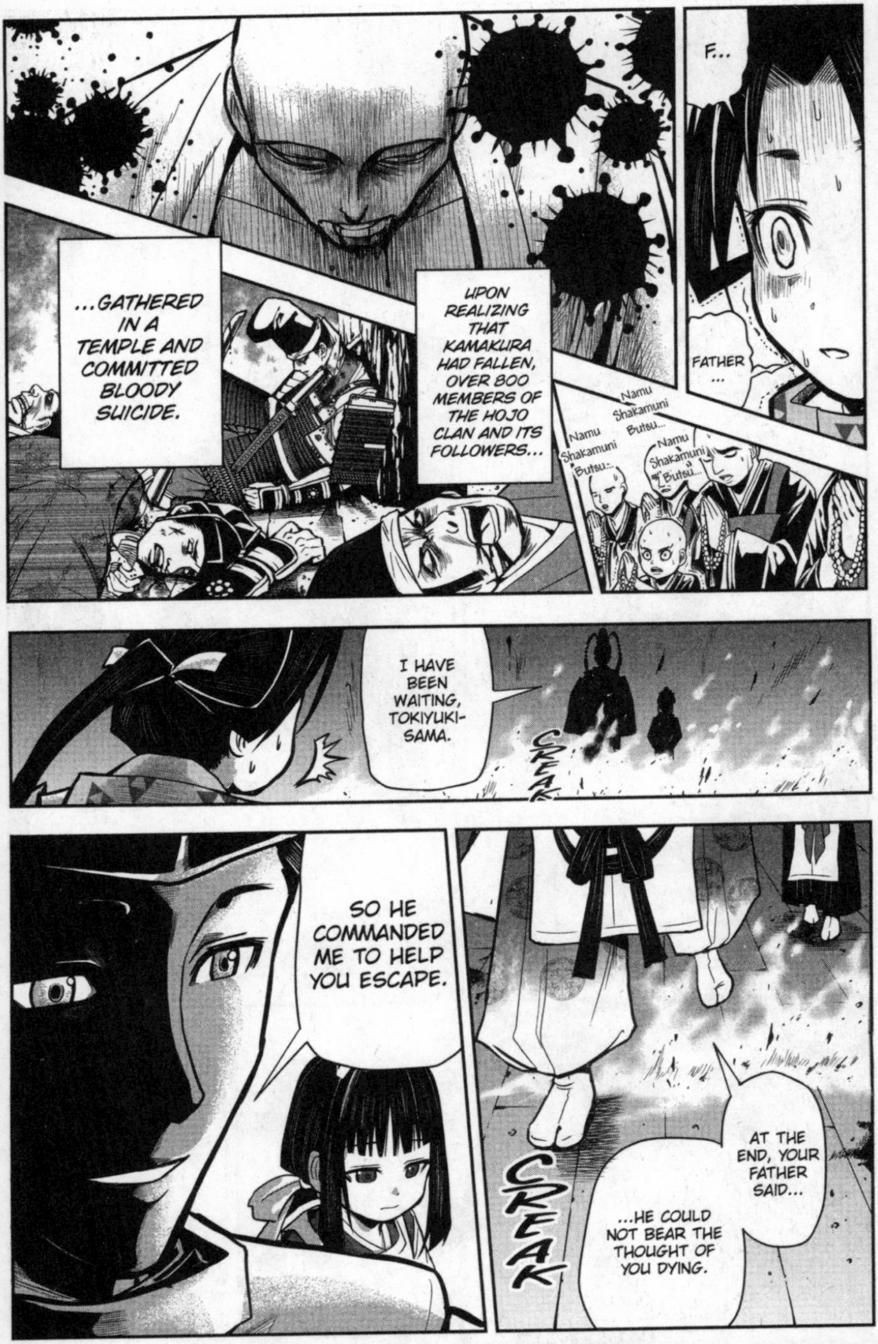
F...
FATHER ...
Namu Shakamuni Butsu...
Namu Shakamuni Butsu...
Namu Shakamuni Butsu...
UPON REALIZING THAT KAMAKURA HAD FALLEN, OVER 800 MEMBERS OF THE HOJO CLAN AND ITS FOLLOWERS...
...GATHERED IN A TEMPLE AND COMMITTED BLOODY SUICIDE.
CREAK
I HAVE BEEN WAITING, TOKIYUKI-SAMA.
AT THE END, YOUR FATHER SAID...
...HE COULD NOT BEAR THE THOUGHT OF YOU DYING.
CREAK
SO HE COMMANDED ME TO HELP YOU ESCAPE.

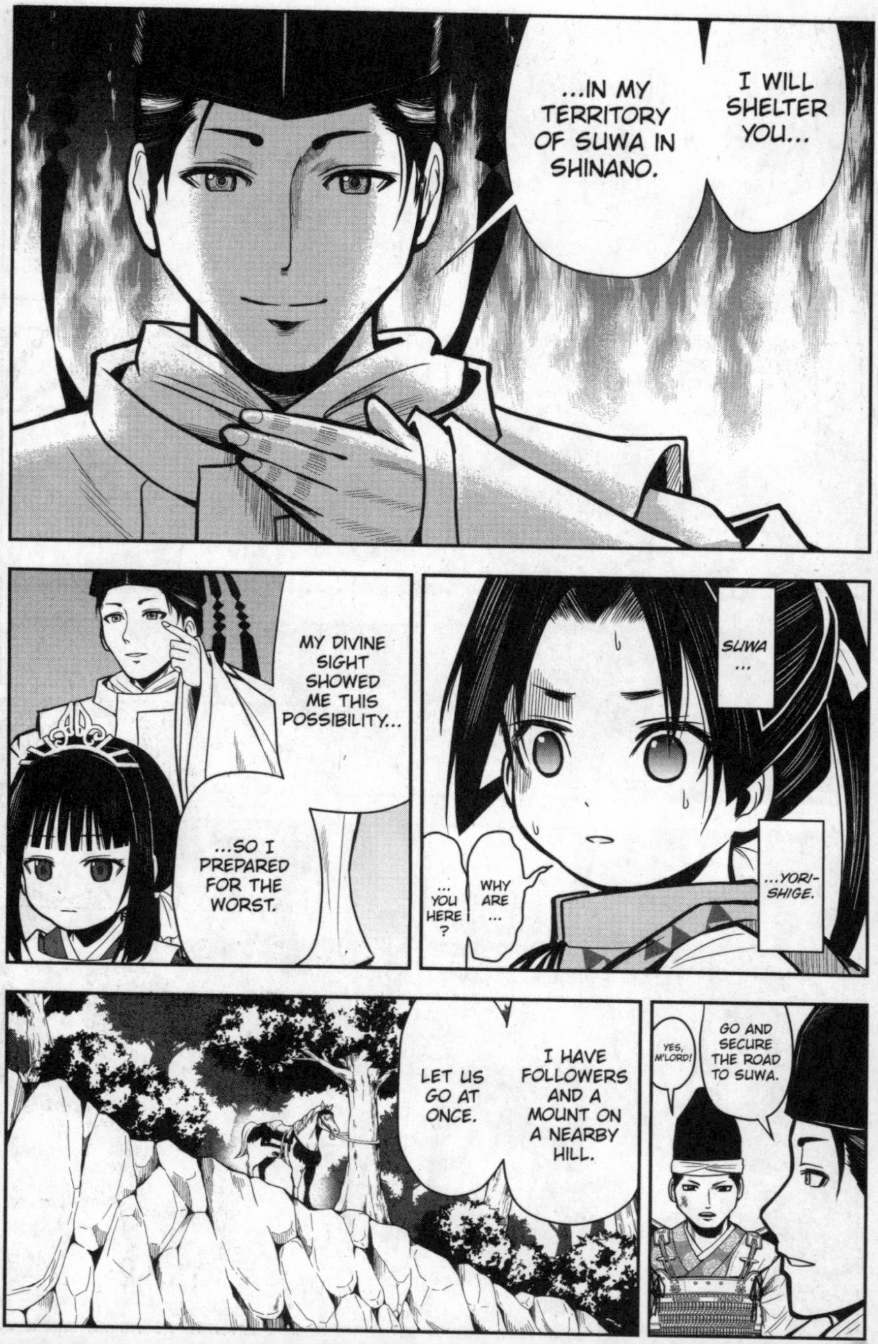
I WILL SHELTER YOU...
...IN MY TERRITORY OF SUWA IN SHINANO.
SUWA ...
...YORI-SHIGE.
WHY ARE ...
... YOU HERE ?
MY DIVINE SIGHT SHOWED ME THIS POSSIBILITY...
...SO I PREPARED FOR THE WORST.
GO AND SECURE THE ROAD TO SUWA.
YES, M'LORD!
I HAVE FOLLOWERS AND A MOUNT ON A NEARBY HILL.
LET US GO AT ONCE.

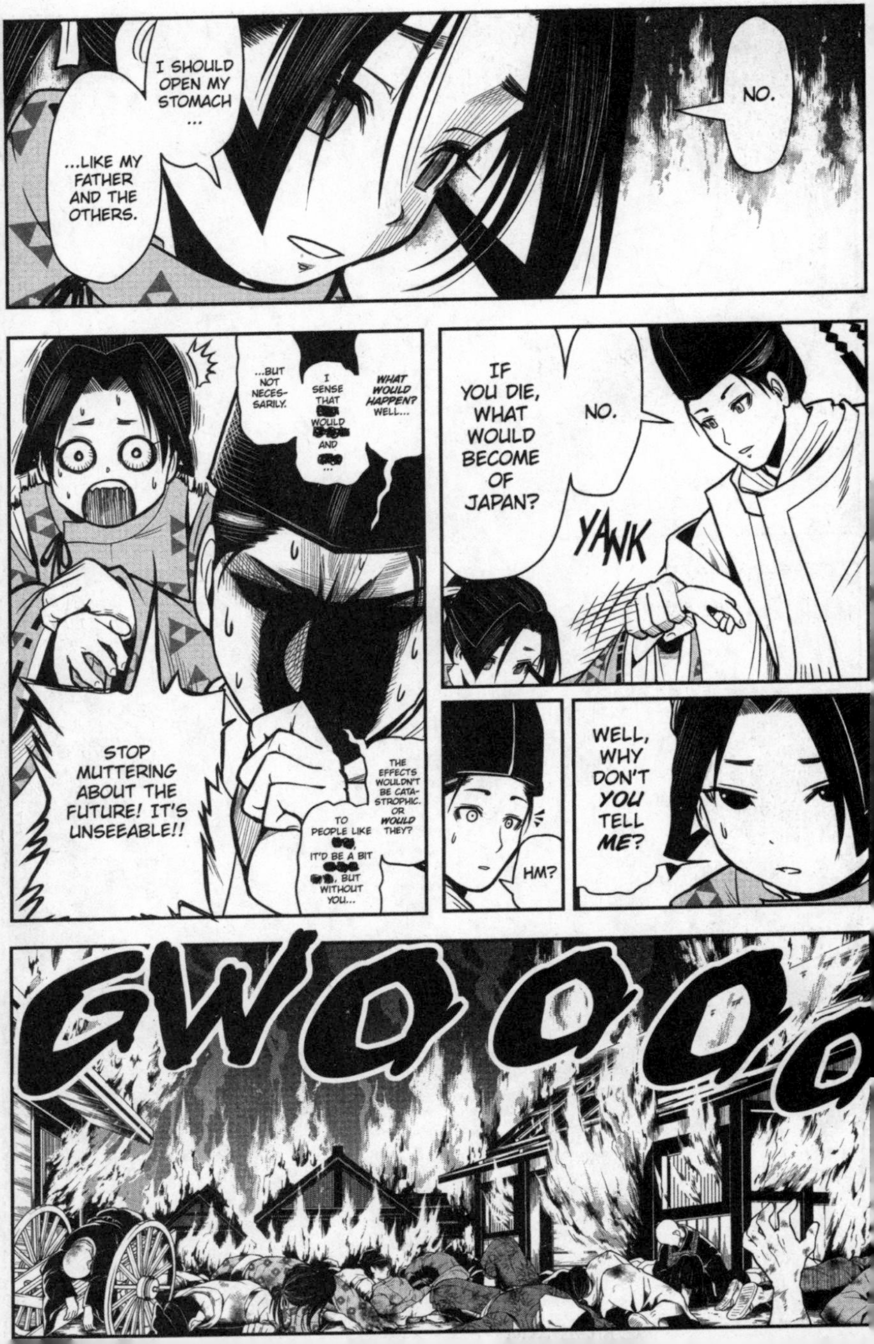
I SHOULD OPEN MY STOMACH ...
...LIKE MY FATHER AND THE OTHERS.
NO.
NO.
IF YOU DIE, WHAT WOULD BECOME OF JAPAN?
YANK
WELL, WHY DON'T *YOU* TELL *ME*?
HM?
WHAT WOULD HAPPEN? WELL...
I SENSE THAT [redacted] WOULD [redacted] AND [redacted] ...
...BUT NOT NECES-SARILY.
THE EFFECTS WOULDN'T BE CATA-STROPHIC. OR *WOULD* THEY?
TO PEOPLE LIKE [redacted], IT'D BE A BIT [redacted], BUT WITHOUT YOU...
STOP MUTTERING ABOUT THE FUTURE! IT'S UNSEEABLE!!
GWOOOO

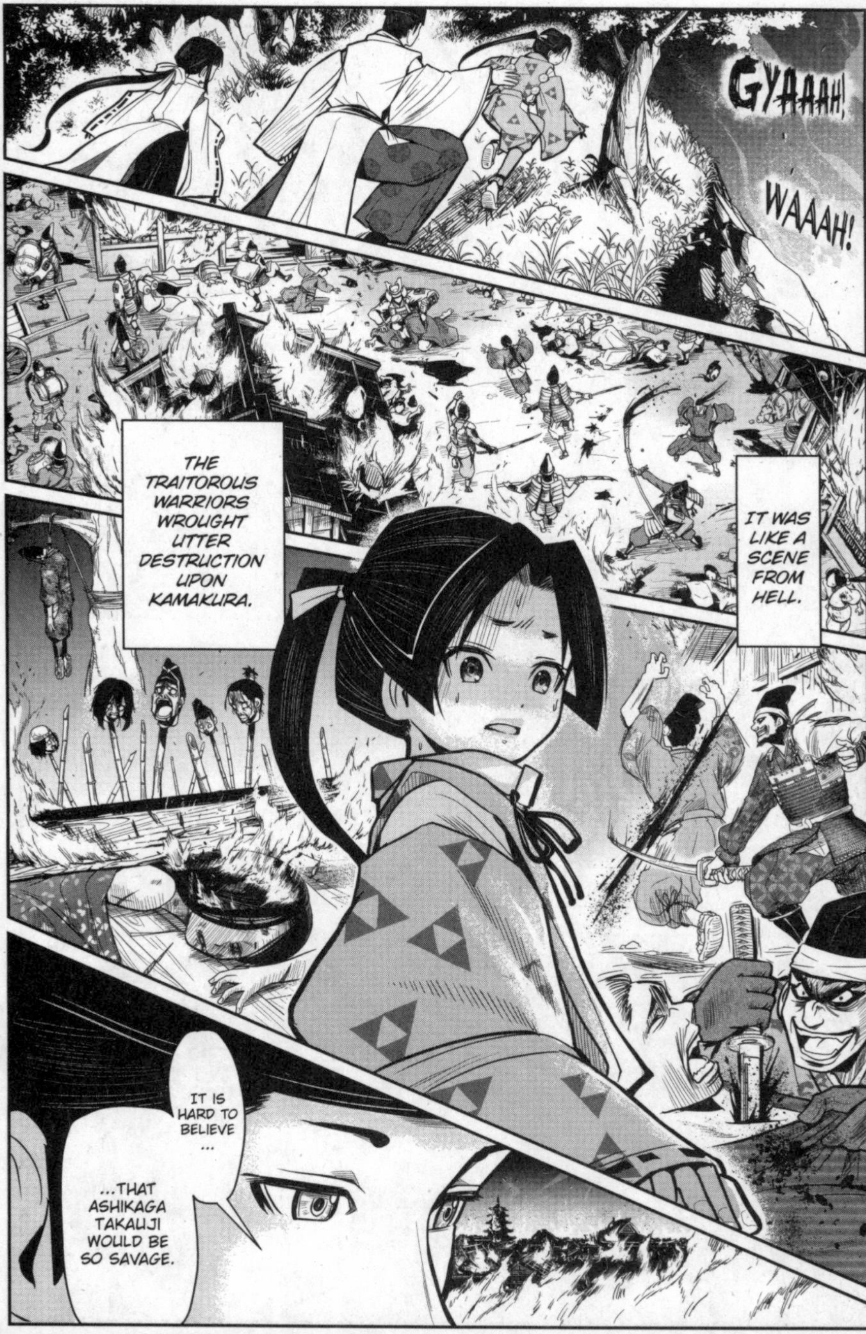
GYAAAH!
WAAAH!
IT WAS LIKE A SCENE FROM HELL.
THE TRAITOROUS WARRIORS WROUGHT UTTER DESTRUCTION UPON KAMAKURA.
IT IS HARD TO BELIEVE ...
...THAT ASHIKAGA TAKAUJI WOULD BE SO SAVAGE.

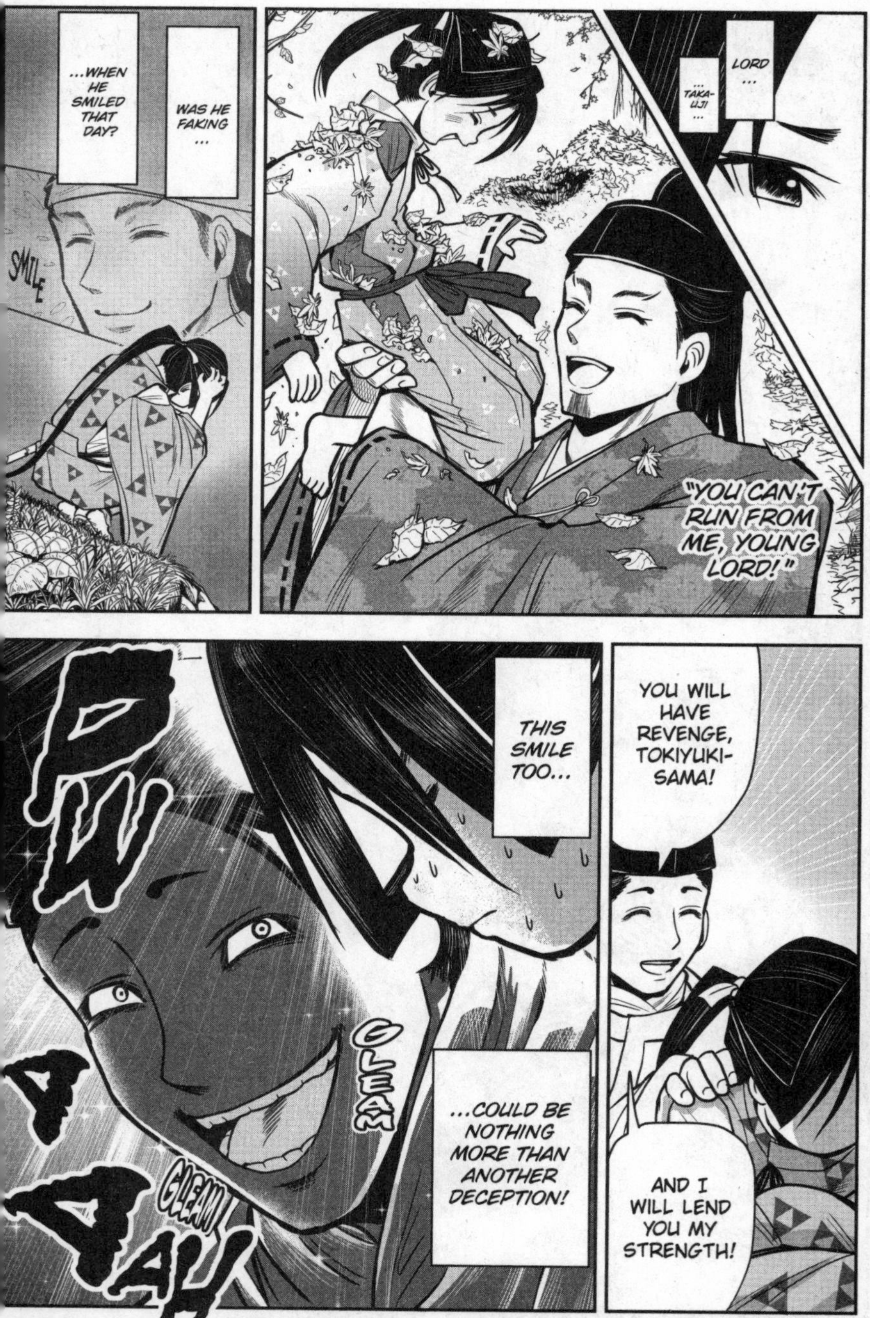
LORD...
...TAKA-UJI...
"YOU CAN'T RUN FROM ME, YOUNG LORD!"
...WHEN HE SMILED THAT DAY?
WAS HE FAKING...
SMILE
YOU WILL HAVE REVENGE, TOKIYUKI-SAMA!
AND I WILL LEND YOU MY STRENGTH!
THIS SMILE TOO...
...COULD BE NOTHING MORE THAN ANOTHER DECEPTION!
GLEAM
GLEAM
PWAAAH!

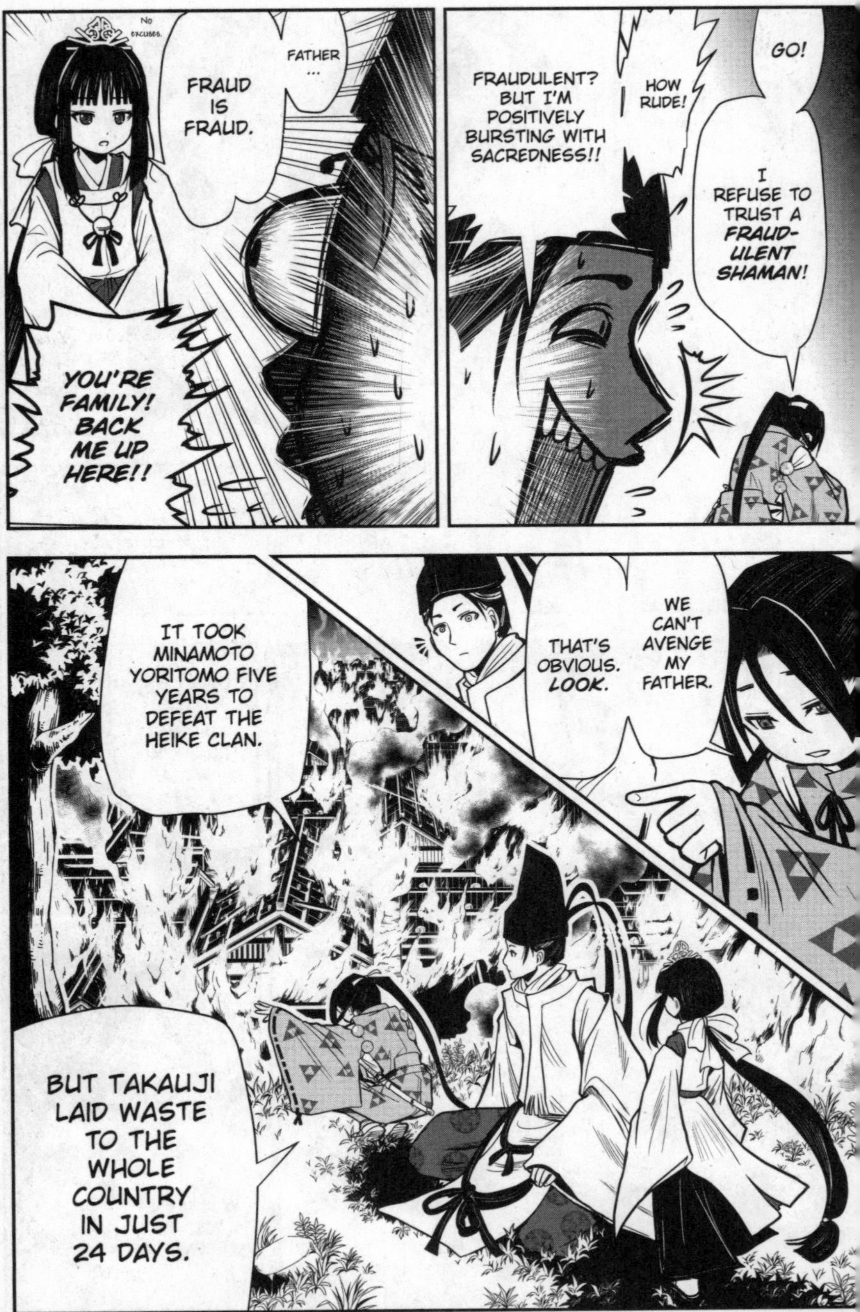
GO!
I REFUSE TO TRUST A FRAUDULENT SHAMAN!
HOW RUDE!
FRAUDULENT? BUT I'M POSITIVELY BURSTING WITH SACREDNESS!!
FATHER ...
FRAUD IS FRAUD.
No excuses.
YOU'RE FAMILY! BACK ME UP HERE!!
WE CAN'T AVENGE MY FATHER.
THAT'S OBVIOUS. LOOK.
IT TOOK MINAMOTO YORITOMO FIVE YEARS TO DEFEAT THE HEIKE CLAN.
BUT TAKAUJI LAID WASTE TO THE WHOLE COUNTRY IN JUST 24 DAYS.

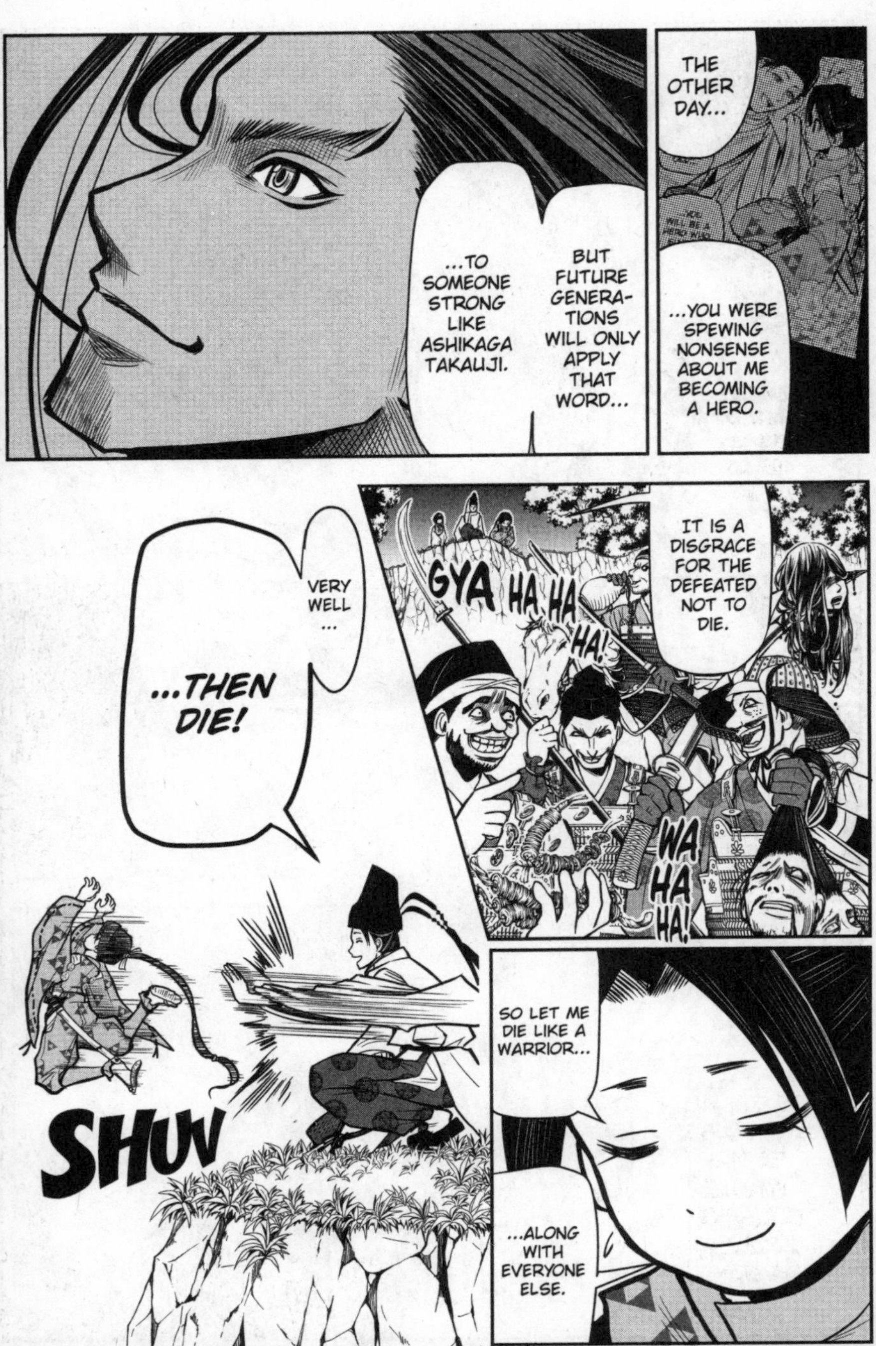
THE OTHER DAY...
...YOU WERE SPEWING NONSENSE ABOUT ME BECOMING A HERO.
BUT FUTURE GENERATIONS WILL ONLY APPLY THAT WORD...
...TO SOMEONE STRONG LIKE ASHIKAGA TAKAUJI.
IT IS A DISGRACE FOR THE DEFEATED NOT TO DIE.
GYA HA HA HA!
WA HA HA HA!
SO LET ME DIE LIKE A WARRIOR...
...ALONG WITH EVERYONE ELSE.
VERY WELL...
...THEN DIE!
SHUV

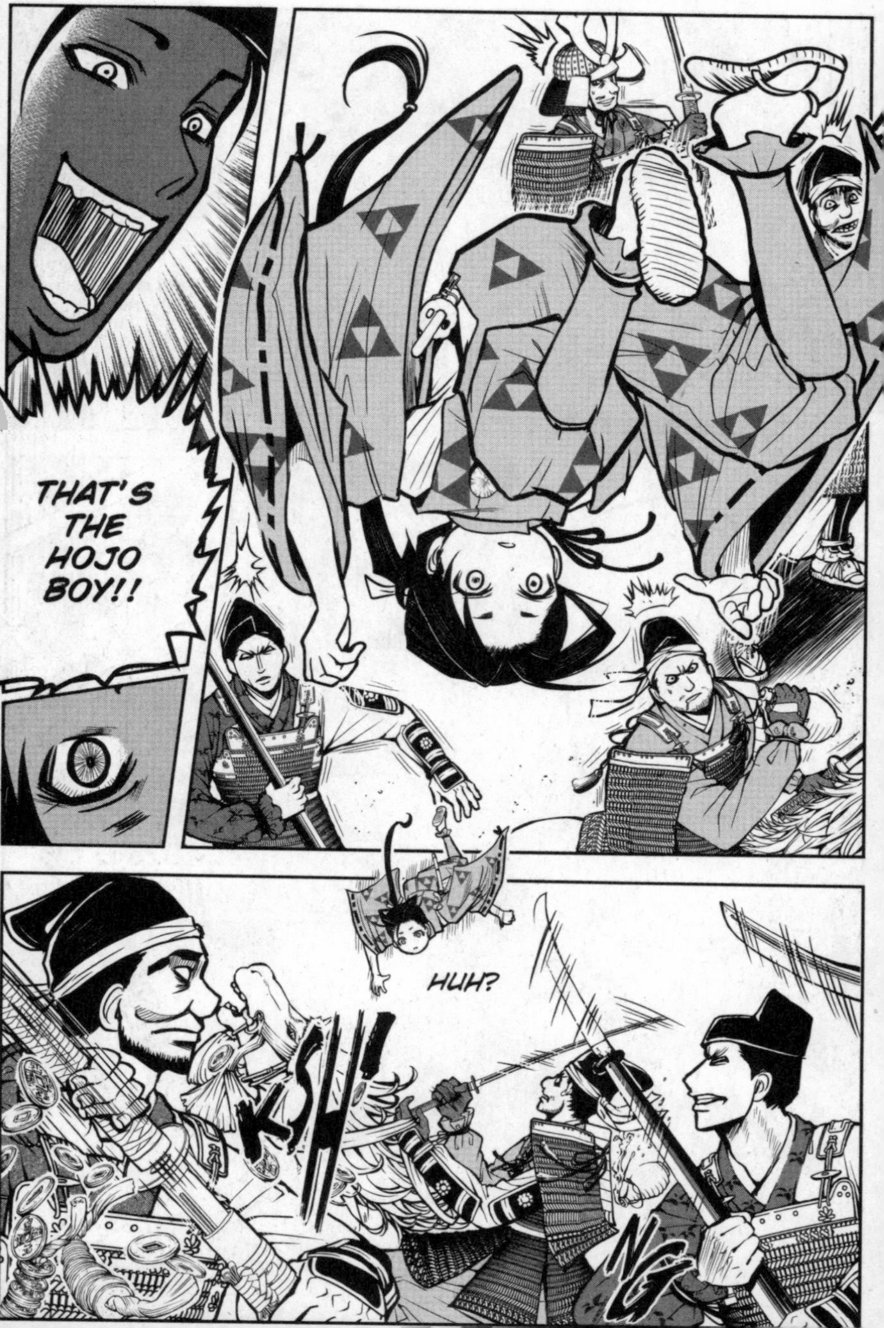
THAT'S THE HOJO BOY!!
HUH?
NG
KSH

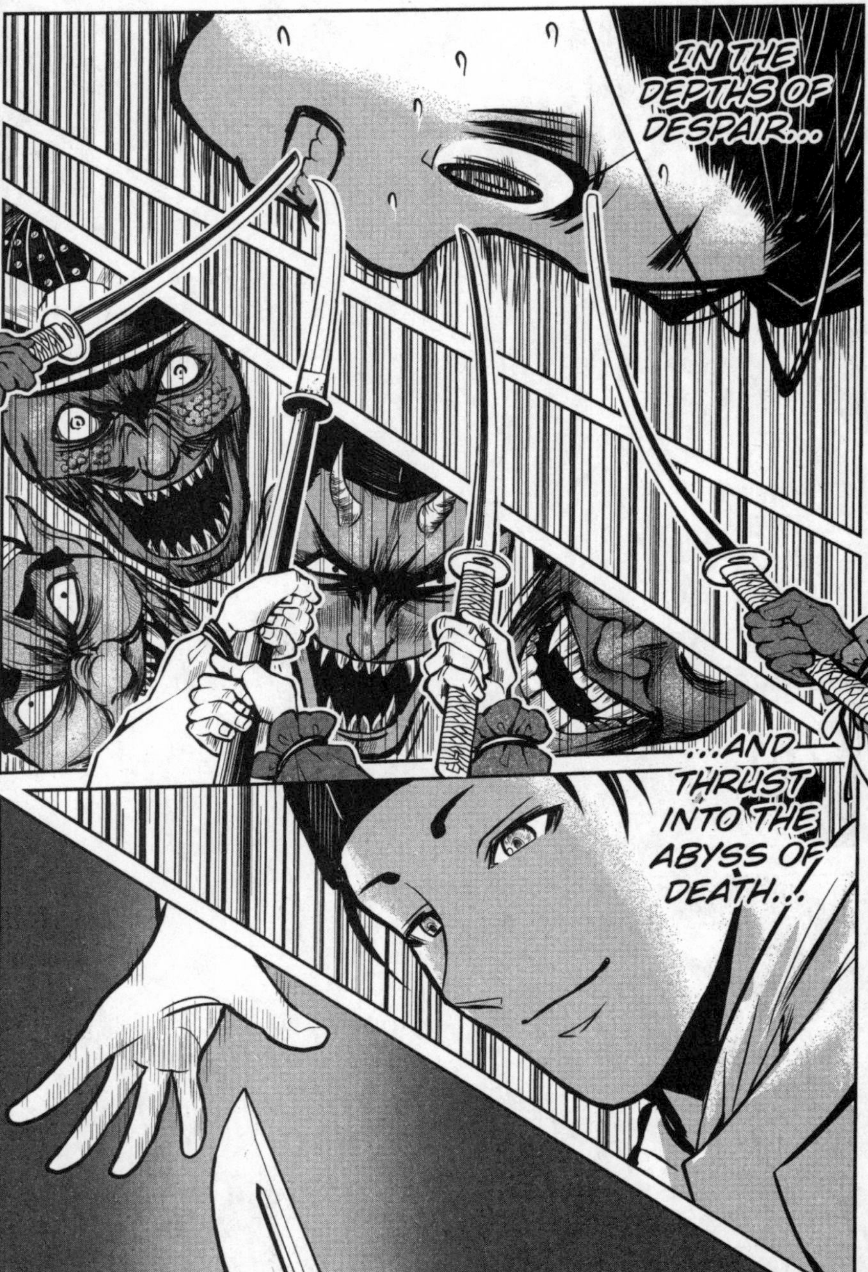
IN THE DEPTHS OF DESPAIR...
...AND THRUST INTO THE ABYSS OF DEATH...!

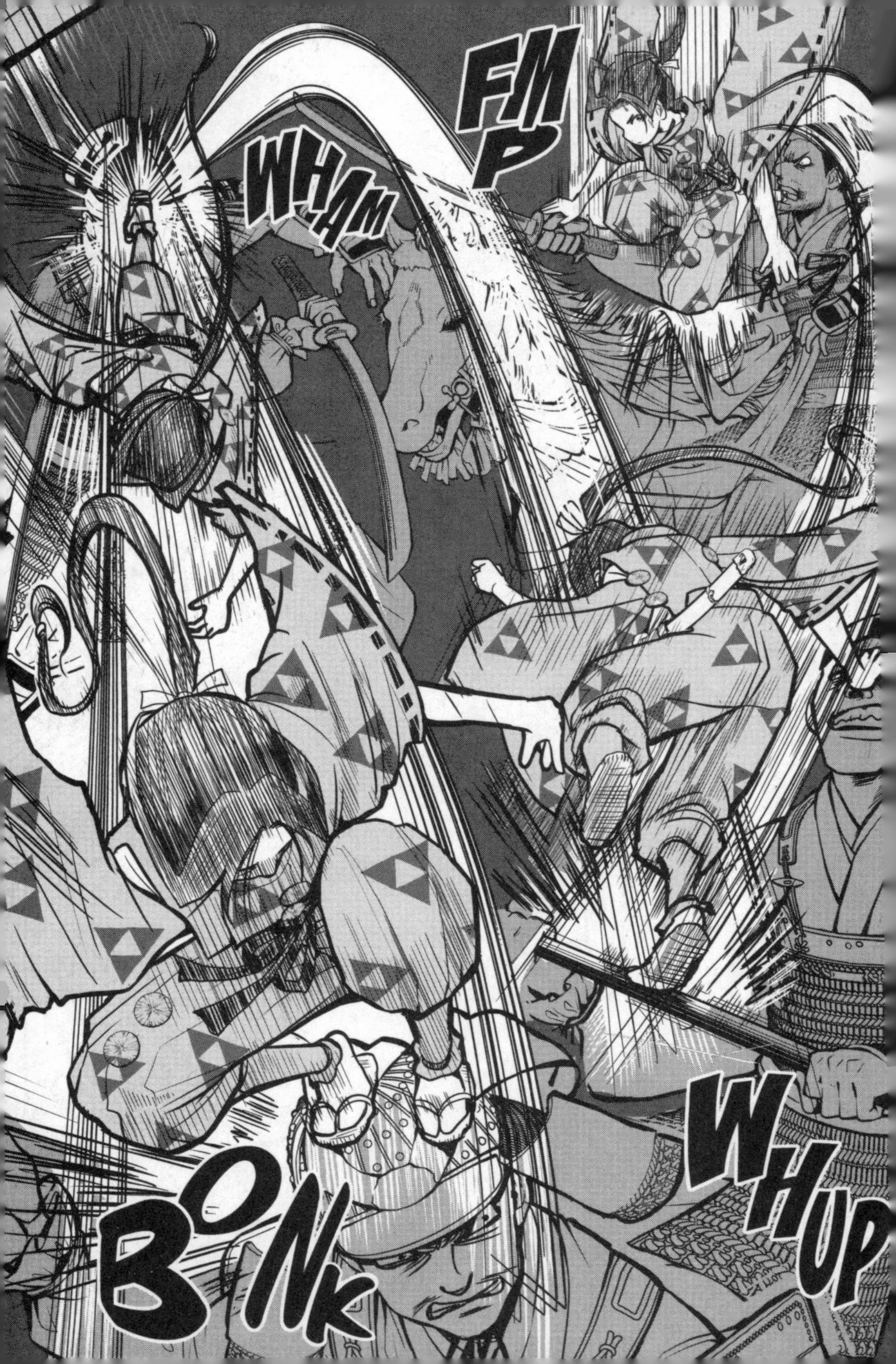
FWIP
WHAM
WHUP
BONK

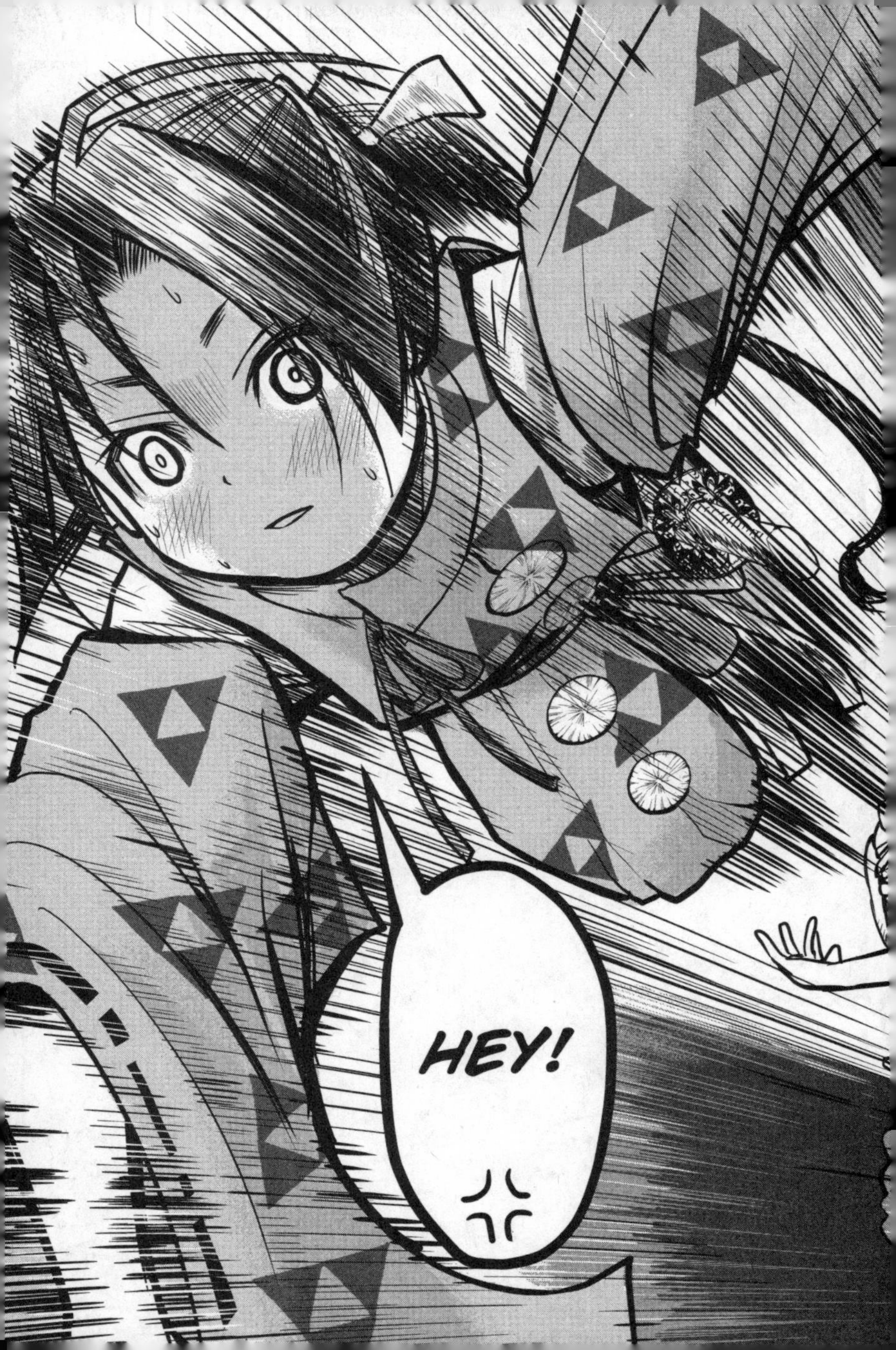
HEY!

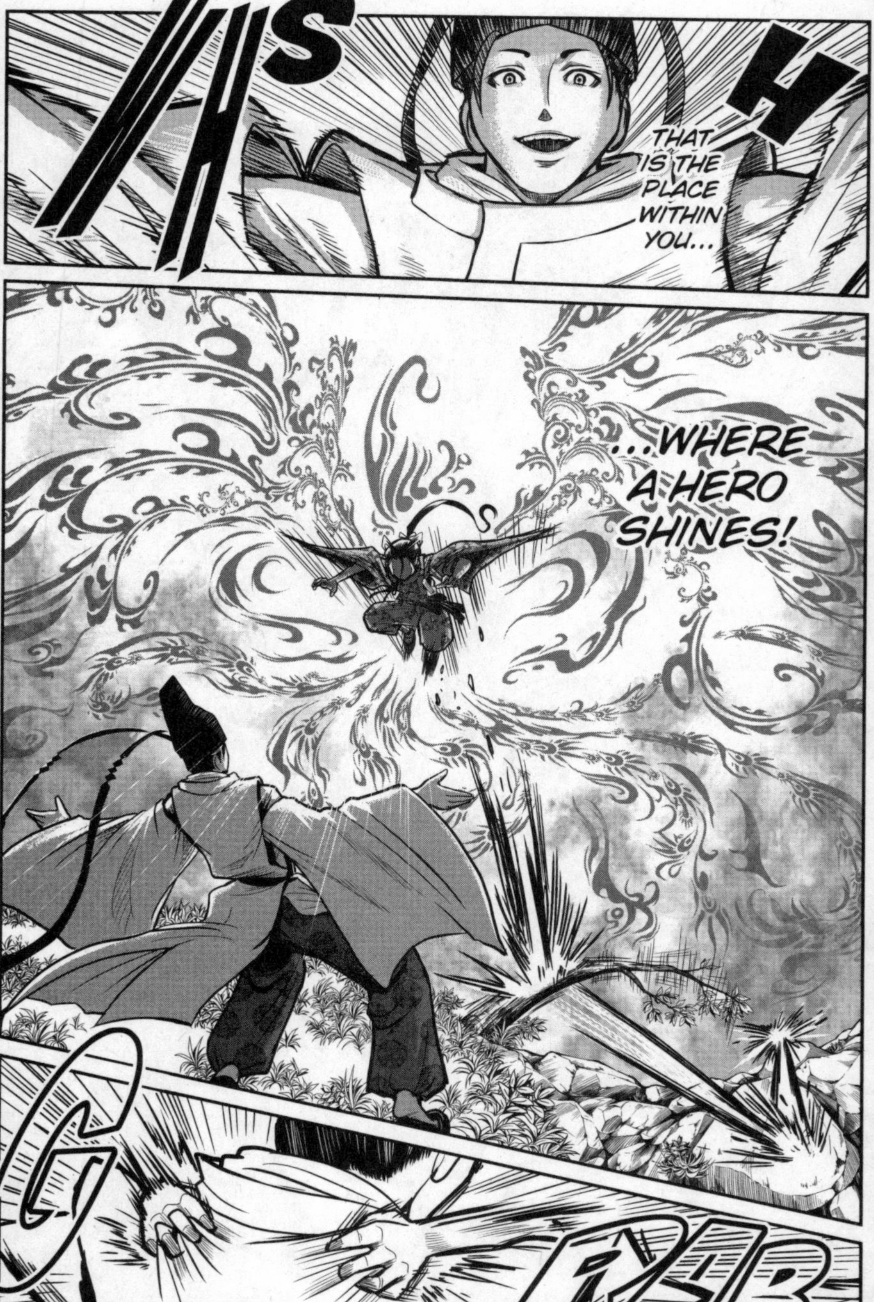
SHHH
THAT IS THE PLACE WITHIN YOU...
...WHERE A HERO SHINES!
GRAB

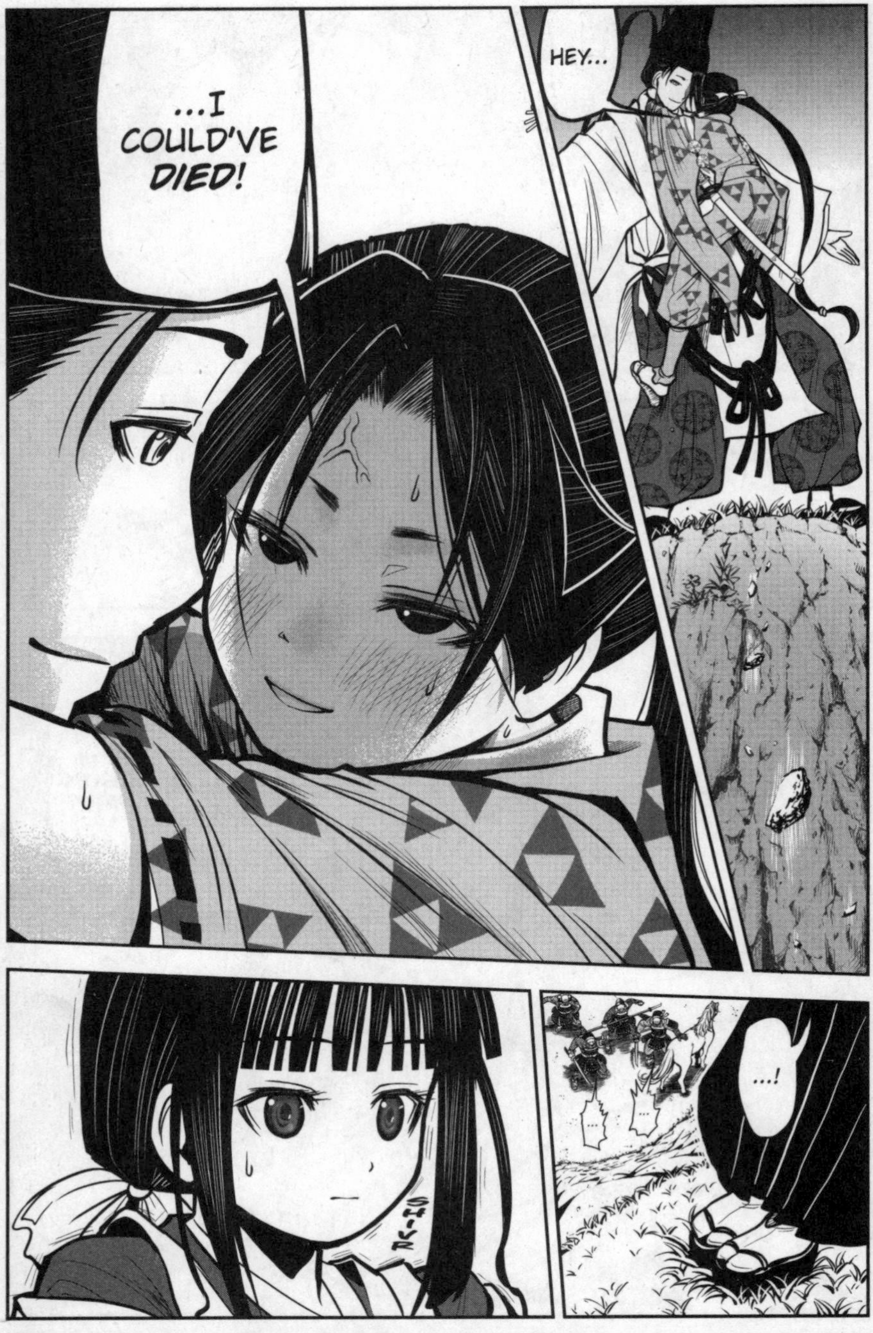
HEY...
...I COULD'VE DIED!
...!
...
...
SHIVR

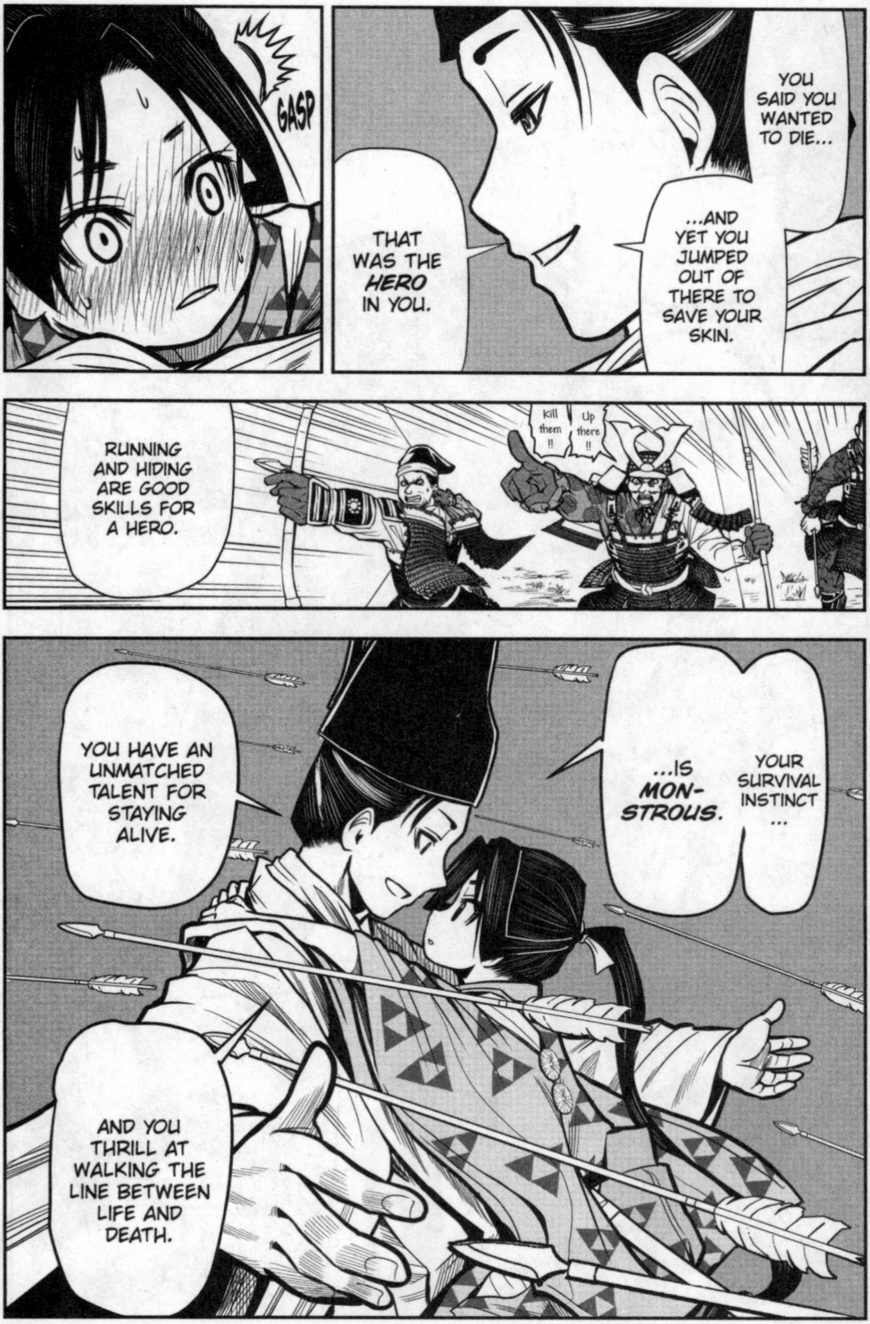
YOU SAID YOU WANTED TO DIE...
...AND YET YOU JUMPED OUT OF THERE TO SAVE YOUR SKIN.
THAT WAS THE *HERO* IN YOU.
GASP
Up there!!
Kill them!!
RUNNING AND HIDING ARE GOOD SKILLS FOR A HERO.
YOUR SURVIVAL INSTINCT...
...IS *MON-STROUS*.
YOU HAVE AN UNMATCHED TALENT FOR STAYING ALIVE.
AND YOU THRILL AT WALKING THE LINE BETWEEN LIFE AND DEATH.

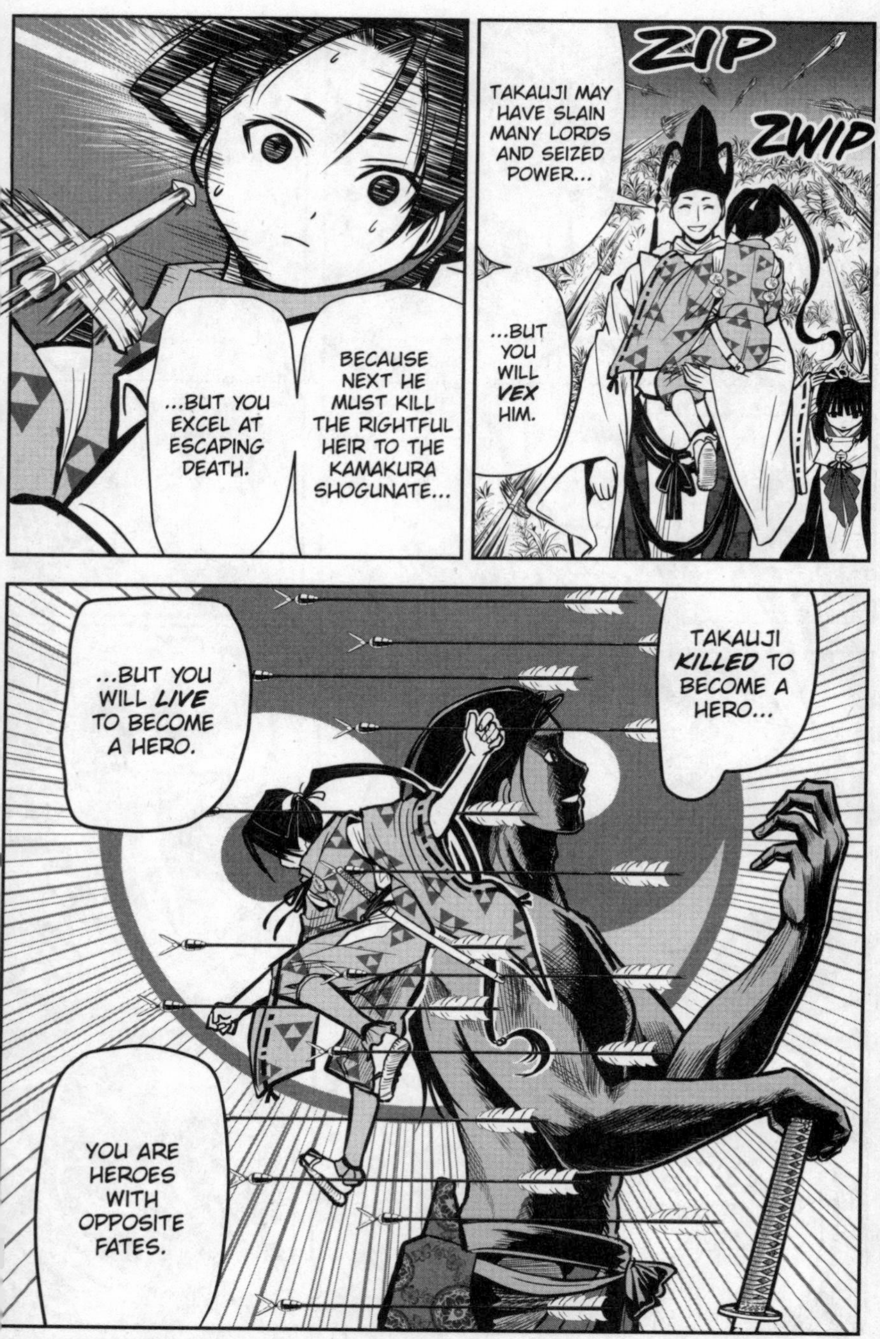
ZIP
TAKAUJI MAY HAVE SLAIN MANY LORDS AND SEIZED POWER...
ZWIP
...BUT YOU WILL VEX HIM.
BECAUSE NEXT HE MUST KILL THE RIGHTFUL HEIR TO THE KAMAKURA SHOGUNATE...
...BUT YOU EXCEL AT ESCAPING DEATH.
TAKAUJI KILLED TO BECOME A HERO...
...BUT YOU WILL LIVE TO BECOME A HERO.
YOU ARE HEROES WITH OPPOSITE FATES.

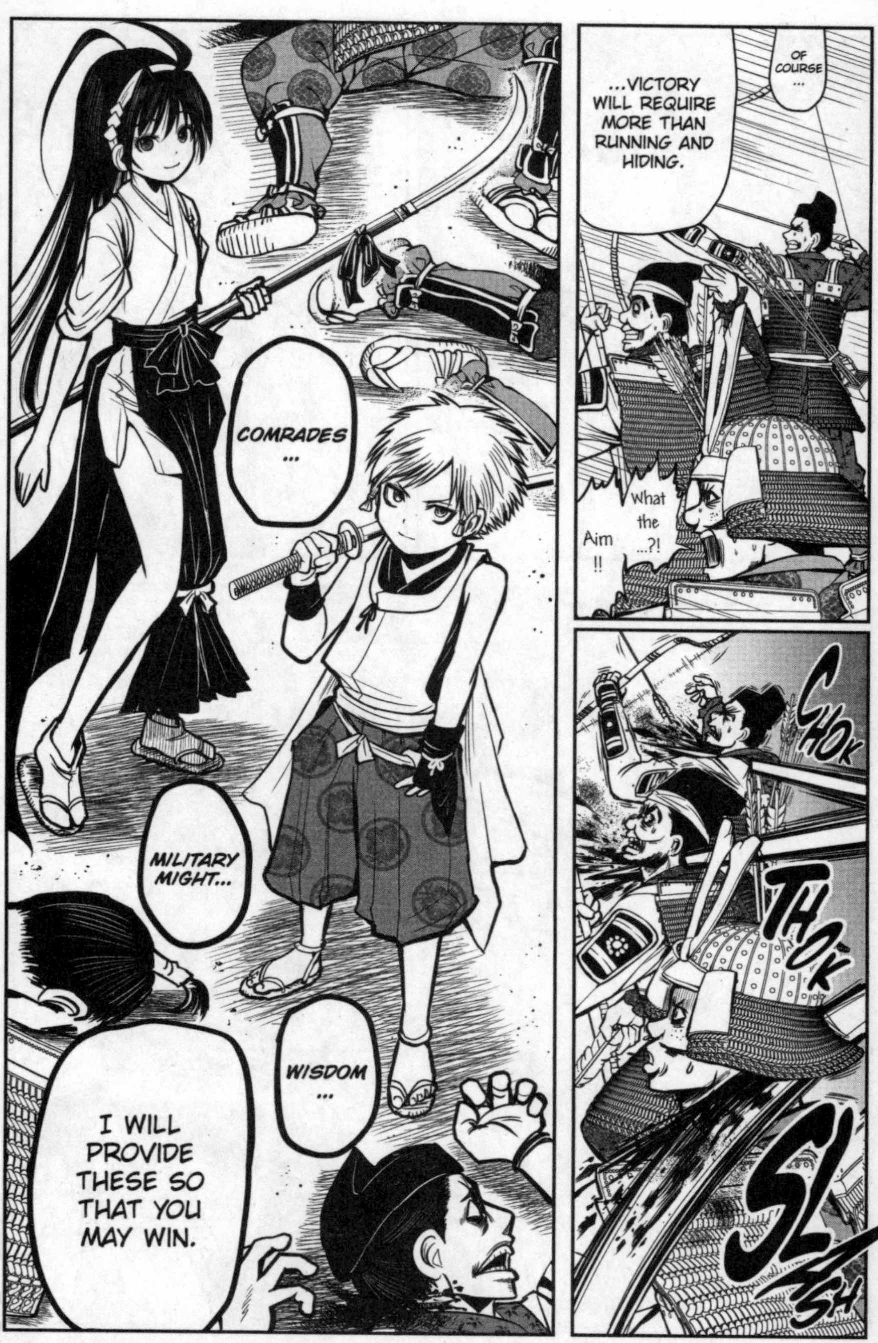
OF COURSE ...
...VICTORY WILL REQUIRE MORE THAN RUNNING AND HIDING.
What the ...?!
Aim !!
CHOK
THOK
SLASH
COMRADES ...
MILITARY MIGHT...
WISDOM ...
I WILL PROVIDE THESE SO THAT YOU MAY WIN.

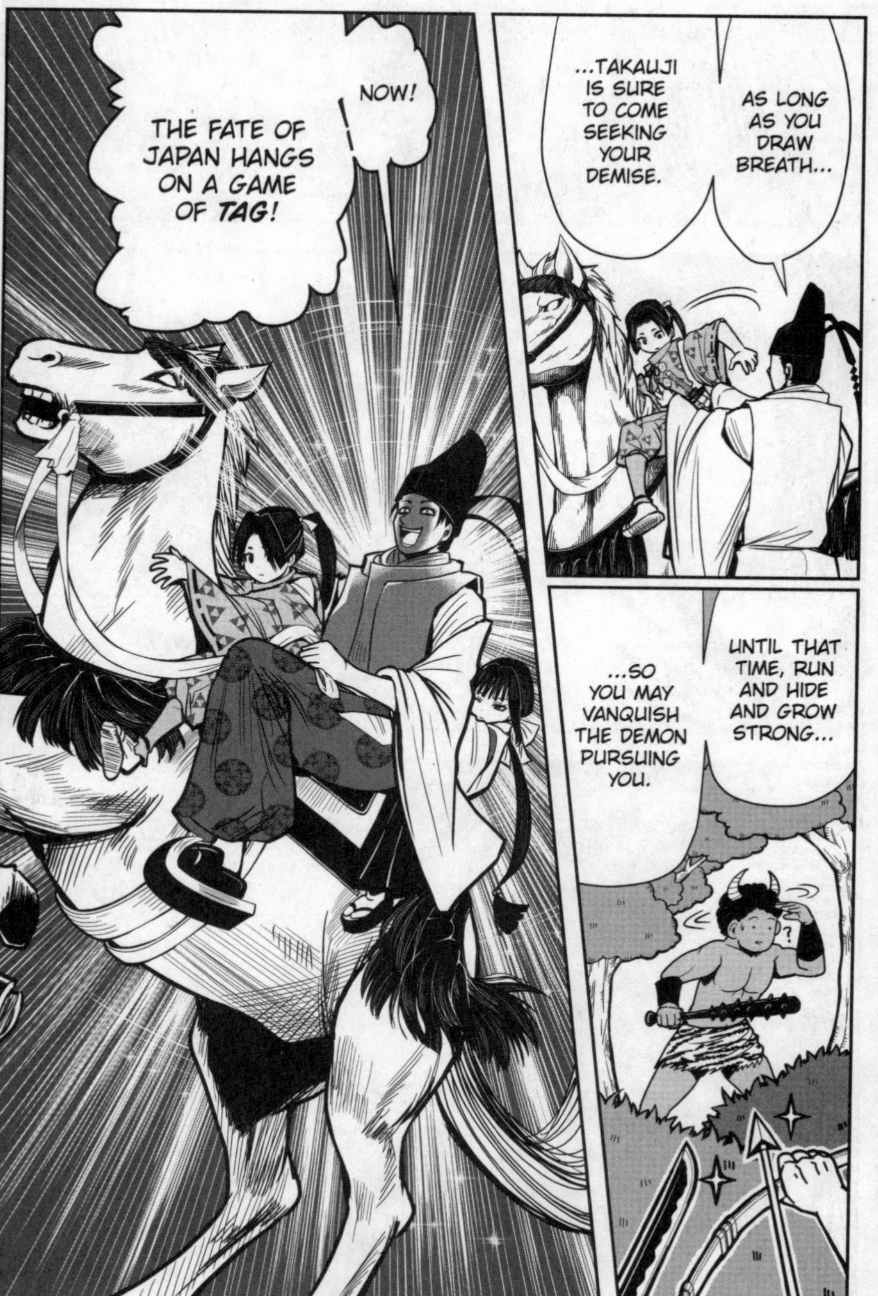
AS LONG AS YOU DRAW BREATH...
...TAKAUJI IS SURE TO COME SEEKING YOUR DEMISE.
UNTIL THAT TIME, RUN AND HIDE AND GROW STRONG...
...SO YOU MAY VANQUISH THE DEMON PURSUING YOU.
?
NOW!
THE FATE OF JAPAN HANGS ON A GAME OF TAG!

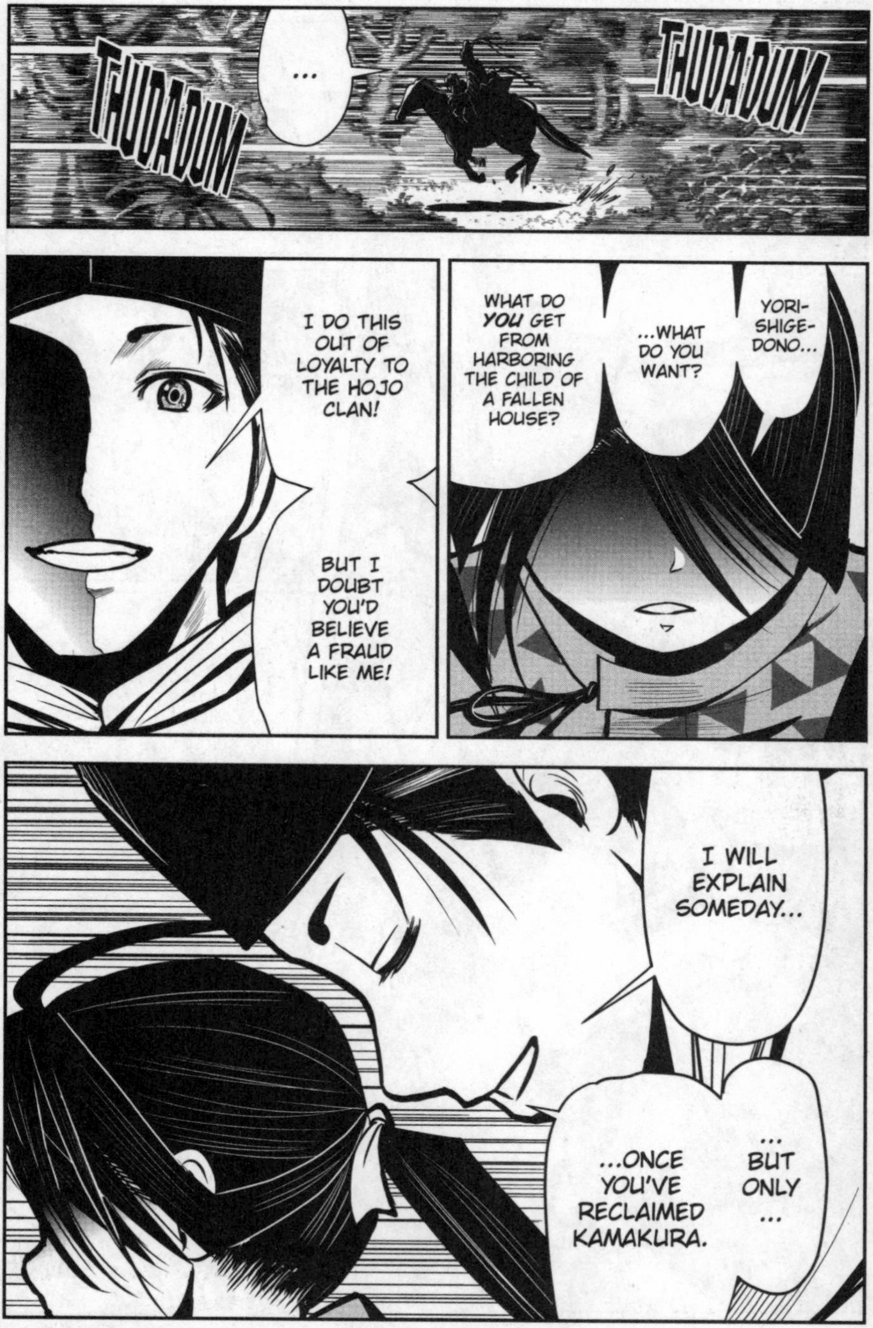
THUDADUM
...
THUDADUM
YORI-SHIGE-DONO...
...WHAT DO YOU WANT?
WHAT DO *YOU* GET FROM HARBORING THE CHILD OF A FALLEN HOUSE?
I DO THIS OUT OF LOYALTY TO THE HOJO CLAN!
BUT I DOUBT YOU'D BELIEVE A FRAUD LIKE ME!
I WILL EXPLAIN SOMEDAY...
... BUT ONLY ...
...ONCE YOU'VE RECLAIMED KAMAKURA.

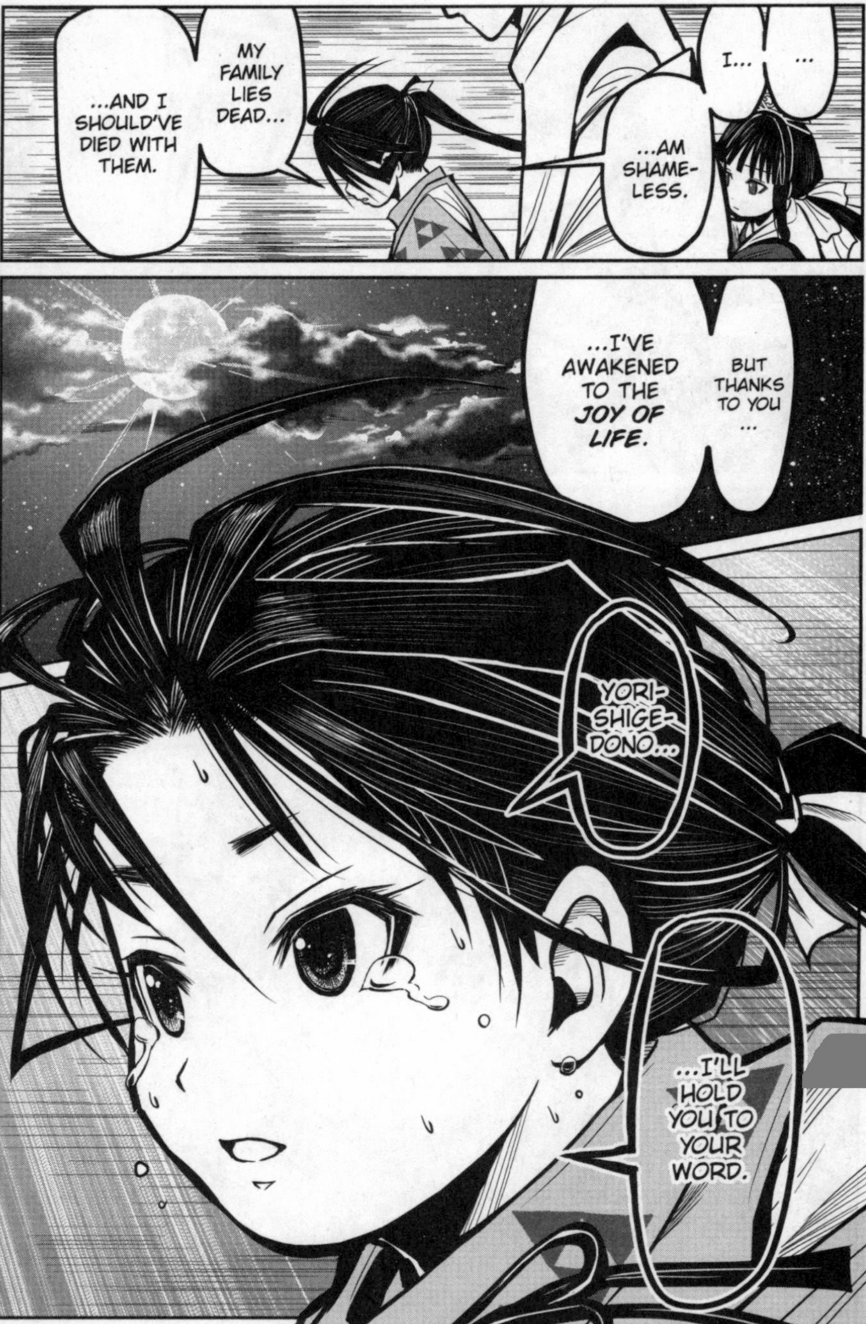
I... ...
...AM SHAMELESS.
MY FAMILY LIES DEAD...
...AND I SHOULD'VE DIED WITH THEM.
BUT THANKS TO YOU ...
...I'VE AWAKENED TO THE *JOY OF LIFE*.
YORISHIGE-DONO...
...I'LL HOLD YOU TO YOUR WORD.

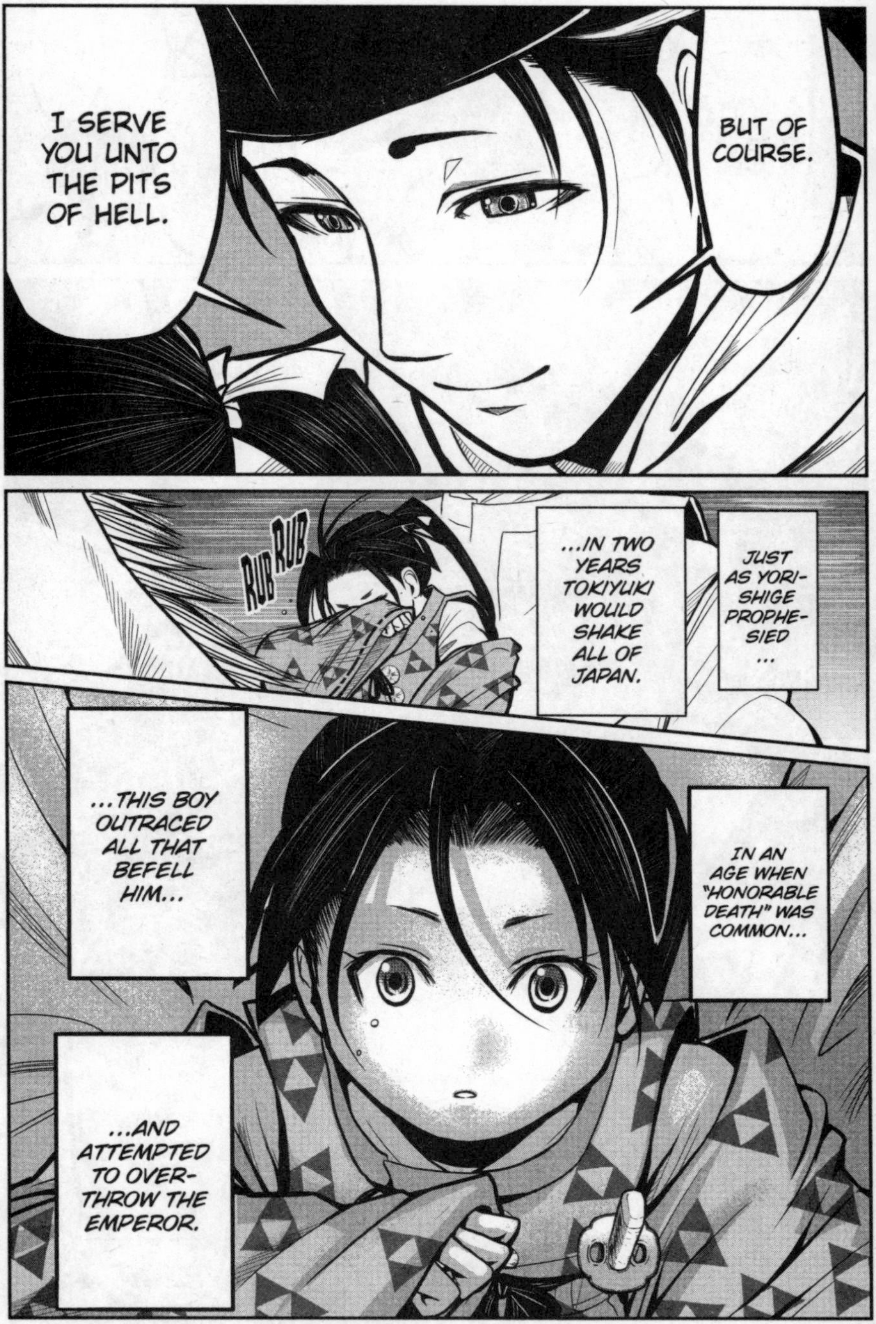
BUT OF COURSE.
I SERVE YOU UNTO THE PITS OF HELL.
JUST AS YORI-SHIGE PROPHE-SIED...
...IN TWO YEARS TOKIYUKI WOULD SHAKE ALL OF JAPAN.
RUB RUB
IN AN AGE WHEN "HONORABLE DEATH" WAS COMMON...
...THIS BOY OUTRACED ALL THAT BEFELL HIM...
...AND ATTEMPTED TO OVER-THROW THE EMPEROR.

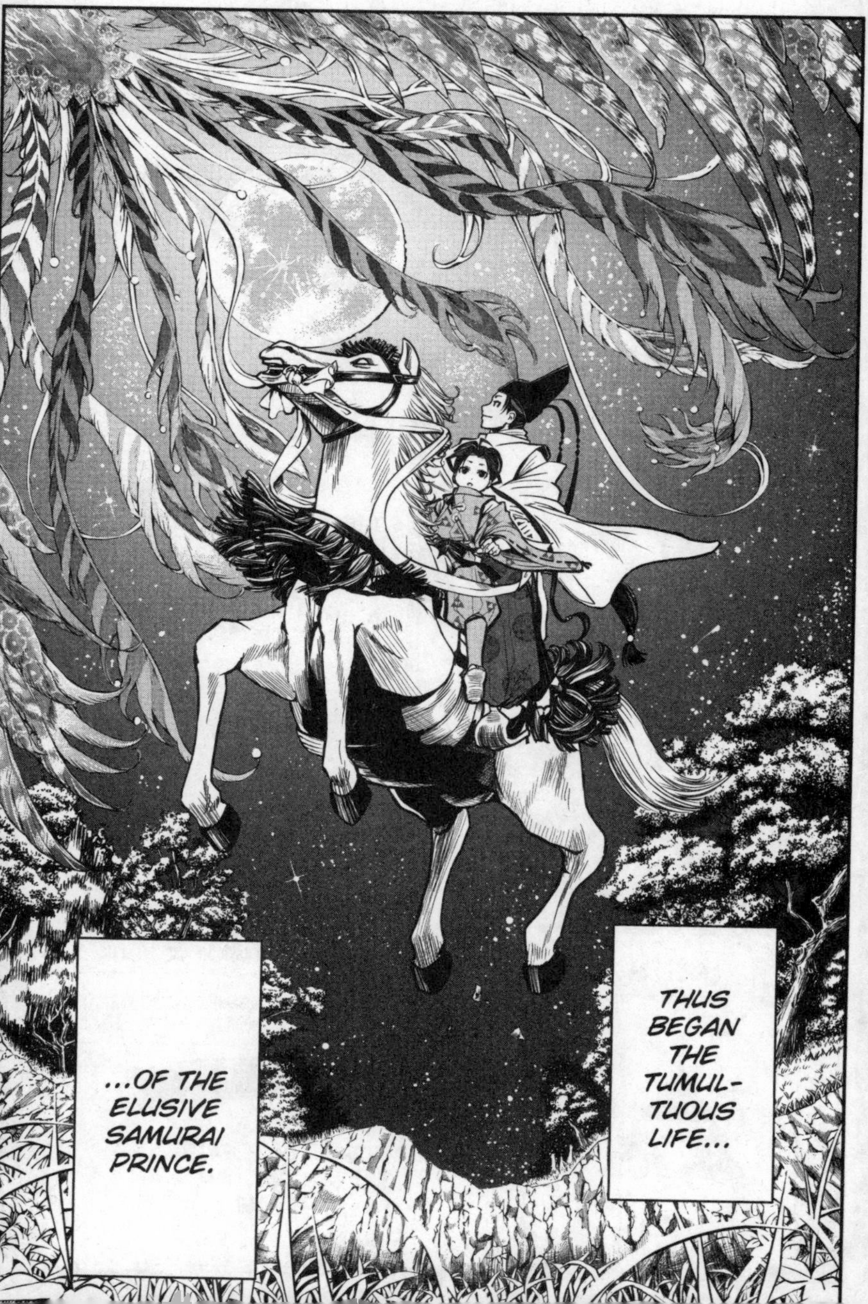
THUS BEGAN THE TUMUL-TUOUS LIFE...
...OF THE ELUSIVE SAMURAI PRINCE.

1333

HOJO TOKIYUKI

★★★★ SSR

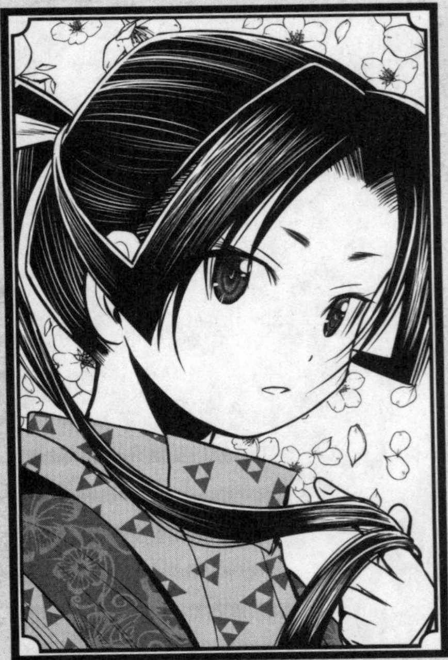

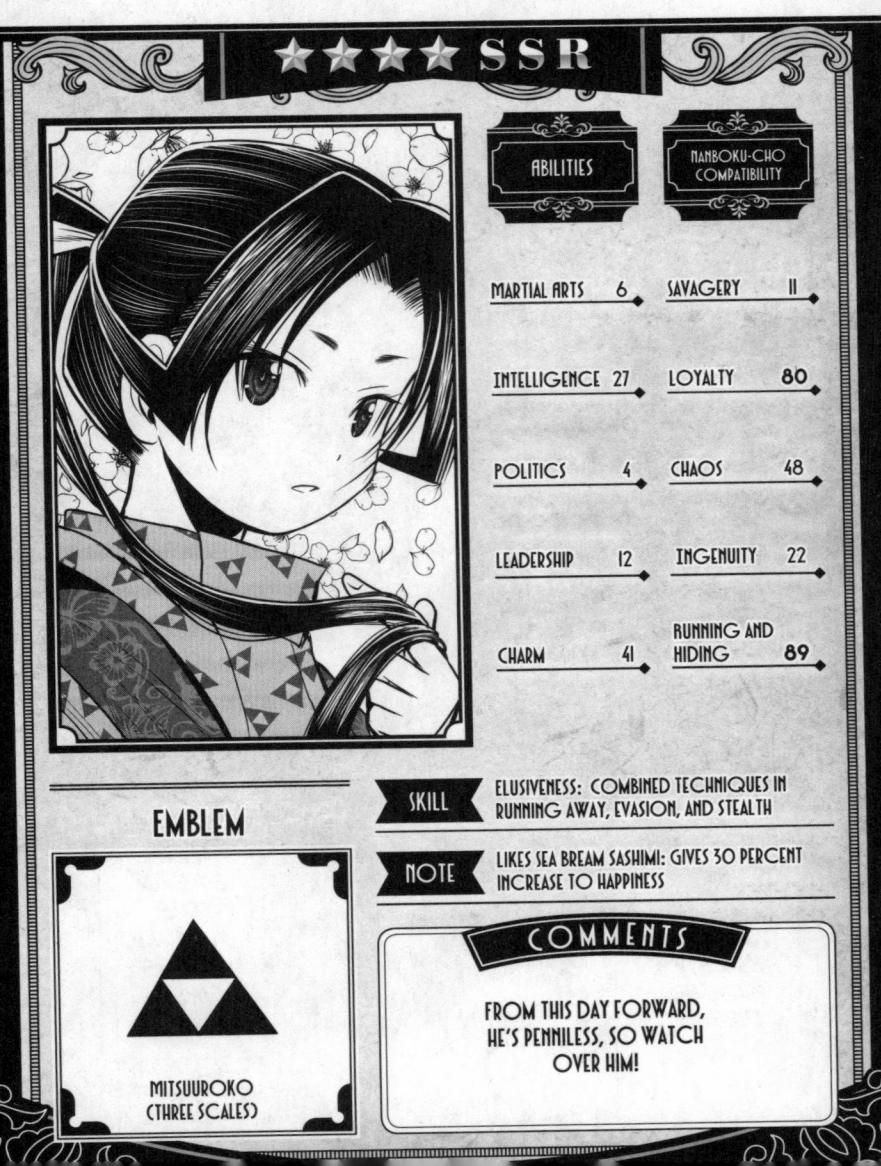

ABILITIES		NANBOKU-CHO COMPATIBILITY	
MARTIAL ARTS	6	SAVAGERY	11
INTELLIGENCE	27	LOYALTY	80
POLITICS	4	CHAOS	48
LEADERSHIP	12	INGENUITY	22
CHARM	41	RUNNING AND HIDING	89

EMBLEM

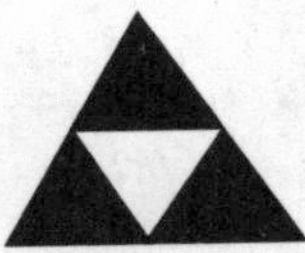

MITSUUROKO
(THREE SCALES)

SKILL ELUSIVENESS: COMBINED TECHNIQUES IN RUNNING AWAY, EVASION, AND STEALTH

NOTE LIKES SEA BREAM SASHIMI: GIVES 30 PERCENT INCREASE TO HAPPINESS

COMMENTS

FROM THIS DAY FORWARD, HE'S PENNILESS, SO WATCH OVER HIM!

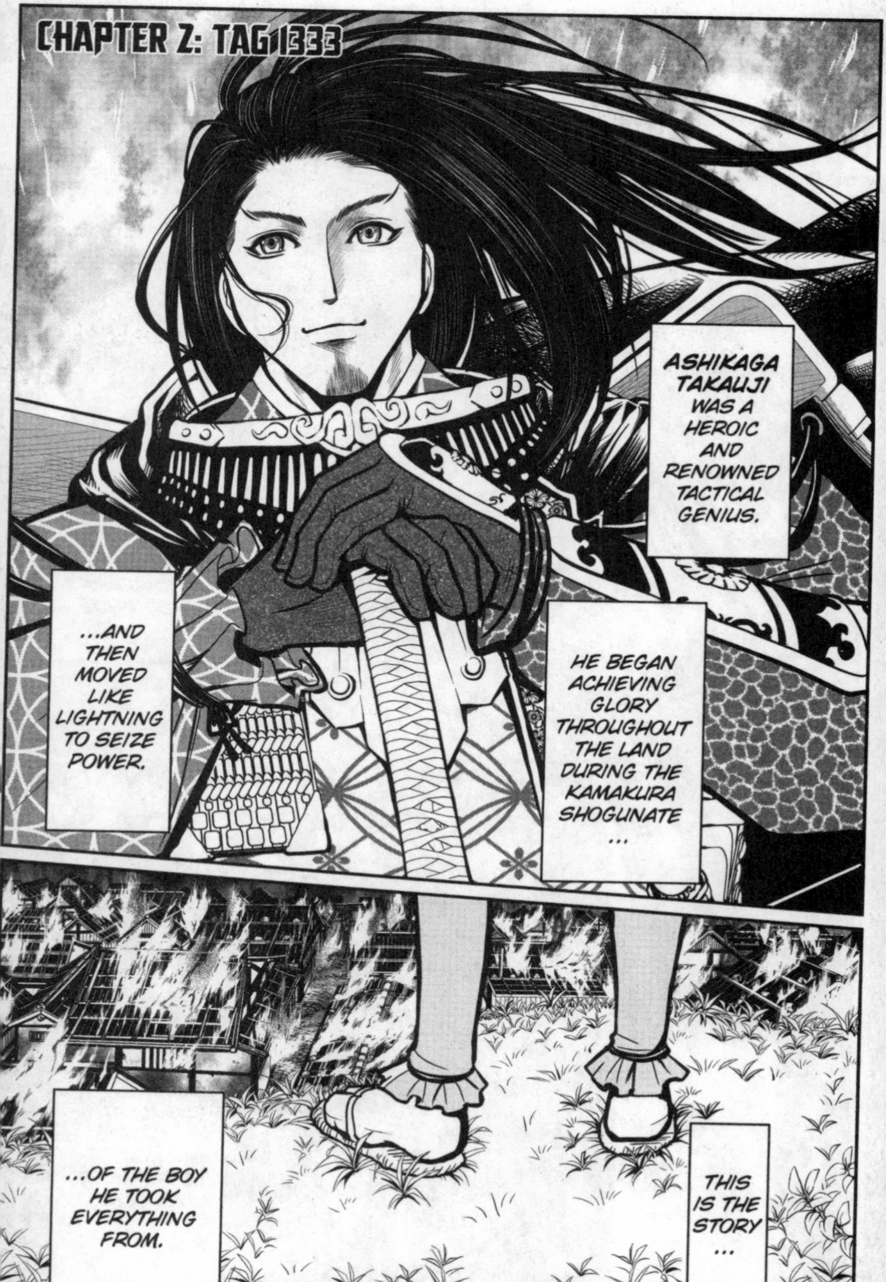
CHAPTER 2: TAG 1333
ASHIKAGA TAKAUJI WAS A HEROIC AND RENOWNED TACTICAL GENIUS.
HE BEGAN ACHIEVING GLORY THROUGHOUT THE LAND DURING THE KAMAKURA SHOGUNATE ...
...AND THEN MOVED LIKE LIGHTNING TO SEIZE POWER.
THIS IS THE STORY ...
...OF THE BOY HE TOOK EVERYTHING FROM.

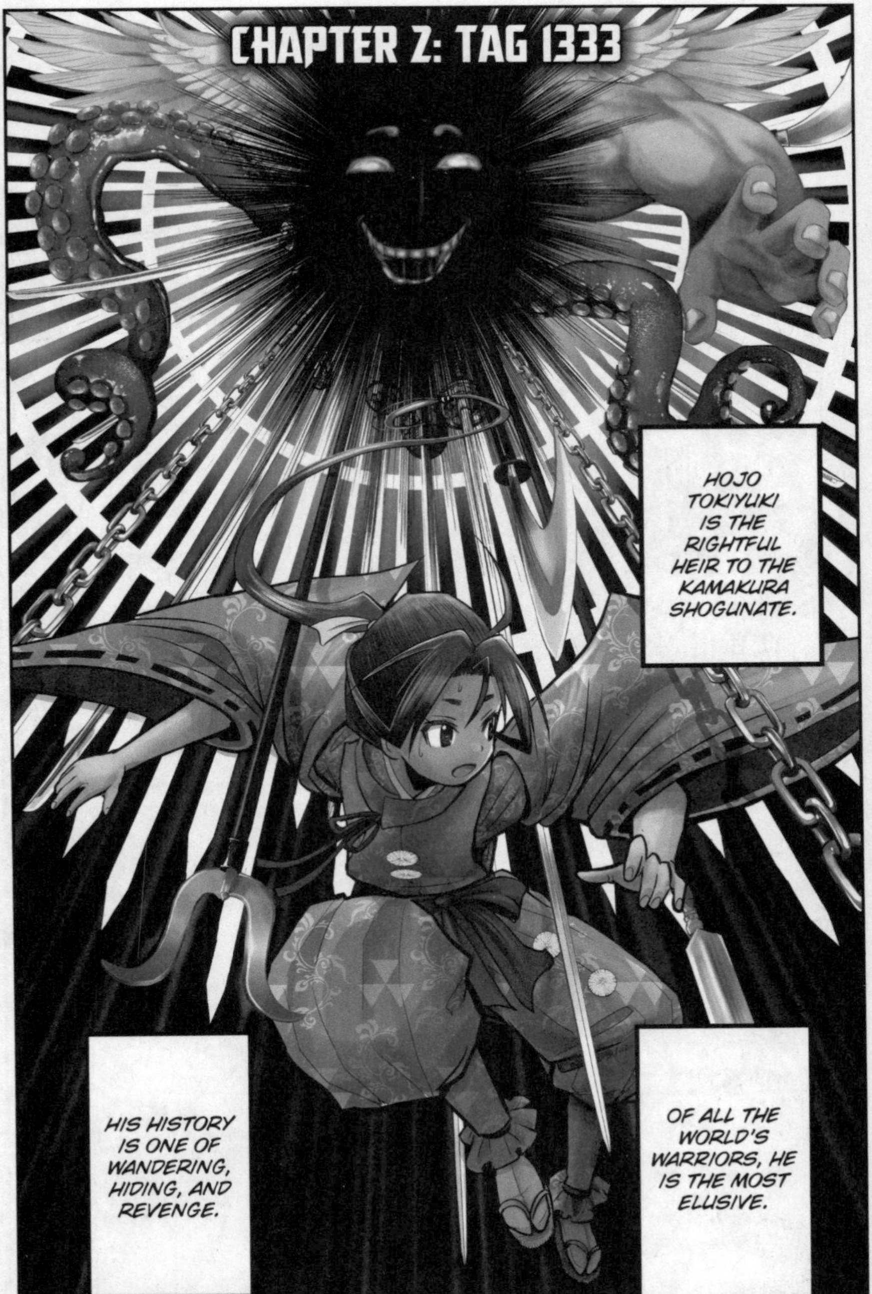
CHAPTER 2: TAG 1333
HOJO TOKIYUKI IS THE RIGHTFUL HEIR TO THE KAMAKURA SHOGUNATE.
OF ALL THE WORLD'S WARRIORS, HE IS THE MOST ELUSIVE.
HIS HISTORY IS ONE OF WANDERING, HIDING, AND REVENGE.

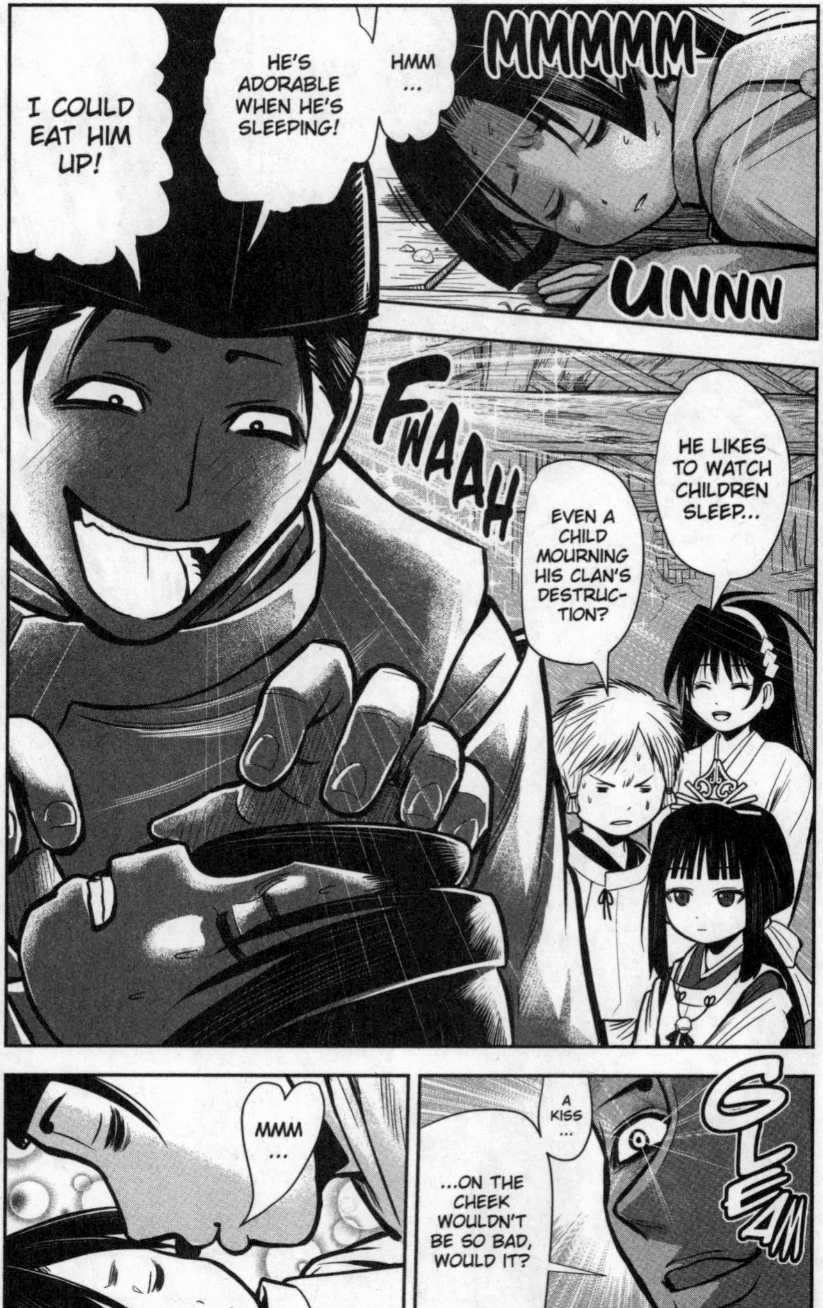
MMMMMM
UNNN
HMM ...
HE'S ADORABLE WHEN HE'S SLEEPING!
I COULD EAT HIM UP!
FWAAH
HE LIKES TO WATCH CHILDREN SLEEP...
EVEN A CHILD MOURNING HIS CLAN'S DESTRUC-TION?
GLEAM
A KISS ...
...ON THE CHEEK WOULDN'T BE SO BAD, WOULD IT?
MMM ...

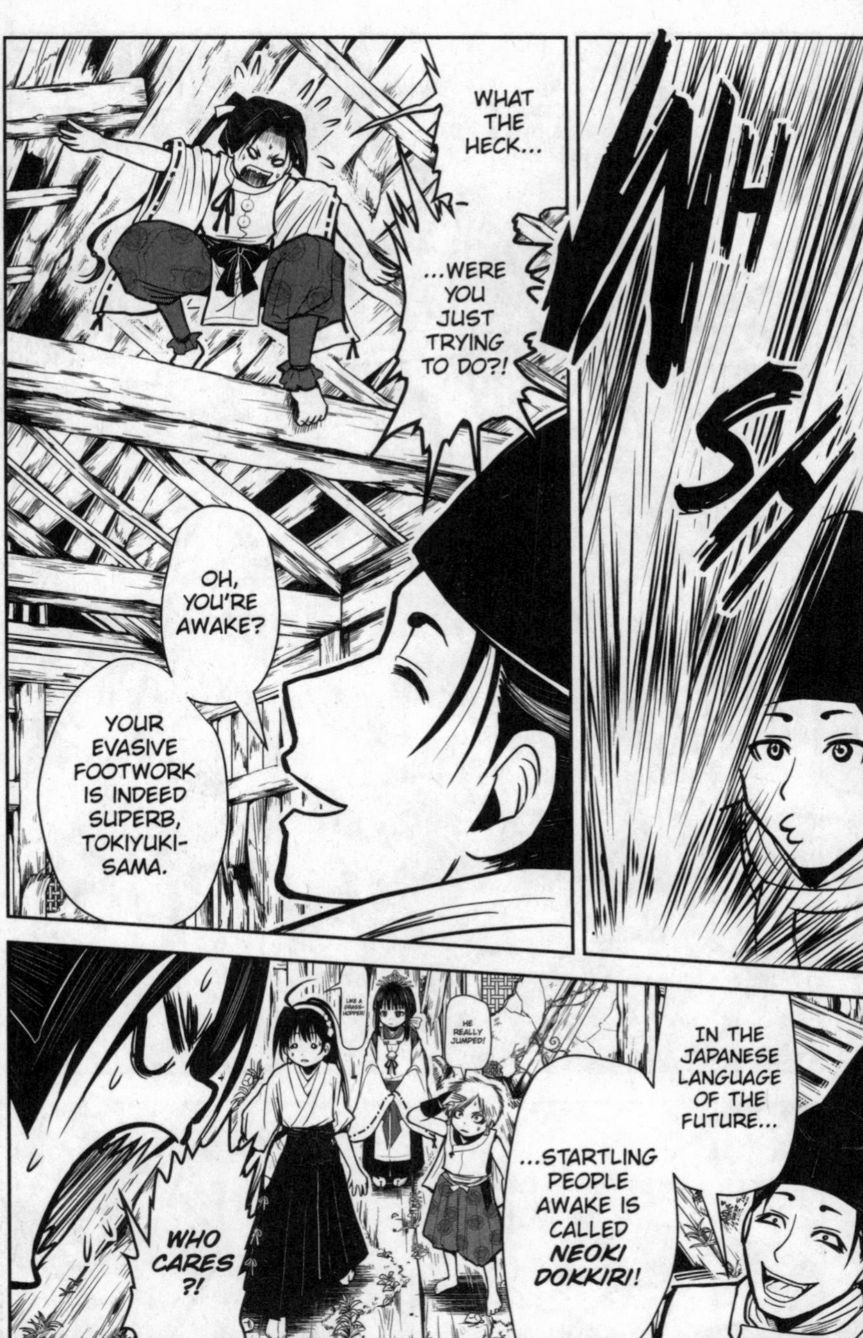
WHSH
WHAT THE HECK...
...WERE YOU JUST TRYING TO DO?!
OH, YOU'RE AWAKE?
YOUR EVASIVE FOOTWORK IS INDEED SUPERB, TOKIYUKI-SAMA.
IN THE JAPANESE LANGUAGE OF THE FUTURE...
...STARTLING PEOPLE AWAKE IS CALLED NEOKI DOKKIRI!
HE REALLY JUMPED!
LIKE A GRASS-HOPPER!
WHO CARES?!

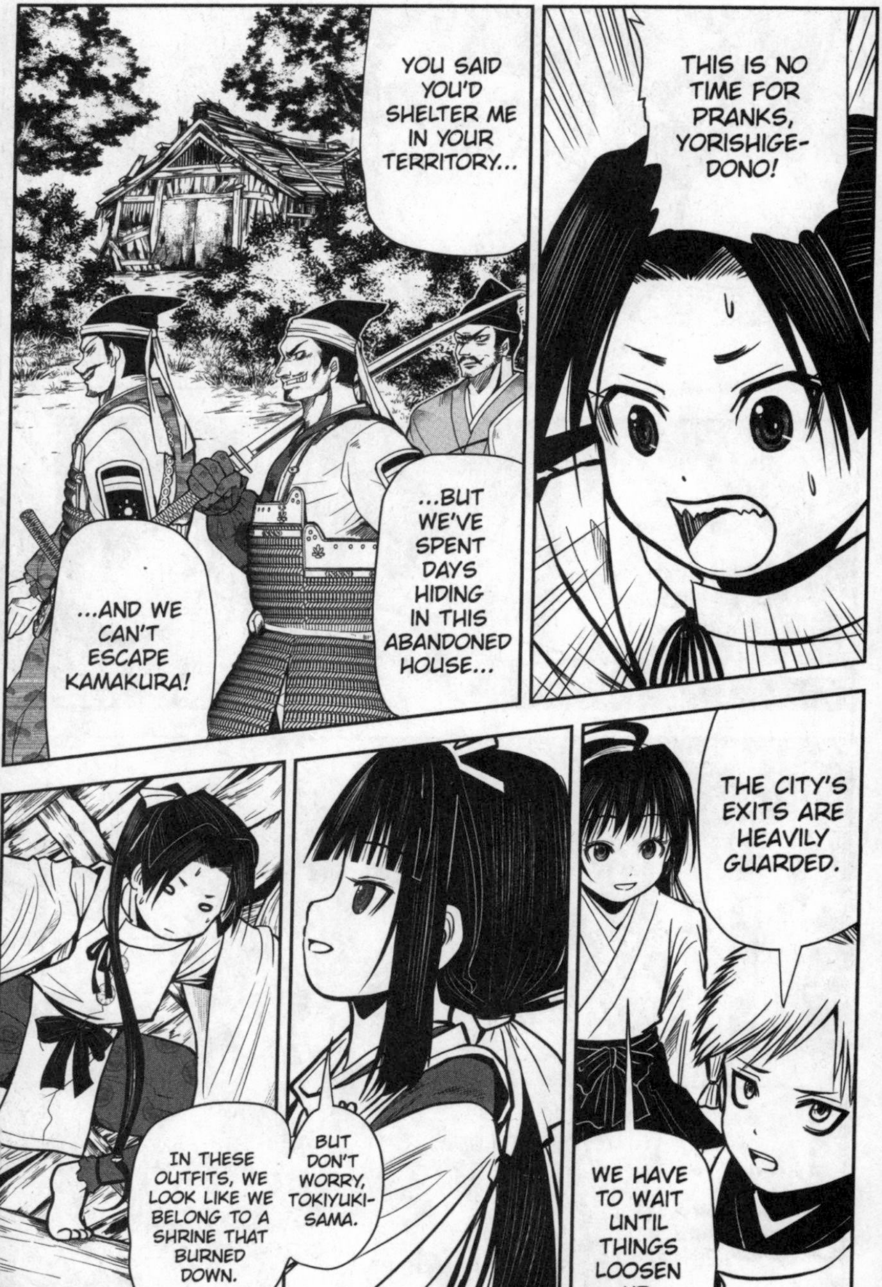
THIS IS NO TIME FOR PRANKS, YORISHIGE-DONO!
YOU SAID YOU'D SHELTER ME IN YOUR TERRITORY...
...BUT WE'VE SPENT DAYS HIDING IN THIS ABANDONED HOUSE...
...AND WE CAN'T ESCAPE KAMAKURA!
THE CITY'S EXITS ARE HEAVILY GUARDED.
WE HAVE TO WAIT UNTIL THINGS LOOSEN UP.
BUT DON'T WORRY, TOKIYUKI-SAMA.
IN THESE OUTFITS, WE LOOK LIKE WE BELONG TO A SHRINE THAT BURNED DOWN.

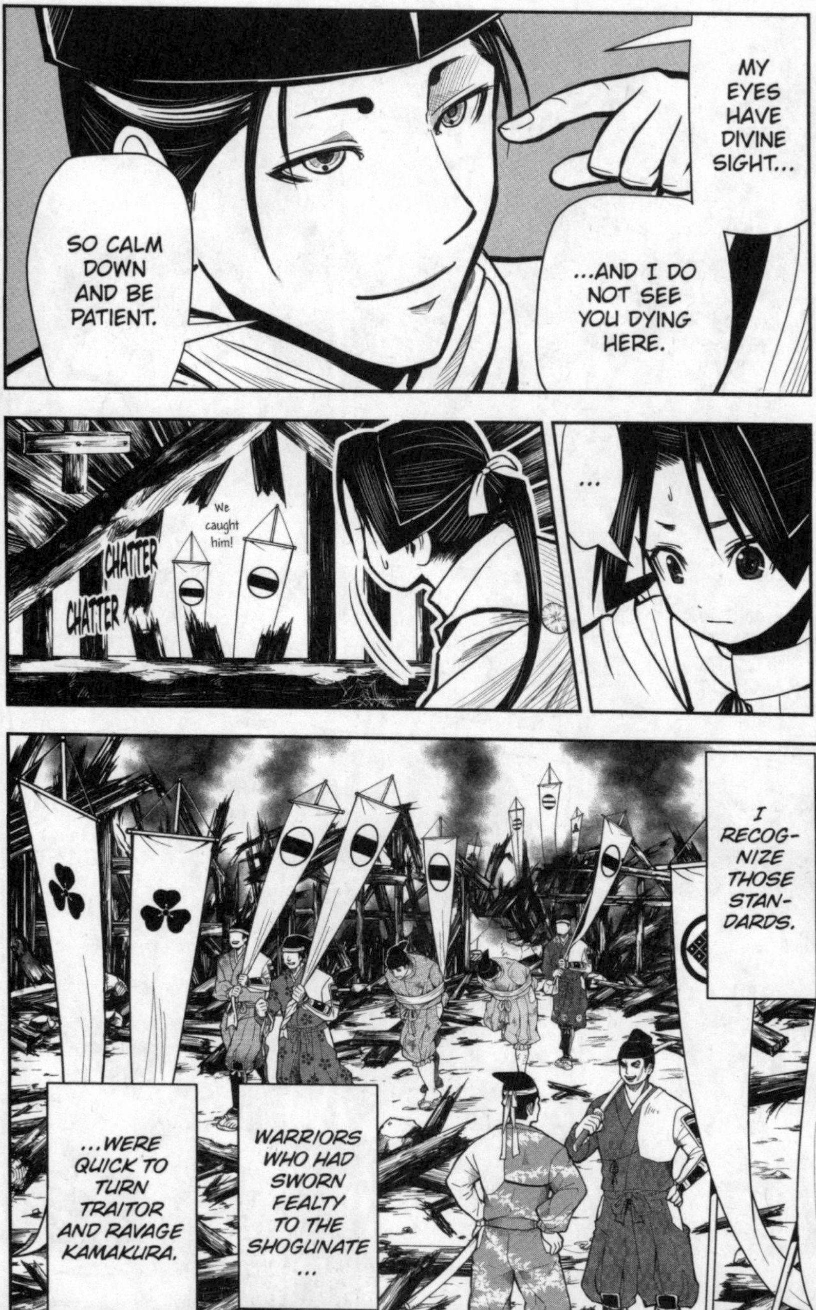
MY EYES HAVE DIVINE SIGHT...
...AND I DO NOT SEE YOU DYING HERE.
SO CALM DOWN AND BE PATIENT.
...
We caught him!
CHATTER
CHATTER
I RECOGNIZE THOSE STANDARDS.
WARRIORS WHO HAD SWORN FEALTY TO THE SHOGUNATE ...
...WERE QUICK TO TURN TRAITOR AND RAVAGE KAMAKURA.

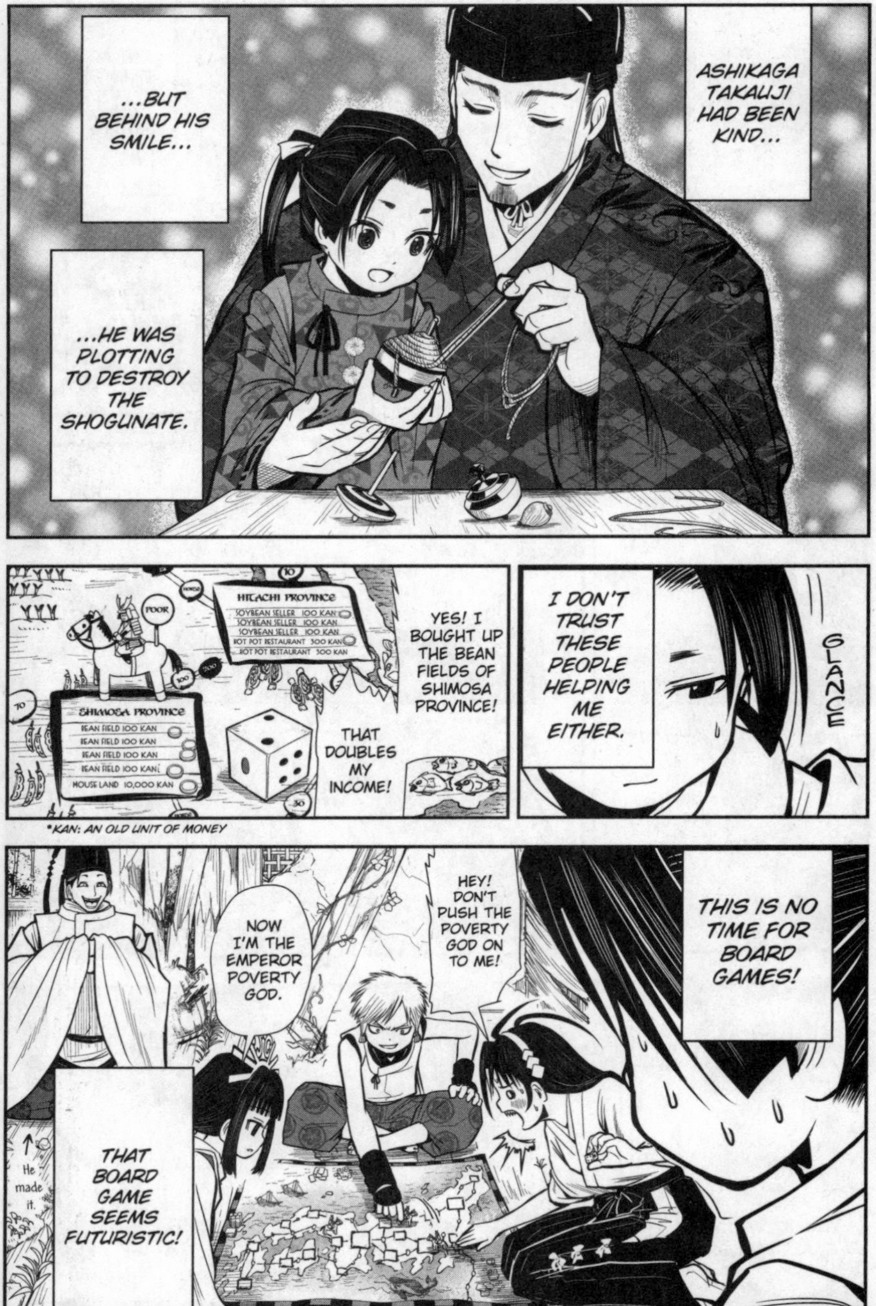
ASHIKAGA TAKAUJI HAD BEEN KIND...
...BUT BEHIND HIS SMILE...
...HE WAS PLOTTING TO DESTROY THE SHOGUNATE.
GLANCE
I DON'T TRUST THESE PEOPLE HELPING ME EITHER.
YES! I BOUGHT UP THE BEAN FIELDS OF SHIMOSA PROVINCE!
THAT DOUBLES MY INCOME!
HITACHI PROVINCE
SOYBEAN SELLER 100 KAN
SOYBEAN SELLER 100 KAN
SOYBEAN SELLER 100 KAN
ROT POT RESTAURANT 300 KAN
ROT POT RESTAURANT 300 KAN
POOR
SHIMOSA PROVINCE
BEAN FIELD 100 KAN
BEAN FIELD 100 KAN
BEAN FIELD 100 KAN
BEAN FIELD 100 KAN
MOUSE LAND 10,000 KAN
*KAN: AN OLD UNIT OF MONEY
THIS IS NO TIME FOR BOARD GAMES!
HEY! DON'T PUSH THE POVERTY GOD ON TO ME!
NOW I'M THE EMPEROR POVERTY GOD.
THAT BOARD GAME SEEMS FUTURISTIC!
← He made it.

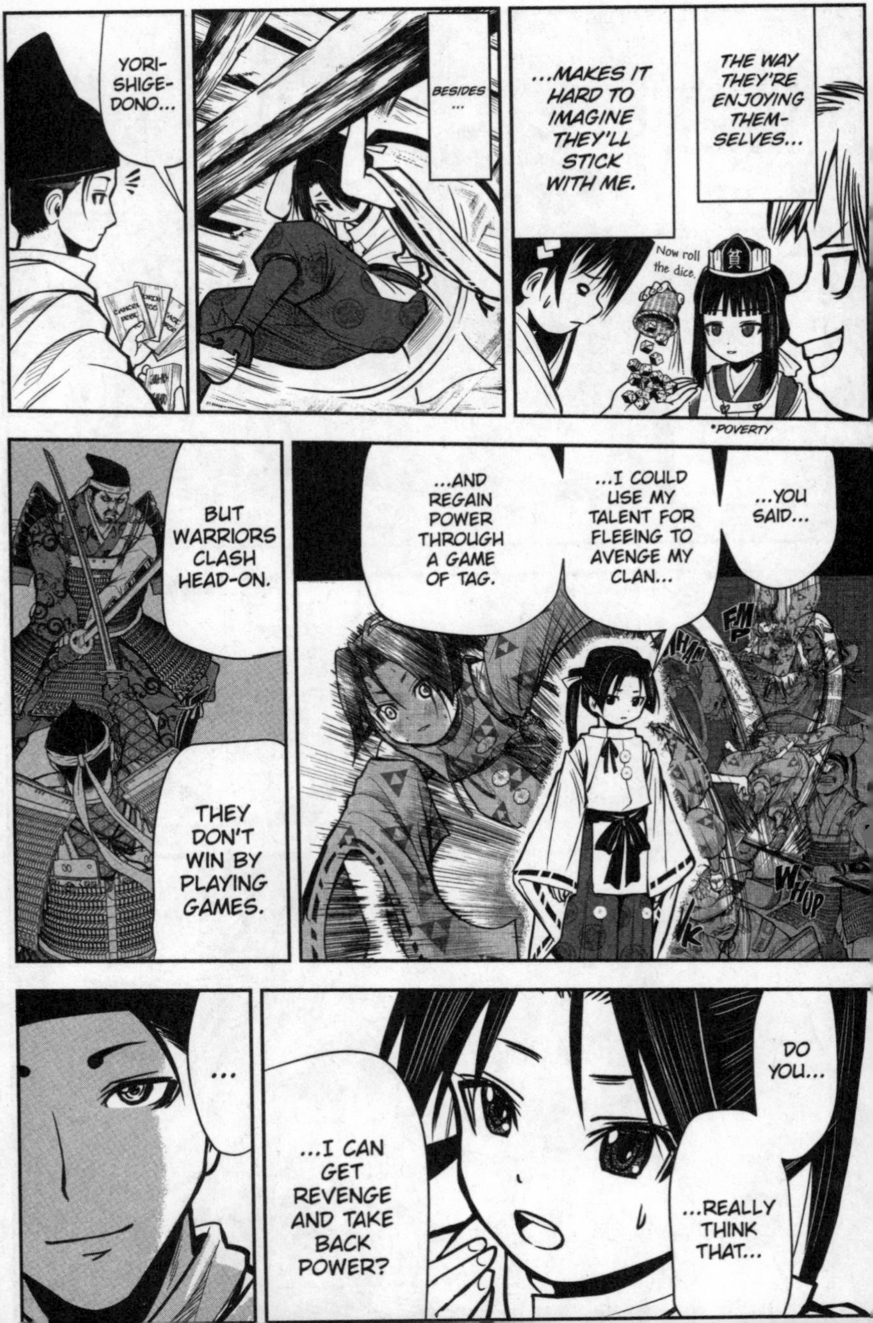
THE WAY THEY'RE ENJOYING THEM-SELVES...
Now roll the dice.
...MAKES IT HARD TO IMAGINE THEY'LL STICK WITH ME.
*POVERTY
BESIDES ...
YORI-SHIGE-DONO...
...YOU SAID...
...I COULD USE MY TALENT FOR FLEEING TO AVENGE MY CLAN...
...AND REGAIN POWER THROUGH A GAME OF TAG.
FMP
WHUP
K
BUT WARRIORS CLASH HEAD-ON.
THEY DON'T WIN BY PLAYING GAMES.
DO YOU...
...REALLY THINK THAT...
...I CAN GET REVENGE AND TAKE BACK POWER?
...

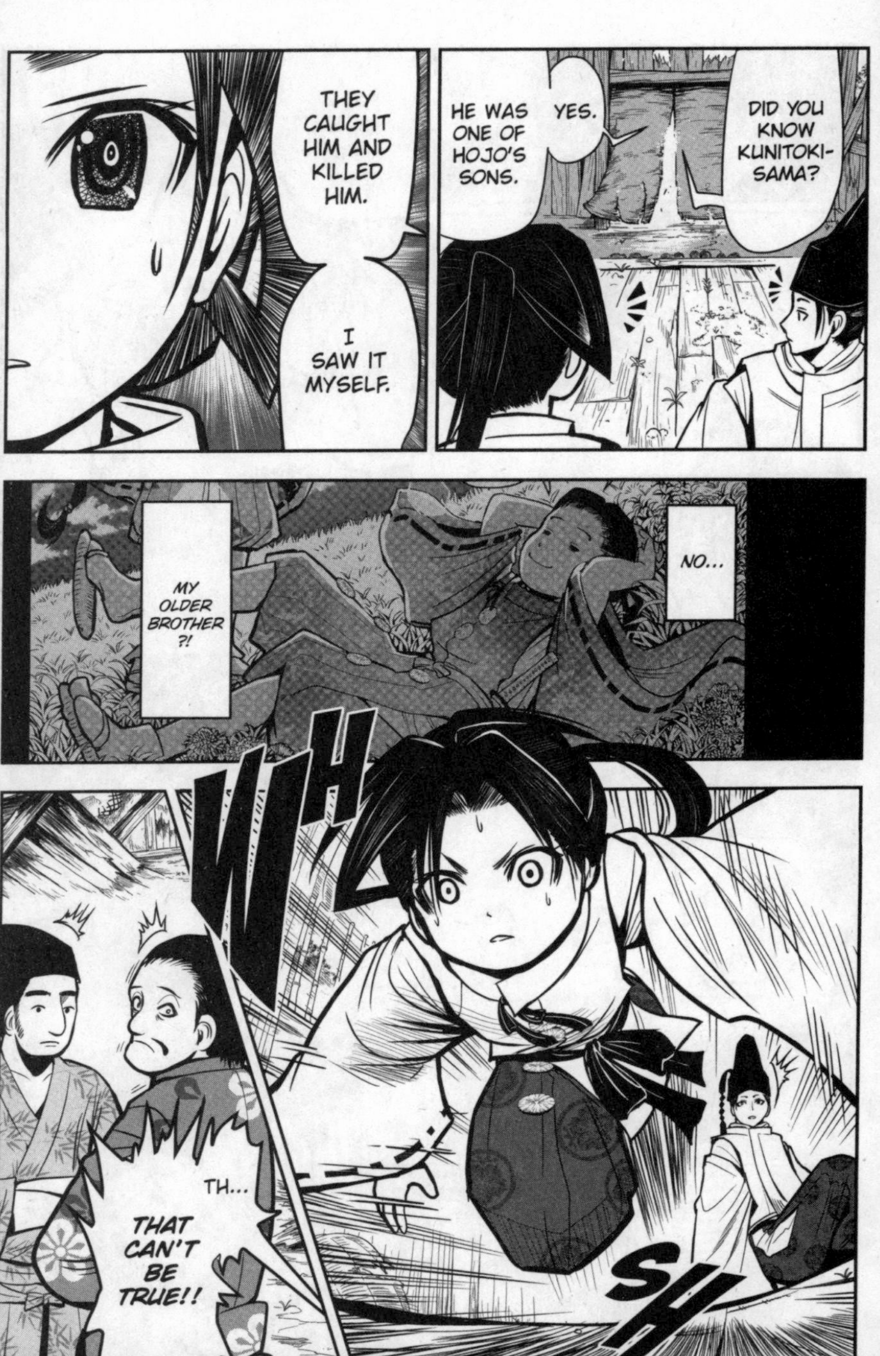
DID YOU KNOW KUNITOKI-SAMA?
YES.
HE WAS ONE OF HOJO'S SONS.
THEY CAUGHT HIM AND KILLED HIM.
I SAW IT MYSELF.
NO...
MY OLDER BROTHER ?!
WHH
SH
TH...
THAT CAN'T BE TRUE!!

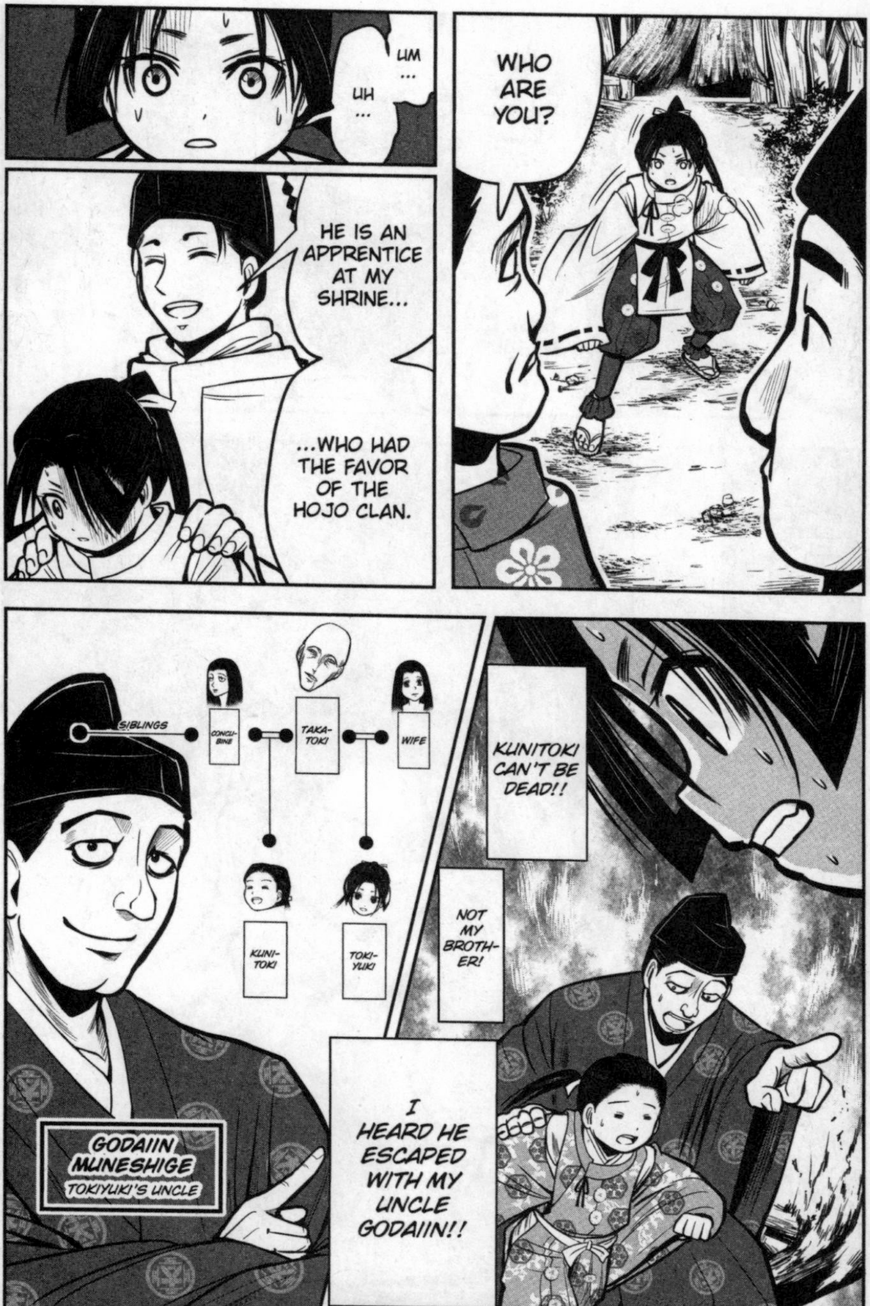
WHO ARE YOU?
UM ...
UH ...
HE IS AN APPRENTICE AT MY SHRINE...
...WHO HAD THE FAVOR OF THE HOJO CLAN.
KUNITOKI CAN'T BE DEAD!!
NOT MY BROTHER!
I HEARD HE ESCAPED WITH MY UNCLE GODAIIN!!
SIBLINGS
CONCUBINE
TAKATOKI
WIFE
KUNITOKI
TOKIYUKI
GODAIIN MUNESHIGE
TOKIYUKI'S UNCLE

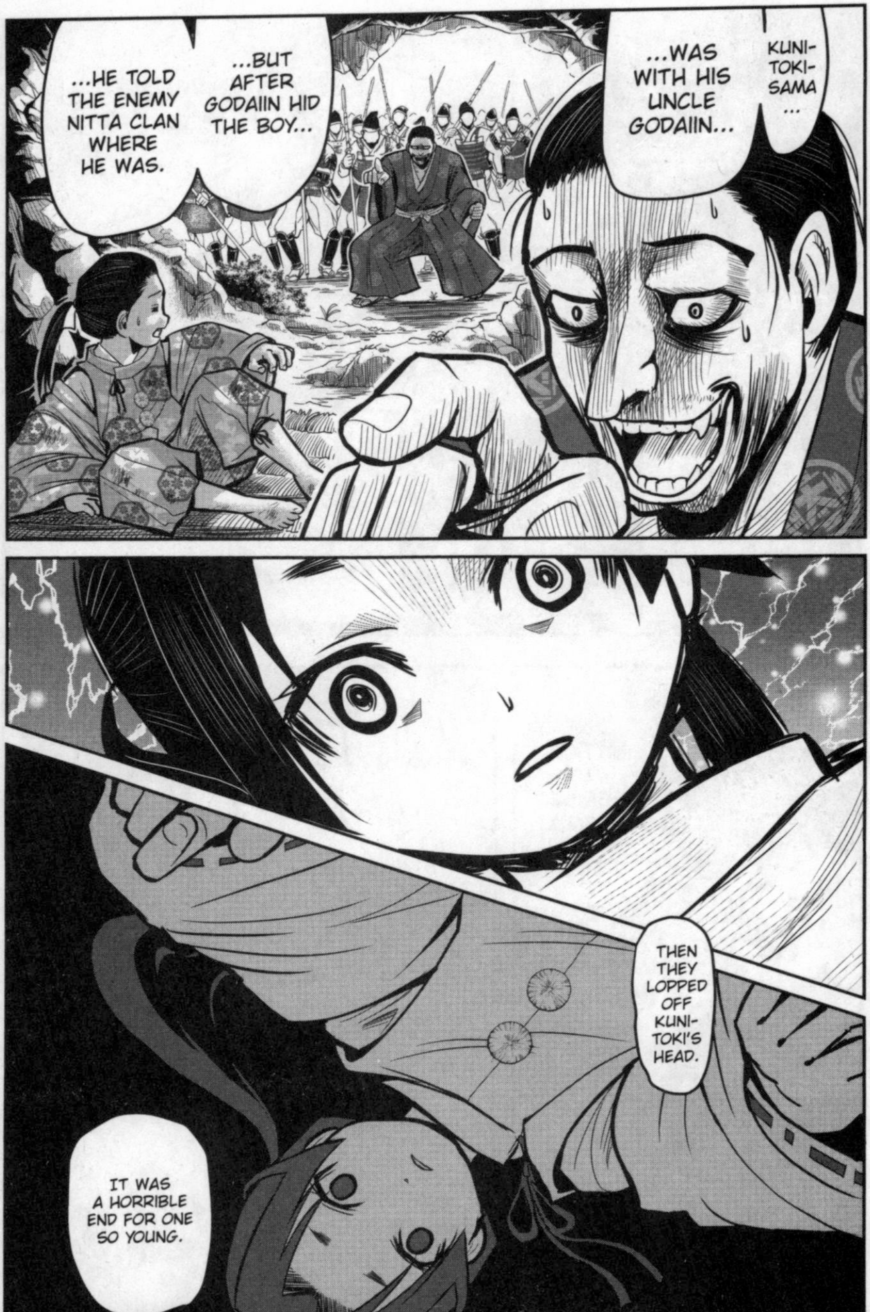
KUNI-TOKI-SAMA...
...WAS WITH HIS UNCLE GODAIIN...
...BUT AFTER GODAIIN HID THE BOY...
...HE TOLD THE ENEMY NITTA CLAN WHERE HE WAS.
THEN THEY LOPPED OFF KUNI-TOKI'S HEAD.
IT WAS A HORRIBLE END FOR ONE SO YOUNG.

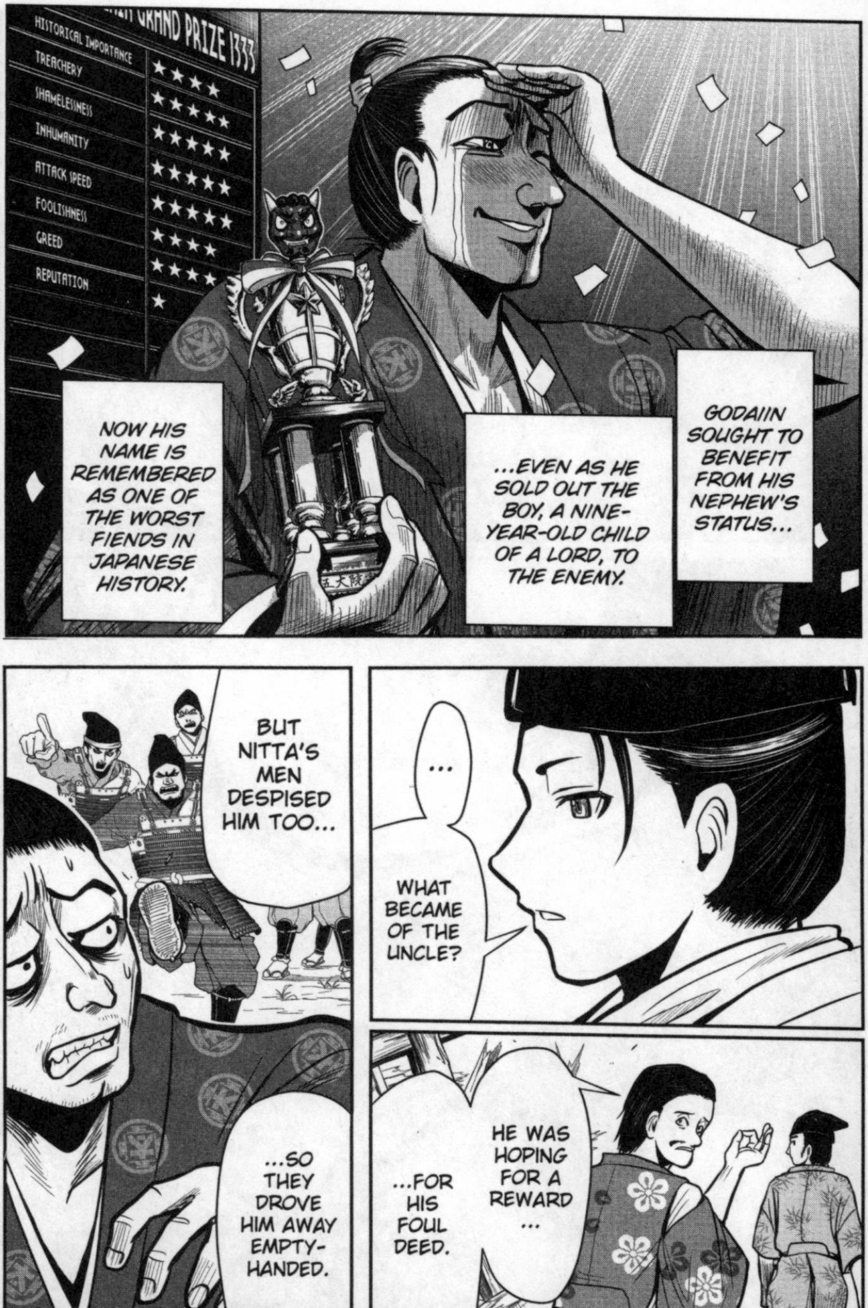
GRAND PRIZE 1333
HISTORICAL IMPORTANCE ★★★★
TREACHERY ★★★★★
SHAMELESSNESS ★★★★★
INHUMANITY ★★★★★
ATTACK SPEED ★★★★★
FOOLISHNESS ★★★★
GREED ★★★★
REPUTATION ★
GODAIIN SOUGHT TO BENEFIT FROM HIS NEPHEW'S STATUS...
...EVEN AS HE SOLD OUT THE BOY, A NINE-YEAR-OLD CHILD OF A LORD, TO THE ENEMY.
NOW HIS NAME IS REMEMBERED AS ONE OF THE WORST FIENDS IN JAPANESE HISTORY.
...
WHAT BECAME OF THE UNCLE?
HE WAS HOPING FOR A REWARD ...
...FOR HIS FOUL DEED.
BUT NITTA'S MEN DESPISED HIM TOO...
...SO THEY DROVE HIM AWAY EMPTY-HANDED.

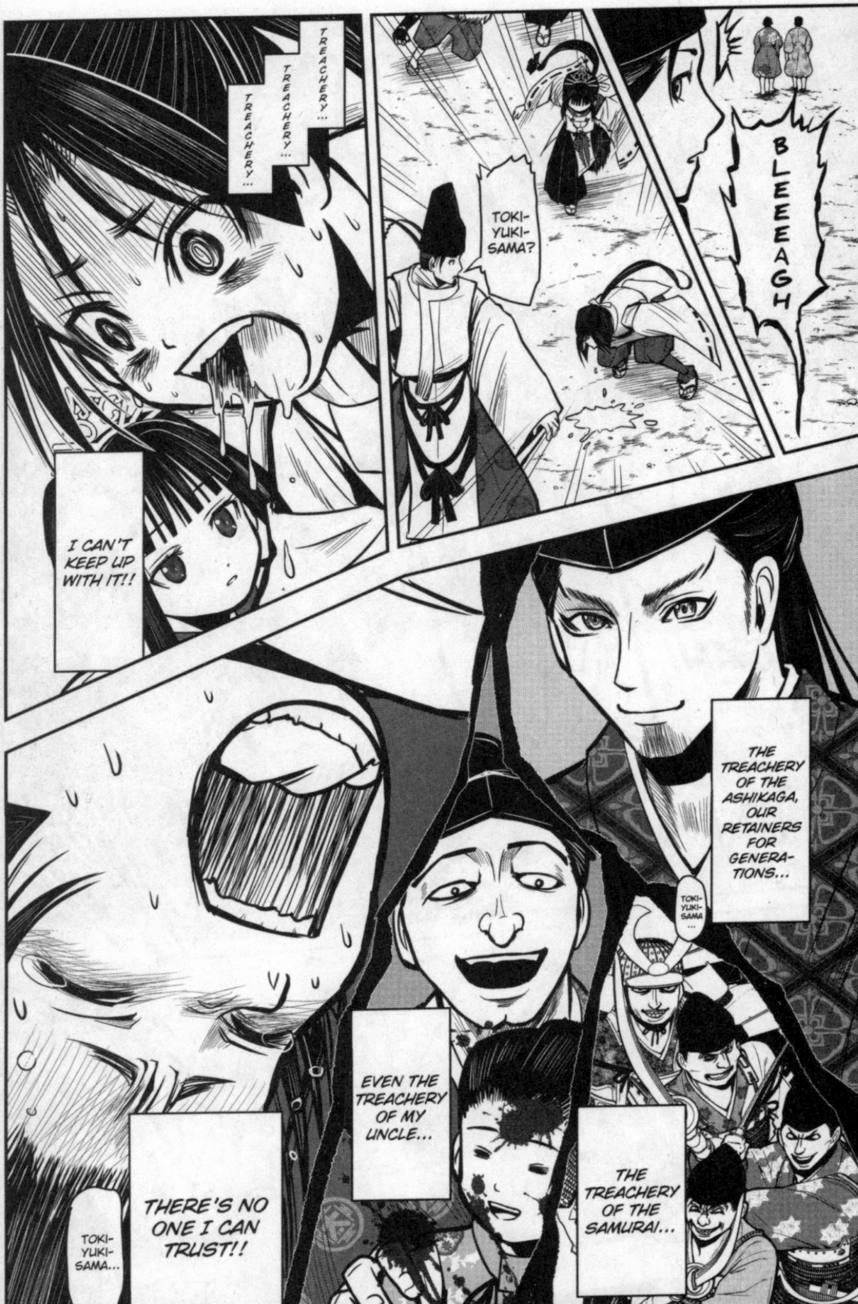
BLEEEAGH
TOKI-YUKI-SAMA?
TREACHERY...
TREACHERY...
TREACHERY...
I CAN'T KEEP UP WITH IT!!
THE TREACHERY OF THE ASHIKAGA, OUR RETAINERS FOR GENERATIONS...
TOKI-YUKI-SAMA...
THE TREACHERY OF THE SAMURAI...
EVEN THE TREACHERY OF MY UNCLE...
THERE'S NO ONE I CAN TRUST!!
TOKI-YUKI-SAMA...

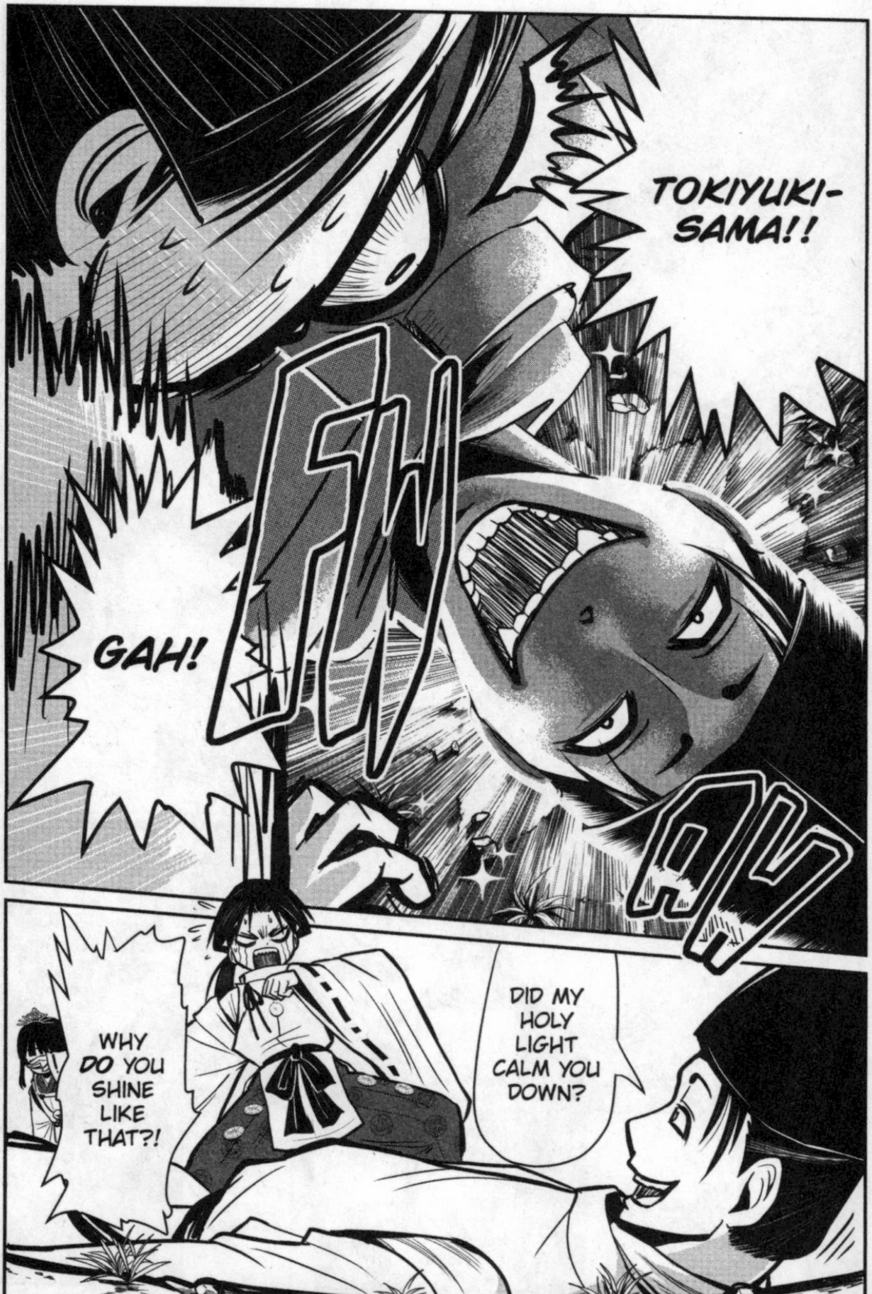
TOKIYUKI-SAMA!!
FW
AH
GAH!
DID MY HOLY LIGHT CALM YOU DOWN?
WHY DO YOU SHINE LIKE THAT?!

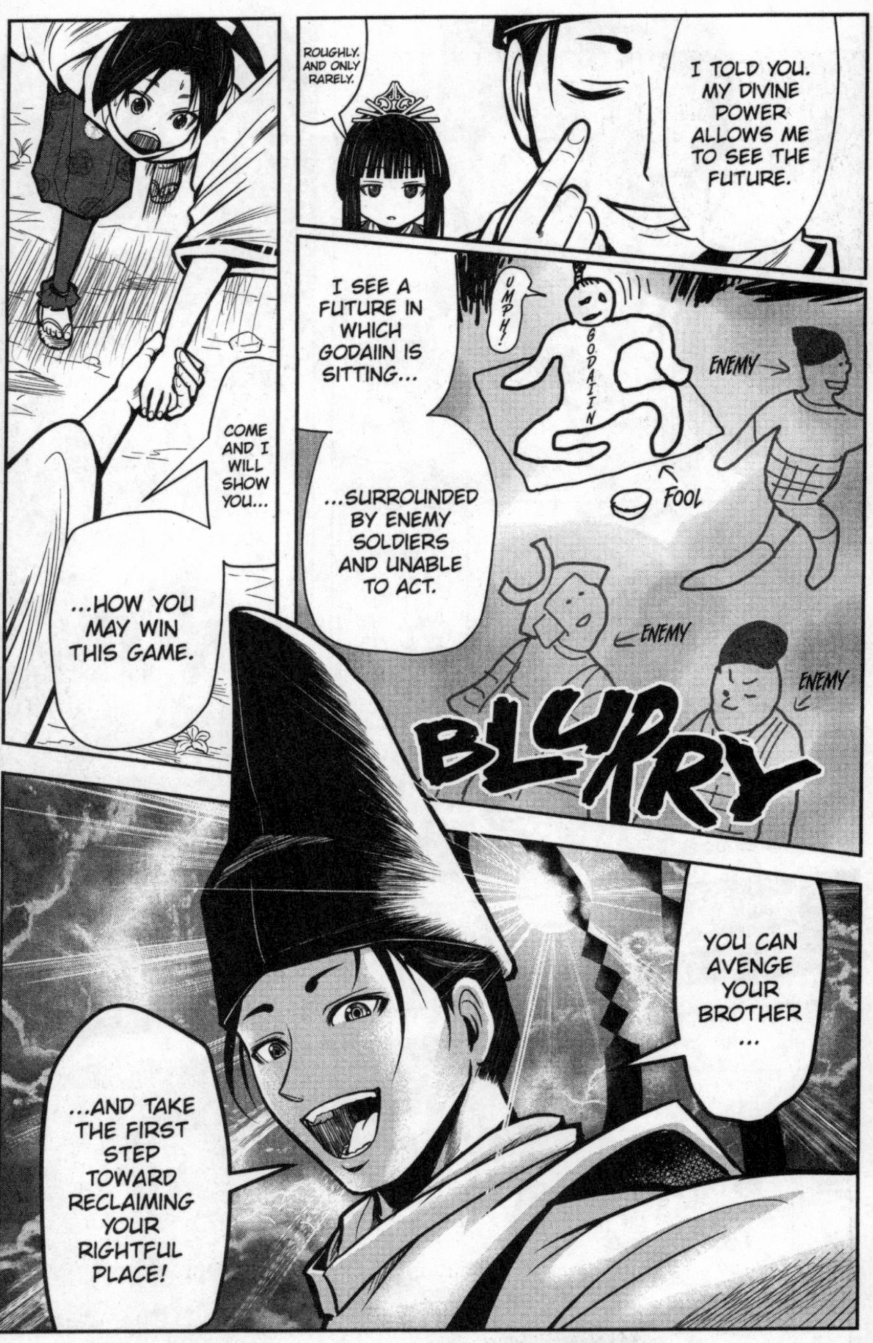
I TOLD YOU. MY DIVINE POWER ALLOWS ME TO SEE THE FUTURE.
ROUGHLY. AND ONLY RARELY.
I SEE A FUTURE IN WHICH GODAIIN IS SITTING...
UMPH!
GODAIIN
ENEMY
FOOL
...SURROUNDED BY ENEMY SOLDIERS AND UNABLE TO ACT.
ENEMY
ENEMY
BLURRY
COME AND I WILL SHOW YOU...
...HOW YOU MAY WIN THIS GAME.
YOU CAN AVENGE YOUR BROTHER ...
...AND TAKE THE FIRST STEP TOWARD RECLAIMING YOUR RIGHTFUL PLACE!

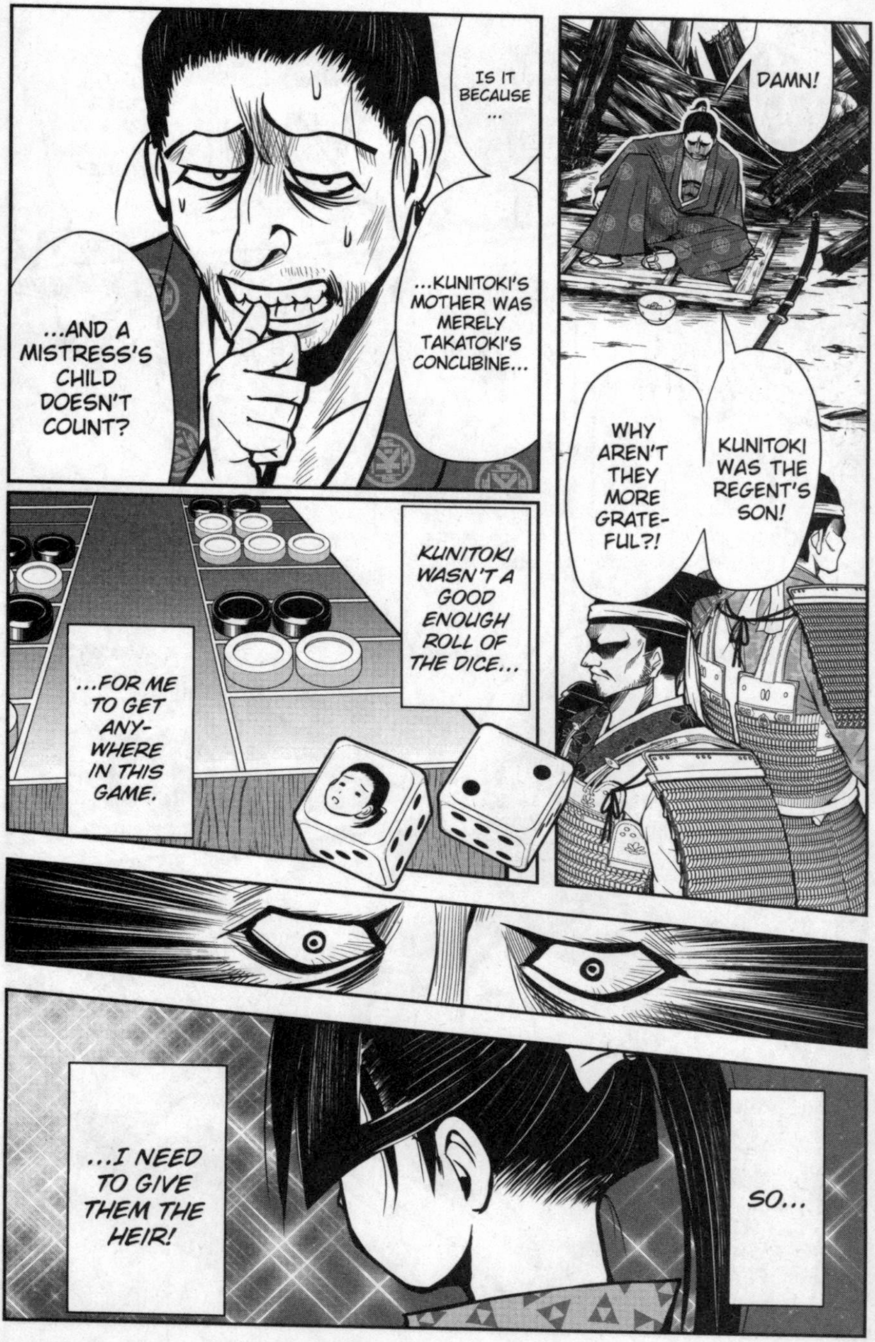
DAMN!
KUNITOKI WAS THE REGENT'S SON!
WHY AREN'T THEY MORE GRATE-FUL?!
IS IT BECAUSE ...
...KUNITOKI'S MOTHER WAS MERELY TAKATOKI'S CONCUBINE...
...AND A MISTRESS'S CHILD DOESN'T COUNT?
KUNITOKI WASN'T A GOOD ENOUGH ROLL OF THE DICE...
...FOR ME TO GET ANY-WHERE IN THIS GAME.
SO...
...I NEED TO GIVE THEM THE HEIR!

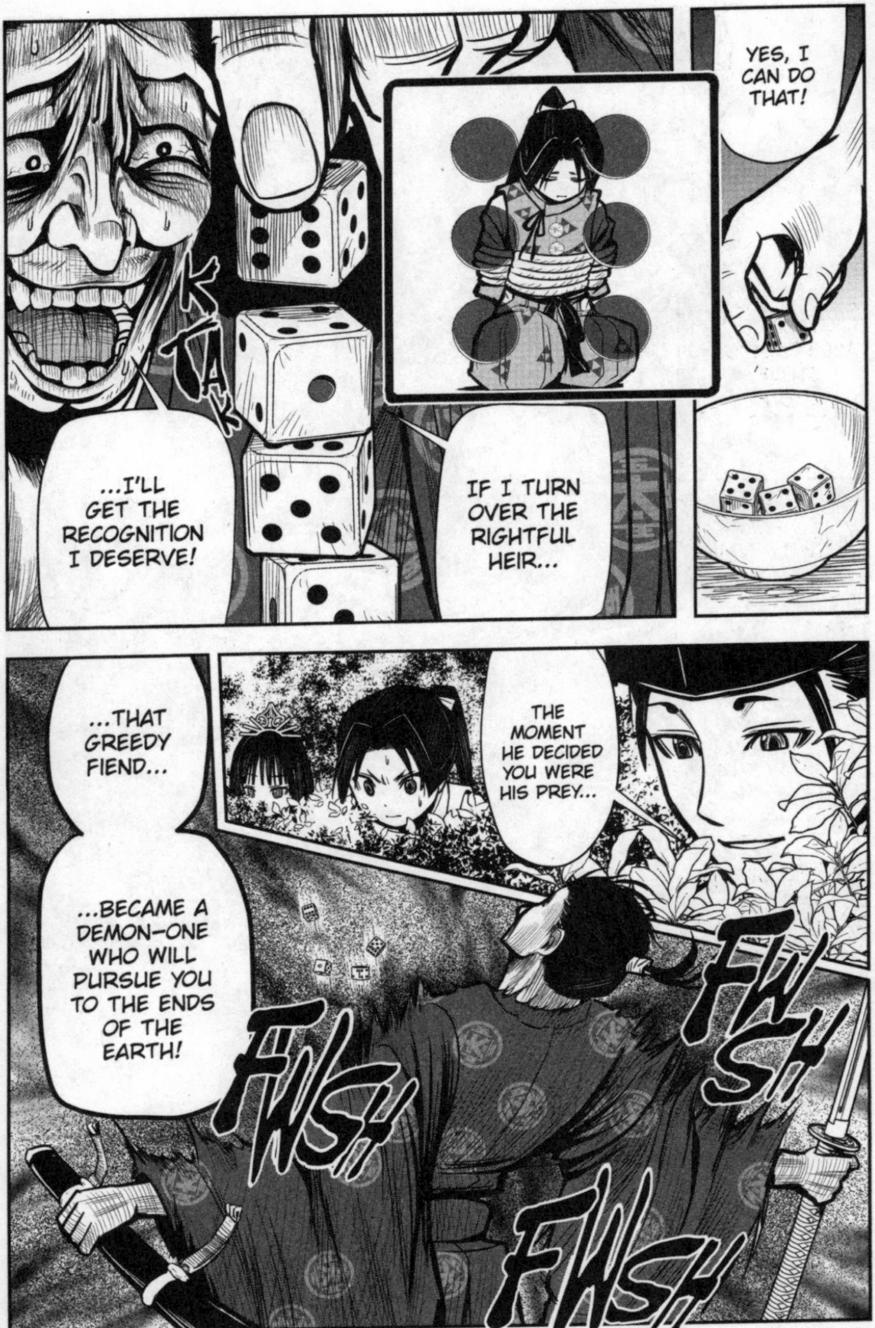
YES, I CAN DO THAT!
IF I TURN OVER THE RIGHTFUL HEIR...
...I'LL GET THE RECOGNITION I DESERVE!
THE MOMENT HE DECIDED YOU WERE HIS PREY...
...THAT GREEDY FIEND...
...BECAME A DEMON—ONE WHO WILL PURSUE YOU TO THE ENDS OF THE EARTH!
FWSH
FWSH
FWSH

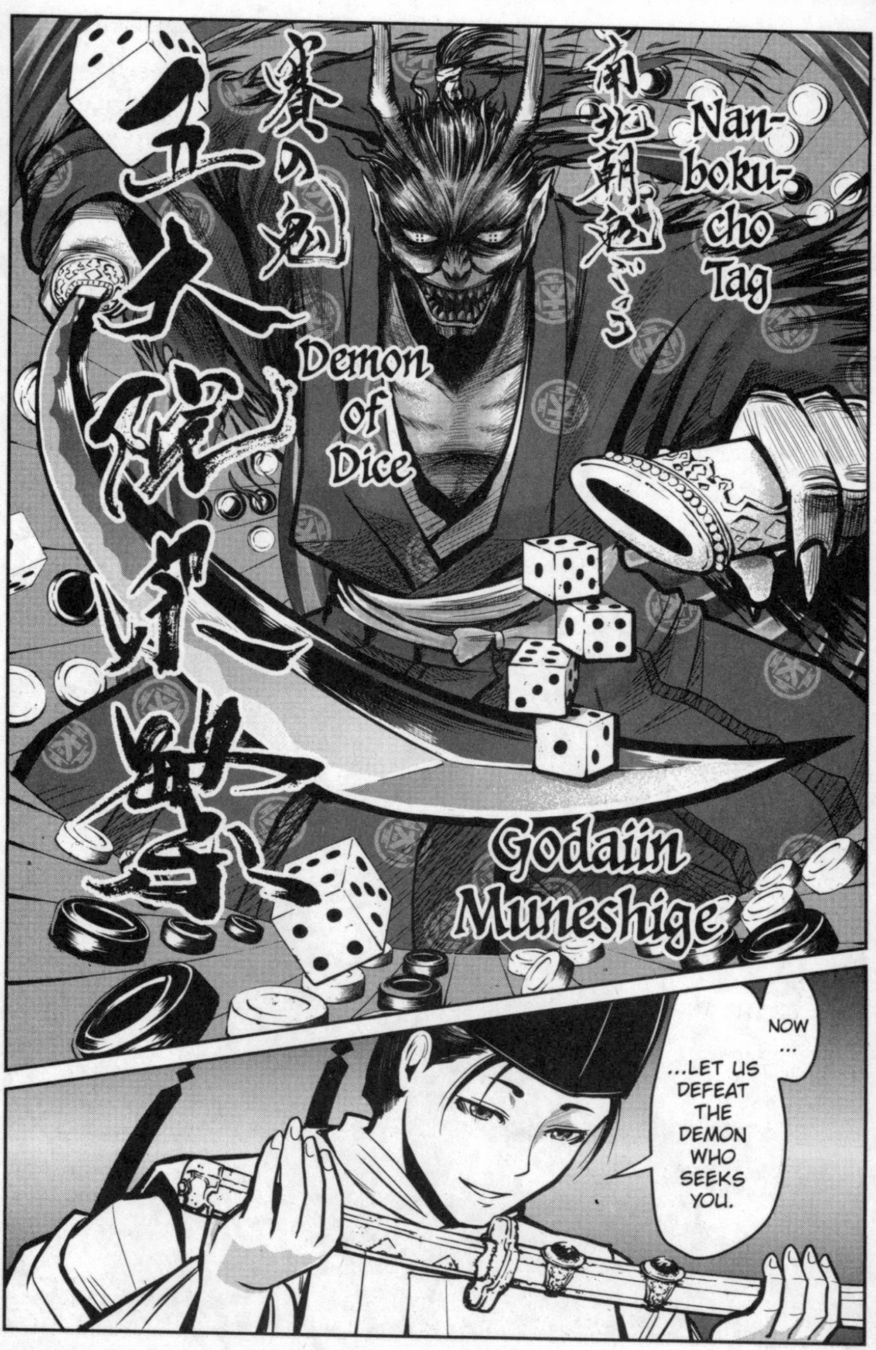
Nan-boku-cho Tag
Demon of Dice
Godaiin Muneshige
NOW ...
...LET US DEFEAT THE DEMON WHO SEEKS YOU.

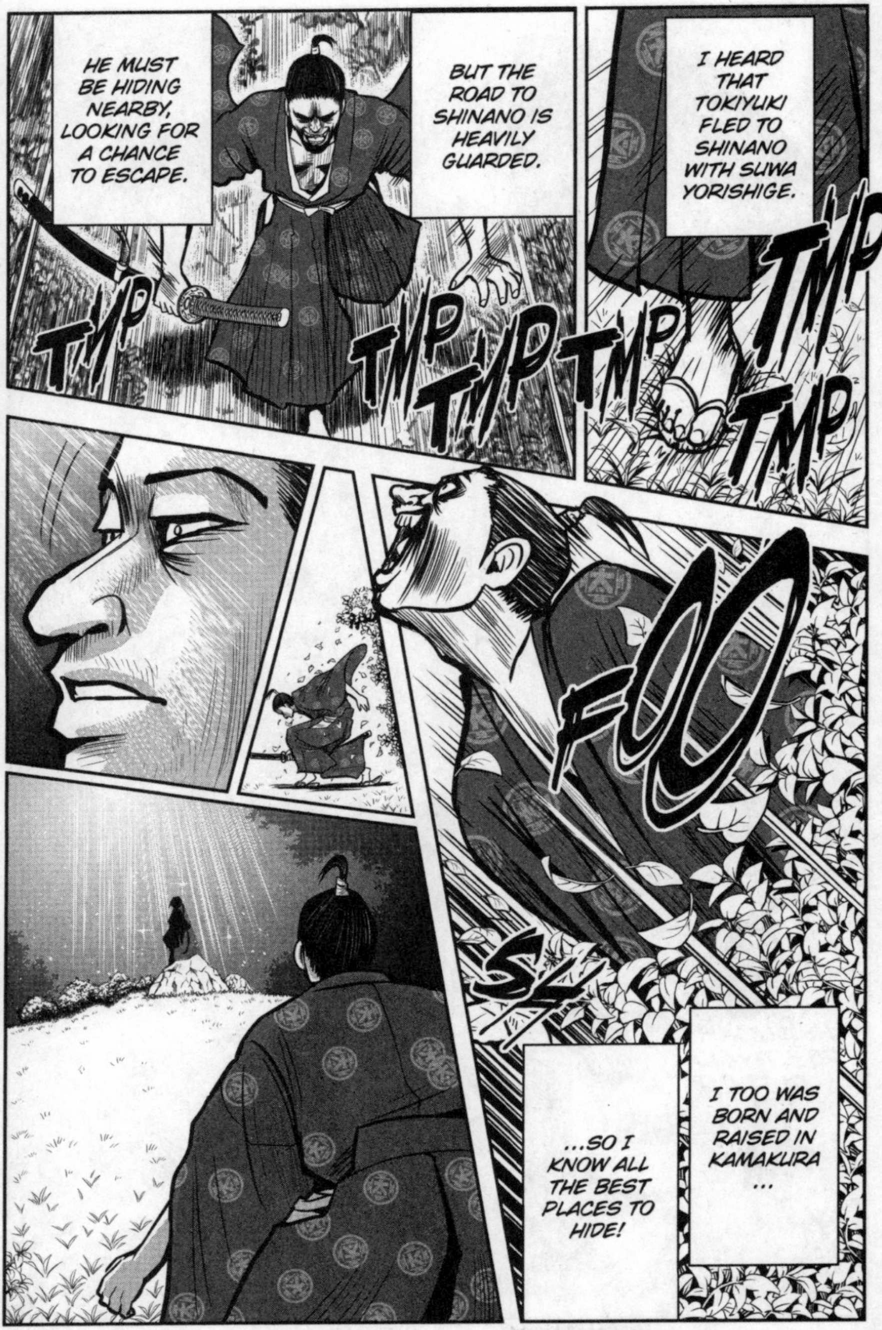
I HEARD THAT TOKIYUKI FLED TO SHINANO WITH SUWA YORISHIGE.
TMP TMP TMP
BUT THE ROAD TO SHINANO IS HEAVILY GUARDED.
TMP TMP TMP
HE MUST BE HIDING NEARBY, LOOKING FOR A CHANCE TO ESCAPE.
TMP
FOO
SH
I TOO WAS BORN AND RAISED IN KAMAKURA ...
...SO I KNOW ALL THE BEST PLACES TO HIDE!

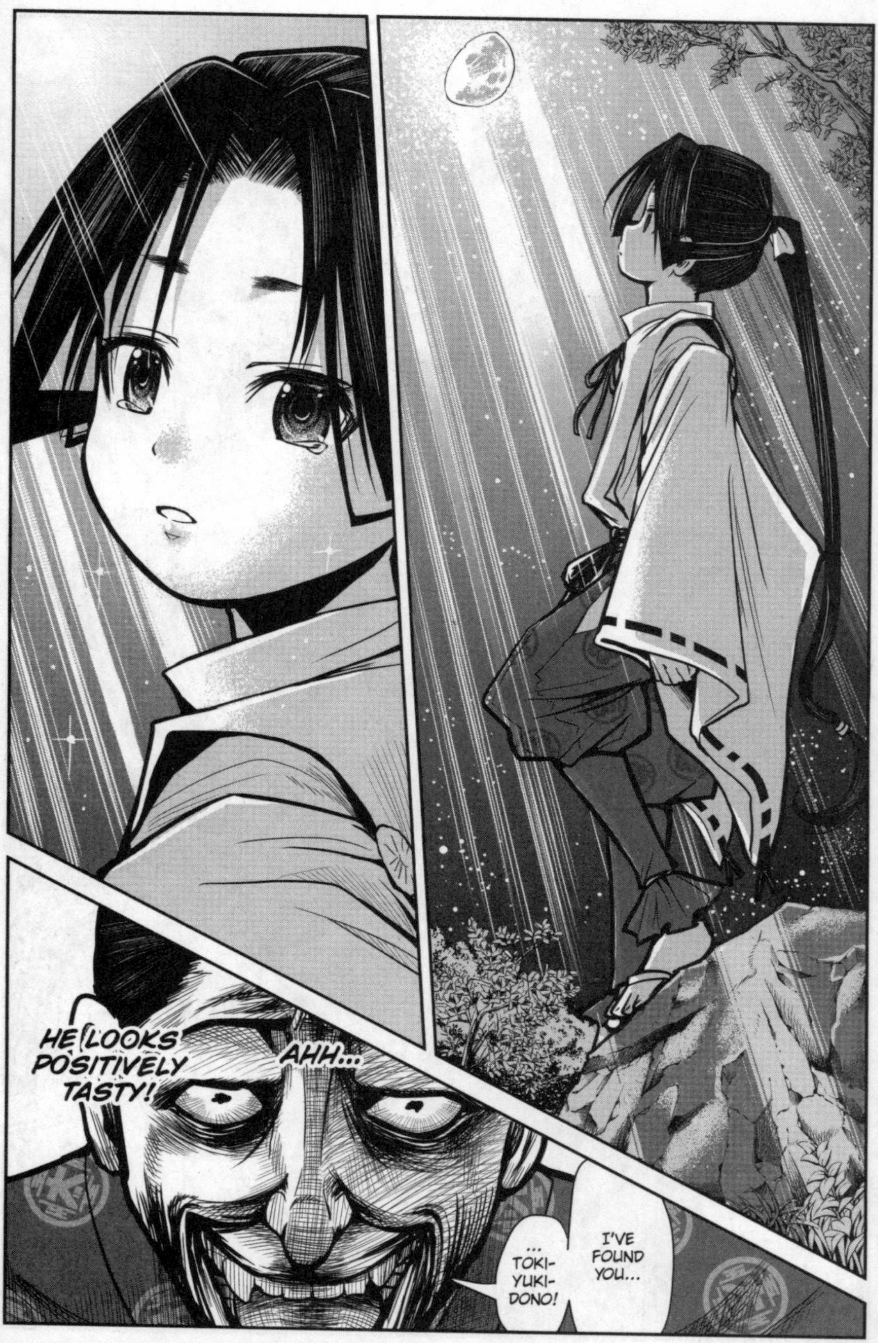
I'VE FOUND YOU...
...TOKI-YUKI-DONO!
AHH...
HE LOOKS POSITIVELY TASTY!

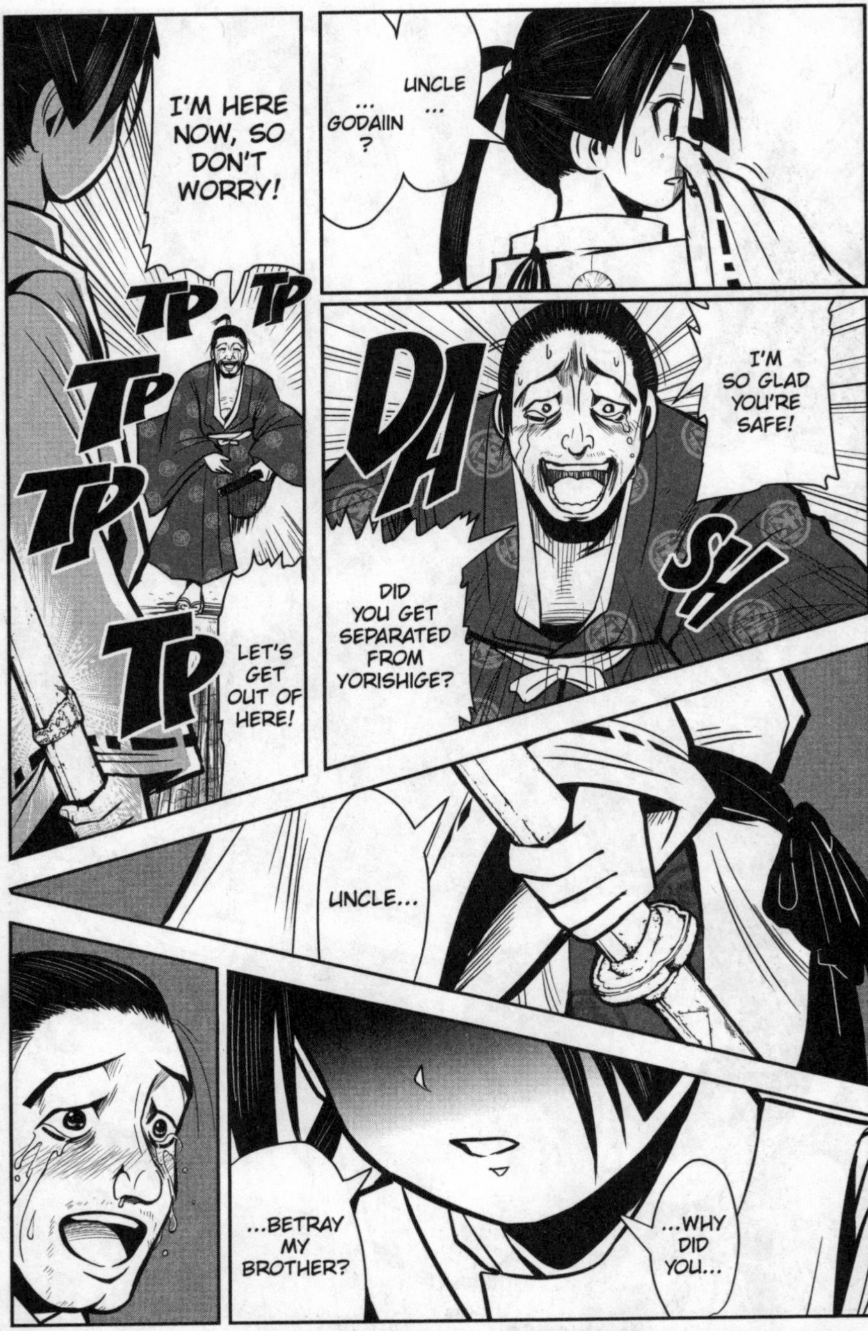
UNCLE ... GODAIIN ...?
I'M SO GLAD YOU'RE SAFE!
DA SH
DID YOU GET SEPARATED FROM YORISHIGE?
I'M HERE NOW, SO DON'T WORRY!
TP TP TP TP TP
LET'S GET OUT OF HERE!
UNCLE...
...WHY DID YOU...
...BETRAY MY BROTHER?

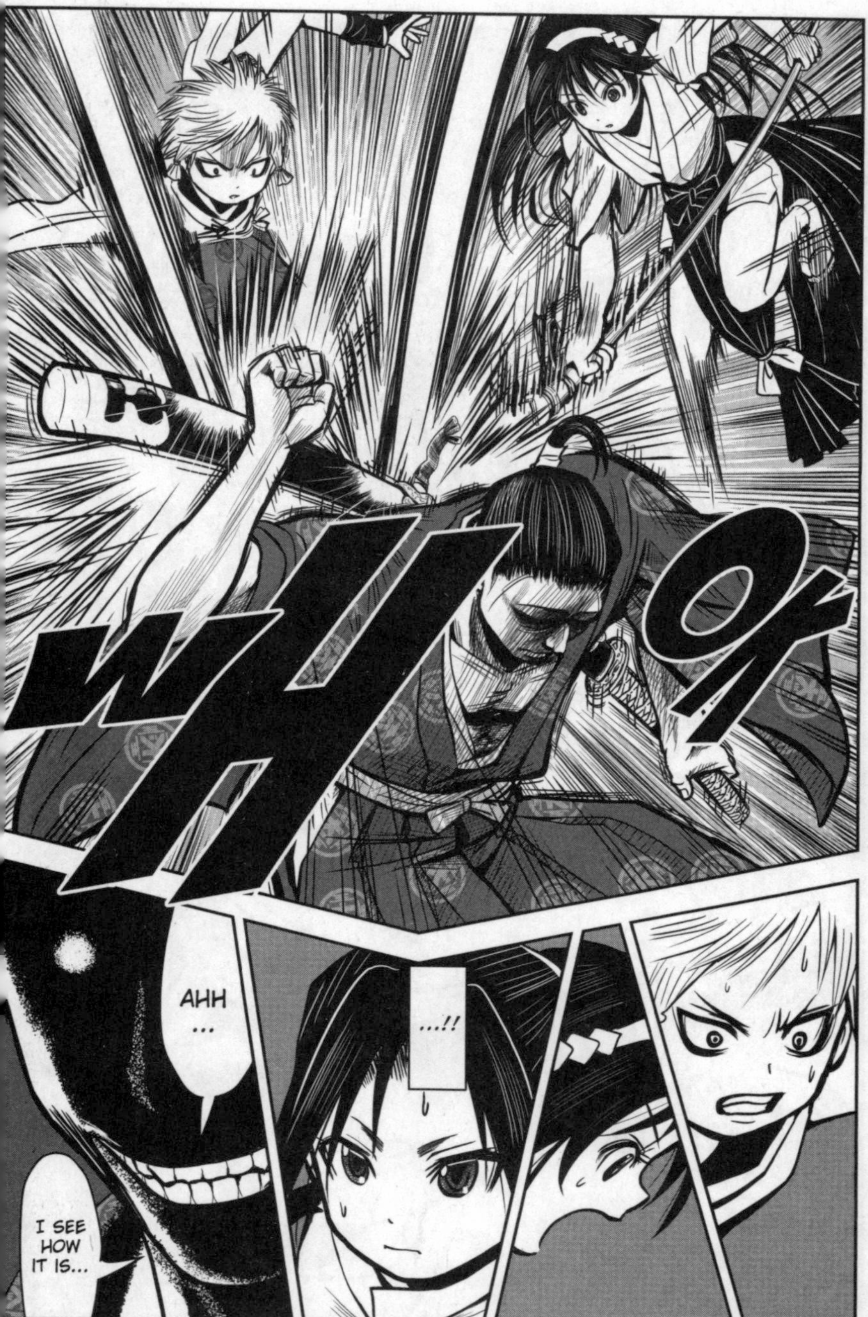
WHO
...!!
AHH
...
I SEE
HOW
IT IS...

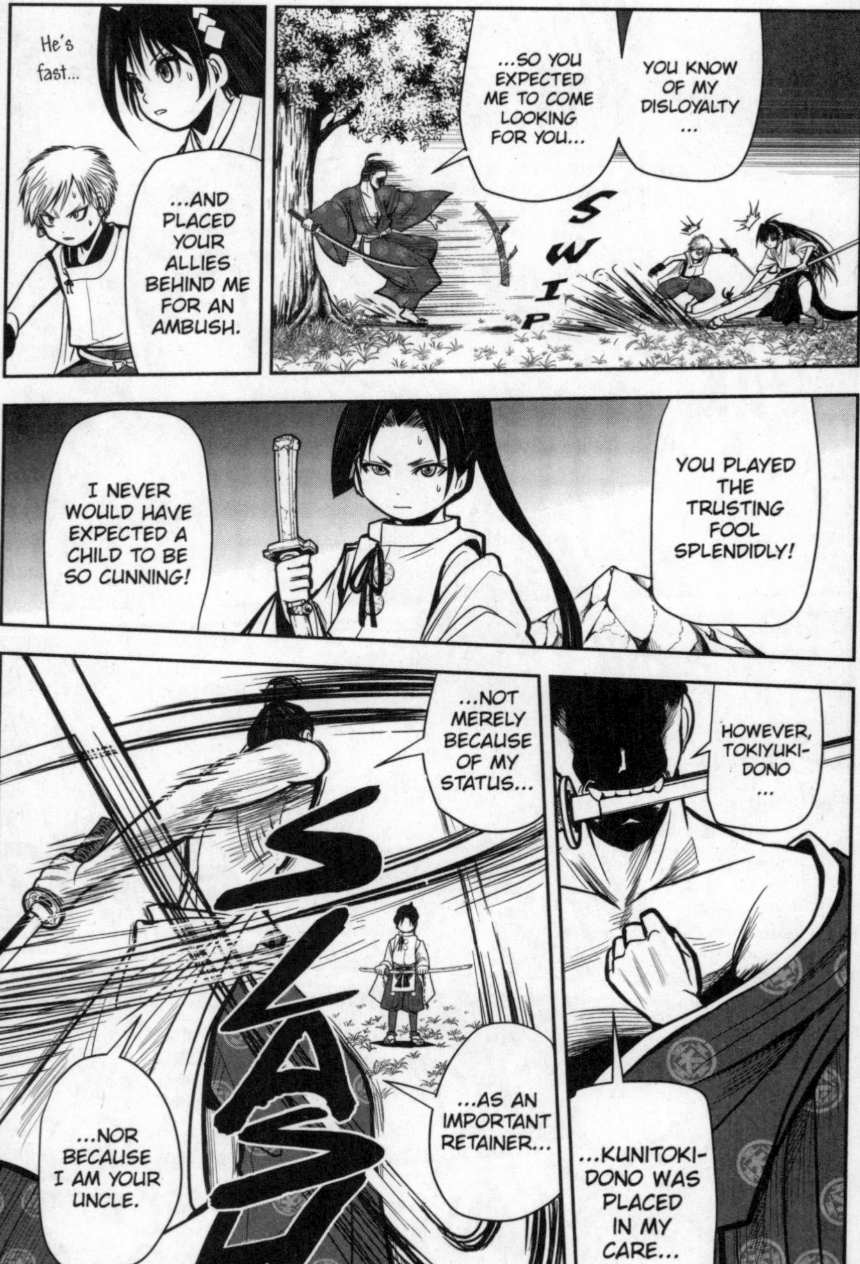
YOU KNOW OF MY DISLOYALTY ...
...SO YOU EXPECTED ME TO COME LOOKING FOR YOU...
SWIP
...AND PLACED YOUR ALLIES BEHIND ME FOR AN AMBUSH.
He's fast...
YOU PLAYED THE TRUSTING FOOL SPLENDIDLY!
I NEVER WOULD HAVE EXPECTED A CHILD TO BE SO CUNNING!
HOWEVER, TOKIYUKI-DONO ...
...KUNITOKI-DONO WAS PLACED IN MY CARE...
...NOT MERELY BECAUSE OF MY STATUS...
...AS AN IMPORTANT RETAINER...
...NOR BECAUSE I AM YOUR UNCLE.
SLASH

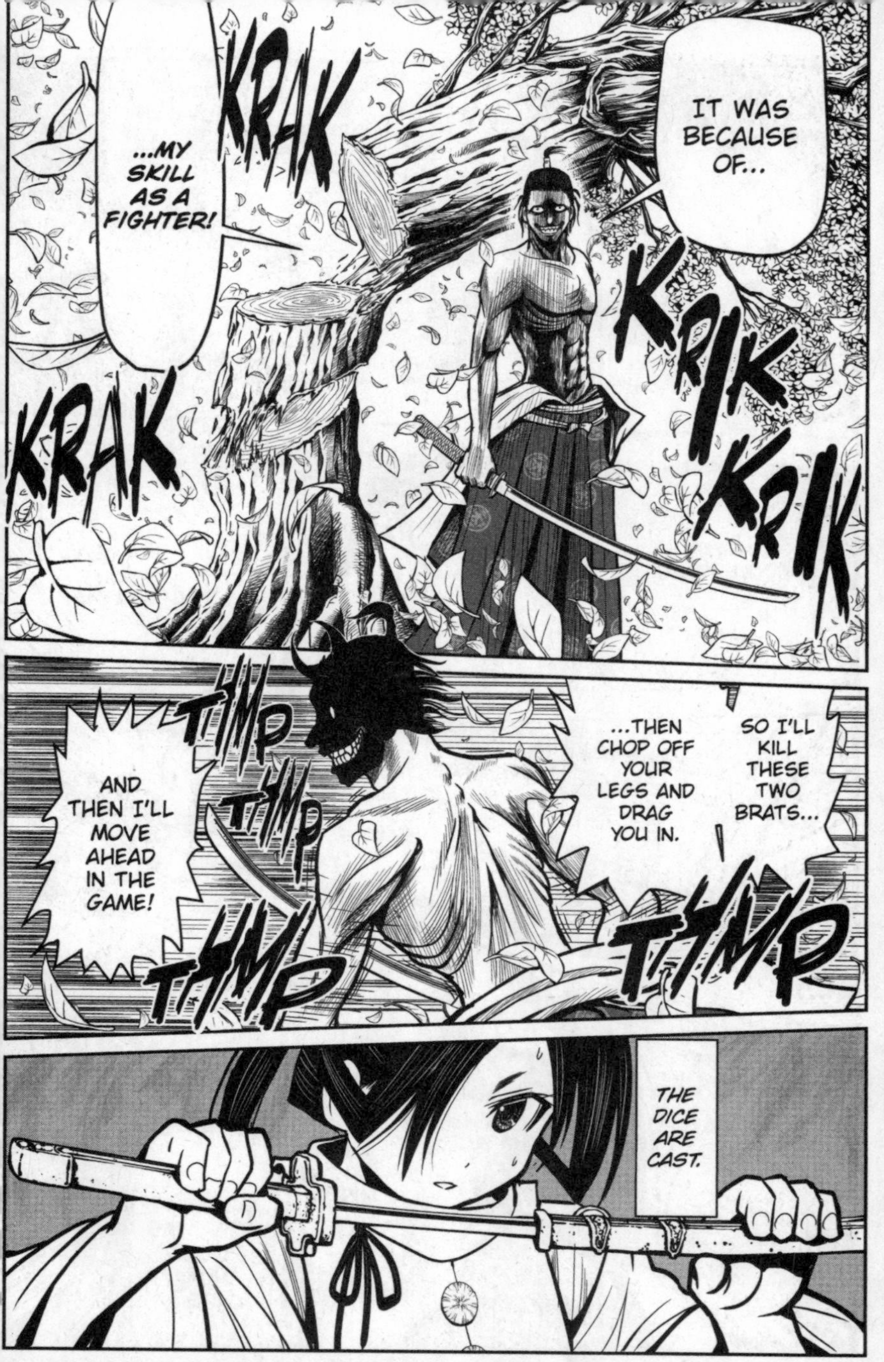
IT WAS BECAUSE OF...
KRIK KRIK
...MY SKILL AS A FIGHTER!
KRAK
KRAK
SO I'LL KILL THESE TWO BRATS...
...THEN CHOP OFF YOUR LEGS AND DRAG YOU IN.
THMP
THMP
AND THEN I'LL MOVE AHEAD IN THE GAME!
THMP
THMP
THE DICE ARE CAST.

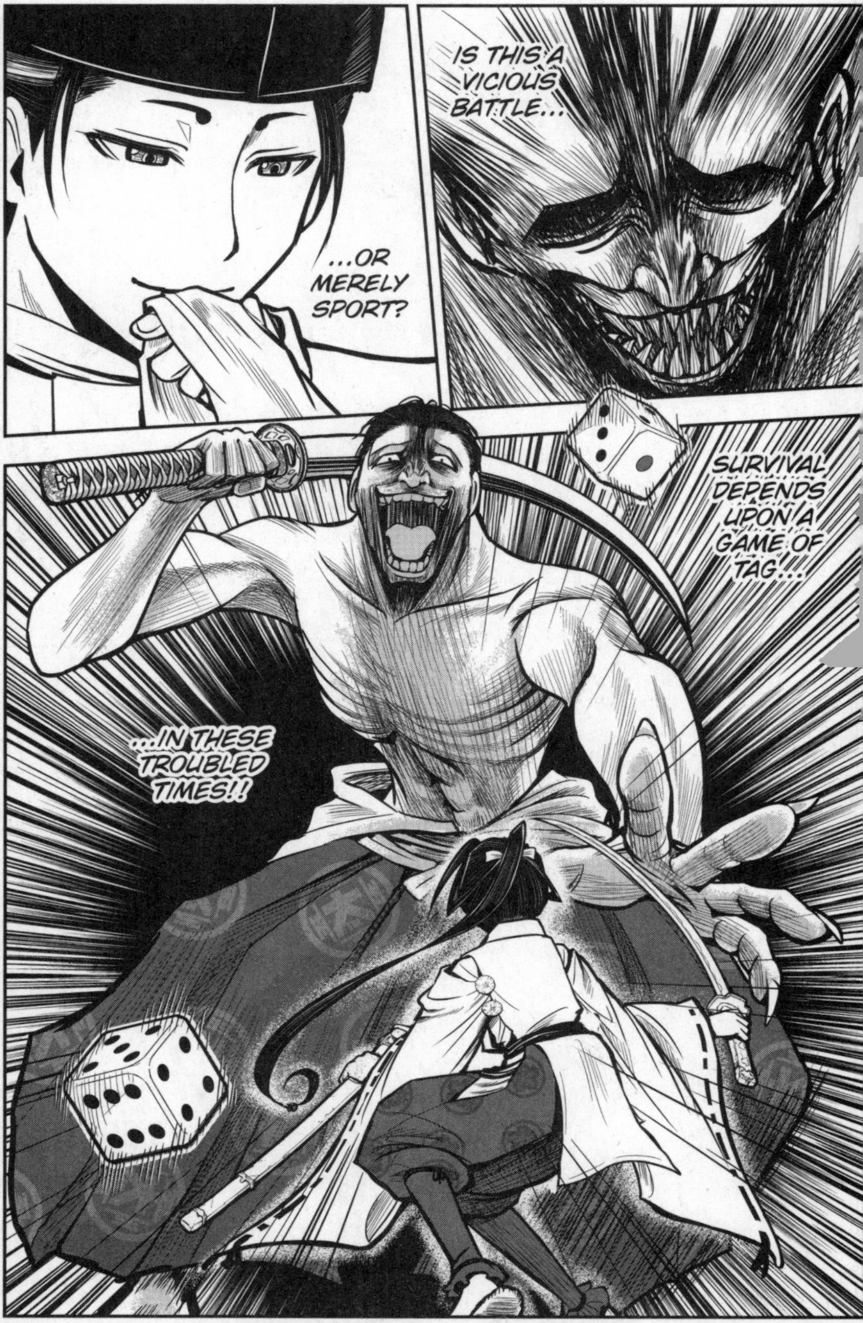
IS THIS A VICIOUS BATTLE...
...OR MERELY SPORT?
SURVIVAL DEPENDS UPON A GAME OF TAG...
...IN THESE TROUBLED TIMES!!

Possibly his first manga appearance ever

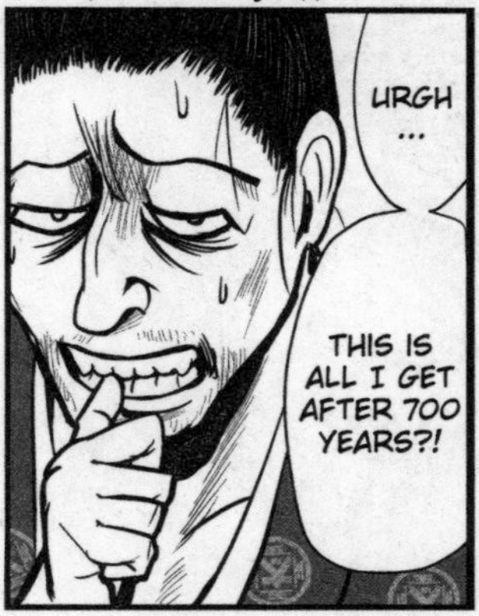
URGH ...
THIS IS ALL I GET AFTER 700 YEARS?!

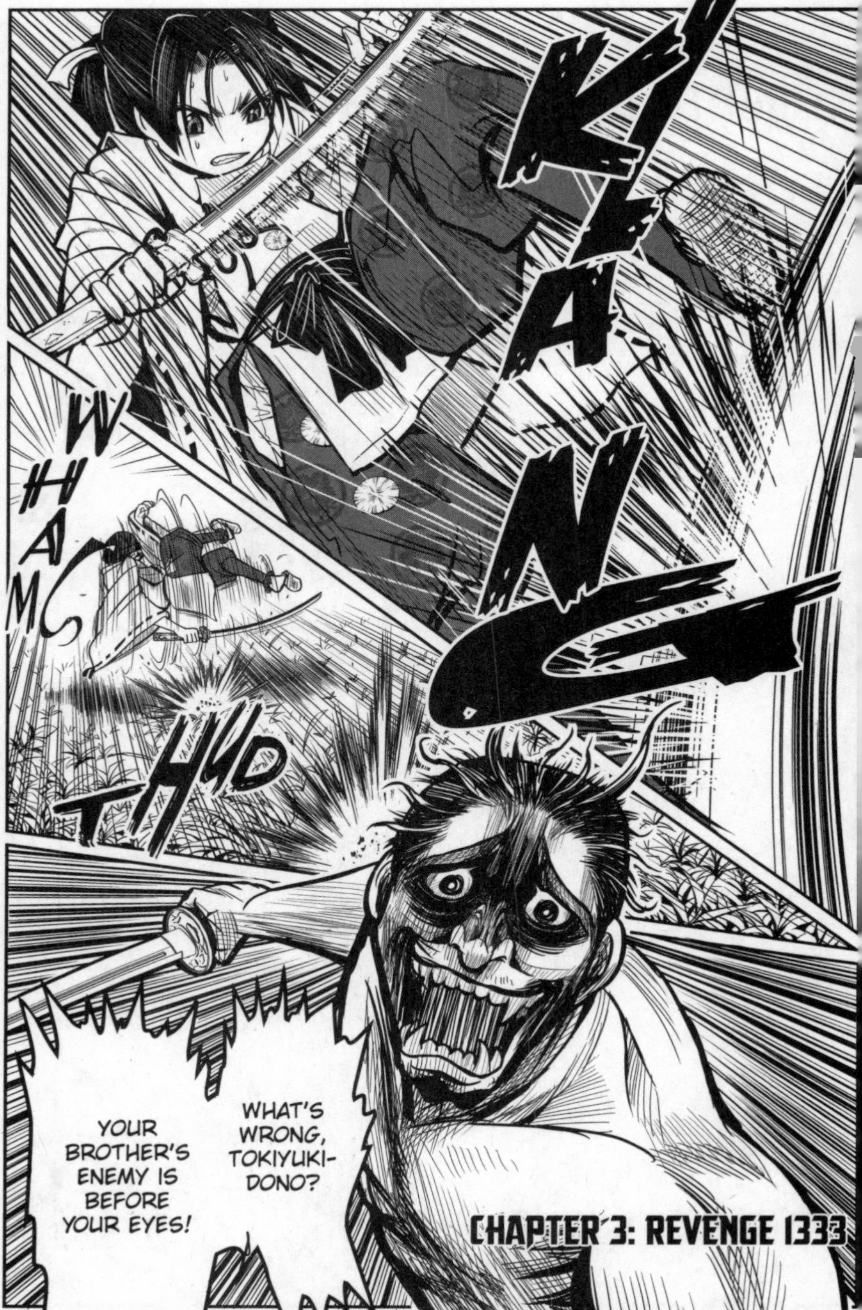
KANG
WHAM
THUD
WHAT'S WRONG, TOKIYUKI-DONO?
YOUR BROTHER'S ENEMY IS BEFORE YOUR EYES!

CHAPTER 3: REVENGE 1333

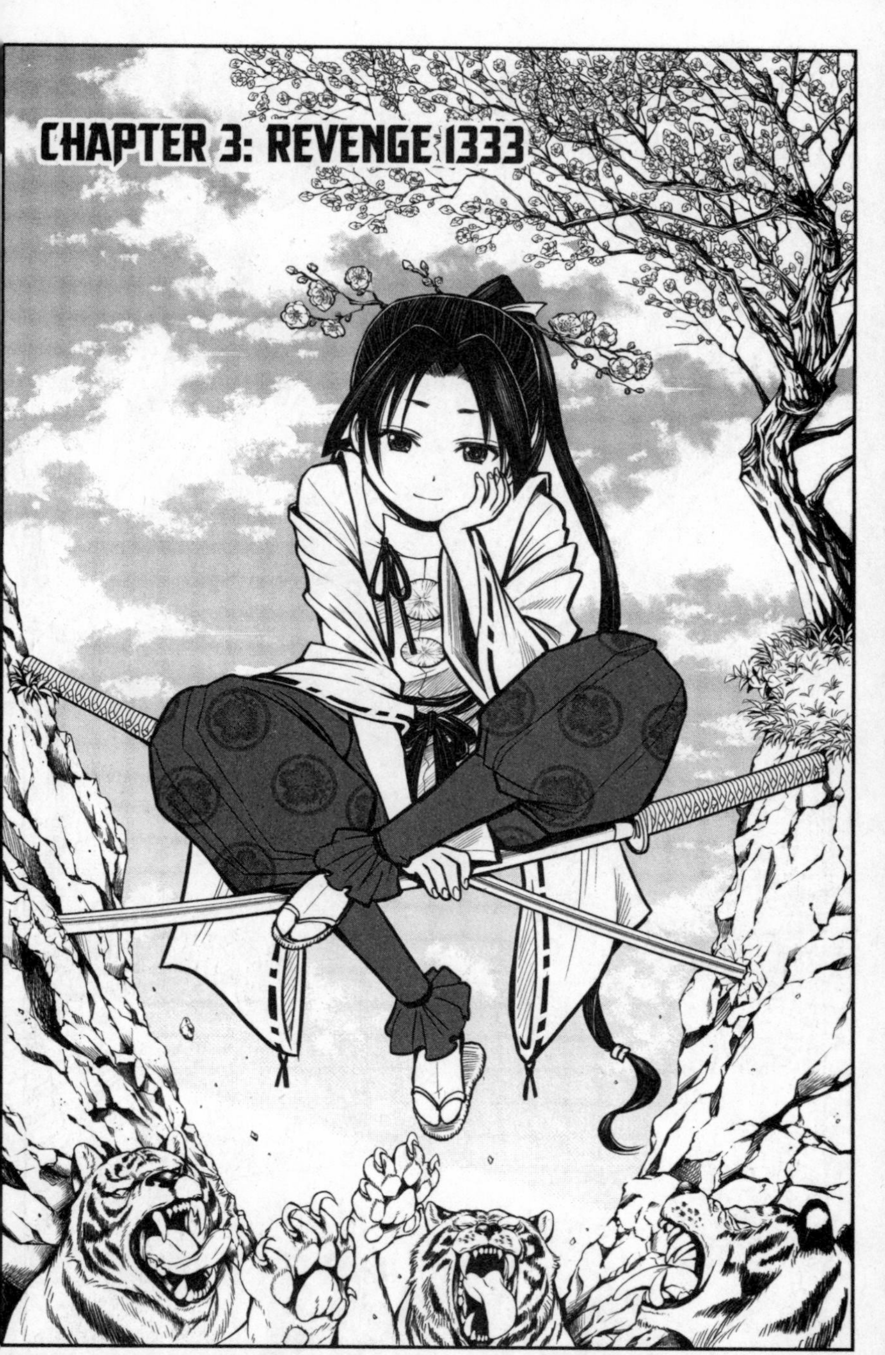
CHAPTER 3: REVENGE 1333

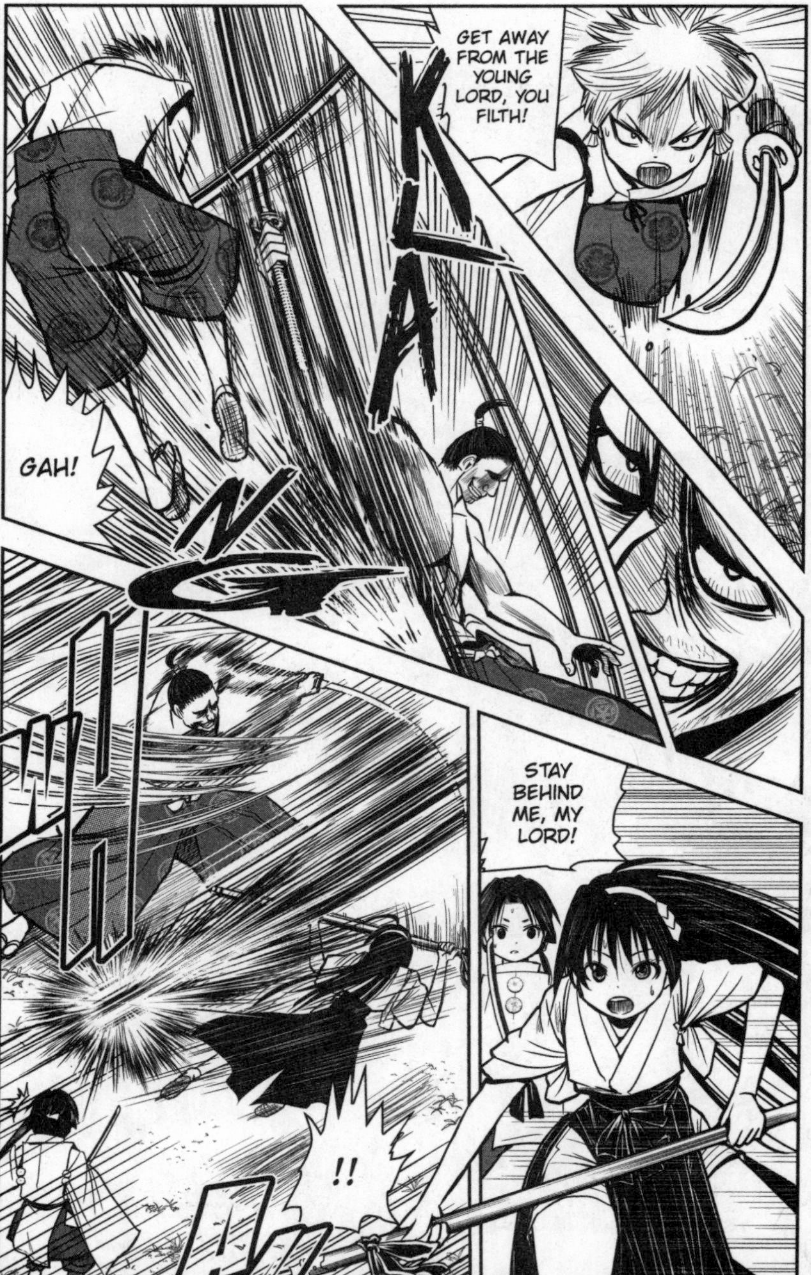
GET AWAY FROM THE YOUNG LORD, YOU FILTH!
KLANG
GAH!
STAY BEHIND ME, MY LORD!
!!

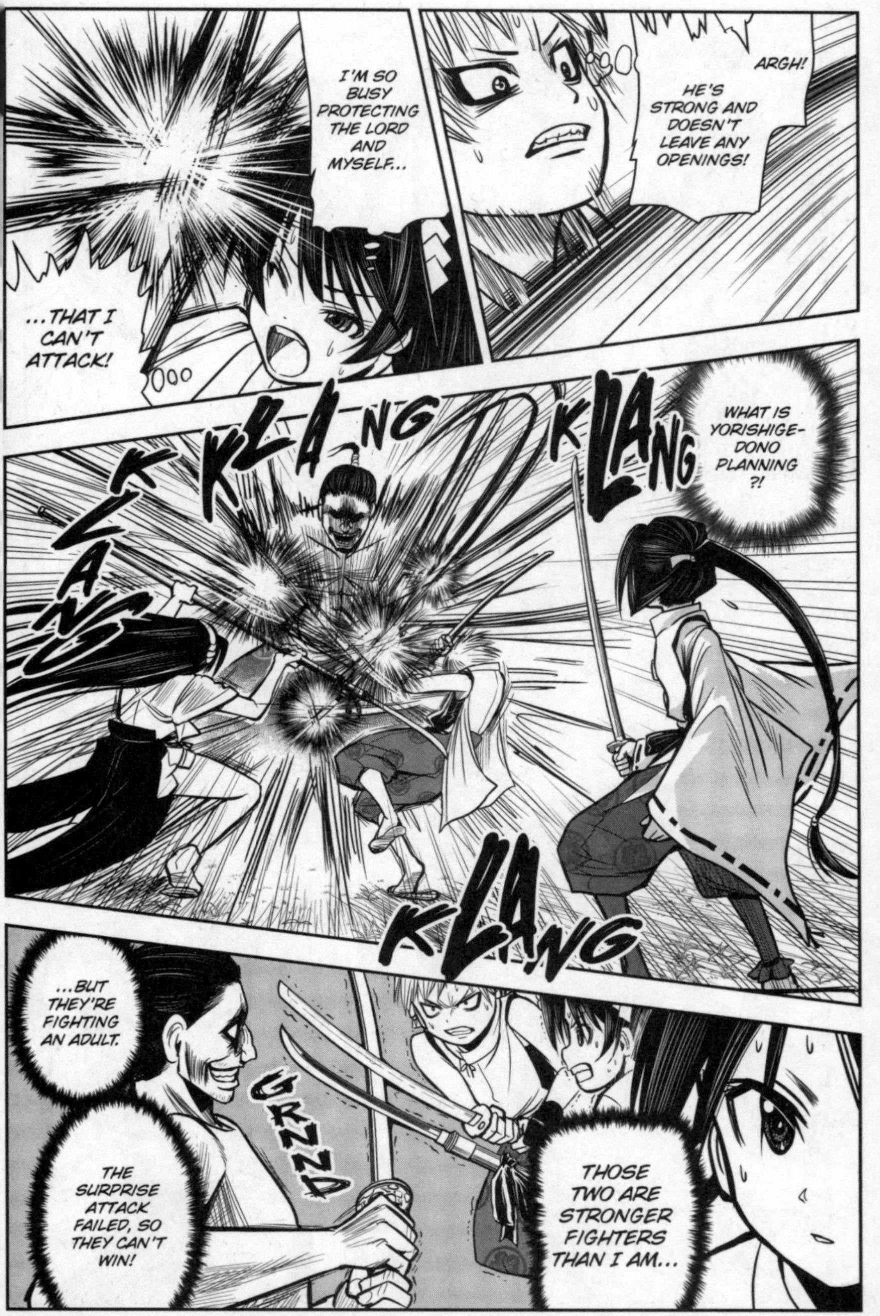
ARGH!
HE'S STRONG AND DOESN'T LEAVE ANY OPENINGS!
I'M SO BUSY PROTECTING THE LORD AND MYSELF...
...THAT I CAN'T ATTACK!
WHAT IS YORISHIGE-DONO PLANNING?!
KLANG
KLANG
KLANG
KLANG
THOSE TWO ARE STRONGER FIGHTERS THAN I AM...
...BUT THEY'RE FIGHTING AN ADULT.
GRNND
THE SURPRISE ATTACK FAILED, SO THEY CAN'T WIN!

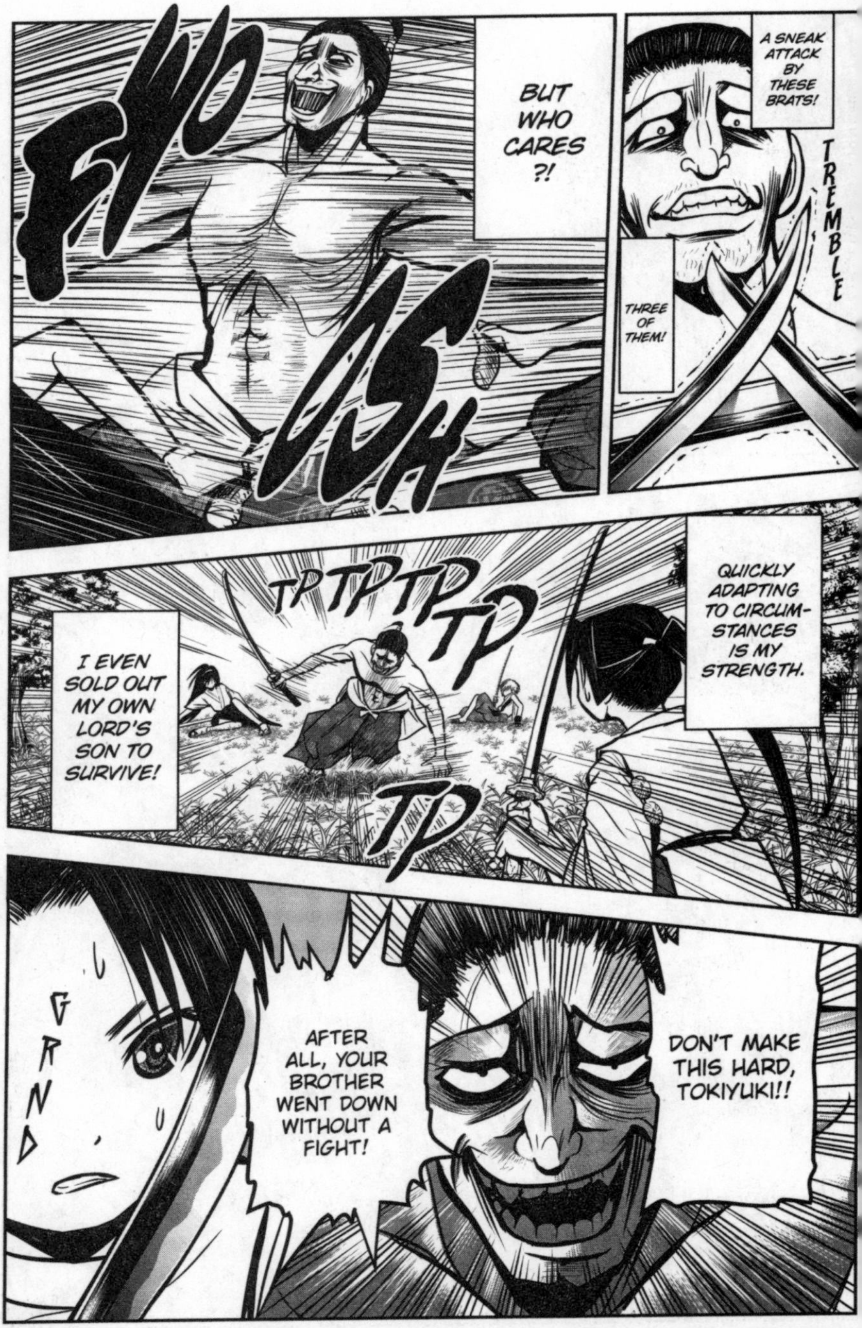
A SNEAK ATTACK BY THESE BRATS!
TREMBLE
THREE OF THEM!
BUT WHO CARES ?!
FWOOSH
QUICKLY ADAPTING TO CIRCUM-STANCES IS MY STRENGTH.
TPTPTPTP TP
TP TP
I EVEN SOLD OUT MY OWN LORD'S SON TO SURVIVE!
DON'T MAKE THIS HARD, TOKIYUKI!!
AFTER ALL, YOUR BROTHER WENT DOWN WITHOUT A FIGHT!
GRND

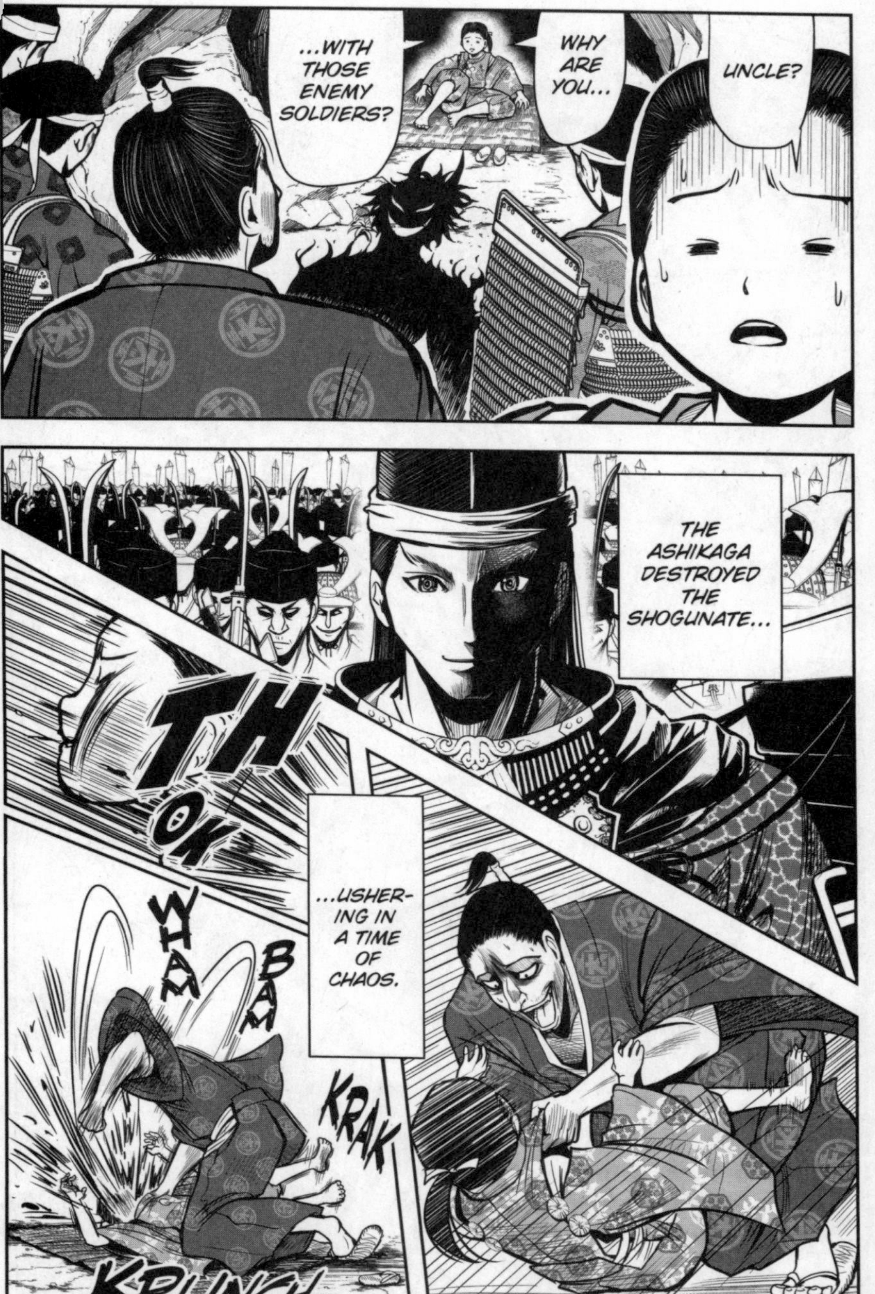
UNCLE?
WHY ARE YOU...
...WITH THOSE ENEMY SOLDIERS?
THE ASHIKAGA DESTROYED THE SHOGUNATE...
THOK
...USHERING IN A TIME OF CHAOS.
KRAK
BAM
WHAM
KRUNCH

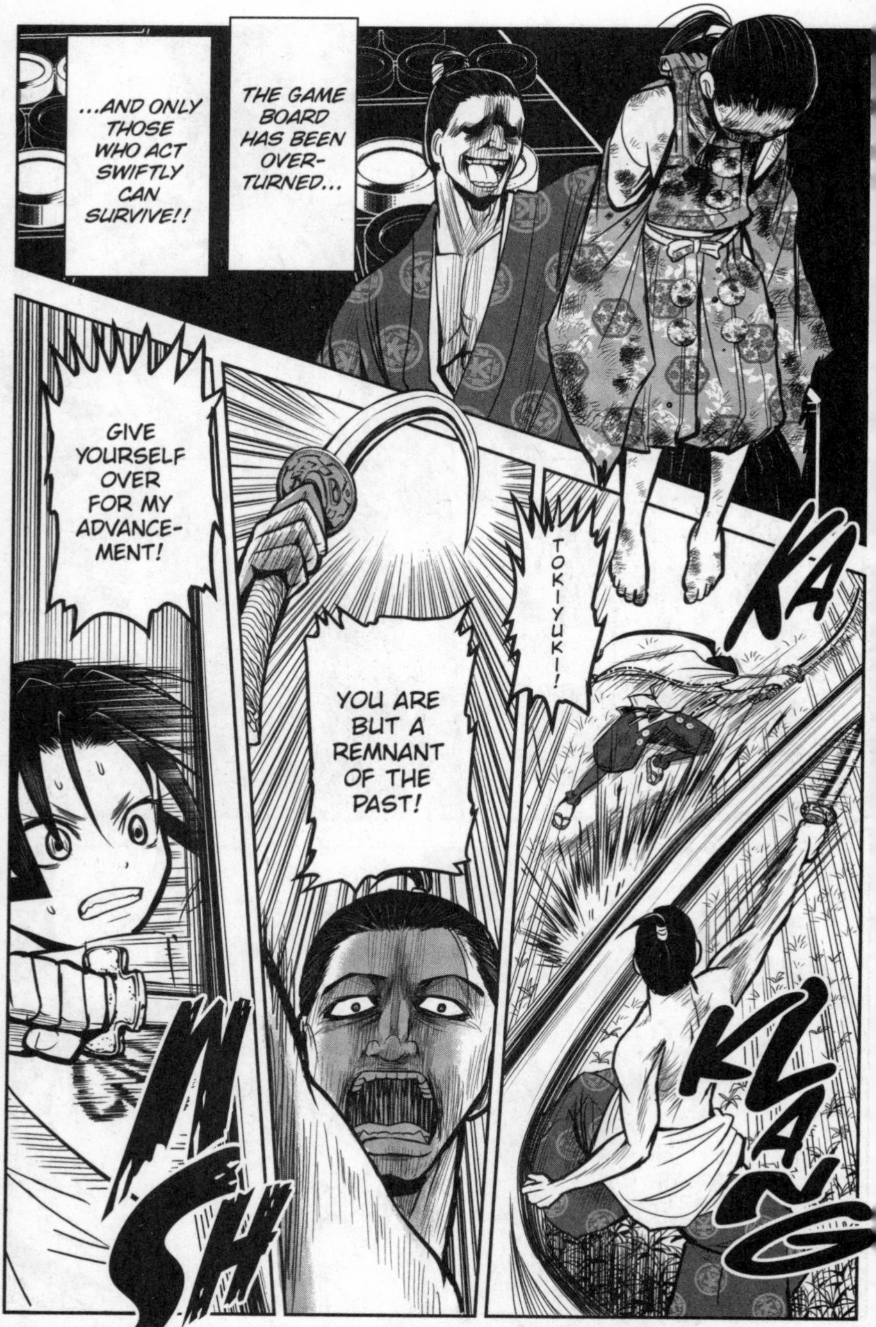
THE GAME BOARD HAS BEEN OVER-TURNED...
...AND ONLY THOSE WHO ACT SWIFTLY CAN SURVIVE!!
KA
TOKIYUKI!
KLANG
YOU ARE BUT A REMNANT OF THE PAST!
GIVE YOURSELF OVER FOR MY ADVANCE-MENT!
WHSH

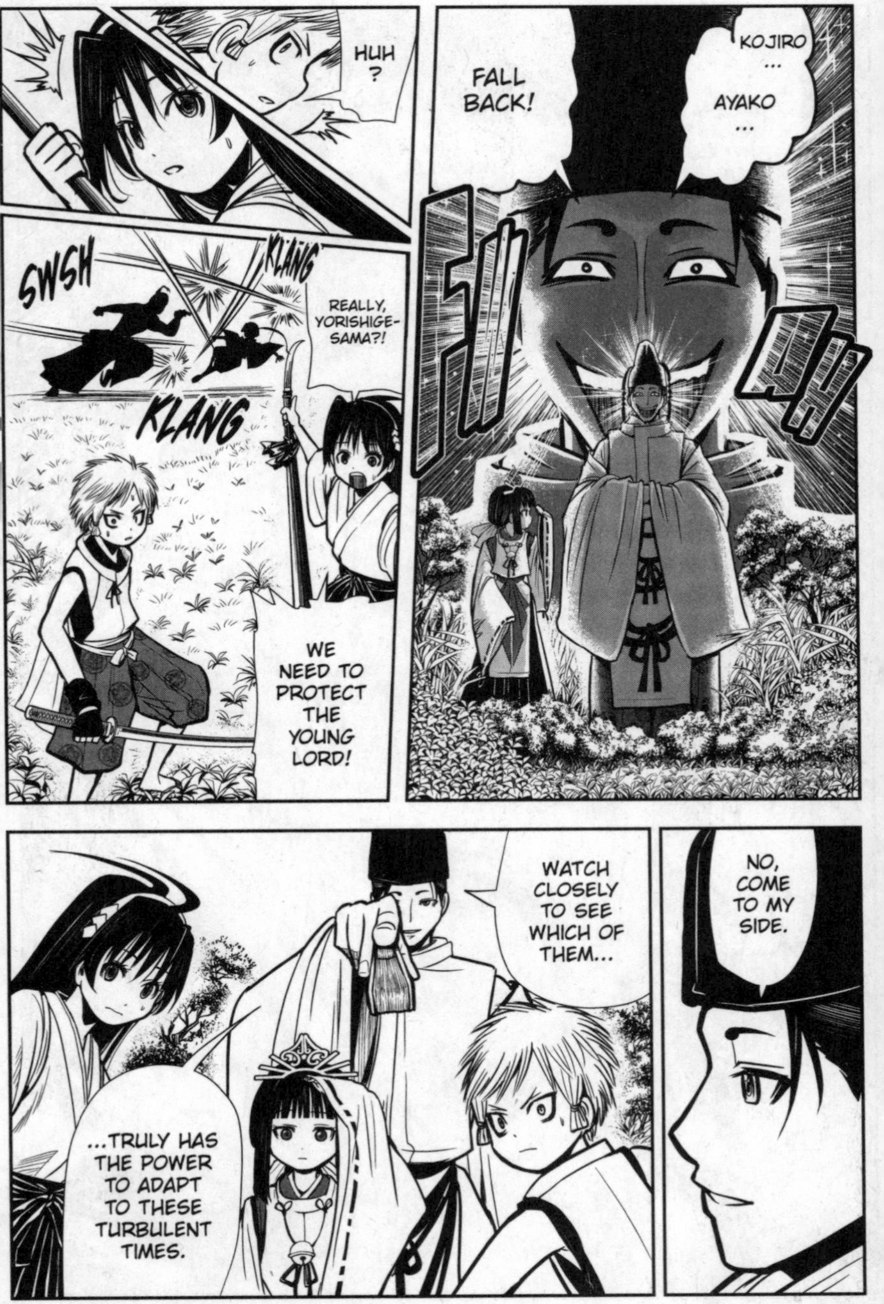

KOJIRO ... AYAKO ...
FALL BACK!
HUH ?
SWSH
KLANG
REALLY, YORISHIGE-SAMA?!
KLANG
WE NEED TO PROTECT THE YOUNG LORD!
NO, COME TO MY SIDE.
WATCH CLOSELY TO SEE WHICH OF THEM...
...TRULY HAS THE POWER TO ADAPT TO THESE TURBULENT TIMES.

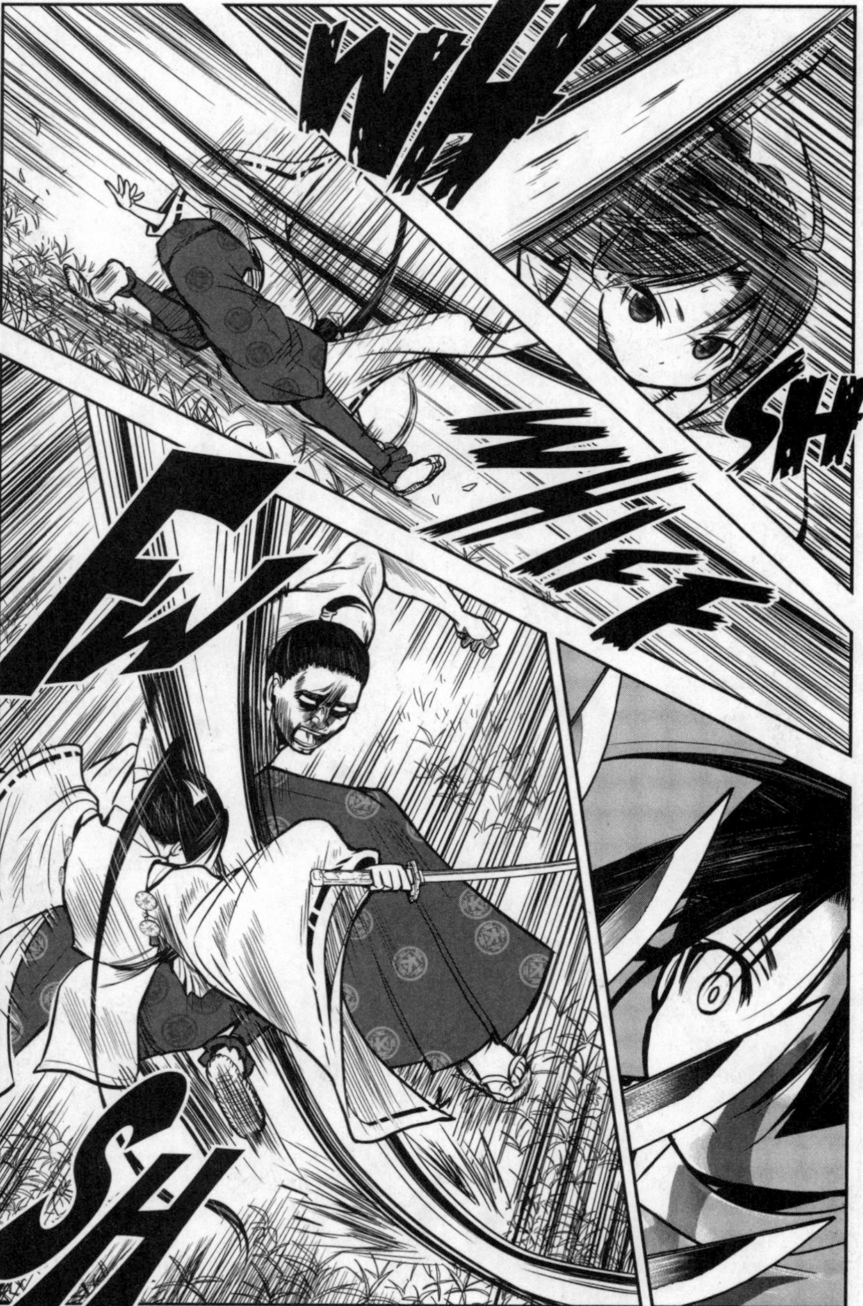
SH
WHA
WHIFF
FW
SH

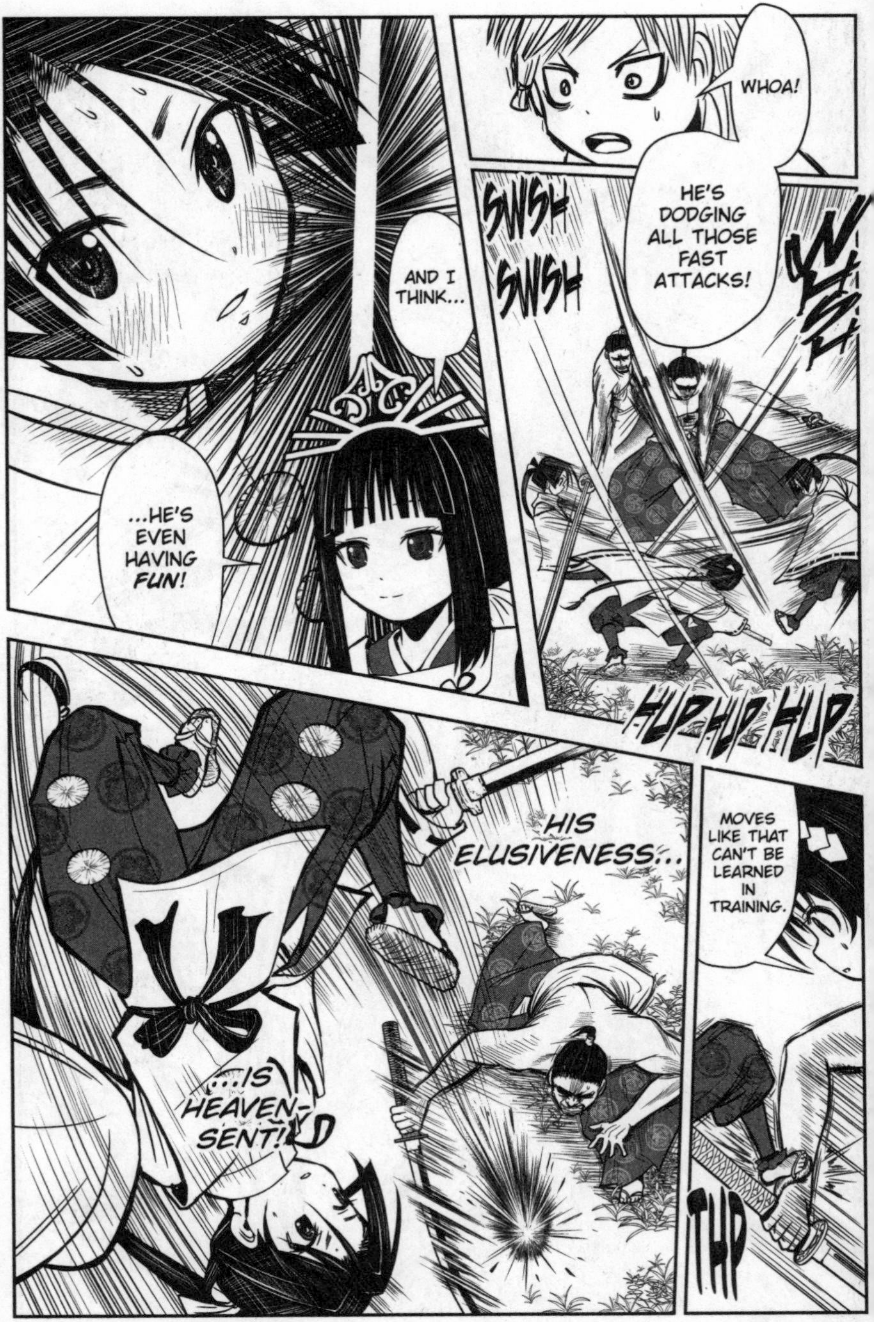
WHOA!
HE'S DODGING ALL THOSE FAST ATTACKS!
SWSH SWSH
WHOOSH
HUP HUP HUP
AND I THINK...
...HE'S EVEN HAVING FUN!
MOVES LIKE THAT CAN'T BE LEARNED IN TRAINING.
THP
HIS ELUSIVENESS...
...IS HEAVEN-SENT!

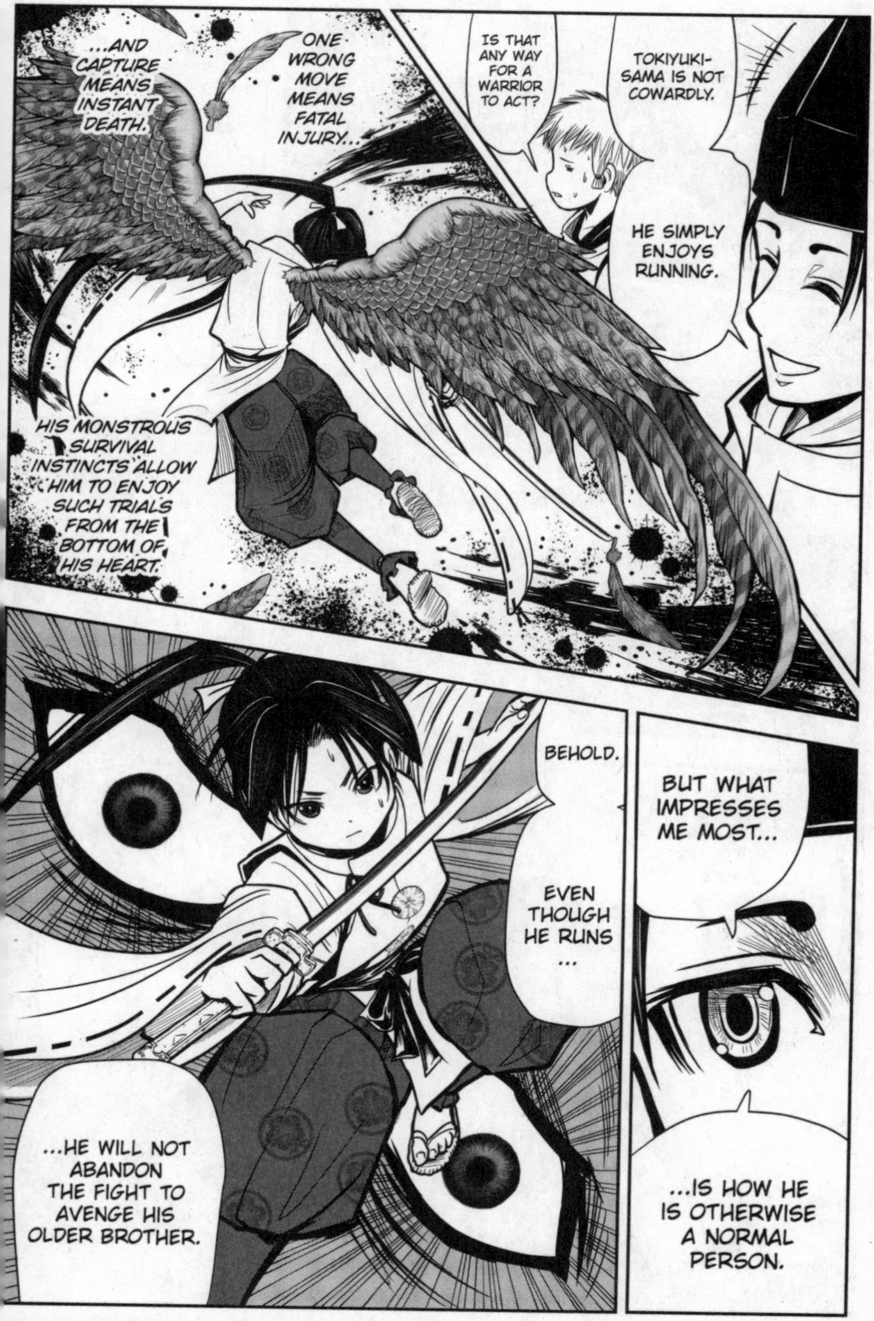
TOKIYUKI-SAMA IS NOT COWARDLY.
IS THAT ANY WAY FOR A WARRIOR TO ACT?
HE SIMPLY ENJOYS RUNNING.
ONE WRONG MOVE MEANS FATAL INJURY...
...AND CAPTURE MEANS INSTANT DEATH.
HIS MONSTROUS SURVIVAL INSTINCTS ALLOW HIM TO ENJOY SUCH TRIALS FROM THE BOTTOM OF HIS HEART.
BUT WHAT IMPRESSES ME MOST...
...IS HOW HE IS OTHERWISE A NORMAL PERSON.
BEHOLD.
EVEN THOUGH HE RUNS...
...HE WILL NOT ABANDON THE FIGHT TO AVENGE HIS OLDER BROTHER.

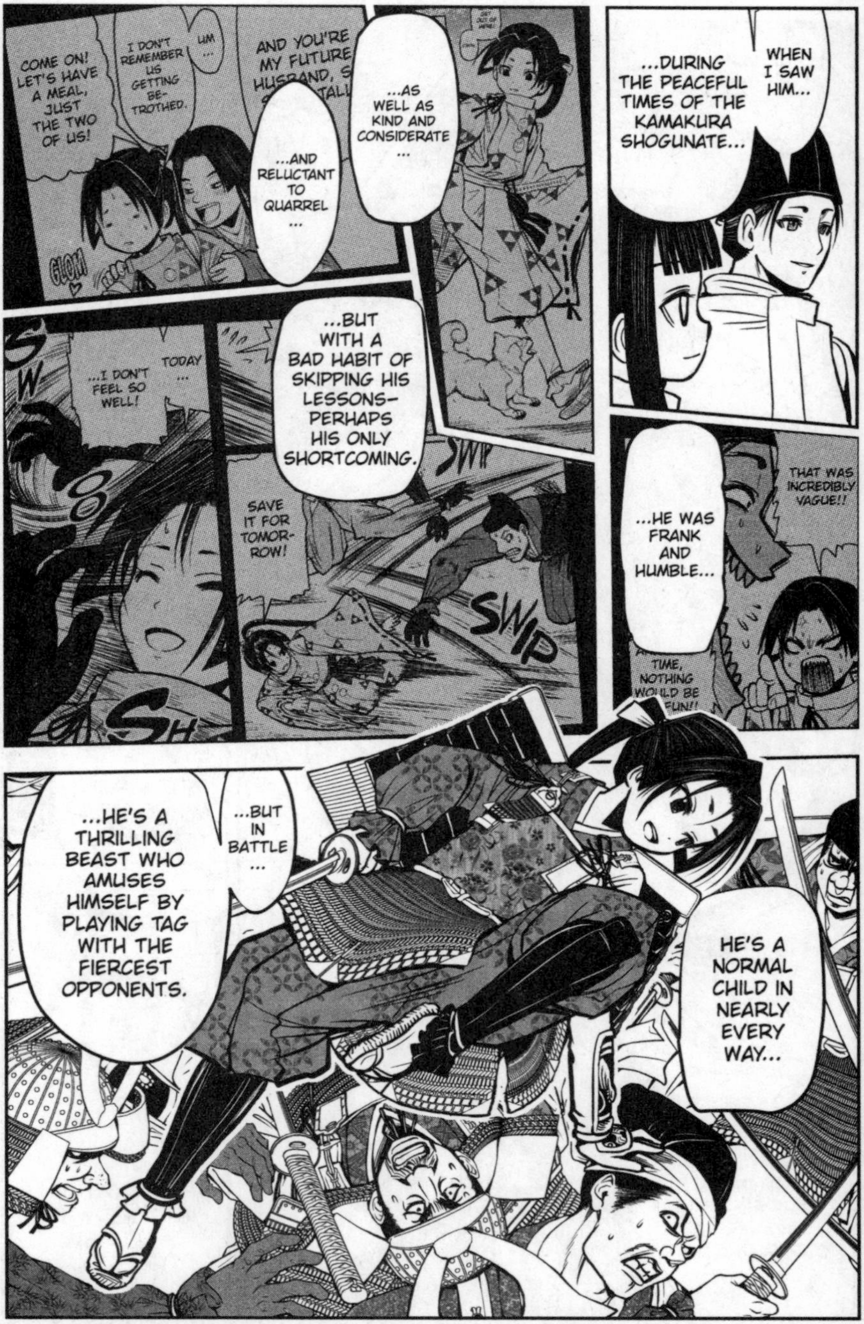
WHEN I SAW HIM...
...DURING THE PEACEFUL TIMES OF THE KAMAKURA SHOGUNATE...
...AS WELL AS KIND AND CONSIDERATE ...
...AND RELUCTANT TO QUARREL ...
AND YOU'RE MY FUTURE HUSBAND, S
UM ...
I DON'T REMEMBER US GETTING BE-TROTHED.
COME ON! LET'S HAVE A MEAL, JUST THE TWO OF US!
GLOM
...HE WAS FRANK AND HUMBLE...
THAT WAS INCREDIBLY VAGUE!!
TIME, NOTHING WOULD BE FUN!!
...BUT WITH A BAD HABIT OF SKIPPING HIS LESSONS—PERHAPS HIS ONLY SHORTCOMING.
SWIP
SAVE IT FOR TOMOR-ROW!
SWIP
TODAY ...
...I DON'T FEEL SO WELL!
HE'S A NORMAL CHILD IN NEARLY EVERY WAY...
...BUT IN BATTLE ...
...HE'S A THRILLING BEAST WHO AMUSES HIMSELF BY PLAYING TAG WITH THE FIERCEST OPPONENTS.

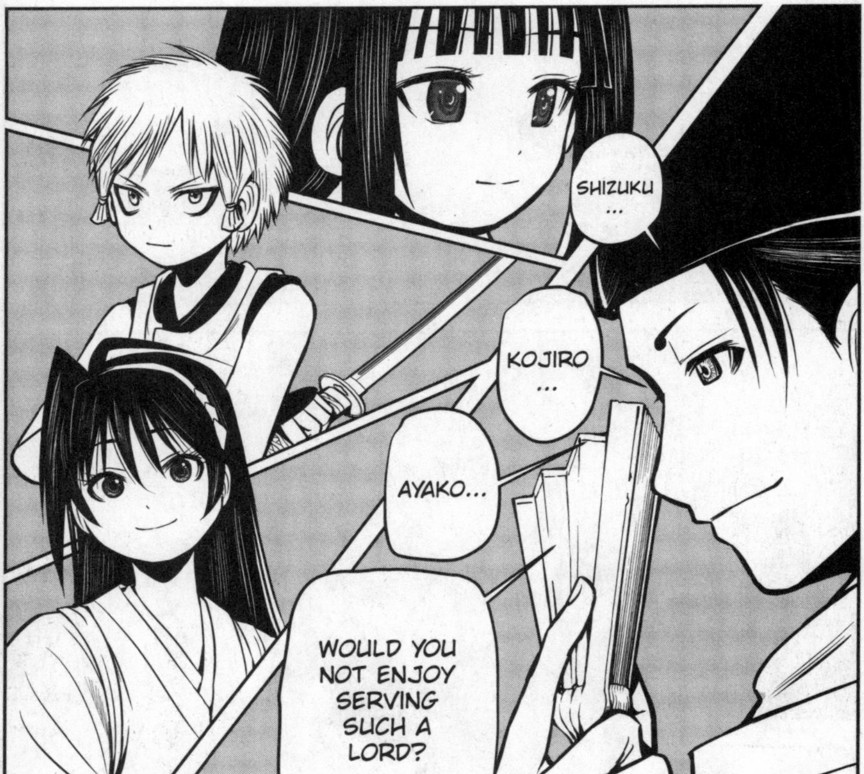
SHIZUKU ...
KOJIRO ...
AYAKO...
WOULD YOU NOT ENJOY SERVING SUCH A LORD?

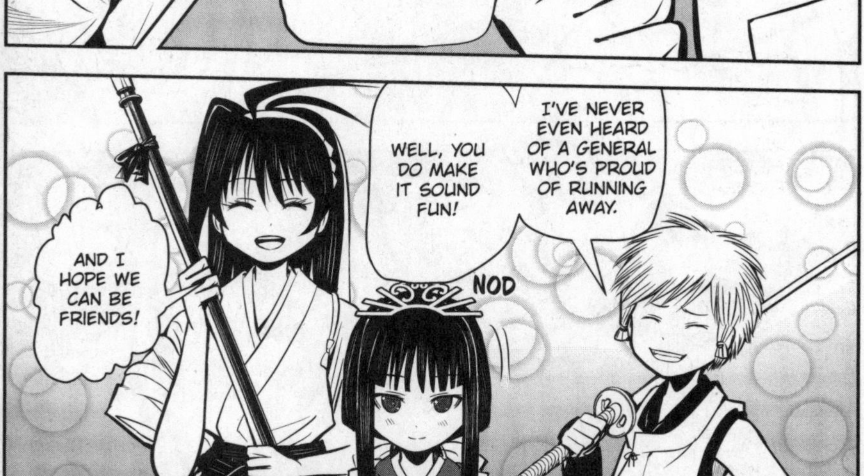
I'VE NEVER EVEN HEARD OF A GENERAL WHO'S PROUD OF RUNNING AWAY.
WELL, YOU DO MAKE IT SOUND FUN!
NOD
AND I HOPE WE CAN BE FRIENDS!

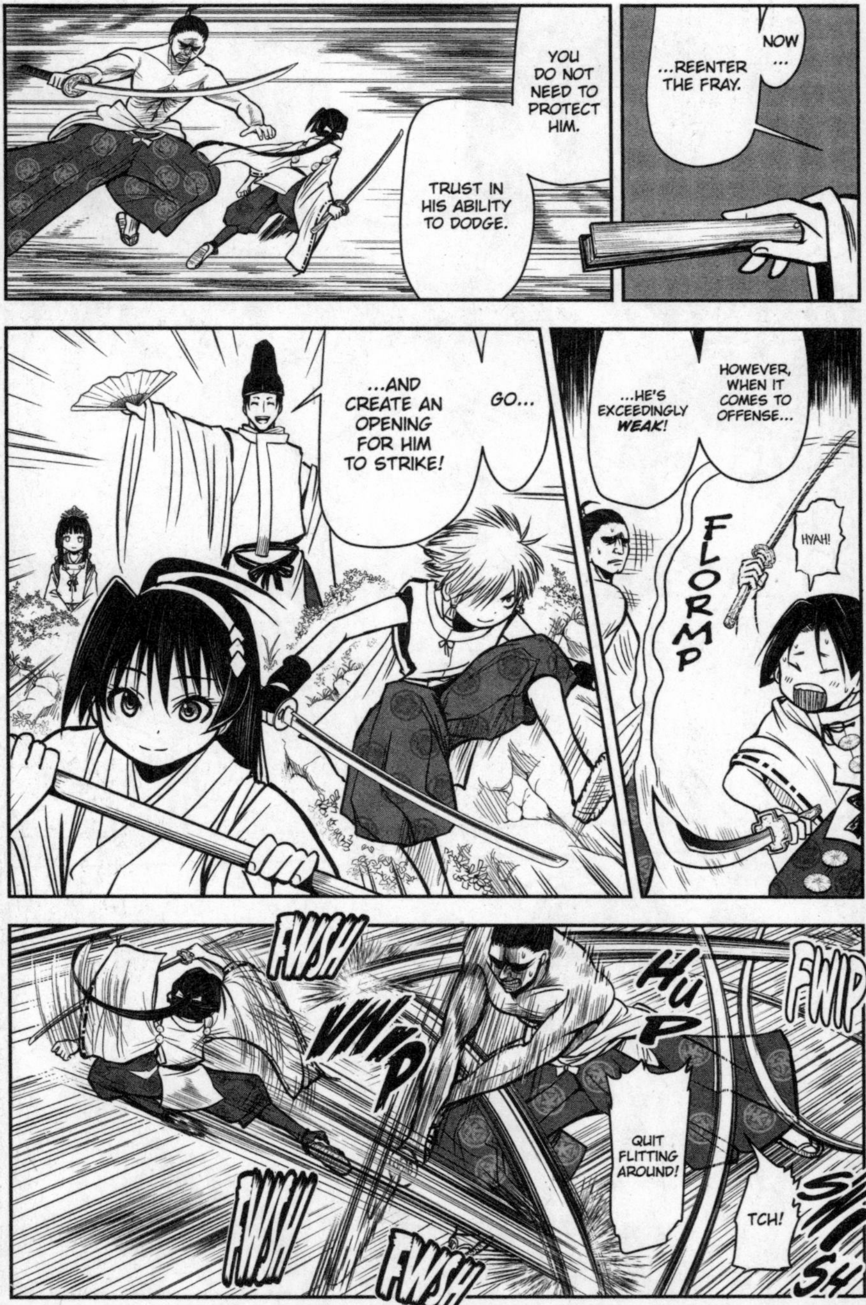
NOW ...
...REENTER THE FRAY.
YOU DO NOT NEED TO PROTECT HIM.
TRUST IN HIS ABILITY TO DODGE.
HOWEVER, WHEN IT COMES TO OFFENSE...
...HE'S EXCEEDINGLY WEAK!
HYAH!
FLORMP
GO...
...AND CREATE AN OPENING FOR HIM TO STRIKE!
FWIP
HUP
FWSH
VWIP
SHSH
TCH!
QUIT FLITTING AROUND!
FWSH
FWSH

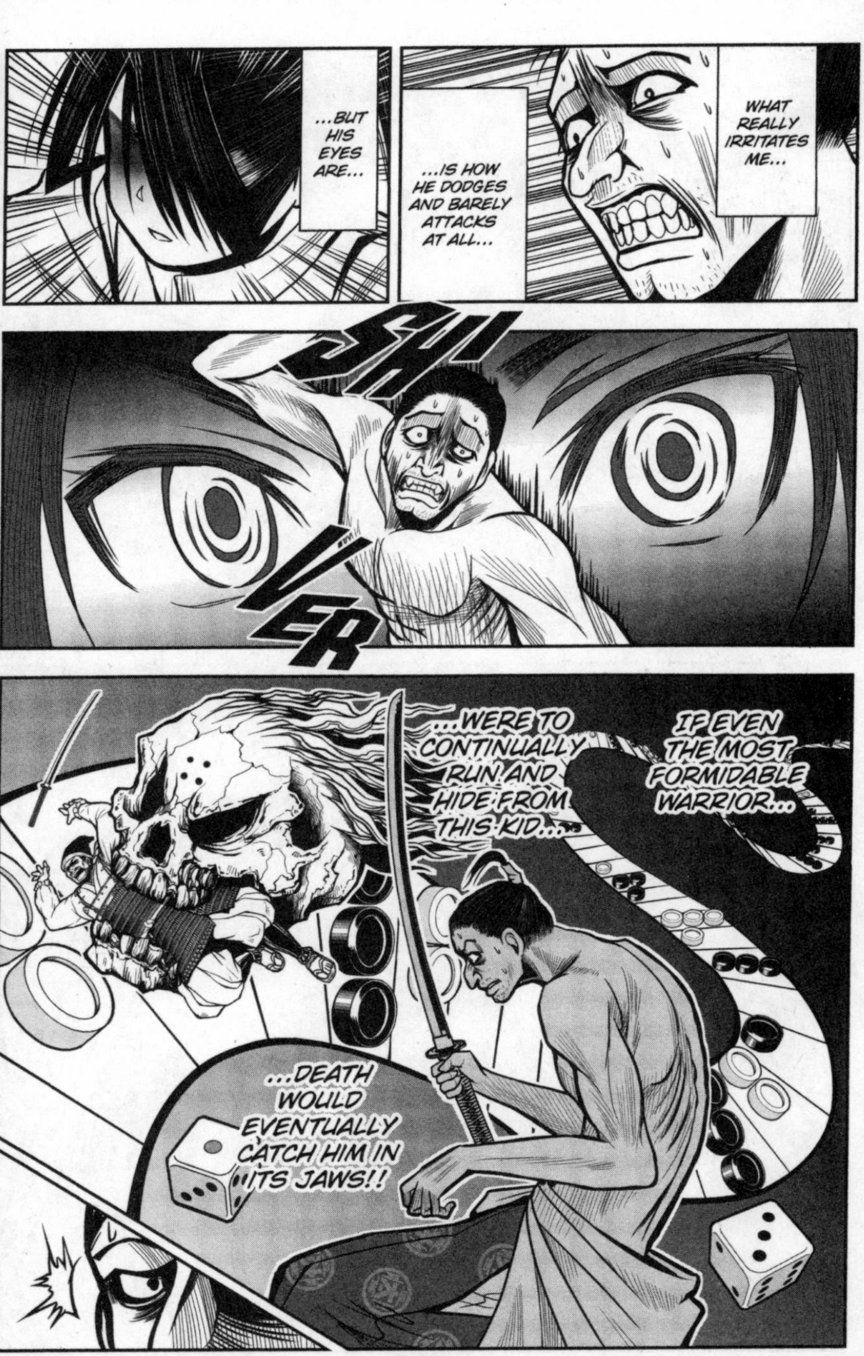
WHAT REALLY IRRITATES ME...
...IS HOW HE DODGES AND BARELY ATTACKS AT ALL...
...BUT HIS EYES ARE...
SHIVER
IF EVEN THE MOST FORMIDABLE WARRIOR...
...WERE TO CONTINUALLY RUN AND HIDE FROM THIS KID...
...DEATH WOULD EVENTUALLY CATCH HIM IN ITS JAWS!!

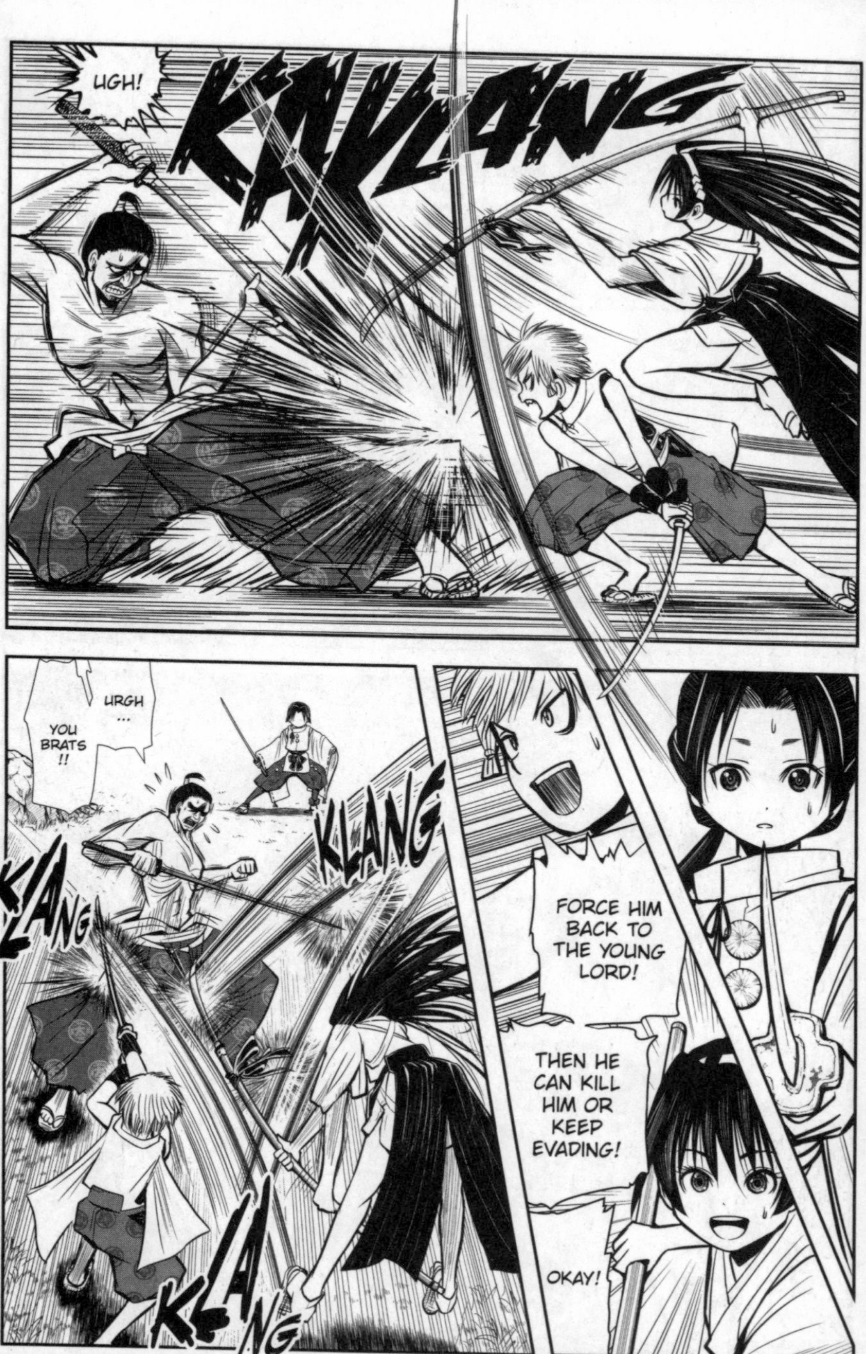
KAVLANG
UGH!
FORCE HIM BACK TO THE YOUNG LORD!
THEN HE CAN KILL HIM OR KEEP EVADING!
OKAY!
URGH ...
YOU BRATS !!
KLANG
KLANG
KLANG

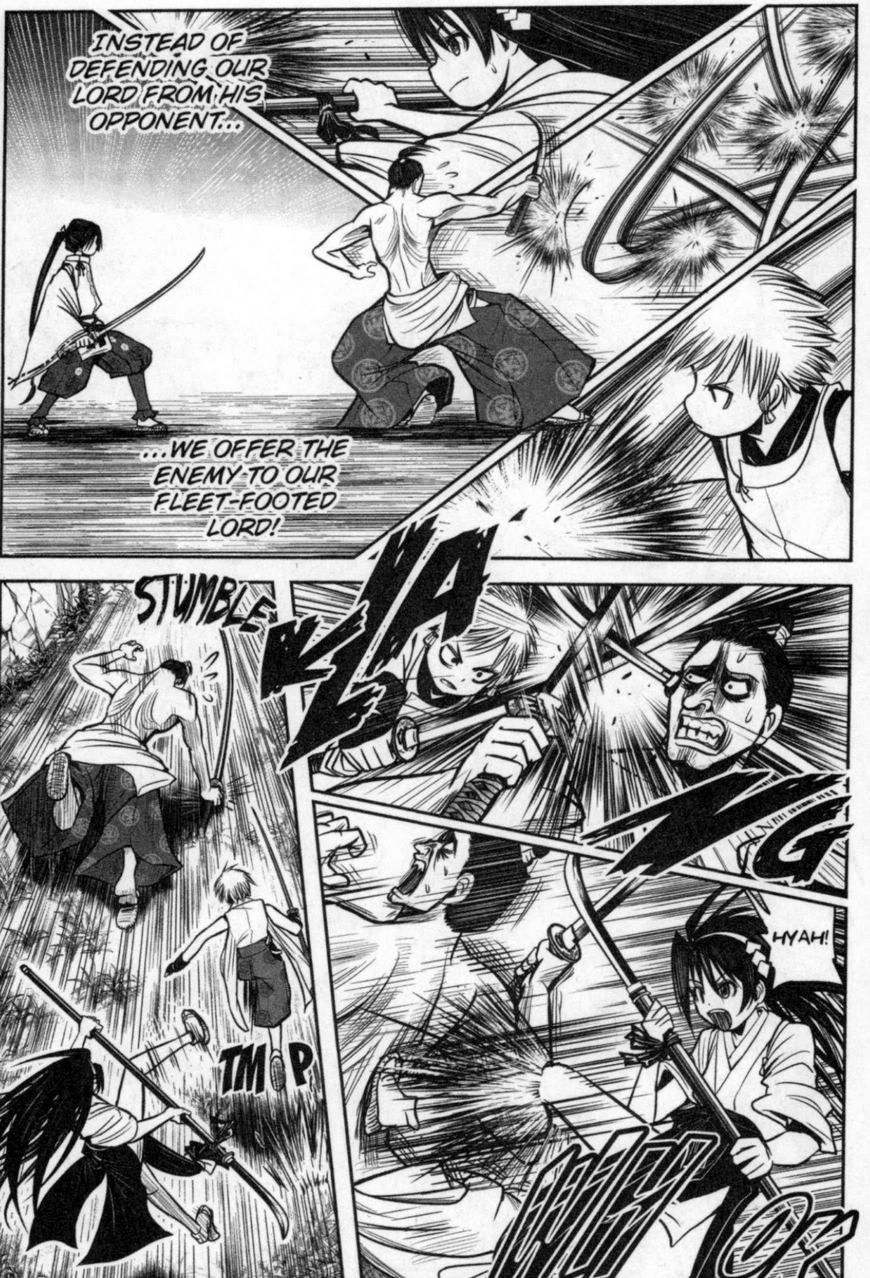
INSTEAD OF DEFENDING OUR LORD FROM HIS OPPONENT...
...WE OFFER THE ENEMY TO OUR FLEET-FOOTED LORD!
HYAH!
STUMBLE
TMP

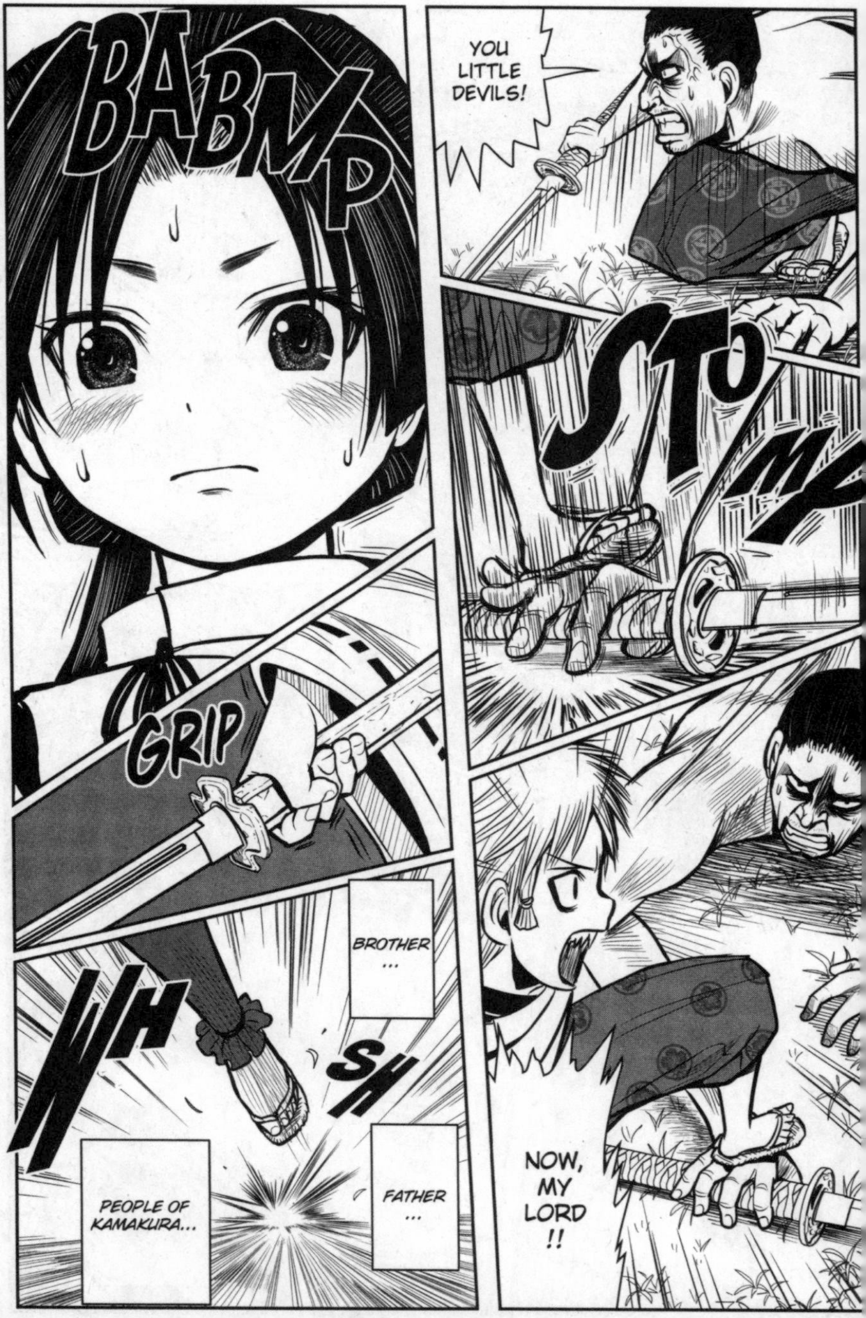
YOU LITTLE DEVILS!
STOM
NOW, MY LORD !!
BABMP
GRIP
BROTHER ...
WH
SH
FATHER ...
PEOPLE OF KAMAKURA...

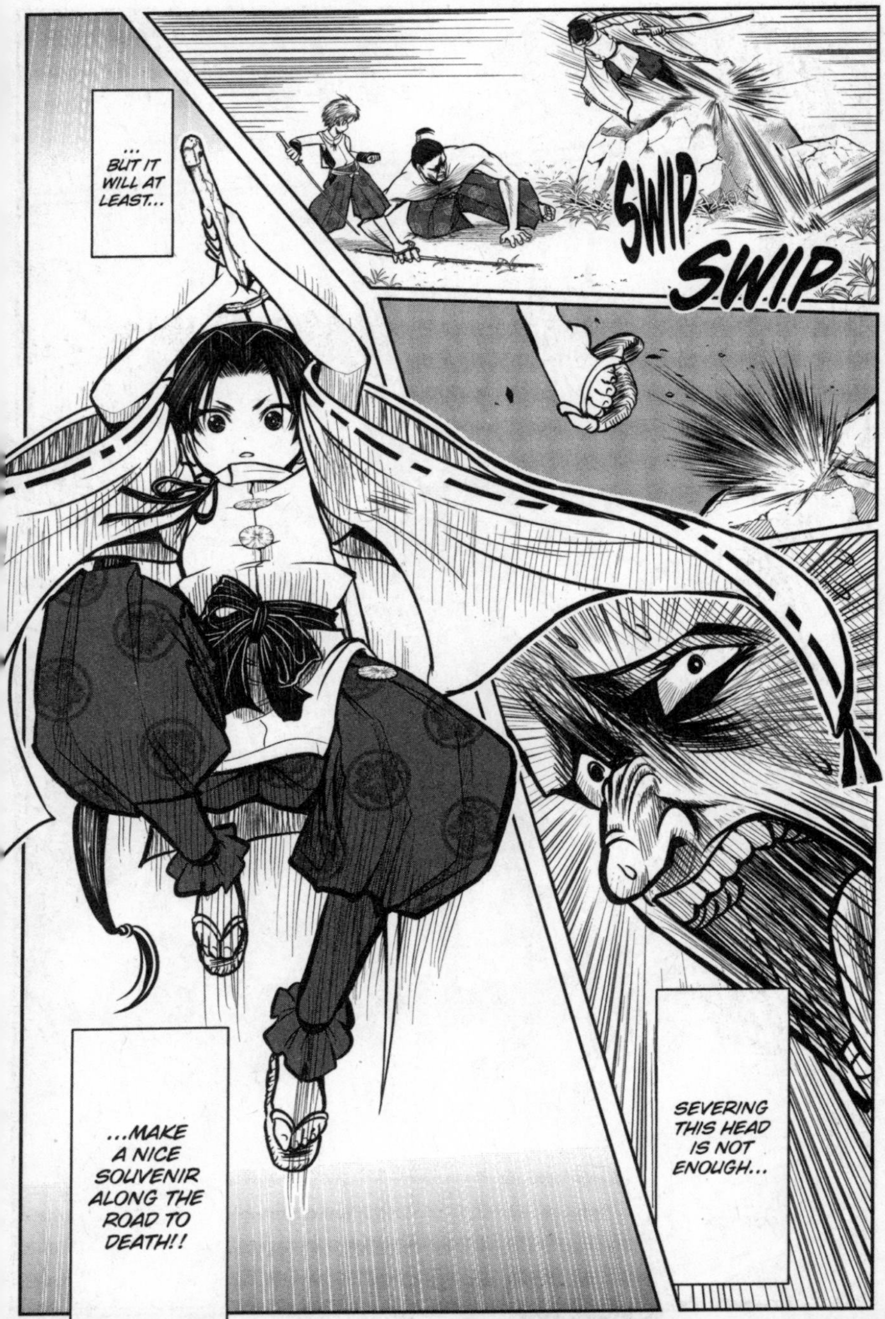
SWIP
SWIP
SEVERING THIS HEAD IS NOT ENOUGH...
...BUT IT WILL AT LEAST...
...MAKE A NICE SOUVENIR ALONG THE ROAD TO DEATH!!

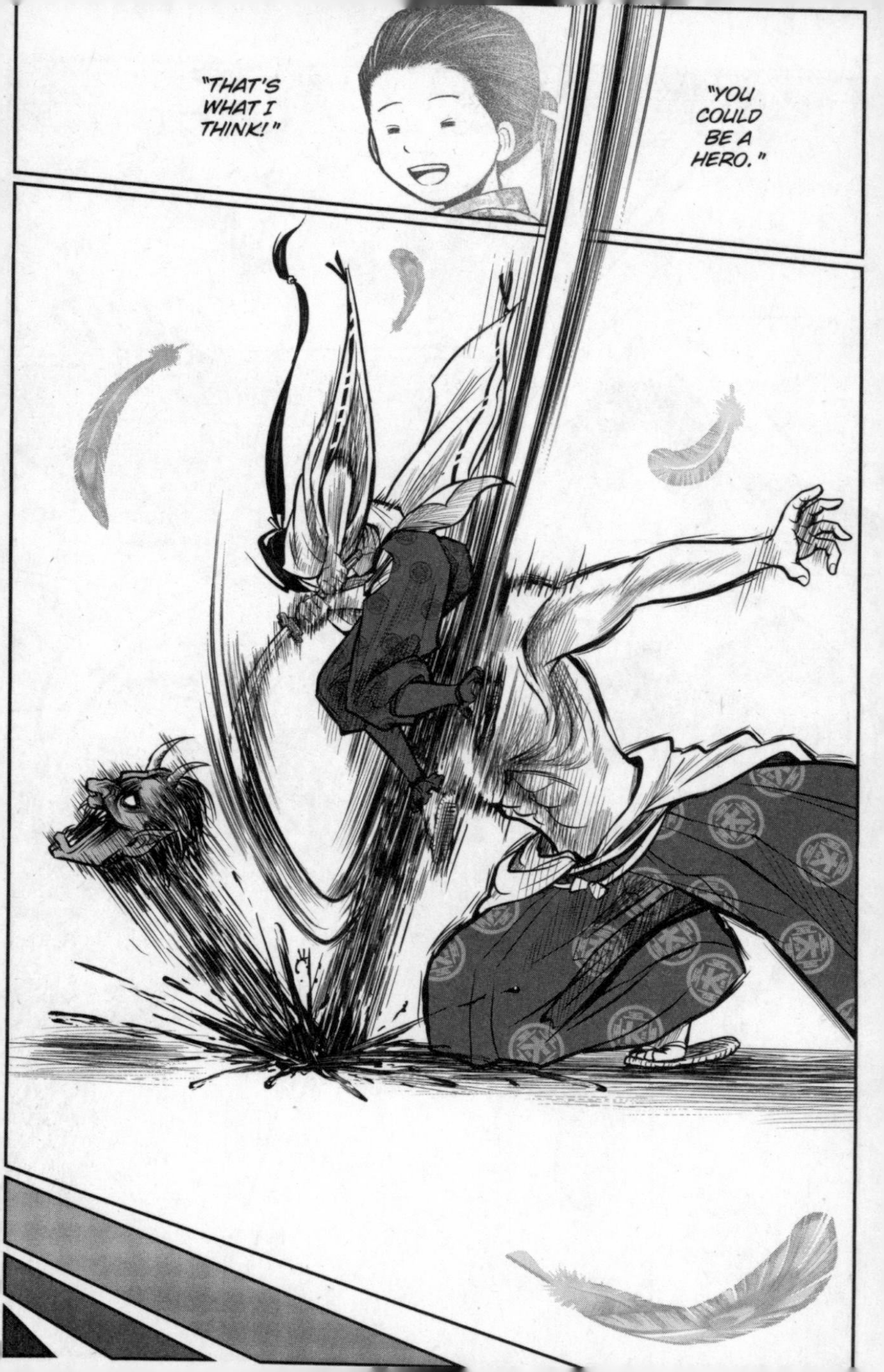
"YOU COULD BE A HERO."
"THAT'S WHAT I THINK!"

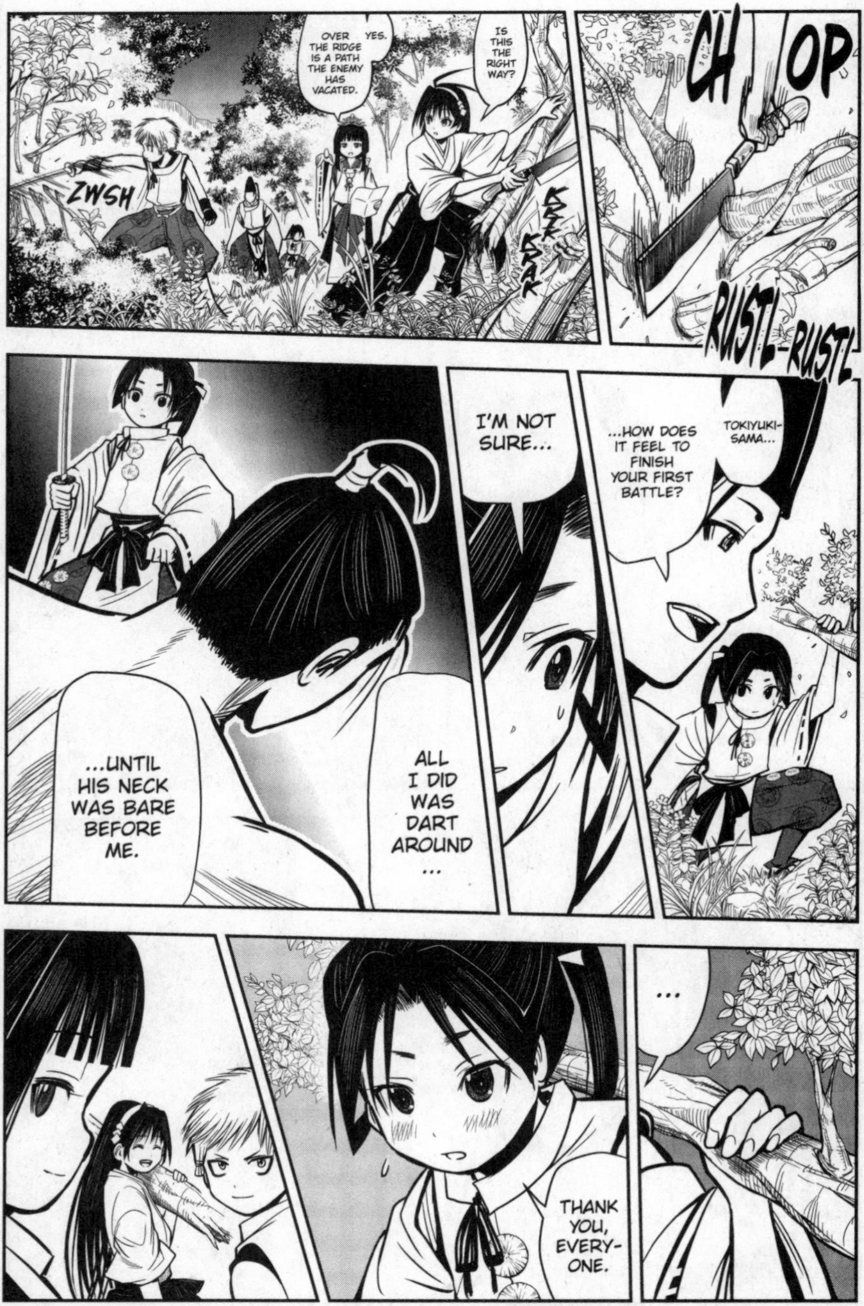
CH OP
RUSTL-RUSTL
IS THIS THE RIGHT WAY?
YES.
OVER THE RIDGE IS A PATH THE ENEMY HAS VACATED.
ZWSH
KSAK KSAK
TOKIYUKI-SAMA...
...HOW DOES IT FEEL TO FINISH YOUR FIRST BATTLE?
I'M NOT SURE...
ALL I DID WAS DART AROUND...
...UNTIL HIS NECK WAS BARE BEFORE ME.
...
THANK YOU, EVERY-ONE.

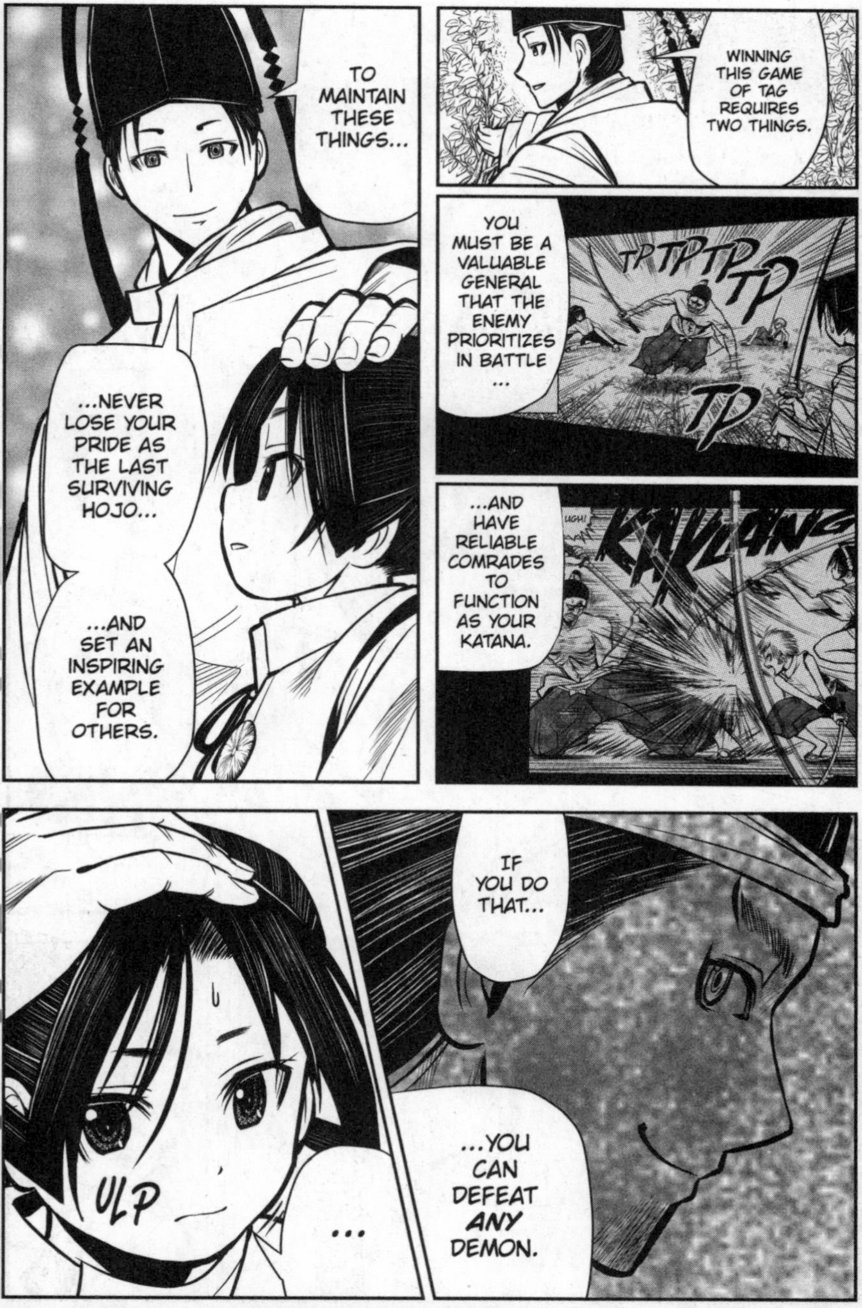
WINNING THIS GAME OF TAG REQUIRES TWO THINGS.
YOU MUST BE A VALUABLE GENERAL THAT THE ENEMY PRIORITIZES IN BATTLE ...
TPTPTPTP TP
TP
...AND HAVE RELIABLE COMRADES TO FUNCTION AS YOUR KATANA.
UGH!
KAWANG
TO MAINTAIN THESE THINGS...
...NEVER LOSE YOUR PRIDE AS THE LAST SURVIVING HOJO...
...AND SET AN INSPIRING EXAMPLE FOR OTHERS.
IF YOU DO THAT...
...YOU CAN DEFEAT *ANY* DEMON.
ULP
...

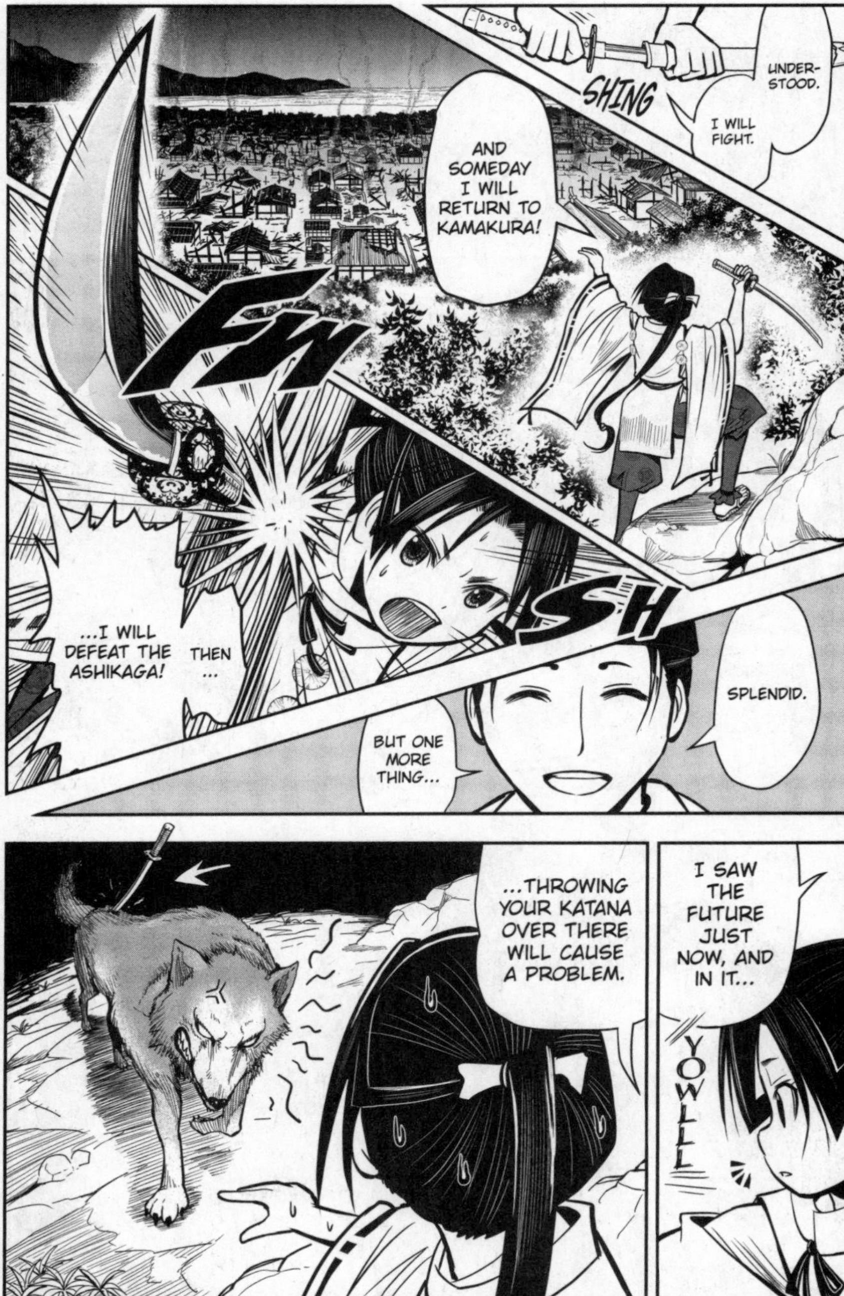
UNDER-STOOD.
I WILL FIGHT.
SHING
AND SOMEDAY I WILL RETURN TO KAMAKURA!
FWN
...I WILL DEFEAT THE ASHIKAGA!
THEN ...
SH
SPLENDID.
BUT ONE MORE THING...
I SAW THE FUTURE JUST NOW, AND IN IT...
YOWLL
...THROWING YOUR KATANA OVER THERE WILL CAUSE A PROBLEM.

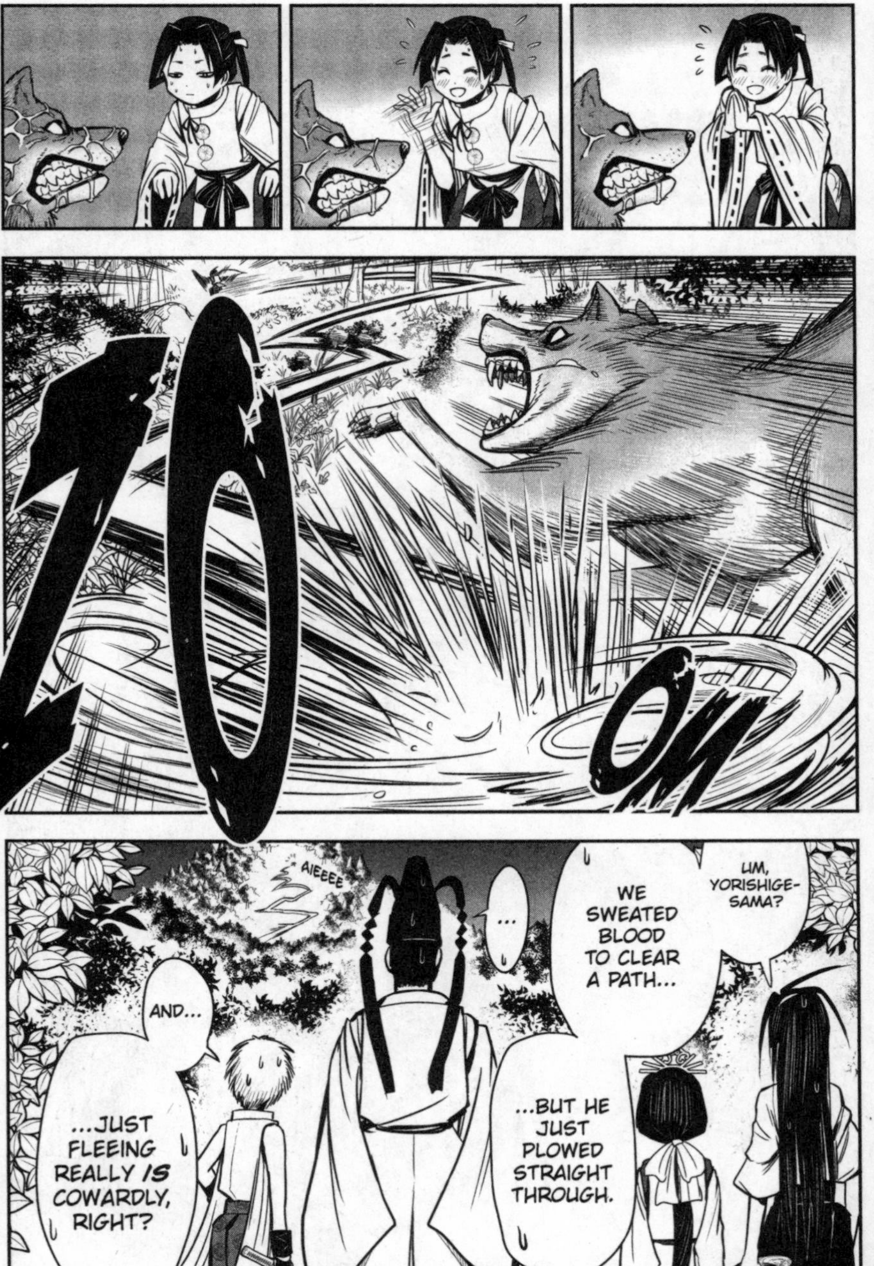
DON
UM, YORISHIGE-SAMA?
WE SWEATED BLOOD TO CLEAR A PATH...
...BUT HE JUST PLOWED STRAIGHT THROUGH.
...
AIEEEE
AND...
...JUST FLEEING REALLY *IS* COWARDLY, RIGHT?

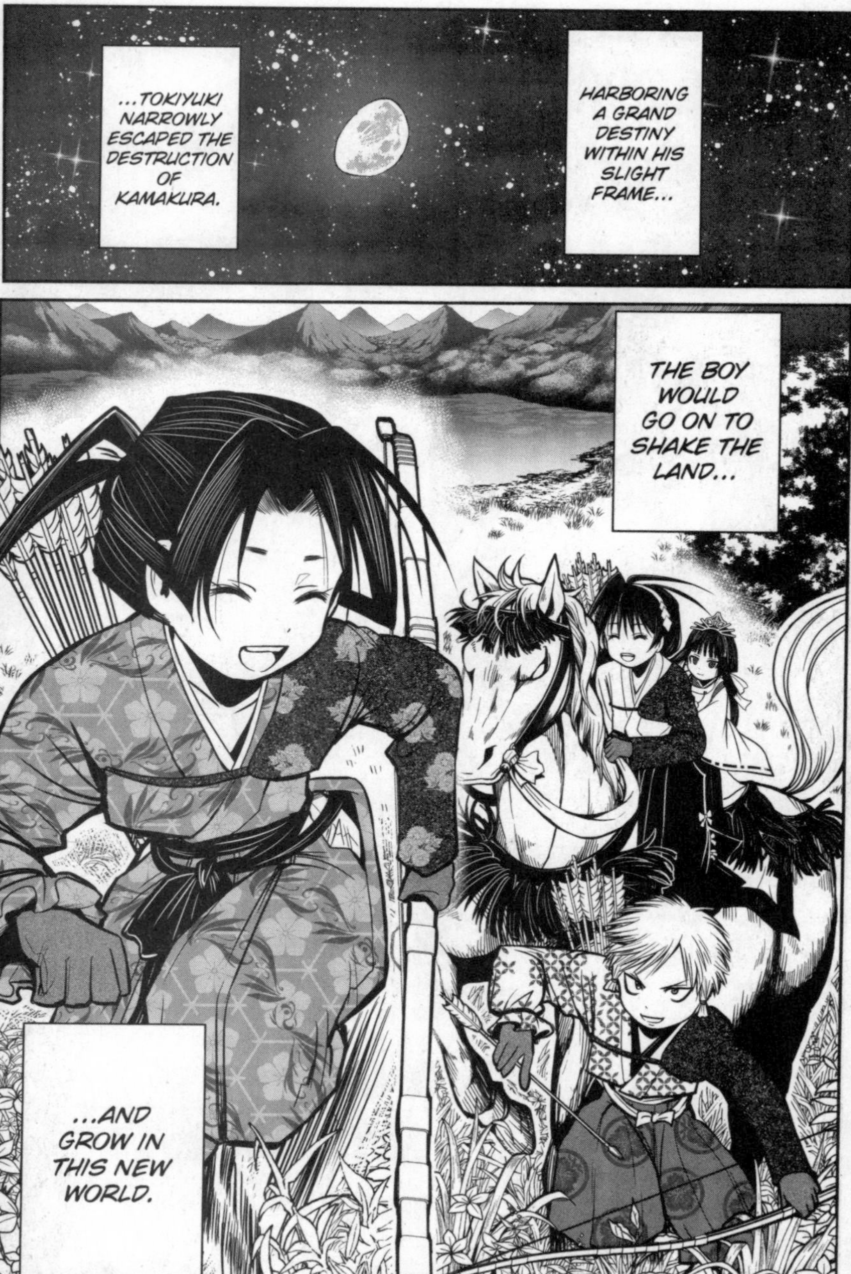
HARBORING A GRAND DESTINY WITHIN HIS SLIGHT FRAME...
...TOKIYUKI NARROWLY ESCAPED THE DESTRUCTION OF KAMAKURA.
THE BOY WOULD GO ON TO SHAKE THE LAND...
...AND GROW IN THIS NEW WORLD.

1333

GODAIIN MUNESHIGE

★★★ SR

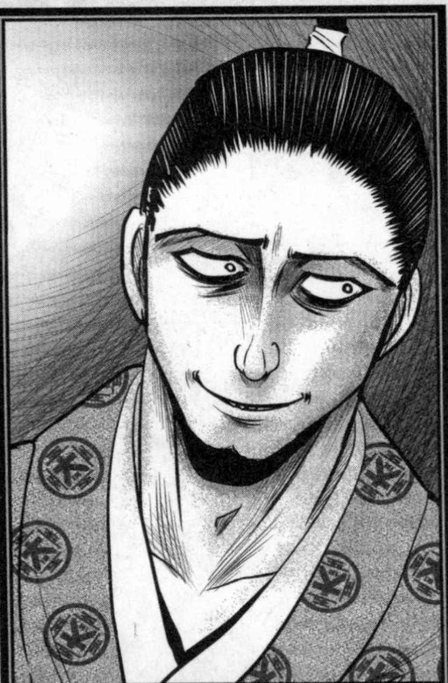

ABILITIES		NANBOKU-CHO COMPATIBILITY	
MARTIAL ARTS	**72**	SAVAGERY	**76**
INTELLIGENCE	37	LOYALTY	3
POLITICS	24	CHAOS	**75**
LEADERSHIP	37	INGENUITY	29
CHARM	15	RUNNING AND HIDING	66

SKILL SWORD FIGHTING: 10 PERCENT INCREASE TO SWORD APTITUDE

SKILL CONSCIENCE VALUE DOESN'T DECREASE EVEN IF HE BETRAYS HIS SUPERIORS

NOTE NO FRIENDS

EMBLEM

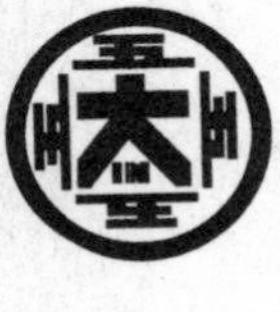

GODAIIN STAMP

CATCHPHRASE

"JUST YOU SAY TAKATOKI'S NAME!!"

CHAPTER 4: SUWA 1333

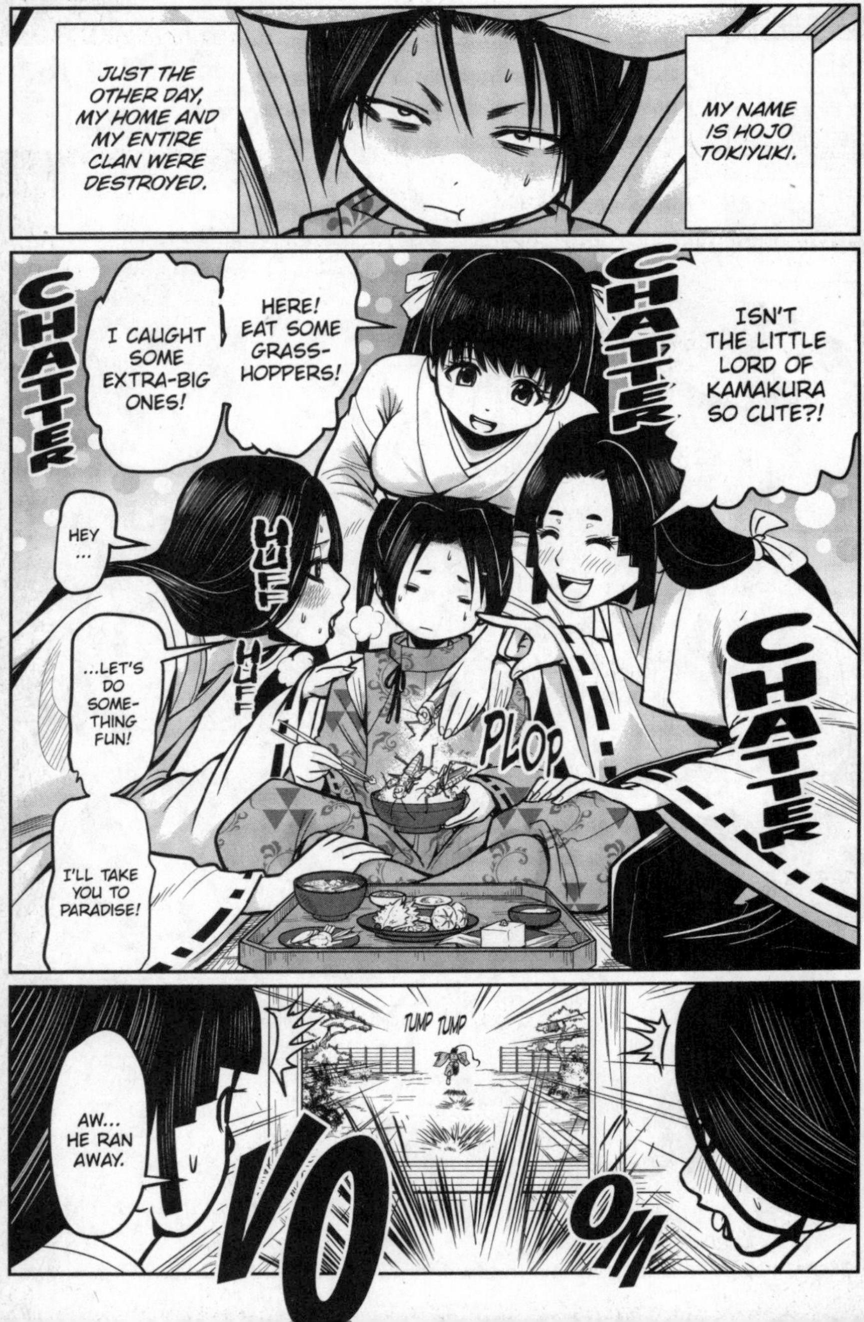
MY NAME IS HOJO TOKIYUKI.
JUST THE OTHER DAY, MY HOME AND MY ENTIRE CLAN WERE DESTROYED.
CHATTER
ISN'T THE LITTLE LORD OF KAMAKURA SO CUTE?!
HERE! EAT SOME GRASS-HOPPERS!
I CAUGHT SOME EXTRA-BIG ONES!
CHATTER
CHATTER
PLOP
HUFF HUFF
HEY ...
...LET'S DO SOME-THING FUN!
I'LL TAKE YOU TO PARADISE!
TUMP TUMP
VOOM
AW... HE RAN AWAY.

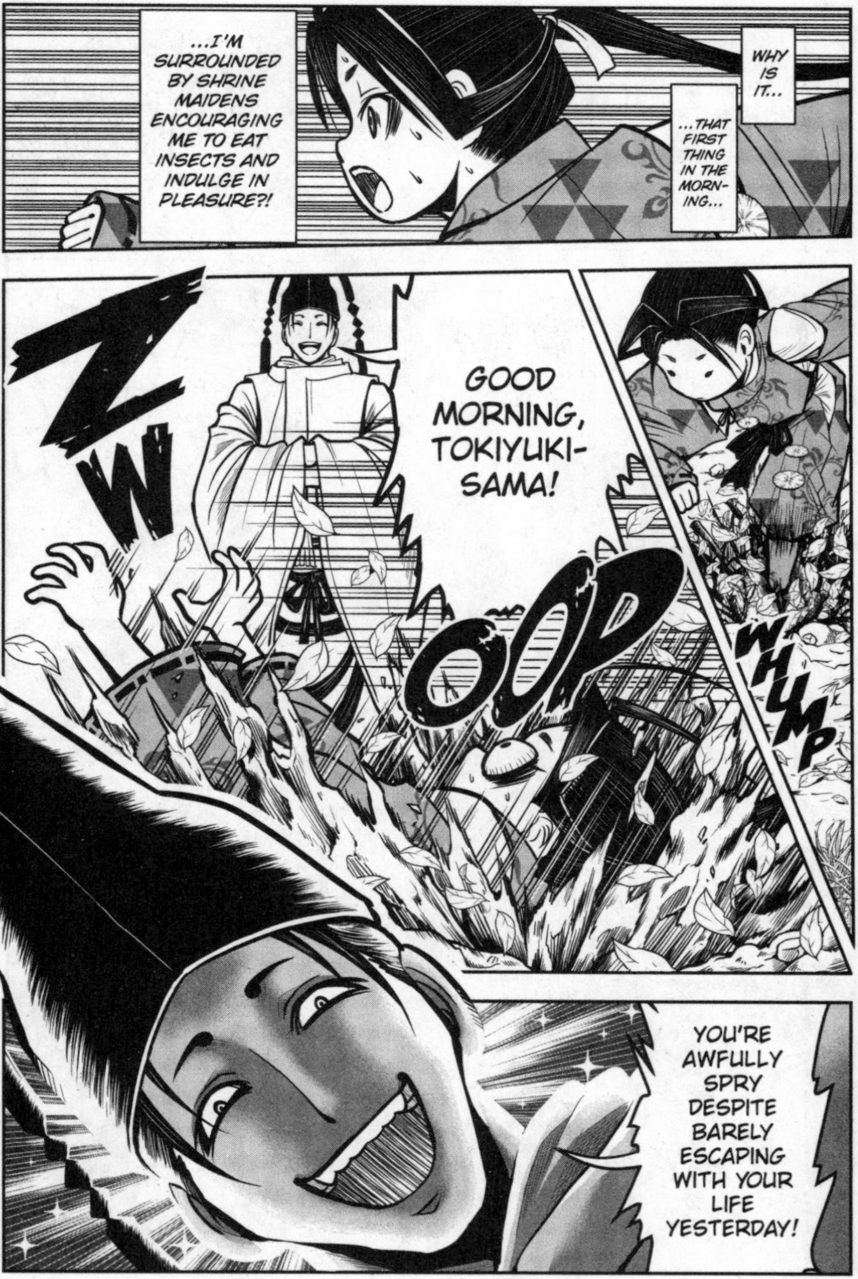
WHY IS IT...
...THAT FIRST THING IN THE MORNING...
...I'M SURROUNDED BY SHRINE MAIDENS ENCOURAGING ME TO EAT INSECTS AND INDULGE IN PLEASURE?!
WHUMP
GOOD MORNING, TOKIYUKI-SAMA!
ZWOOP
YOU'RE AWFULLY SPRY DESPITE BARELY ESCAPING WITH YOUR LIFE YESTERDAY!

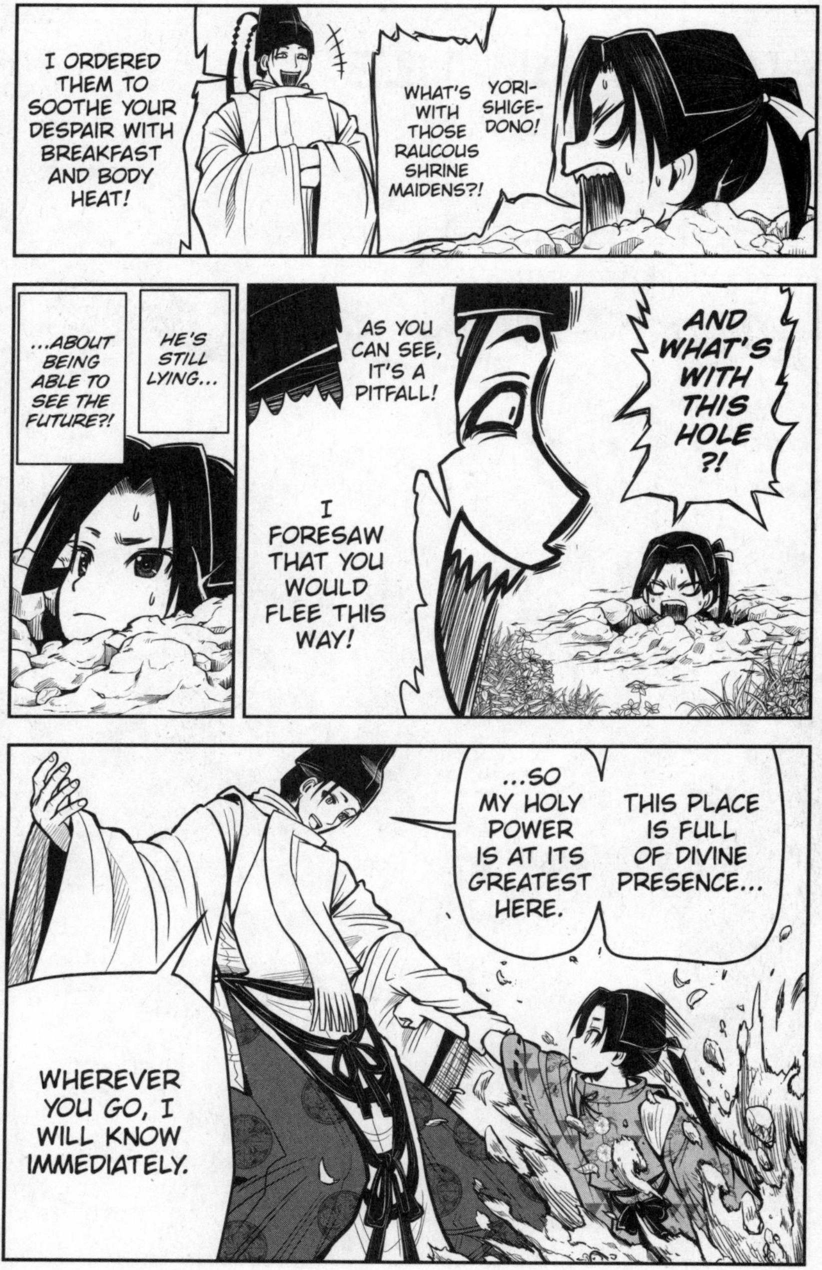
YORI-SHIGE-DONO!
WHAT'S WITH THOSE RAUCOUS SHRINE MAIDENS?!
I ORDERED THEM TO SOOTHE YOUR DESPAIR WITH BREAKFAST AND BODY HEAT!
AND WHAT'S WITH THIS HOLE ?!
AS YOU CAN SEE, IT'S A PITFALL!
I FORESAW THAT YOU WOULD FLEE THIS WAY!
HE'S STILL LYING...
...ABOUT BEING ABLE TO SEE THE FUTURE?!
THIS PLACE IS FULL OF DIVINE PRESENCE...
...SO MY HOLY POWER IS AT ITS GREATEST HERE.
WHEREVER YOU GO, I WILL KNOW IMMEDIATELY.

CHAPTER 4: SUWA 1333

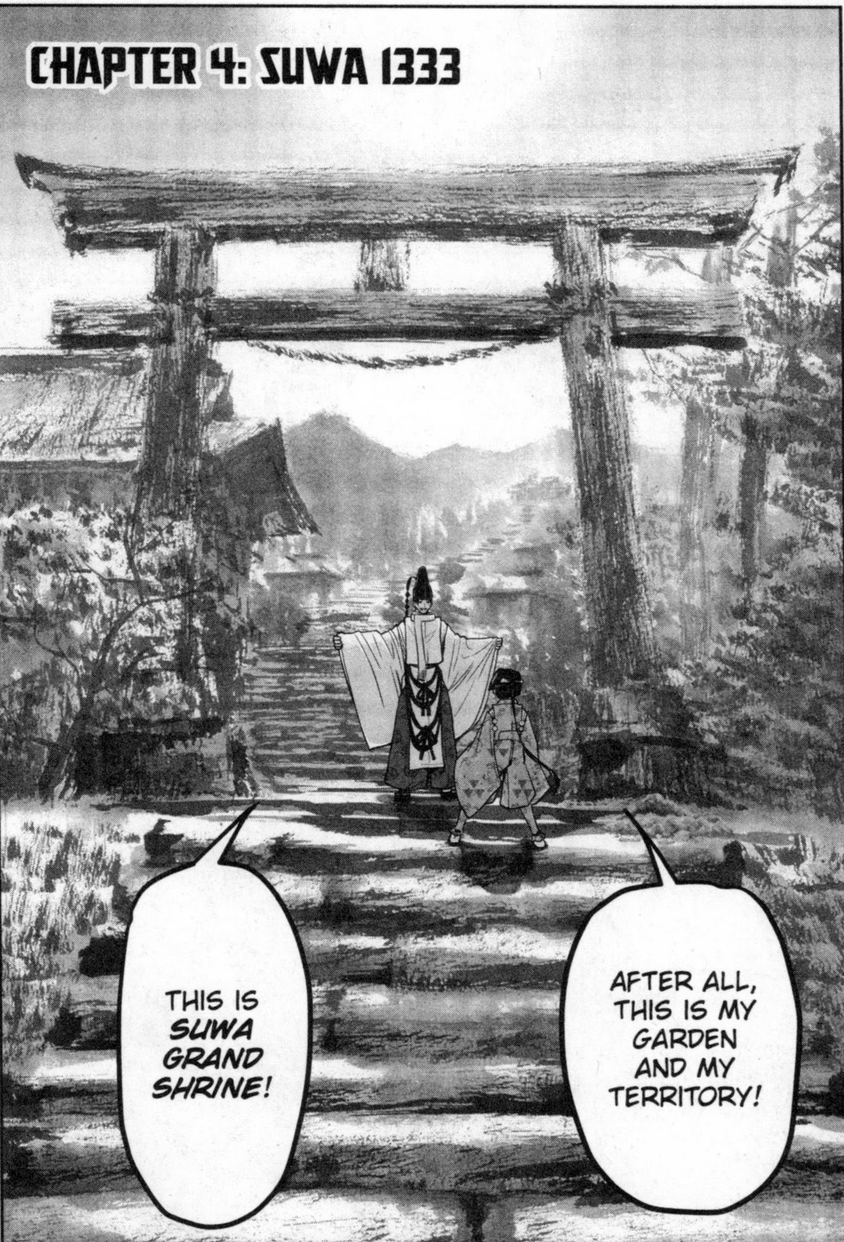
AFTER ALL, THIS IS MY GARDEN AND MY TERRITORY!
THIS IS SUWA GRAND SHRINE!

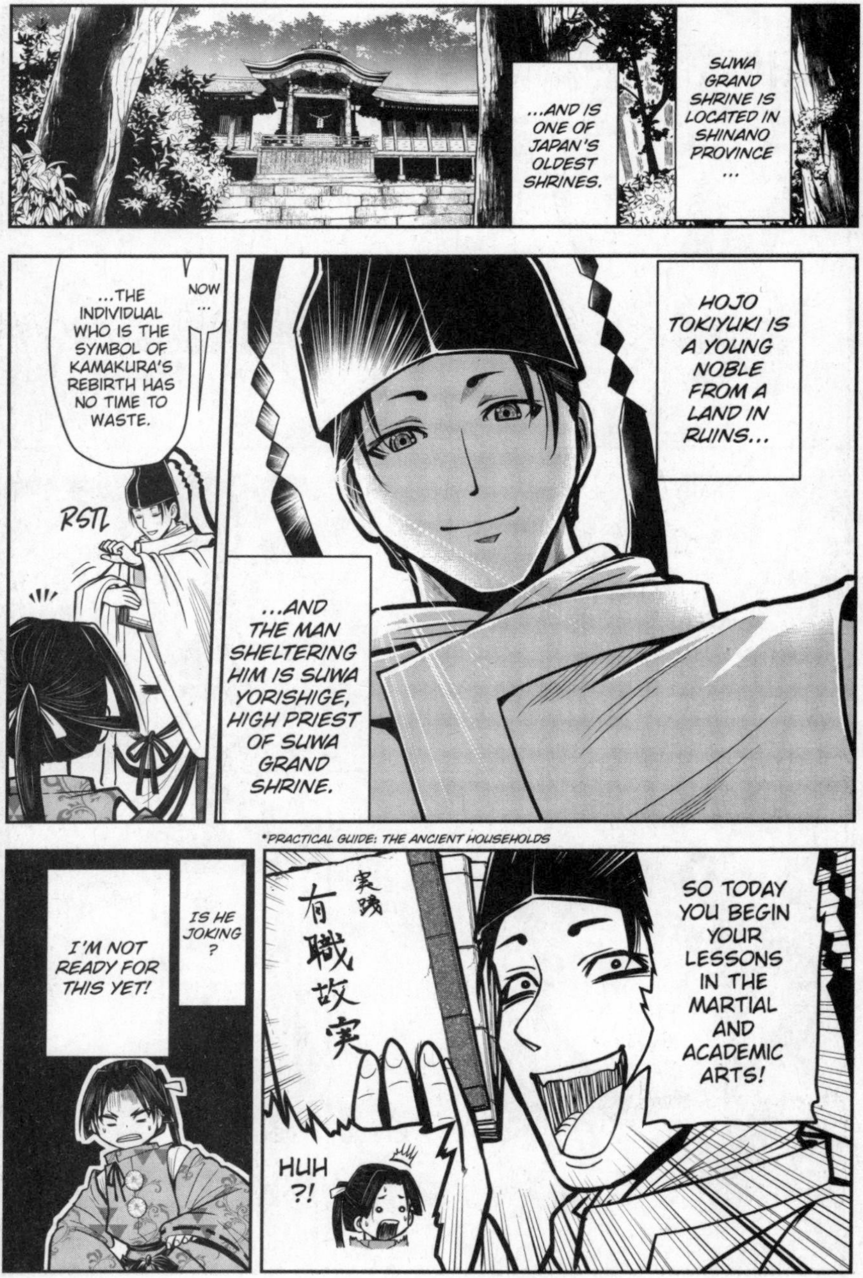
SUWA GRAND SHRINE IS LOCATED IN SHINANO PROVINCE ...
...AND IS ONE OF JAPAN'S OLDEST SHRINES.
HOJO TOKIYUKI IS A YOUNG NOBLE FROM A LAND IN RUINS...
...AND THE MAN SHELTERING HIM IS SUWA YORISHIGE, HIGH PRIEST OF SUWA GRAND SHRINE.
NOW ...
...THE INDIVIDUAL WHO IS THE SYMBOL OF KAMAKURA'S REBIRTH HAS NO TIME TO WASTE.
RSTL
SO TODAY YOU BEGIN YOUR LESSONS IN THE MARTIAL AND ACADEMIC ARTS!
実践
有職故実
HUH ?!
IS HE JOKING ?
I'M NOT READY FOR THIS YET!

*PRACTICAL GUIDE: THE ANCIENT HOUSEHOLDS

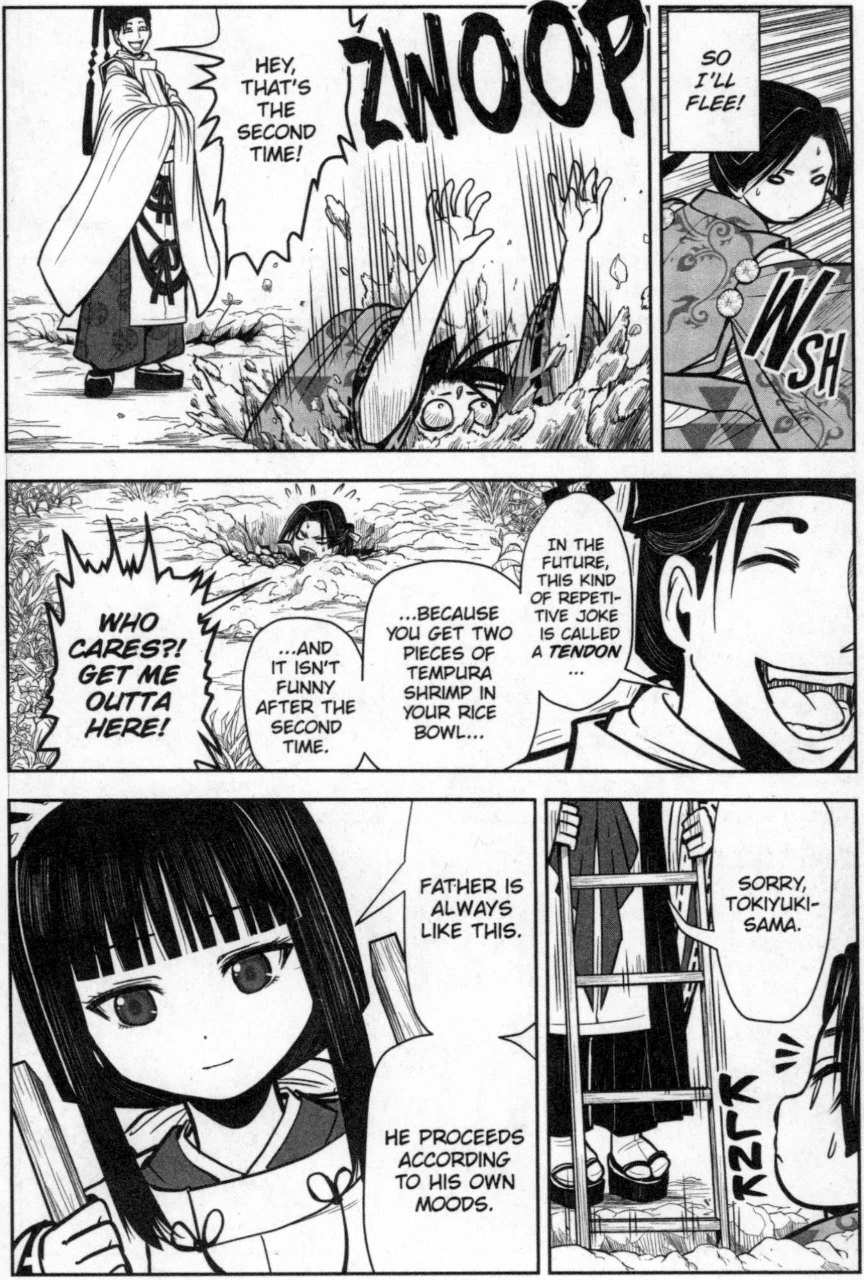
SO I'LL FLEE!
WSH
ZWOOP
HEY, THAT'S THE SECOND TIME!
IN THE FUTURE, THIS KIND OF REPETITIVE JOKE IS CALLED A TENDON ...
...BECAUSE YOU GET TWO PIECES OF TEMPURA SHRIMP IN YOUR RICE BOWL...
...AND IT ISN'T FUNNY AFTER THE SECOND TIME.
WHO CARES?! GET ME OUTTA HERE!
SORRY, TOKIYUKI-SAMA.
KLNK
FATHER IS ALWAYS LIKE THIS.
HE PROCEEDS ACCORDING TO HIS OWN MOODS.

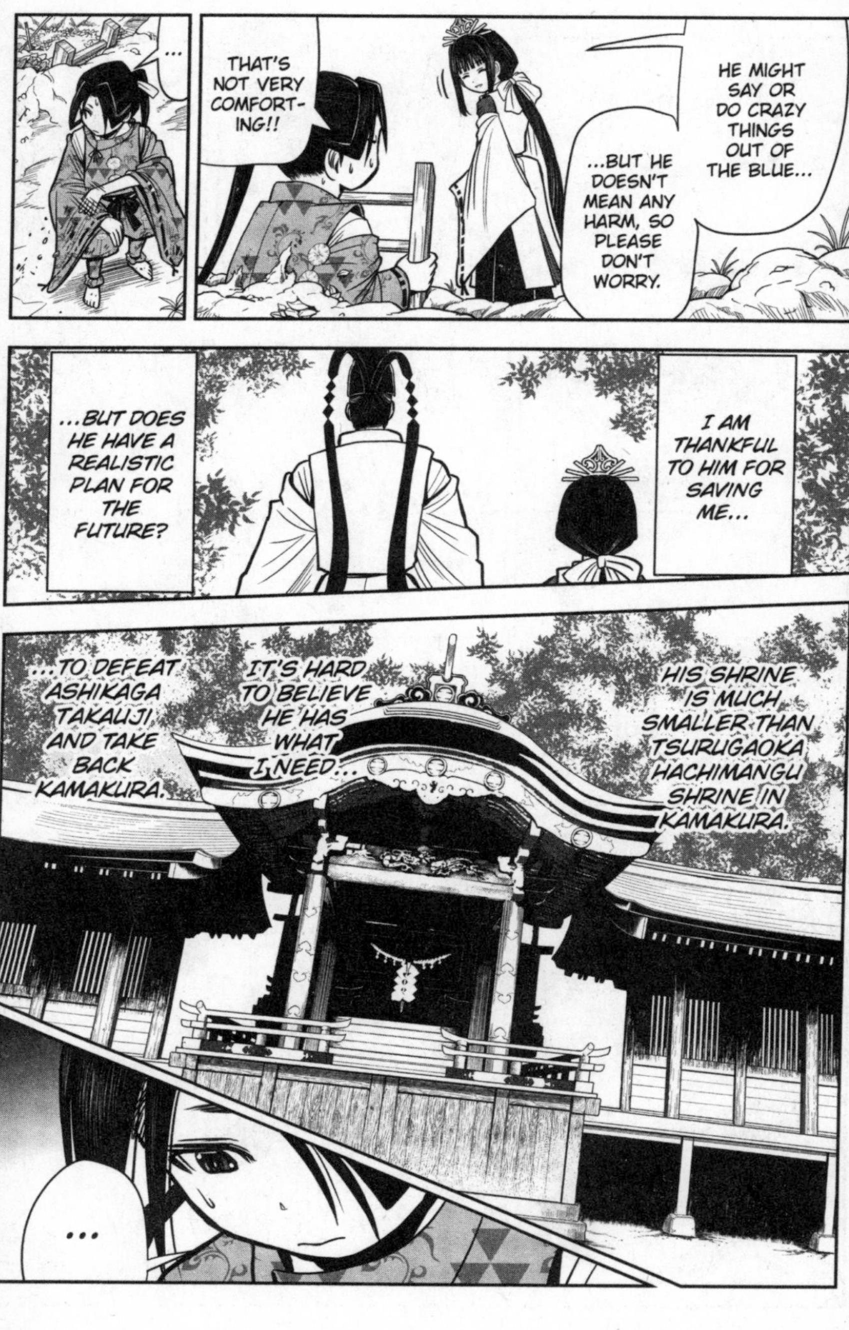
HE MIGHT SAY OR DO CRAZY THINGS OUT OF THE BLUE...
...BUT HE DOESN'T MEAN ANY HARM, SO PLEASE DON'T WORRY.
THAT'S NOT VERY COMFORT-ING!!
...
I AM THANKFUL TO HIM FOR SAVING ME...
...BUT DOES HE HAVE A REALISTIC PLAN FOR THE FUTURE?
HIS SHRINE IS MUCH SMALLER THAN TSURUGAOKA HACHIMANGU SHRINE IN KAMAKURA.
IT'S HARD TO BELIEVE HE HAS WHAT I NEED...
...TO DEFEAT ASHIKAGA TAKAUJI AND TAKE BACK KAMAKURA.
...

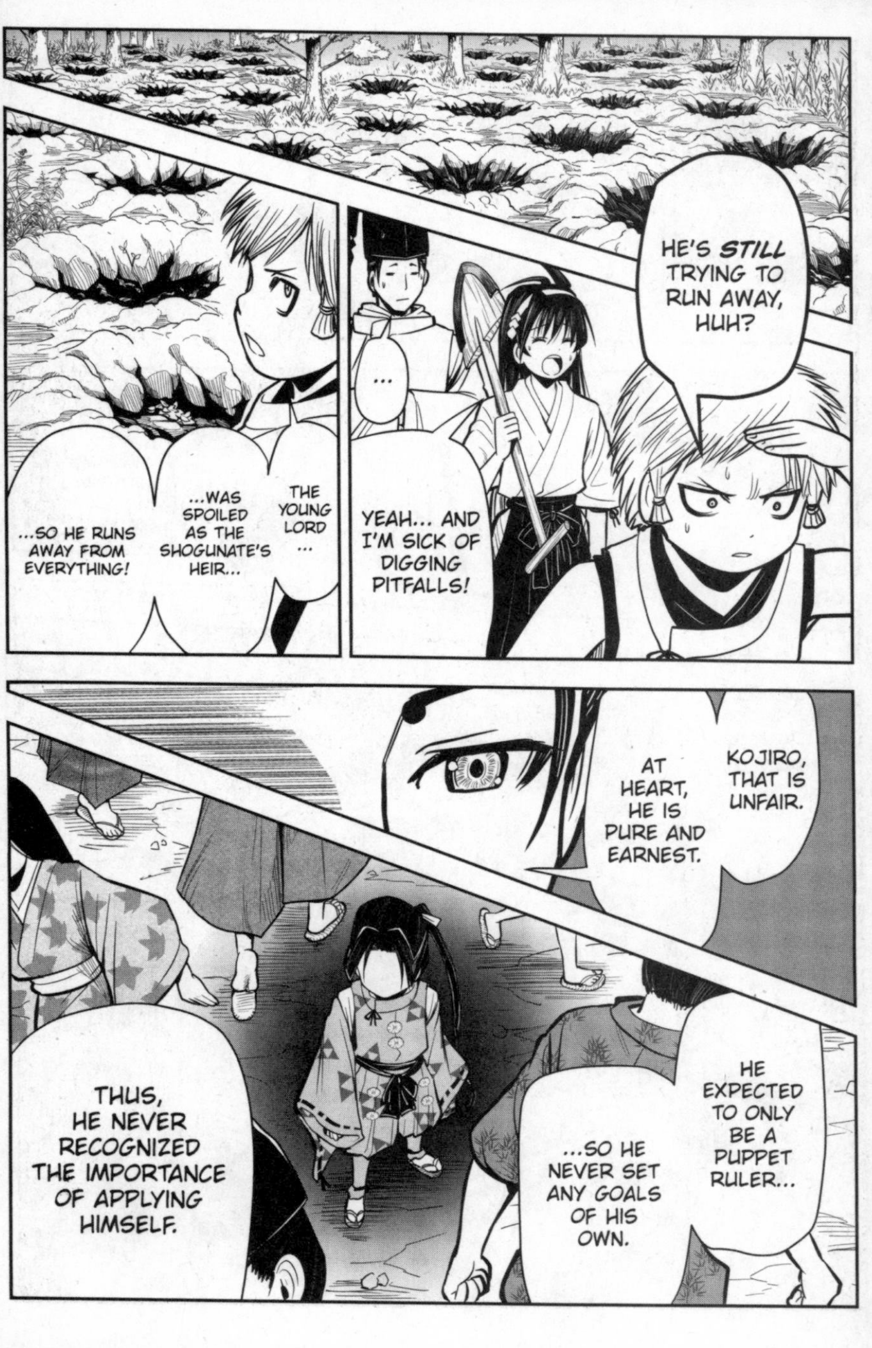
HE'S *STILL* TRYING TO RUN AWAY, HUH?
YEAH... AND I'M SICK OF DIGGING PITFALLS!
...
THE YOUNG LORD ...
...WAS SPOILED AS THE SHOGUNATE'S HEIR...
...SO HE RUNS AWAY FROM EVERYTHING!
KOJIRO, THAT IS UNFAIR.
AT HEART, HE IS PURE AND EARNEST.
HE EXPECTED TO ONLY BE A PUPPET RULER...
...SO HE NEVER SET ANY GOALS OF HIS OWN.
THUS, HE NEVER RECOGNIZED THE IMPORTANCE OF APPLYING HIMSELF.

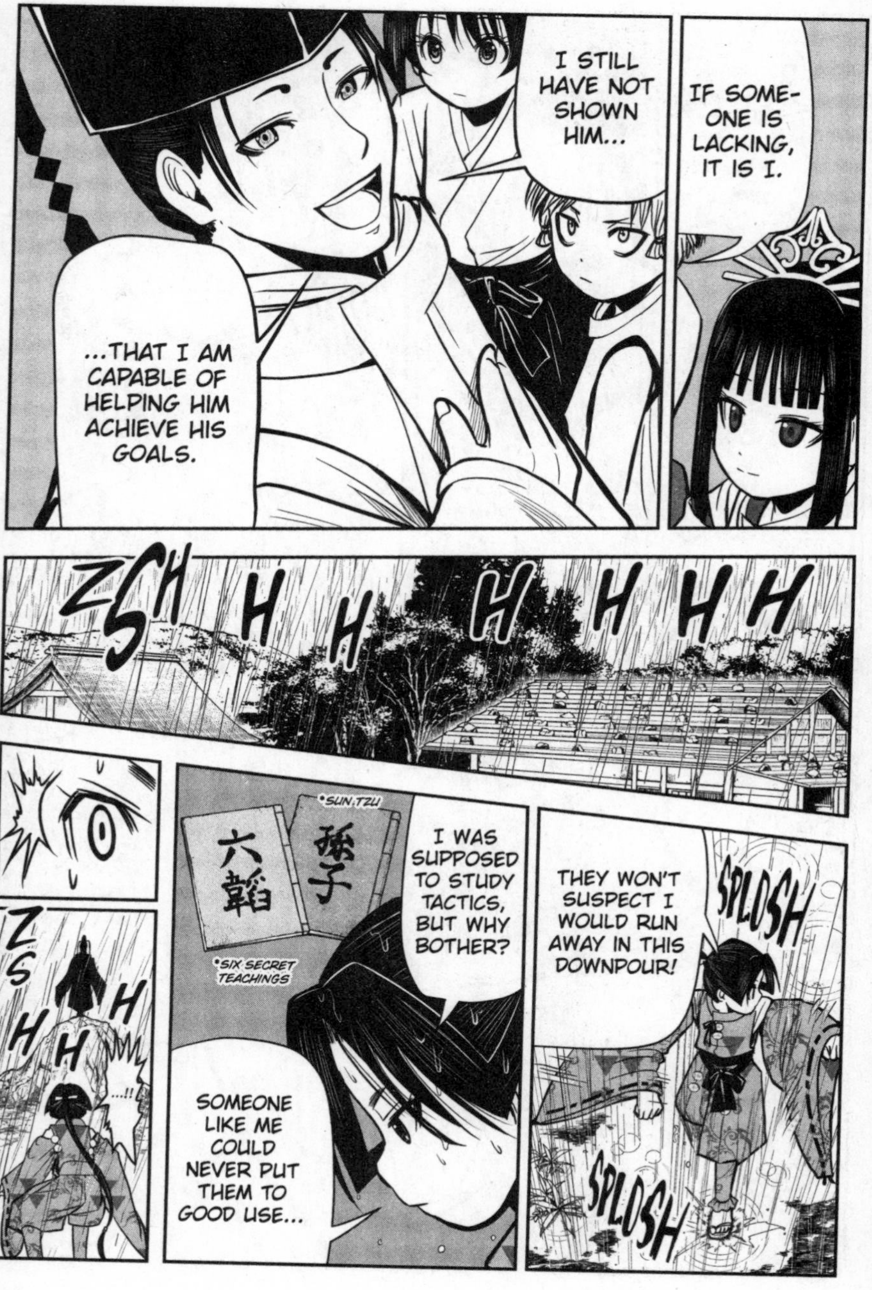
IF SOME-ONE IS LACKING, IT IS I.
I STILL HAVE NOT SHOWN HIM...
...THAT I AM CAPABLE OF HELPING HIM ACHIEVE HIS GOALS.
ZSHHHHHHH
SPLOSH
THEY WON'T SUSPECT I WOULD RUN AWAY IN THIS DOWNPOUR!
SPLOSH
孫子
*SUN TZU
六韜
*SIX SECRET TEACHINGS
I WAS SUPPOSED TO STUDY TACTICS, BUT WHY BOTHER?
SOMEONE LIKE ME COULD NEVER PUT THEM TO GOOD USE...
ZSHHHH
...!!

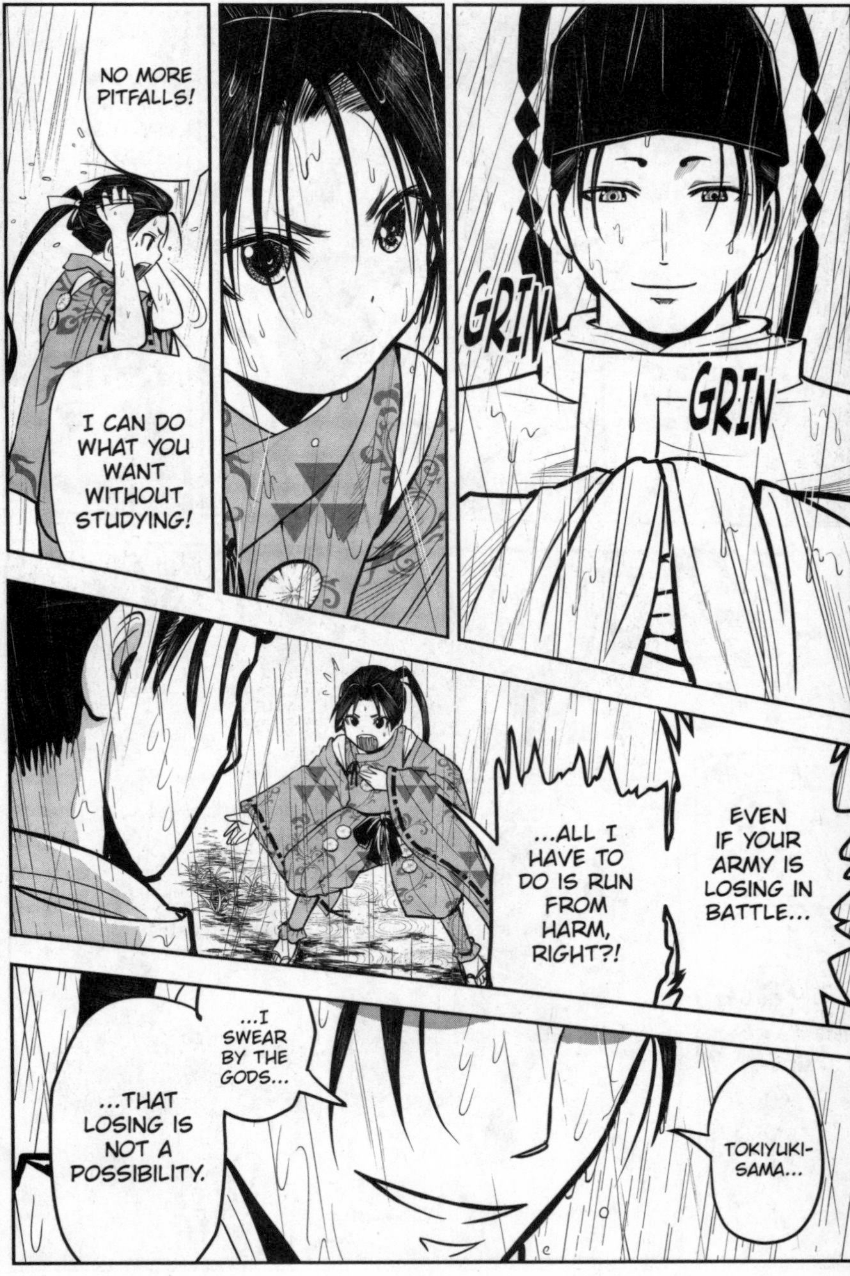
GRIN
GRIN
NO MORE PITFALLS!
I CAN DO WHAT YOU WANT WITHOUT STUDYING!
EVEN IF YOUR ARMY IS LOSING IN BATTLE...
...ALL I HAVE TO DO IS RUN FROM HARM, RIGHT?!
TOKIYUKI-SAMA...
...I SWEAR BY THE GODS...
...THAT LOSING IS NOT A POSSIBILITY.

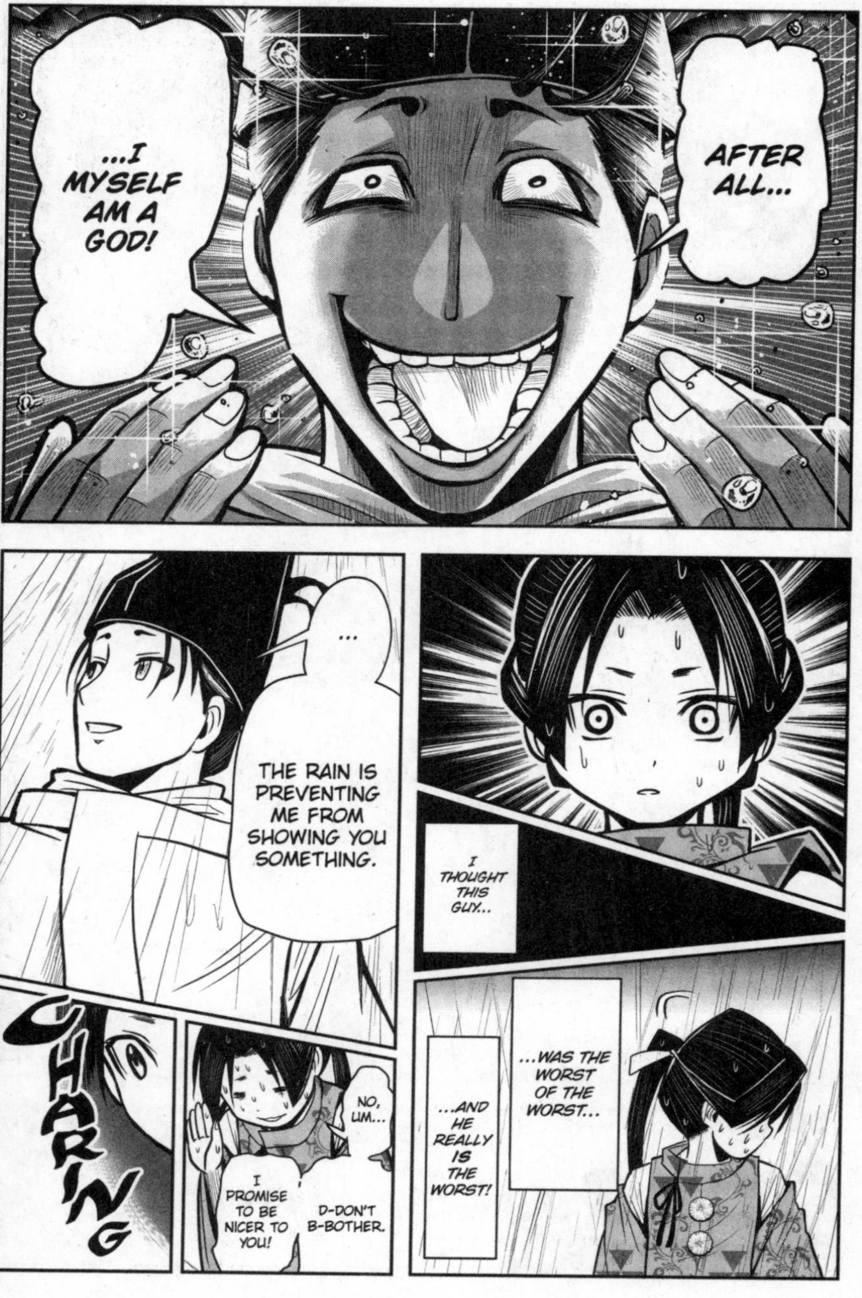
AFTER ALL...
...I MYSELF AM A GOD!
I THOUGHT THIS GUY...
...
THE RAIN IS PREVENTING ME FROM SHOWING YOU SOMETHING.
...WAS THE WORST OF THE WORST...
...AND HE REALLY IS THE WORST!
NO, UM...
D-DON'T B-BOTHER.
I PROMISE TO BE NICER TO YOU!
CHARING

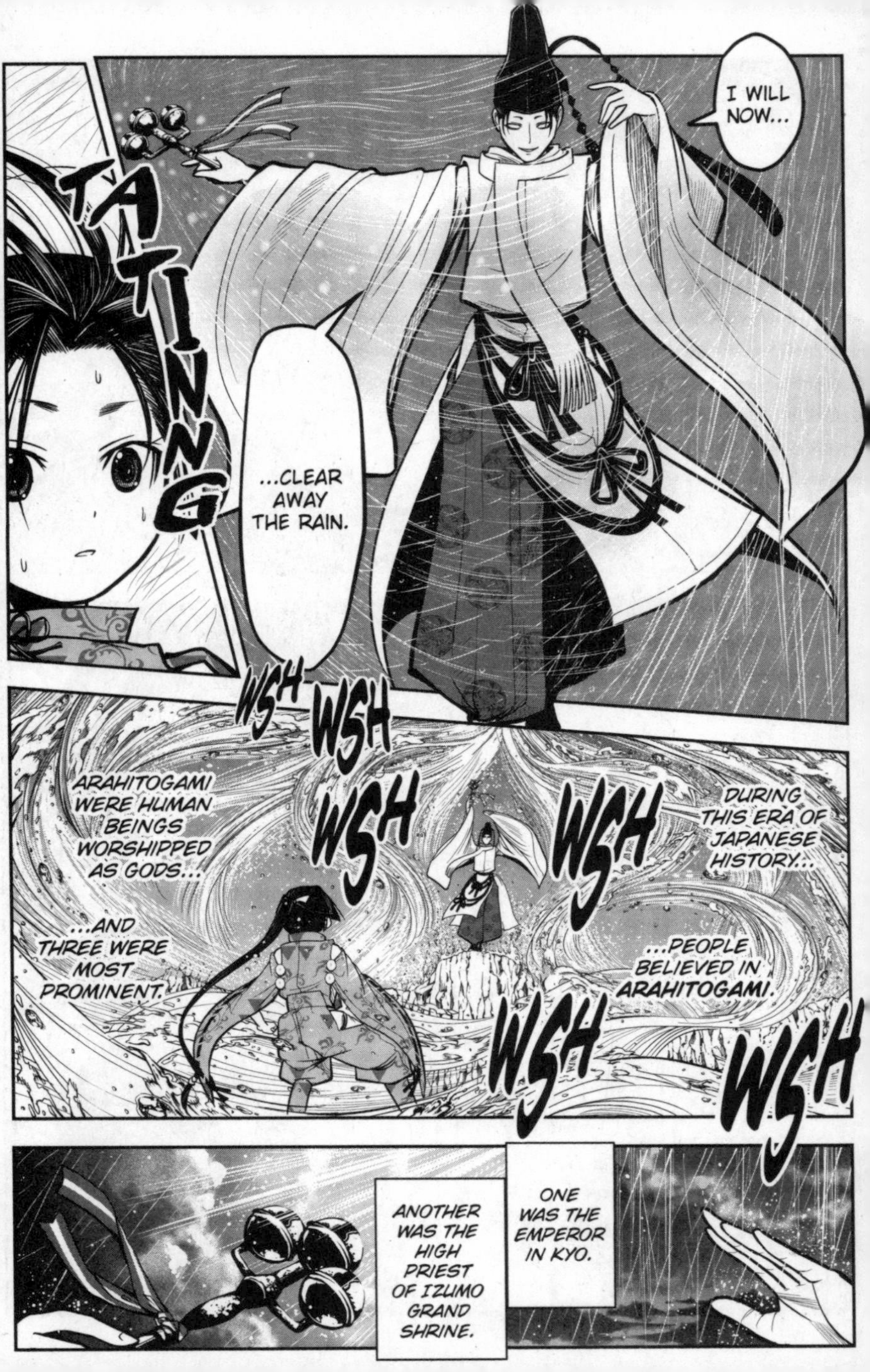
I WILL NOW...
...CLEAR AWAY THE RAIN.
TATINNG
WSH WSH
DURING THIS ERA OF JAPANESE HISTORY...
...PEOPLE BELIEVED IN ARAHITOGAMI.
WSH WSH
ARAHITOGAMI WERE HUMAN BEINGS WORSHIPPED AS GODS...
...AND THREE WERE MOST PROMINENT.
WSH WSH
ONE WAS THE EMPEROR IN KYO.
ANOTHER WAS THE HIGH PRIEST OF IZUMO GRAND SHRINE.

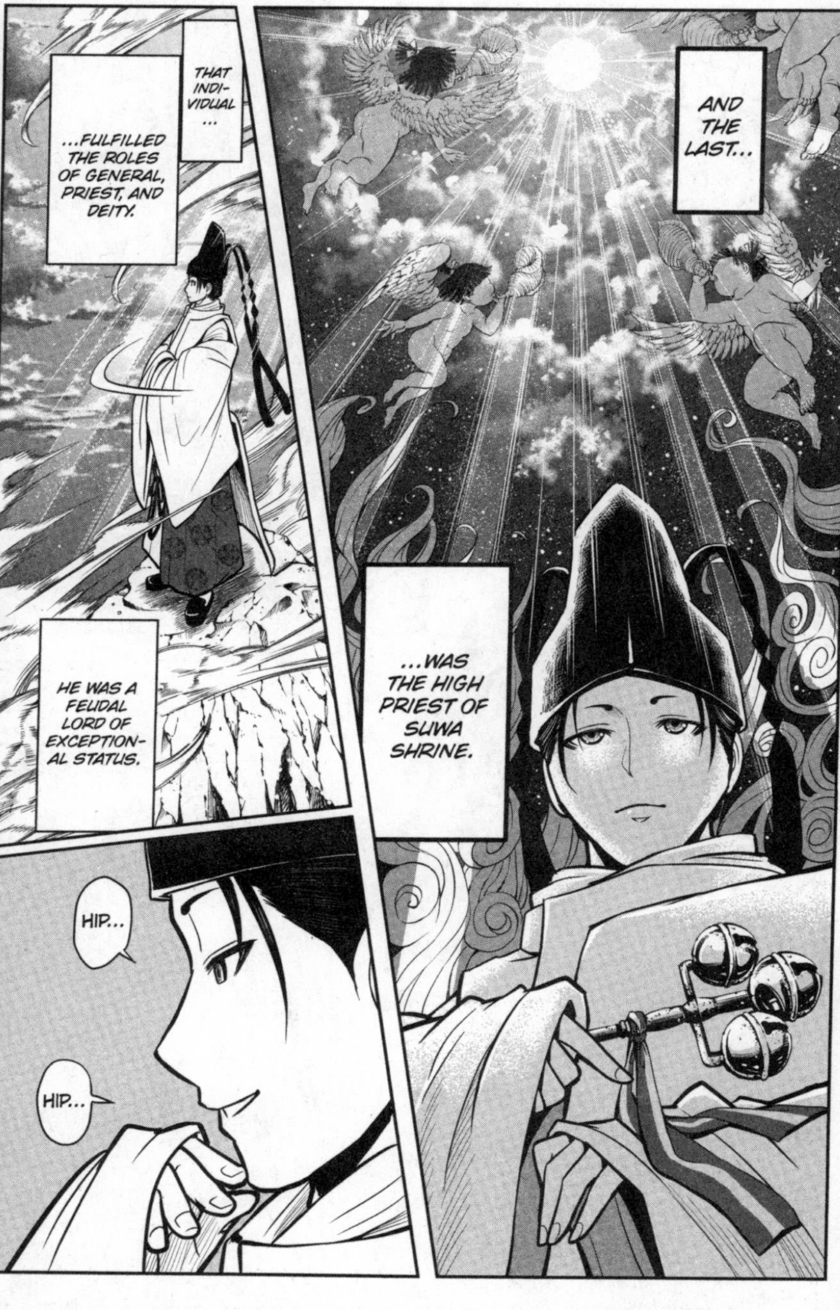
AND THE LAST...
...WAS THE HIGH PRIEST OF SUWA SHRINE.
THAT INDI-VIDUAL ...
...FULFILLED THE ROLES OF GENERAL, PRIEST, AND DEITY.
HE WAS A FEUDAL LORD OF EXCEPTION-AL STATUS.
HIP...
HIP...

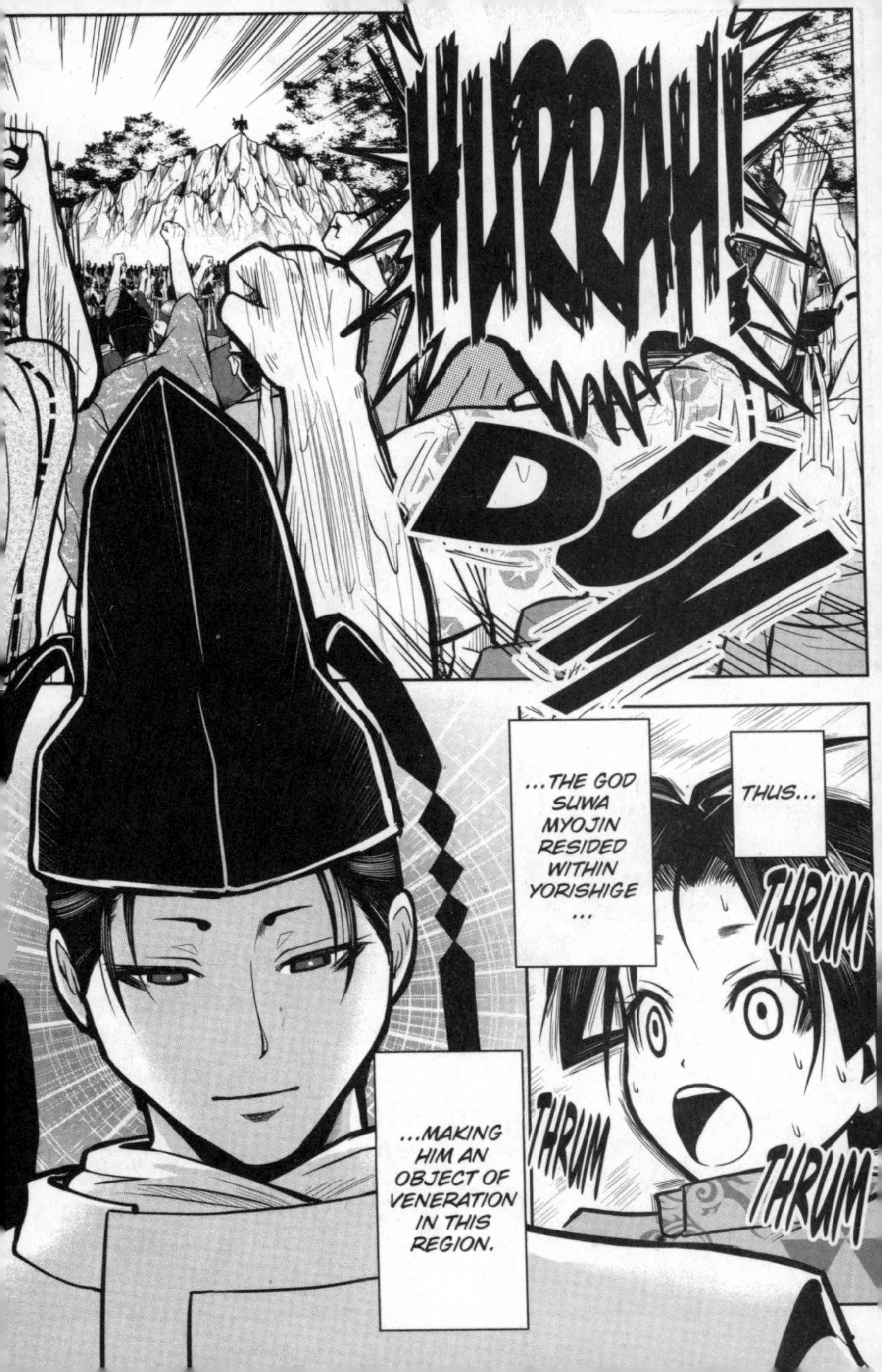
HURRAH!
DUH
THUS...
...THE GOD SUWA MYOJIN RESIDED WITHIN YORISHIGE ...
THRUM
THRUM
THRUM
...MAKING HIM AN OBJECT OF VENERATION IN THIS REGION.

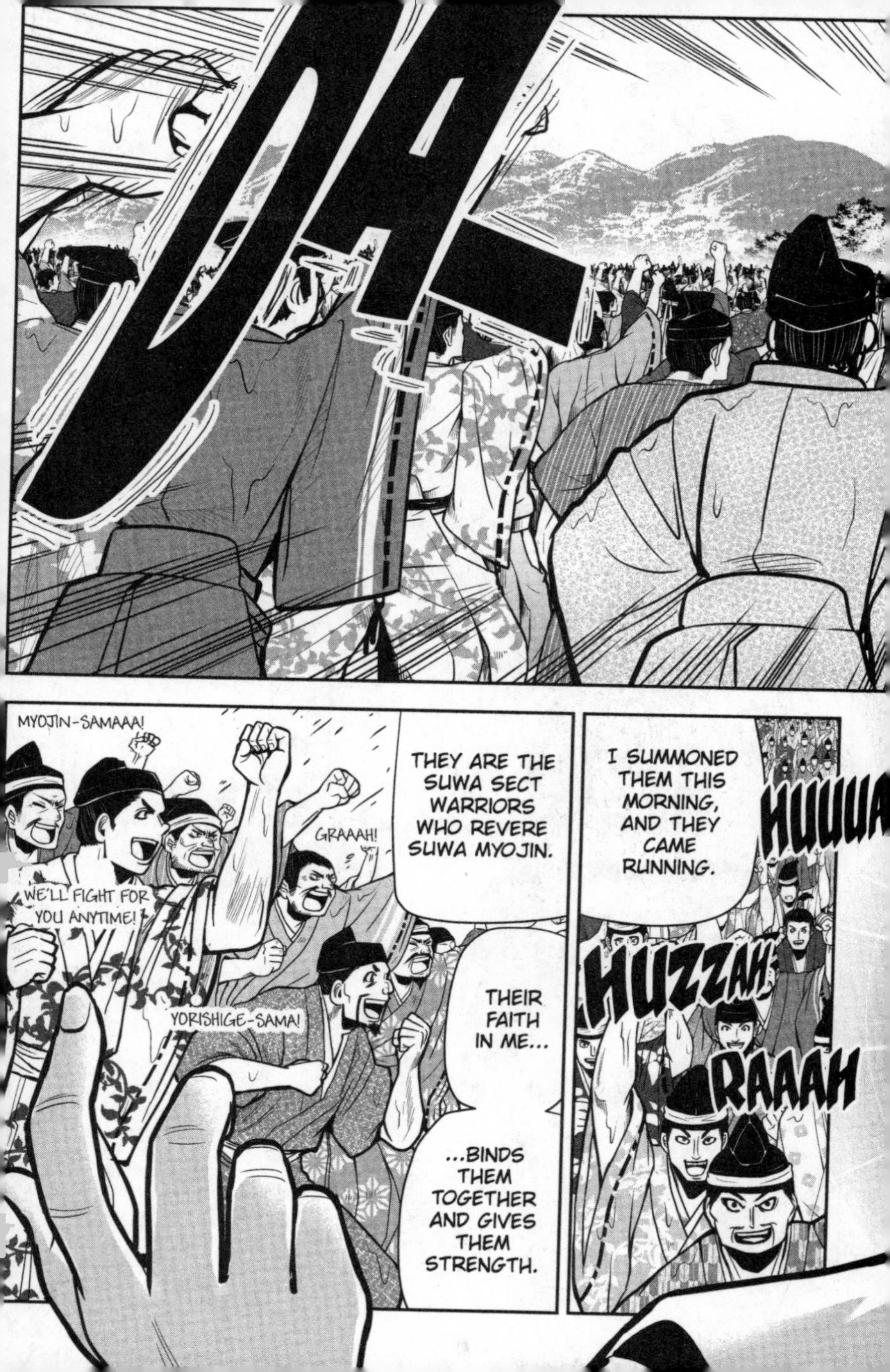
OH--
I SUMMONED THEM THIS MORNING, AND THEY CAME RUNNING.
HUUUA
HUZZAH
RAAAH
THEY ARE THE SUWA SECT WARRIORS WHO REVERE SUWA MYOJIN.
THEIR FAITH IN ME...
...BINDS THEM TOGETHER AND GIVES THEM STRENGTH.
GRAAAH!
MYOJIN-SAMAAA!
WE'LL FIGHT FOR YOU ANYTIME!
YORISHIGE-SAMA!

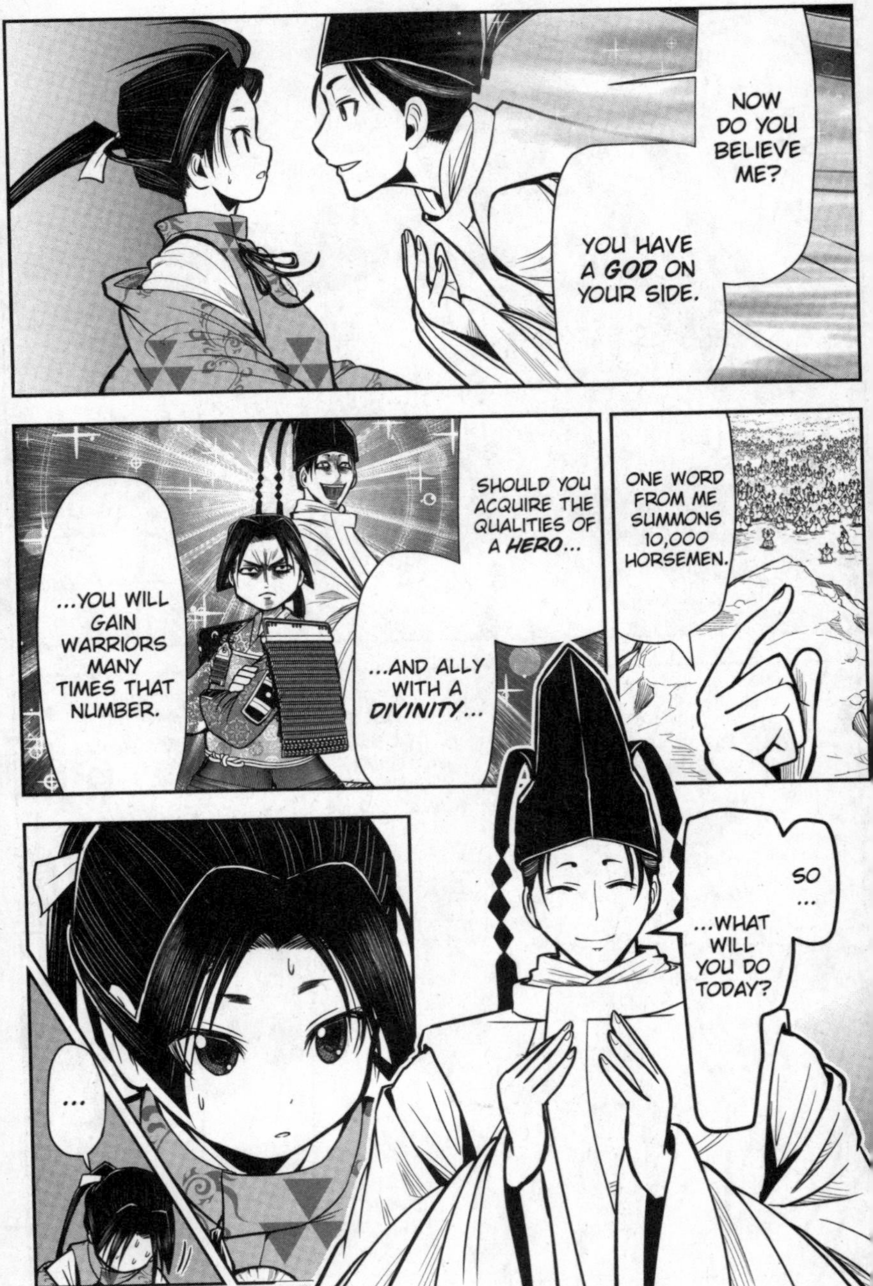
NOW DO YOU BELIEVE ME?
YOU HAVE A **GOD** ON YOUR SIDE.
ONE WORD FROM ME SUMMONS 10,000 HORSEMEN.
SHOULD YOU ACQUIRE THE QUALITIES OF A **HERO**...
...AND ALLY WITH A ***DIVINITY***...
...YOU WILL GAIN WARRIORS MANY TIMES THAT NUMBER.
SO ...
...WHAT WILL YOU DO TODAY?
...

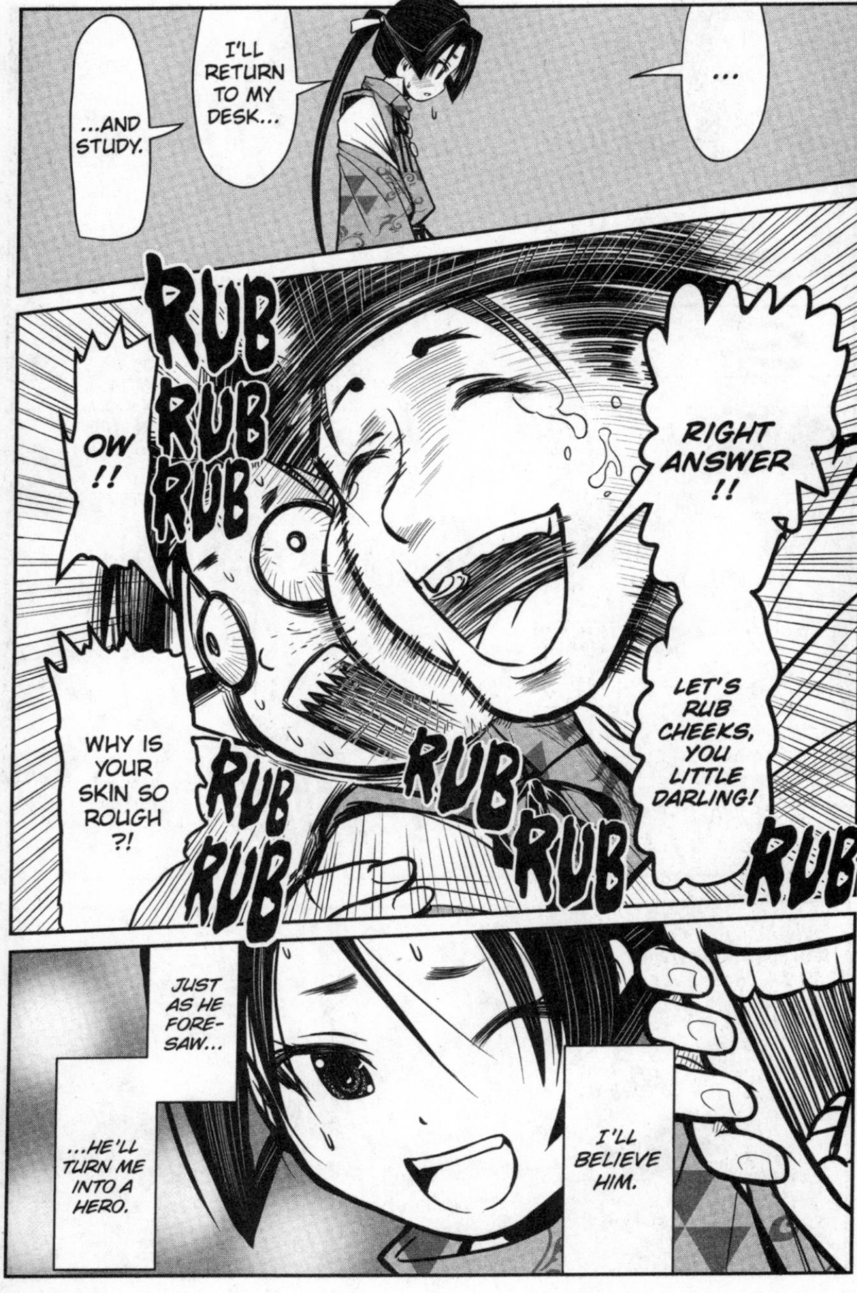
...
I'LL RETURN TO MY DESK...
...AND STUDY.
RIGHT ANSWER !!
LET'S RUB CHEEKS, YOU LITTLE DARLING!
RUB
RUB RUB
RUB RUB RUB
OW !!
WHY IS YOUR SKIN SO ROUGH ?!
RUB RUB
I'LL BELIEVE HIM.
JUST AS HE FORE-SAW...
...HE'LL TURN ME INTO A HERO.

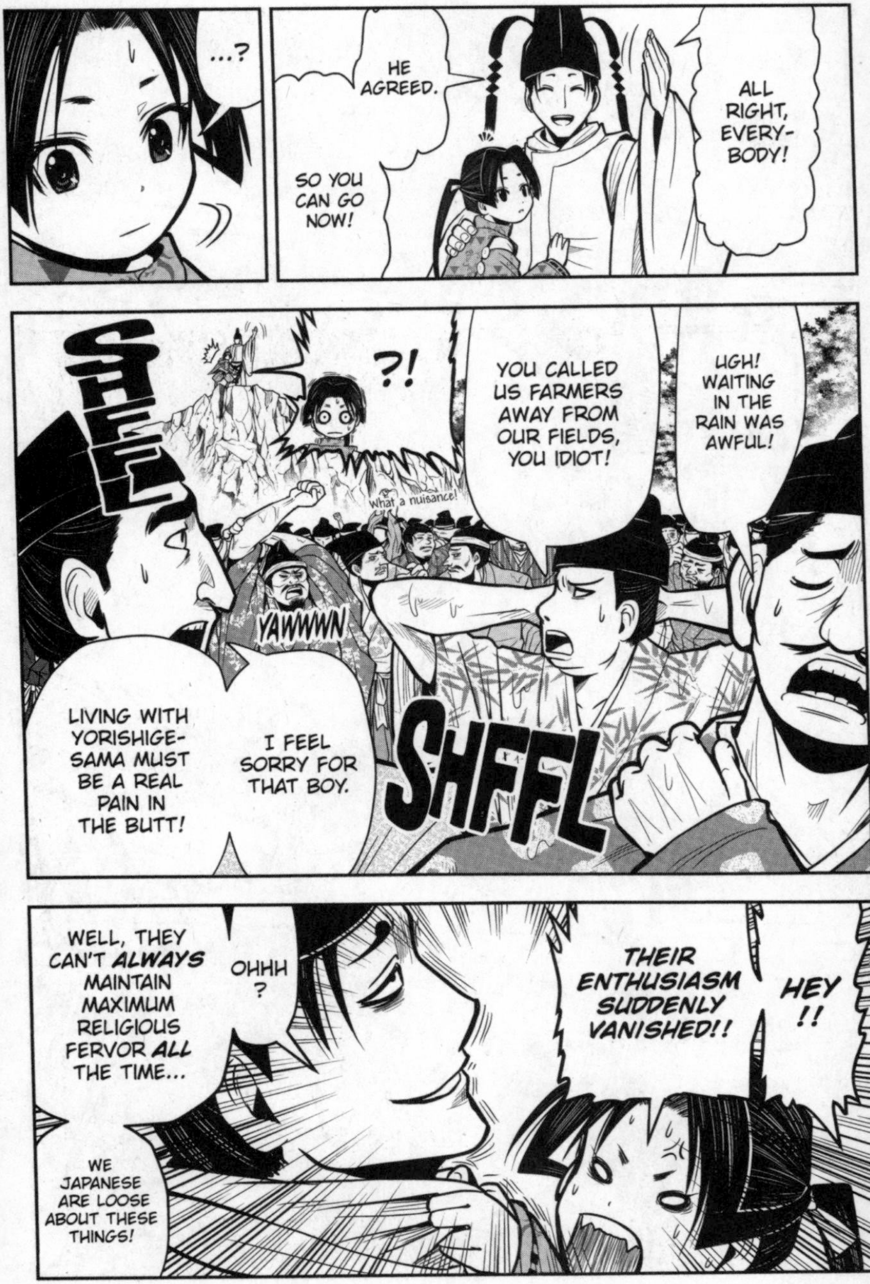
ALL RIGHT, EVERY-BODY!
HE AGREED.
SO YOU CAN GO NOW!
...?
UGH! WAITING IN THE RAIN WAS AWFUL!
YOU CALLED US FARMERS AWAY FROM OUR FIELDS, YOU IDIOT!
?!
What a nuisance!
SHFFL
YAWWWN
SHFFL
I FEEL SORRY FOR THAT BOY.
LIVING WITH YORISHIGE-SAMA MUST BE A REAL PAIN IN THE BUTT!
HEY!!
THEIR ENTHUSIASM SUDDENLY VANISHED!!
OHHH?
WELL, THEY CAN'T ALWAYS MAINTAIN MAXIMUM RELIGIOUS FERVOR ALL THE TIME...
WE JAPANESE ARE LOOSE ABOUT THESE THINGS!

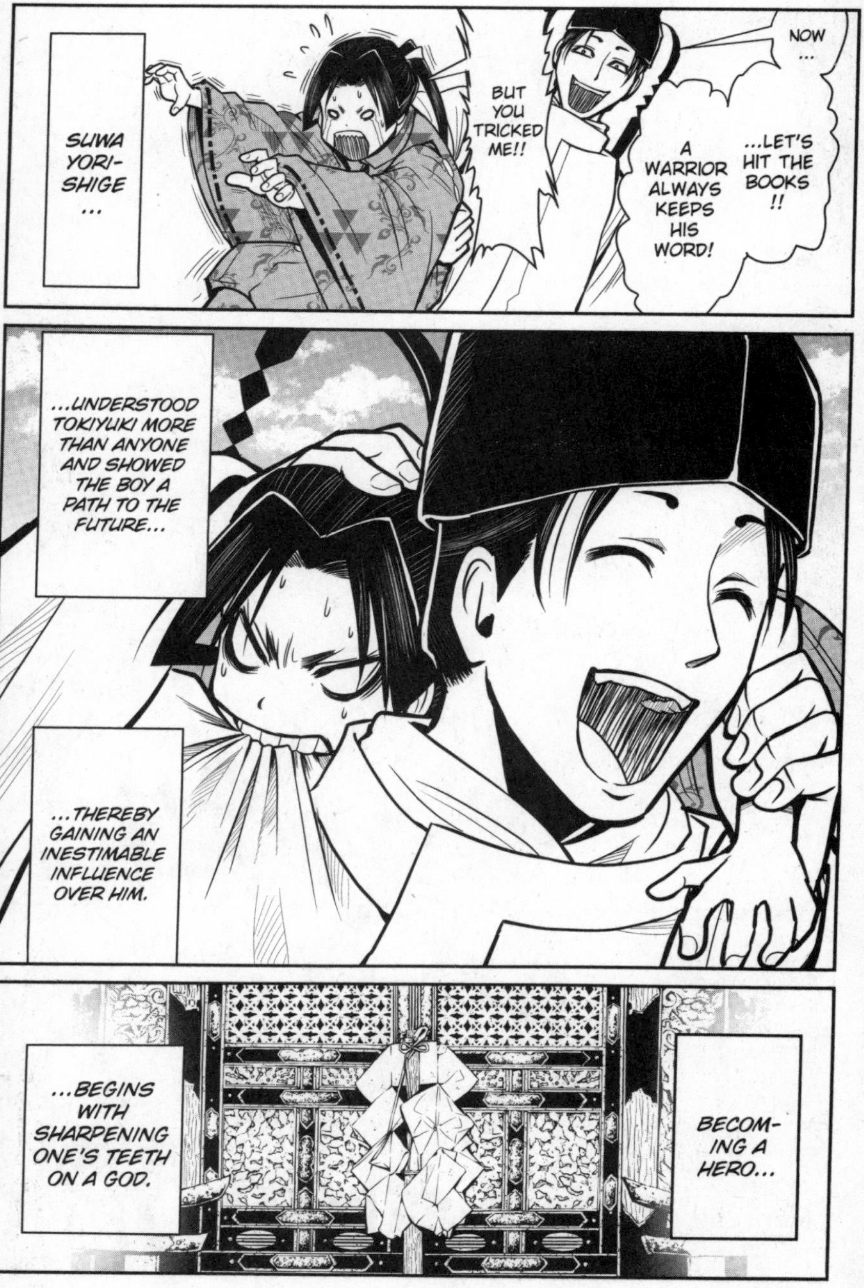
NOW...
...LET'S HIT THE BOOKS!!
A WARRIOR ALWAYS KEEPS HIS WORD!
BUT YOU TRICKED ME!!
SUWA YORI-SHIGE...
...UNDERSTOOD TOKIYUKI MORE THAN ANYONE AND SHOWED THE BOY A PATH TO THE FUTURE...
...THEREBY GAINING AN INESTIMABLE INFLUENCE OVER HIM.
BECOM-ING A HERO...
...BEGINS WITH SHARPENING ONE'S TEETH ON A GOD.

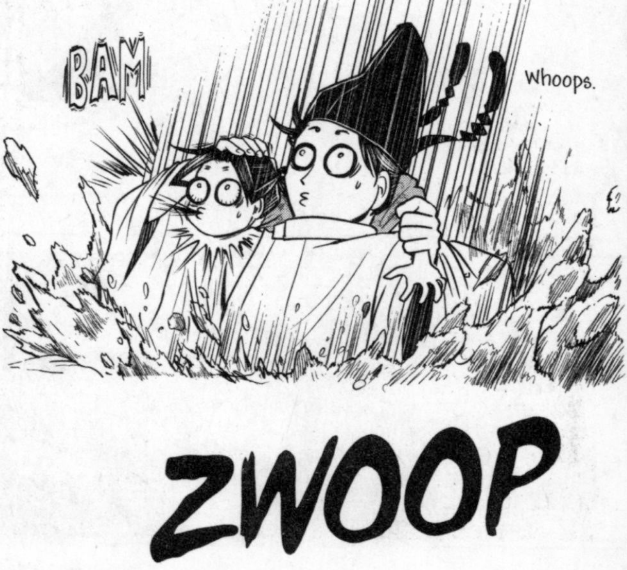
Whoops.
BAM
ZWOOP

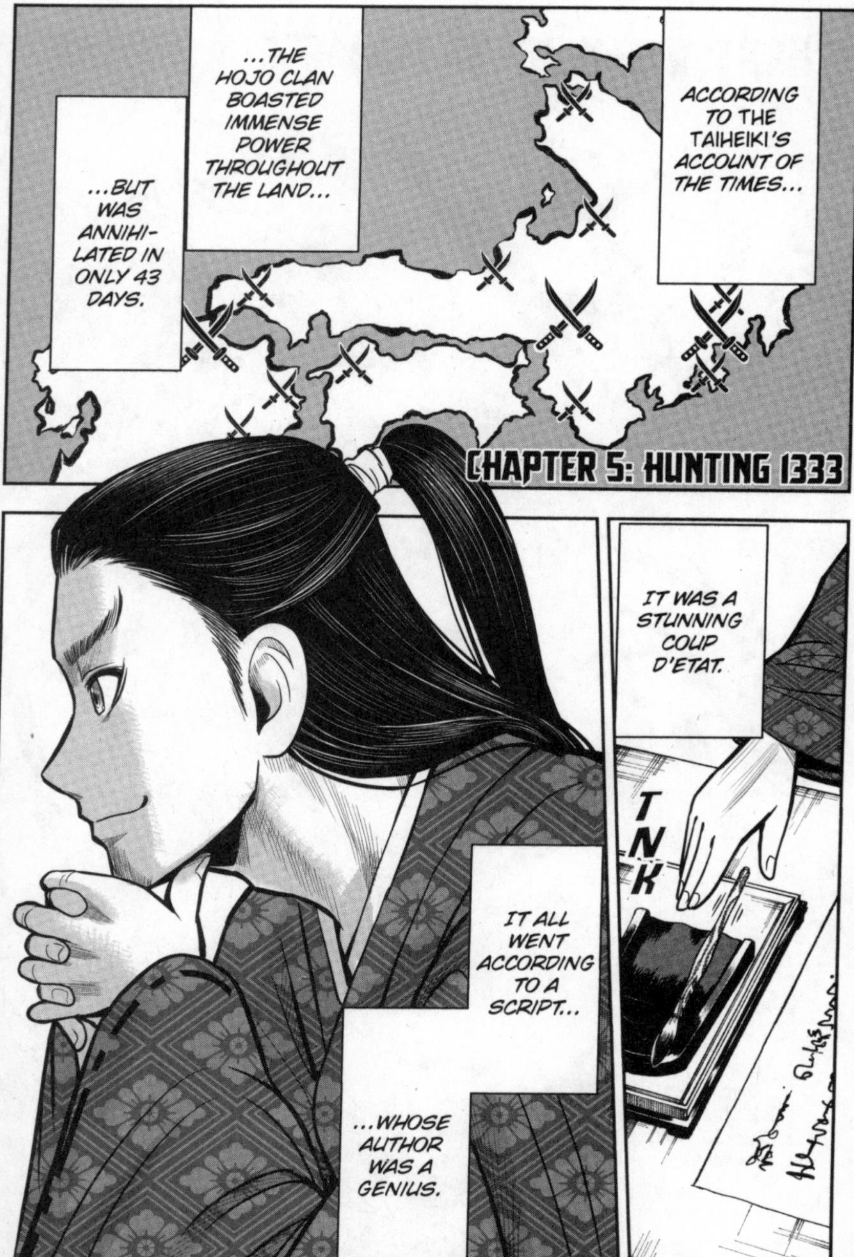
ACCORDING TO THE TAIHEIKI'S ACCOUNT OF THE TIMES...
...THE HOJO CLAN BOASTED IMMENSE POWER THROUGHOUT THE LAND...
...BUT WAS ANNIHI-LATED IN ONLY 43 DAYS.
CHAPTER 5: HUNTING 1333
IT WAS A STUNNING COUP D'ETAT.
TNK
IT ALL WENT ACCORDING TO A SCRIPT...
...WHOSE AUTHOR WAS A GENIUS.

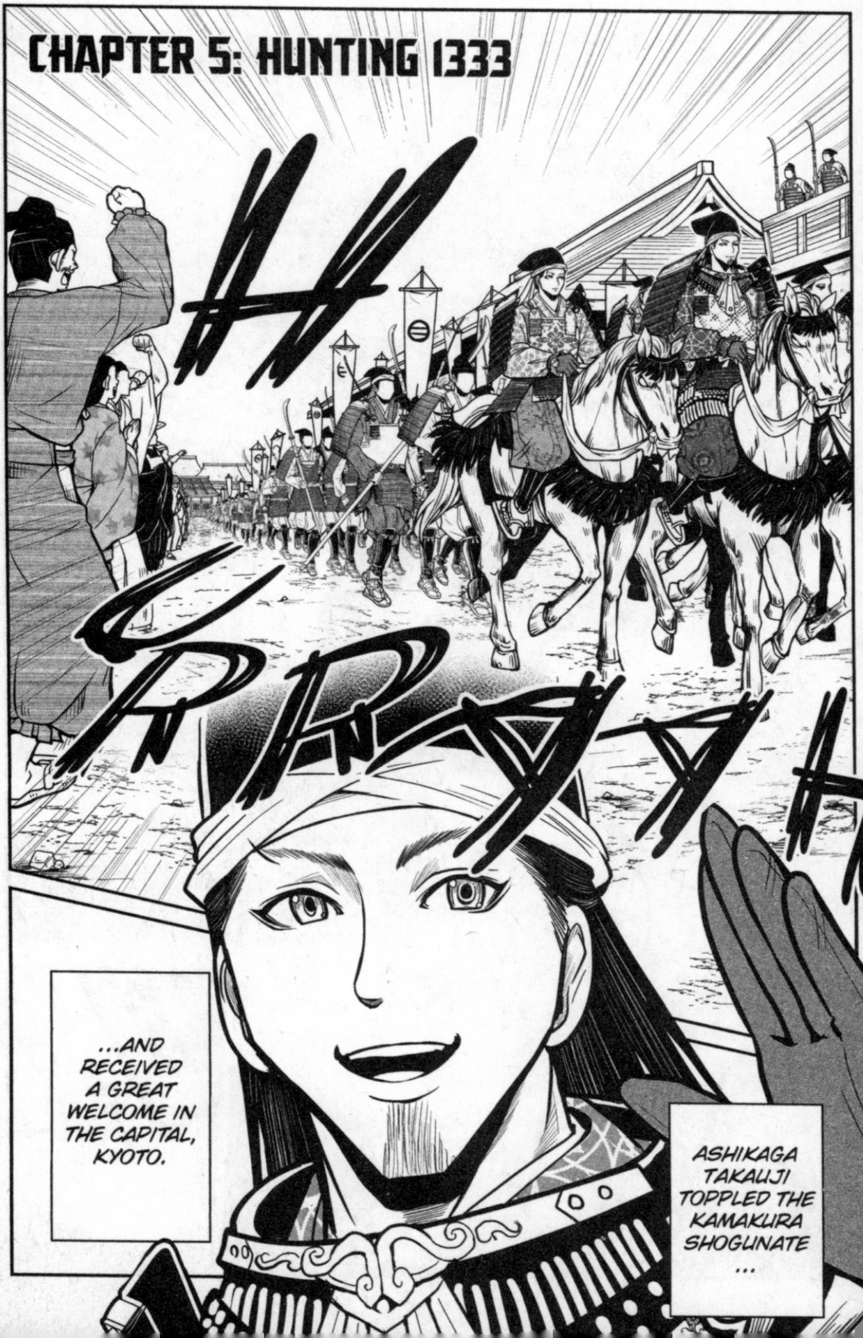
CHAPTER 5: HUNTING 1333
ASHIKAGA TAKAUJI TOPPLED THE KAMAKURA SHOGUNATE ...
...AND RECEIVED A GREAT WELCOME IN THE CAPITAL, KYOTO.

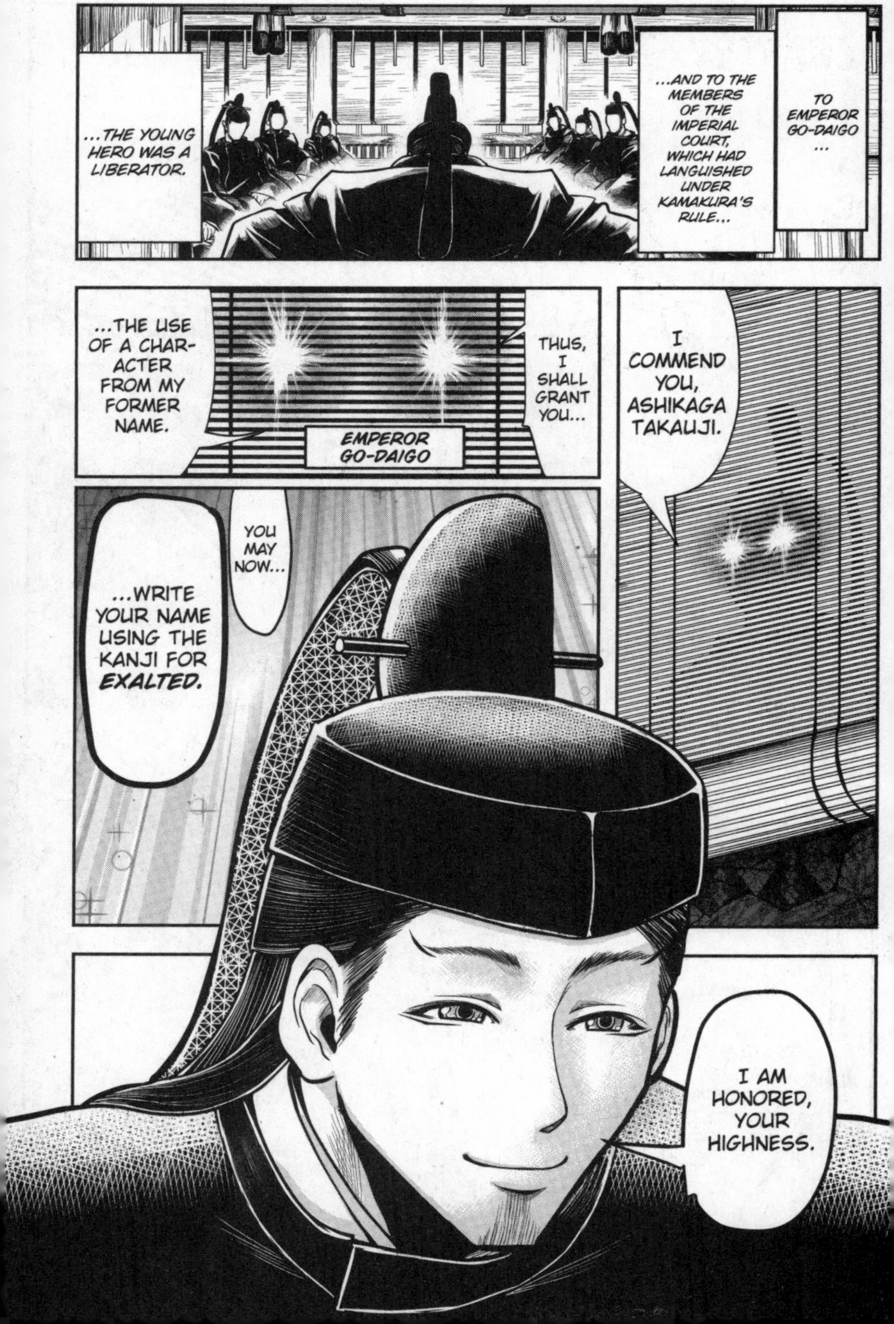
TO EMPEROR GO-DAIGO ...
...AND TO THE MEMBERS OF THE IMPERIAL COURT, WHICH HAD LANGUISHED UNDER KAMAKURA'S RULE...
...THE YOUNG HERO WAS A LIBERATOR.
I COMMEND YOU, ASHIKAGA TAKAUJI.
THUS, I SHALL GRANT YOU...
EMPEROR GO-DAIGO
...THE USE OF A CHARACTER FROM MY FORMER NAME.
YOU MAY NOW...
...WRITE YOUR NAME USING THE KANJI FOR EXALTED.
I AM HONORED, YOUR HIGHNESS.

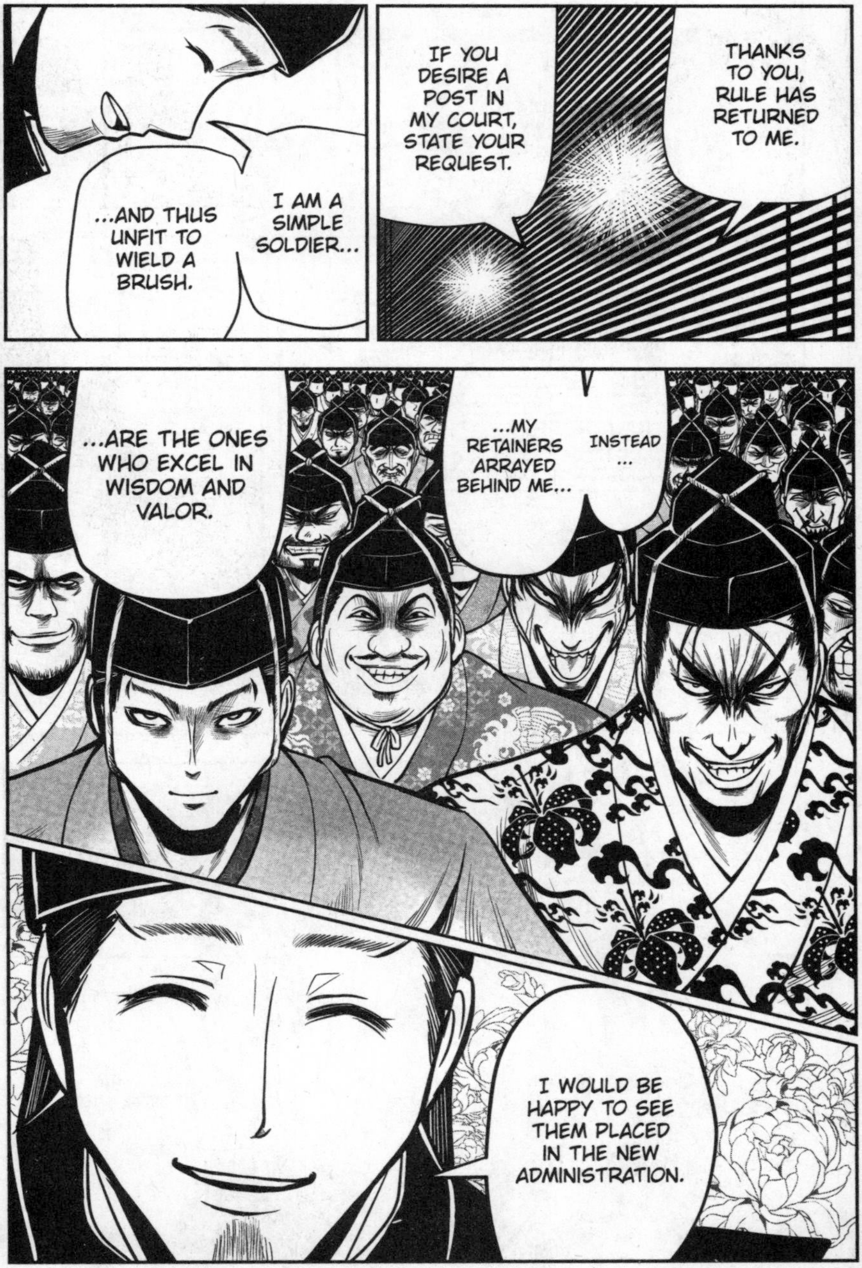
THANKS TO YOU, RULE HAS RETURNED TO ME.
IF YOU DESIRE A POST IN MY COURT, STATE YOUR REQUEST.
I AM A SIMPLE SOLDIER...
...AND THUS UNFIT TO WIELD A BRUSH.
INSTEAD ...
...MY RETAINERS ARRAYED BEHIND ME...
...ARE THE ONES WHO EXCEL IN WISDOM AND VALOR.
I WOULD BE HAPPY TO SEE THEM PLACED IN THE NEW ADMINISTRATION.

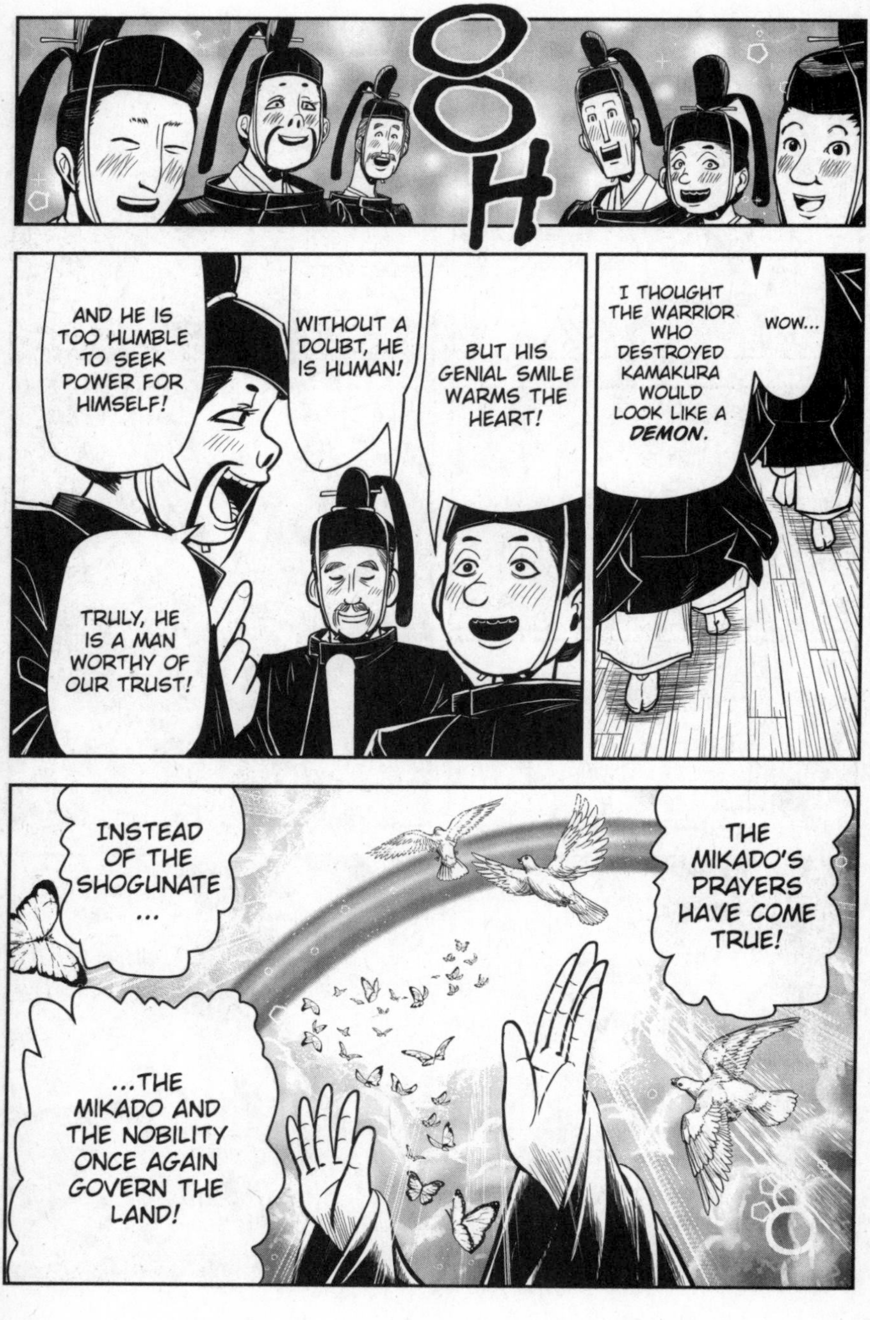
OH
WOW...
I THOUGHT THE WARRIOR WHO DESTROYED KAMAKURA WOULD LOOK LIKE A *DEMON*.
BUT HIS GENIAL SMILE WARMS THE HEART!
WITHOUT A DOUBT, HE IS HUMAN!
AND HE IS TOO HUMBLE TO SEEK POWER FOR HIMSELF!
TRULY, HE IS A MAN WORTHY OF OUR TRUST!
THE MIKADO'S PRAYERS HAVE COME TRUE!
INSTEAD OF THE SHOGUNATE ...
...THE MIKADO AND THE NOBILITY ONCE AGAIN GOVERN THE LAND!

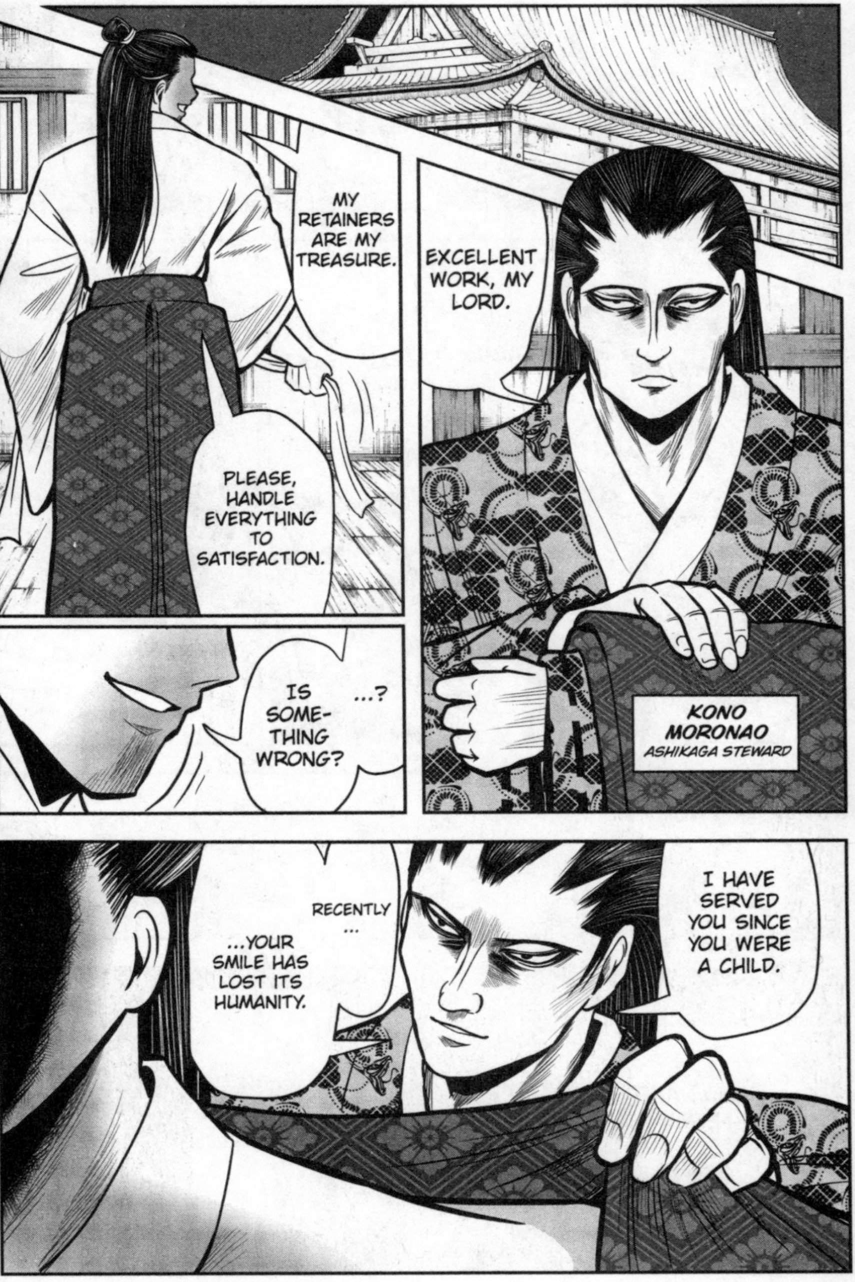
EXCELLENT WORK, MY LORD.
KONO MORONAO
ASHIKAGA STEWARD
MY RETAINERS ARE MY TREASURE.
PLEASE, HANDLE EVERYTHING TO SATISFACTION.
...?
IS SOMETHING WRONG?
I HAVE SERVED YOU SINCE YOU WERE A CHILD.
RECENTLY ...
...YOUR SMILE HAS LOST ITS HUMANITY.

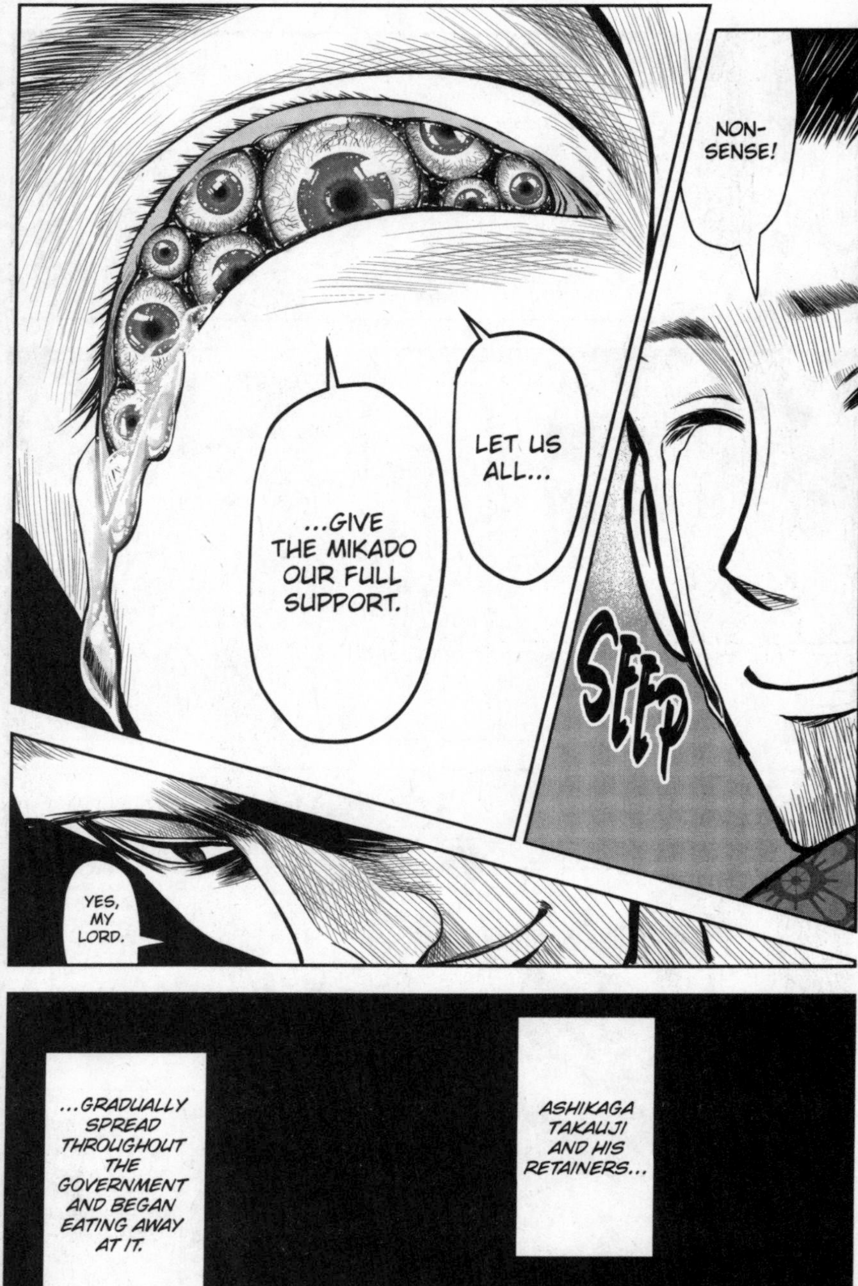
NON-SENSE!
SEEP
LET US ALL...
...GIVE THE MIKADO OUR FULL SUPPORT.
YES, MY LORD.
ASHIKAGA TAKAUJI AND HIS RETAINERS...
...GRADUALLY SPREAD THROUGHOUT THE GOVERNMENT AND BEGAN EATING AWAY AT IT.

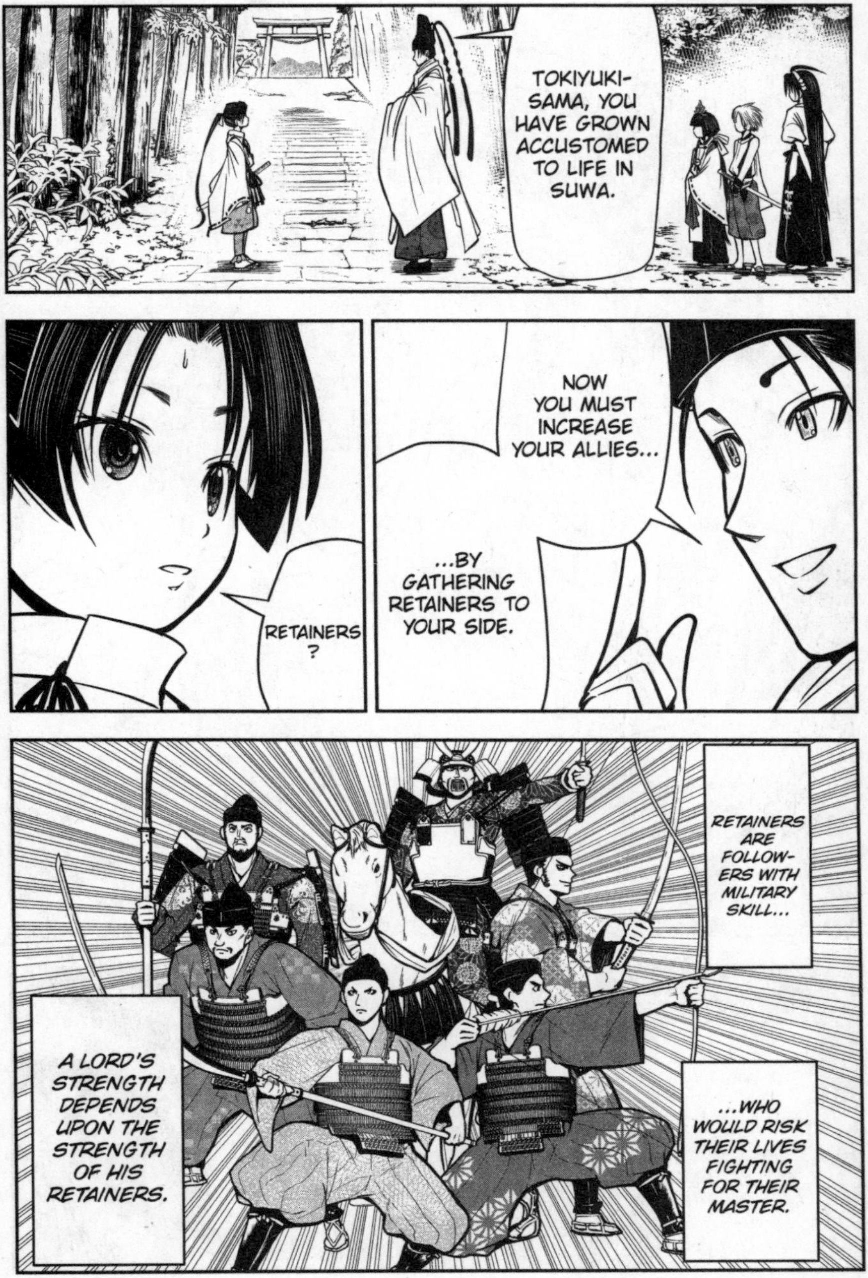
TOKIYUKI-SAMA, YOU HAVE GROWN ACCUSTOMED TO LIFE IN SUWA.
NOW YOU MUST INCREASE YOUR ALLIES...
...BY GATHERING RETAINERS TO YOUR SIDE.
RETAINERS?
RETAINERS ARE FOLLOWERS WITH MILITARY SKILL...
...WHO WOULD RISK THEIR LIVES FIGHTING FOR THEIR MASTER.
A LORD'S STRENGTH DEPENDS UPON THE STRENGTH OF HIS RETAINERS.

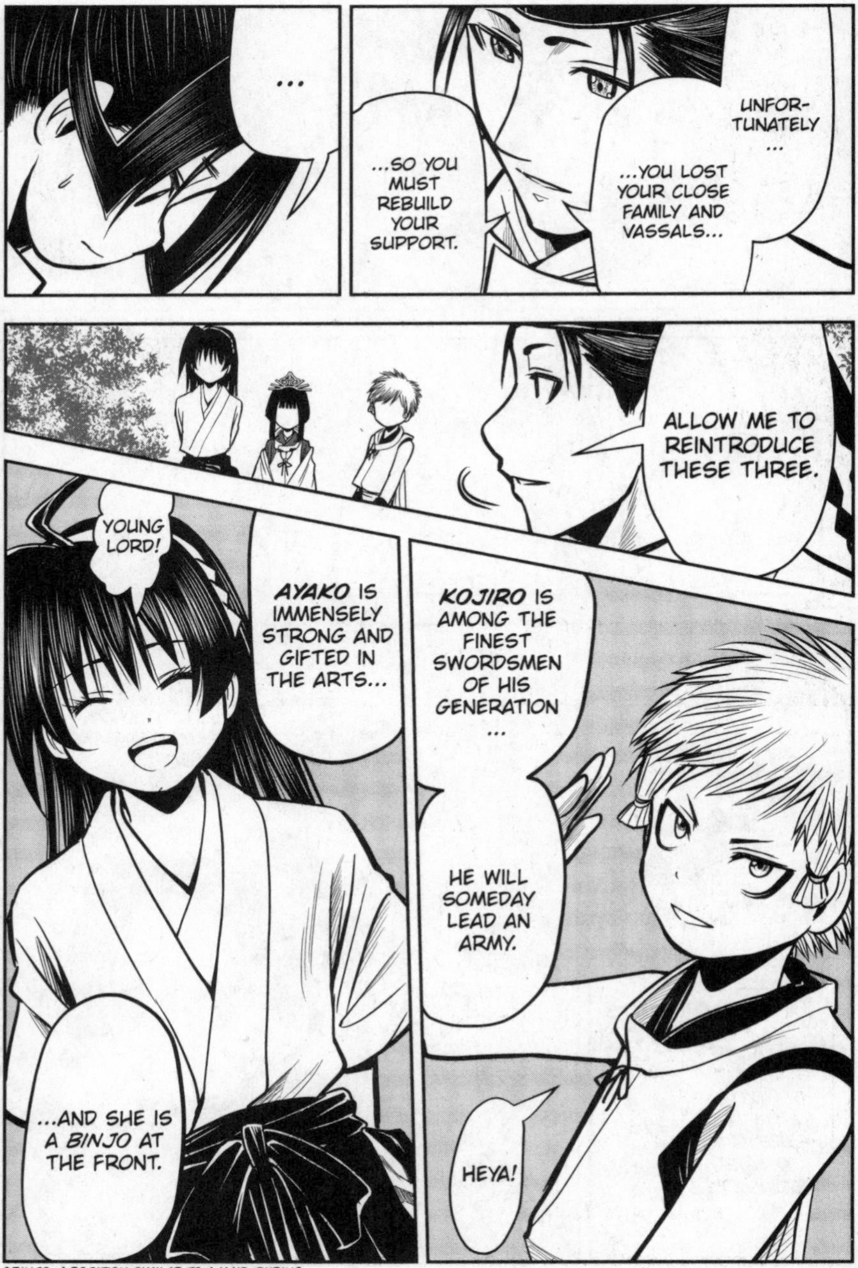
UNFOR-TUNATELY ...
...YOU LOST YOUR CLOSE FAMILY AND VASSALS...
...SO YOU MUST REBUILD YOUR SUPPORT.
...
ALLOW ME TO REINTRODUCE THESE THREE.
KOJIRO IS AMONG THE FINEST SWORDSMEN OF HIS GENERATION ...
HE WILL SOMEDAY LEAD AN ARMY.
HEYA!
AYAKO IS IMMENSELY STRONG AND GIFTED IN THE ARTS...
YOUNG LORD!
...AND SHE IS A BINJO AT THE FRONT.

*BINJO: A POSITION SIMILAR TO A MAID. DURING THE MIDDLE AGES, SOME ALSO FOUGHT.

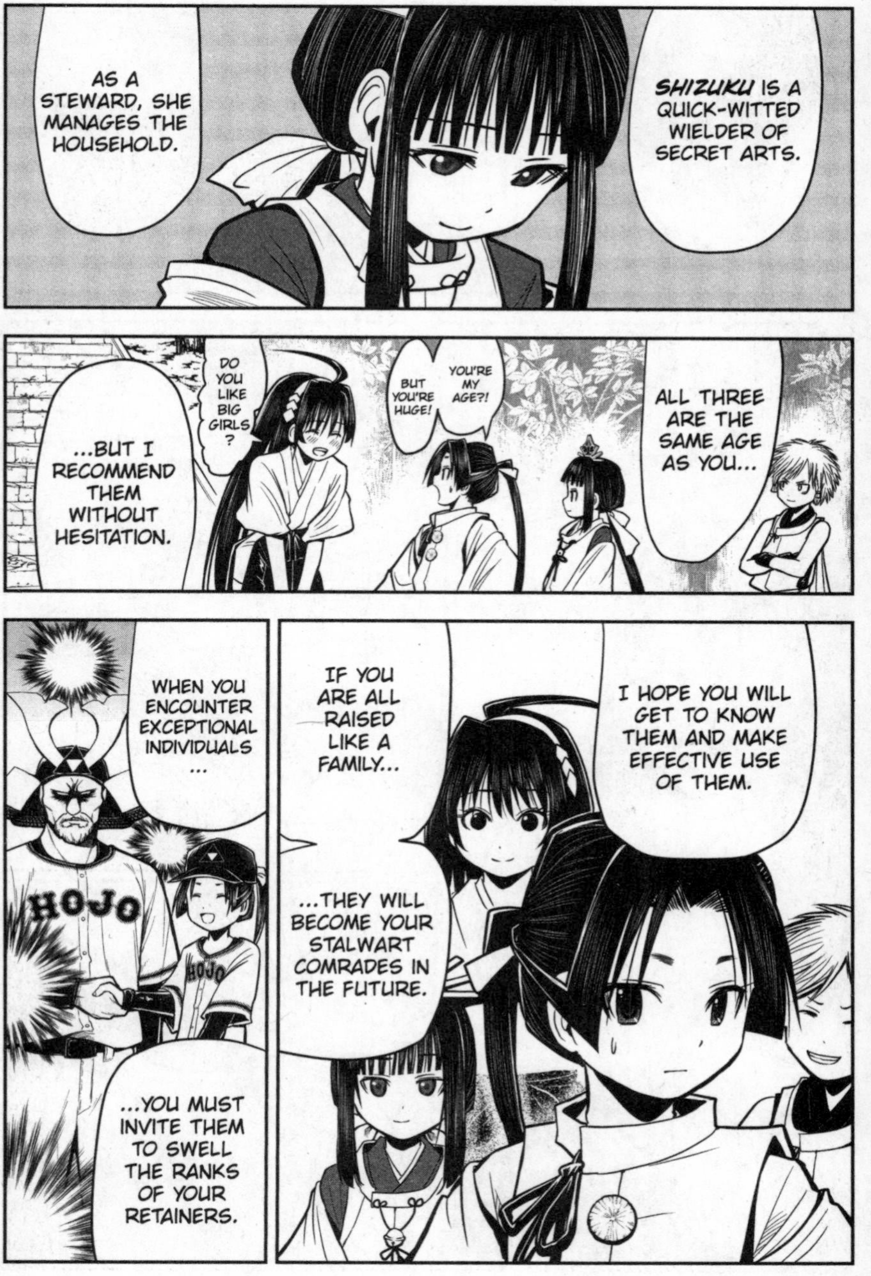
SHIZUKU IS A QUICK-WITTED WIELDER OF SECRET ARTS.
AS A STEWARD, SHE MANAGES THE HOUSEHOLD.
ALL THREE ARE THE SAME AGE AS YOU...
YOU'RE MY AGE?!
BUT YOU'RE HUGE!
DO YOU LIKE BIG GIRLS ?
...BUT I RECOMMEND THEM WITHOUT HESITATION.
I HOPE YOU WILL GET TO KNOW THEM AND MAKE EFFECTIVE USE OF THEM.
IF YOU ARE ALL RAISED LIKE A FAMILY...
...THEY WILL BECOME YOUR STALWART COMRADES IN THE FUTURE.
WHEN YOU ENCOUNTER EXCEPTIONAL INDIVIDUALS ...
HOJO
HOJO
...YOU MUST INVITE THEM TO SWELL THE RANKS OF YOUR RETAINERS.

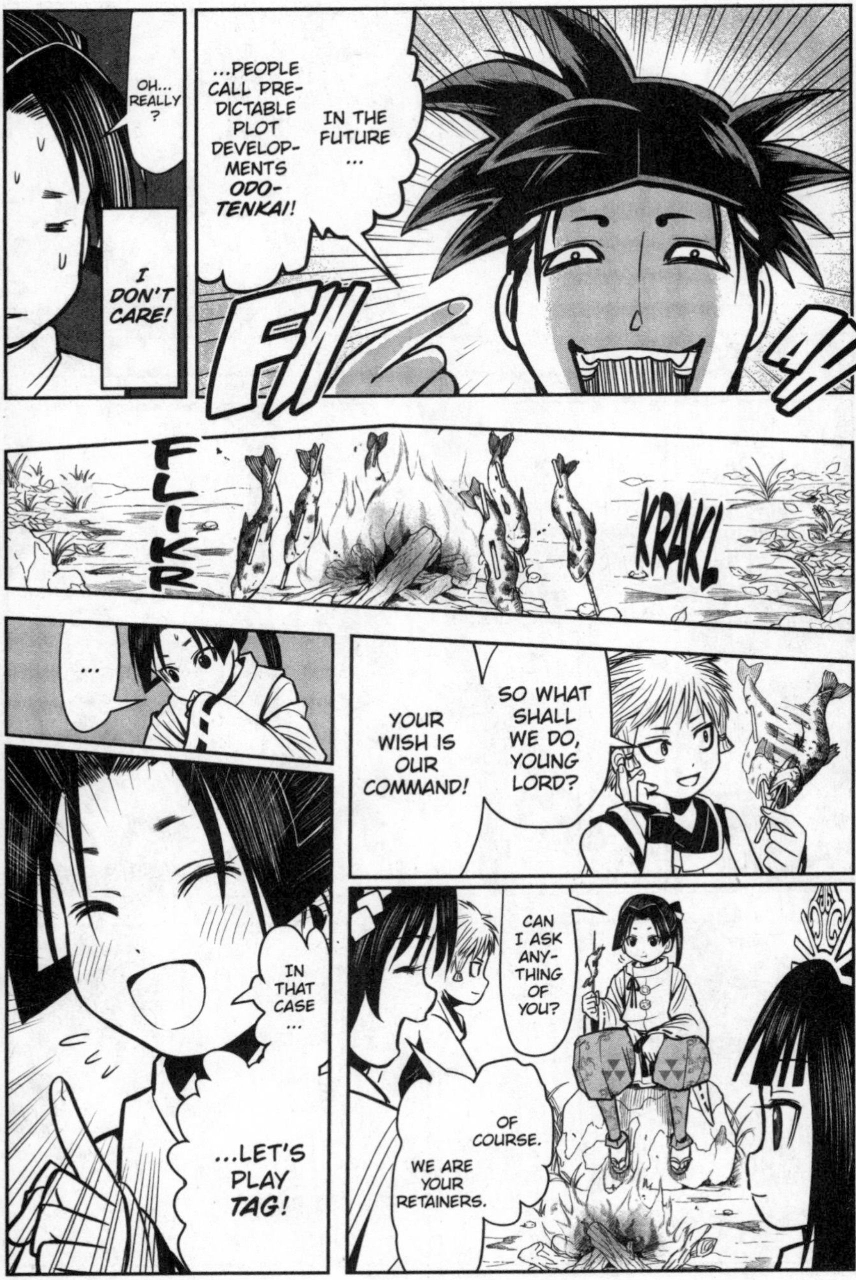
IN THE FUTURE...
...PEOPLE CALL PREDICTABLE PLOT DEVELOPMENTS ODO-TENKAI!
AH
FH
OH... REALLY?
I DON'T CARE!
KRAKL
FLIKR
SO WHAT SHALL WE DO, YOUNG LORD?
YOUR WISH IS OUR COMMAND!
...
CAN I ASK ANYTHING OF YOU?
OF COURSE.
WE ARE YOUR RETAINERS.
IN THAT CASE...
...LET'S PLAY TAG!

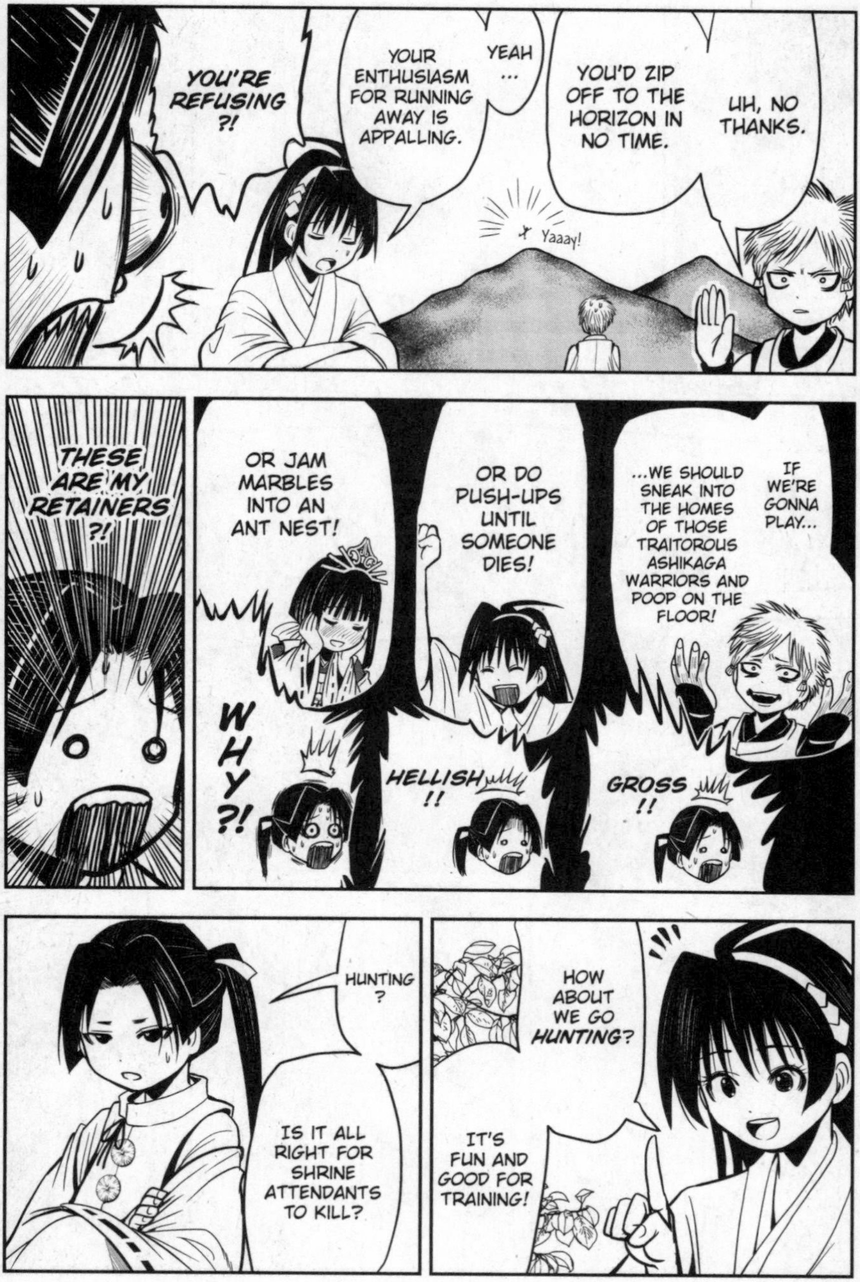
UH, NO THANKS.
YOU'D ZIP OFF TO THE HORIZON IN NO TIME.
Yaaay!
YEAH ...
YOUR ENTHUSIASM FOR RUNNING AWAY IS APPALLING.
YOU'RE REFUSING ?!
IF WE'RE GONNA PLAY...
...WE SHOULD SNEAK INTO THE HOMES OF THOSE TRAITOROUS ASHIKAGA WARRIORS AND POOP ON THE FLOOR!
GROSS !!
OR DO PUSH-UPS UNTIL SOMEONE DIES!
HELLISH !!
OR JAM MARBLES INTO AN ANT NEST!
WHY ?!
THESE ARE MY RETAINERS ?!
HOW ABOUT WE GO HUNTING?
IT'S FUN AND GOOD FOR TRAINING!
HUNTING ?
IS IT ALL RIGHT FOR SHRINE ATTENDANTS TO KILL?

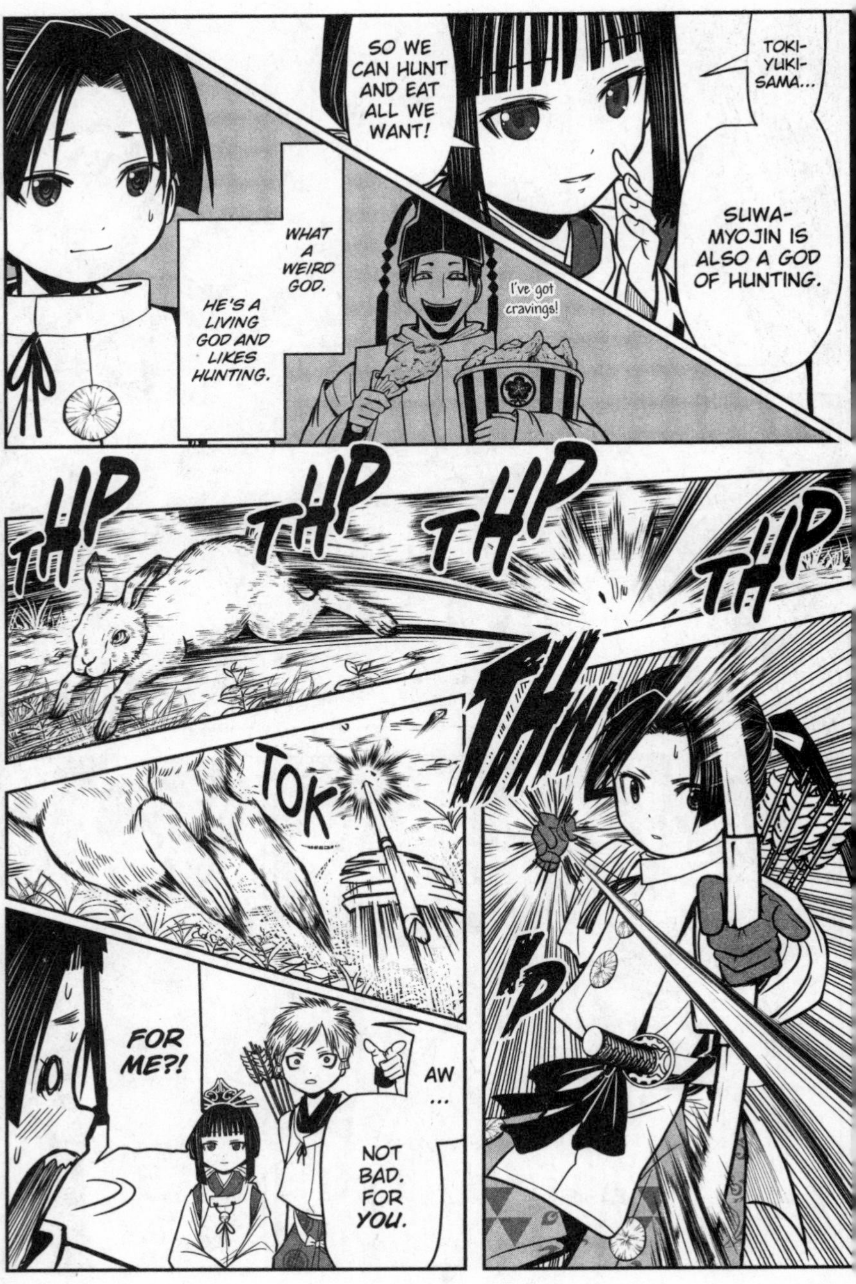
TOKI-YUKI-SAMA...
SUWA-MYOJIN IS ALSO A GOD OF HUNTING.
SO WE CAN HUNT AND EAT ALL WE WANT!
I've got cravings!
WHAT A WEIRD GOD.
HE'S A LIVING GOD AND LIKES HUNTING.
THP
THP
THP
THP
THWP
TOK
AW...
NOT BAD. FOR YOU.
FOR ME?!

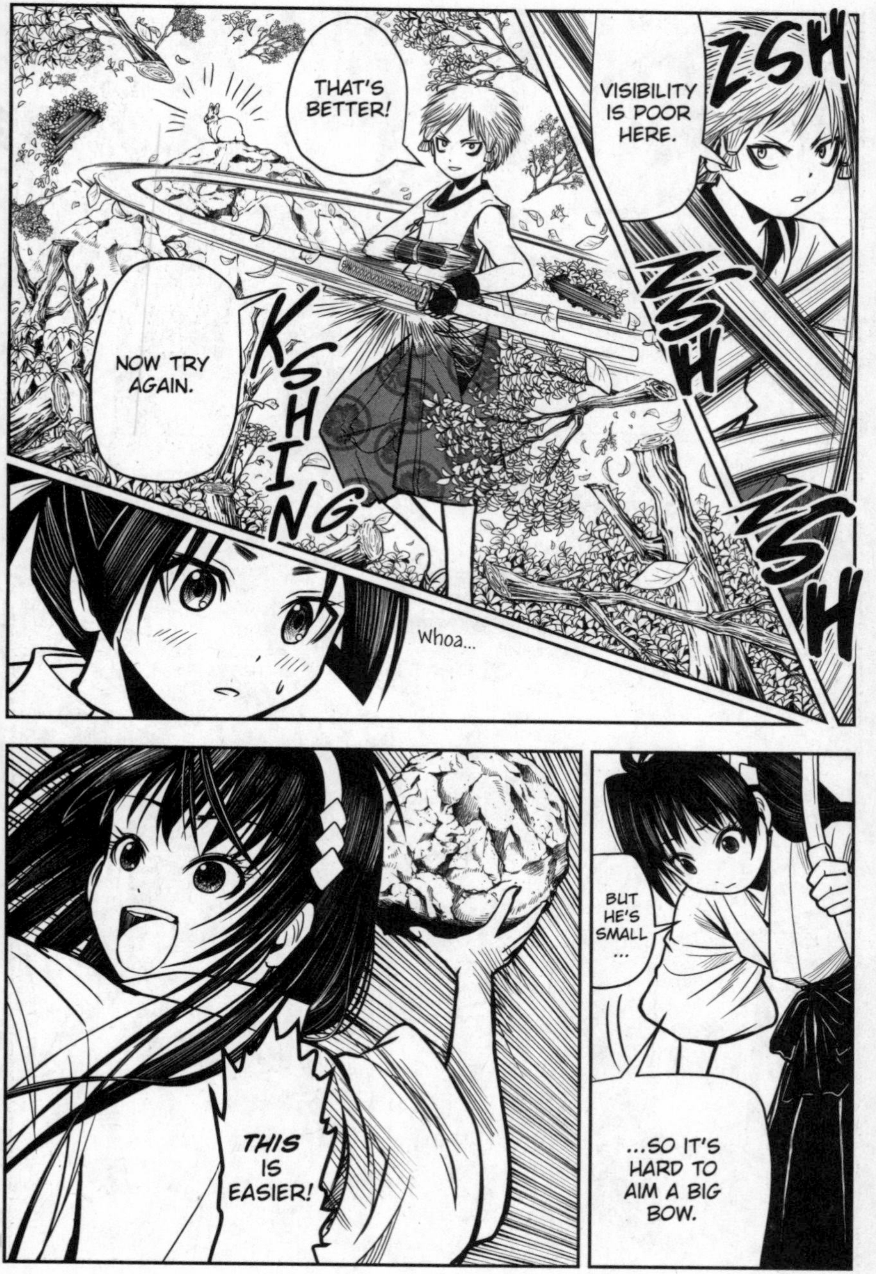
ZSH
VISIBILITY IS POOR HERE.
ZSH
ZSH
THAT'S BETTER!
KSHING
NOW TRY AGAIN.
Whoa...
BUT HE'S SMALL ...
...SO IT'S HARD TO AIM A BIG BOW.
THIS IS EASIER!

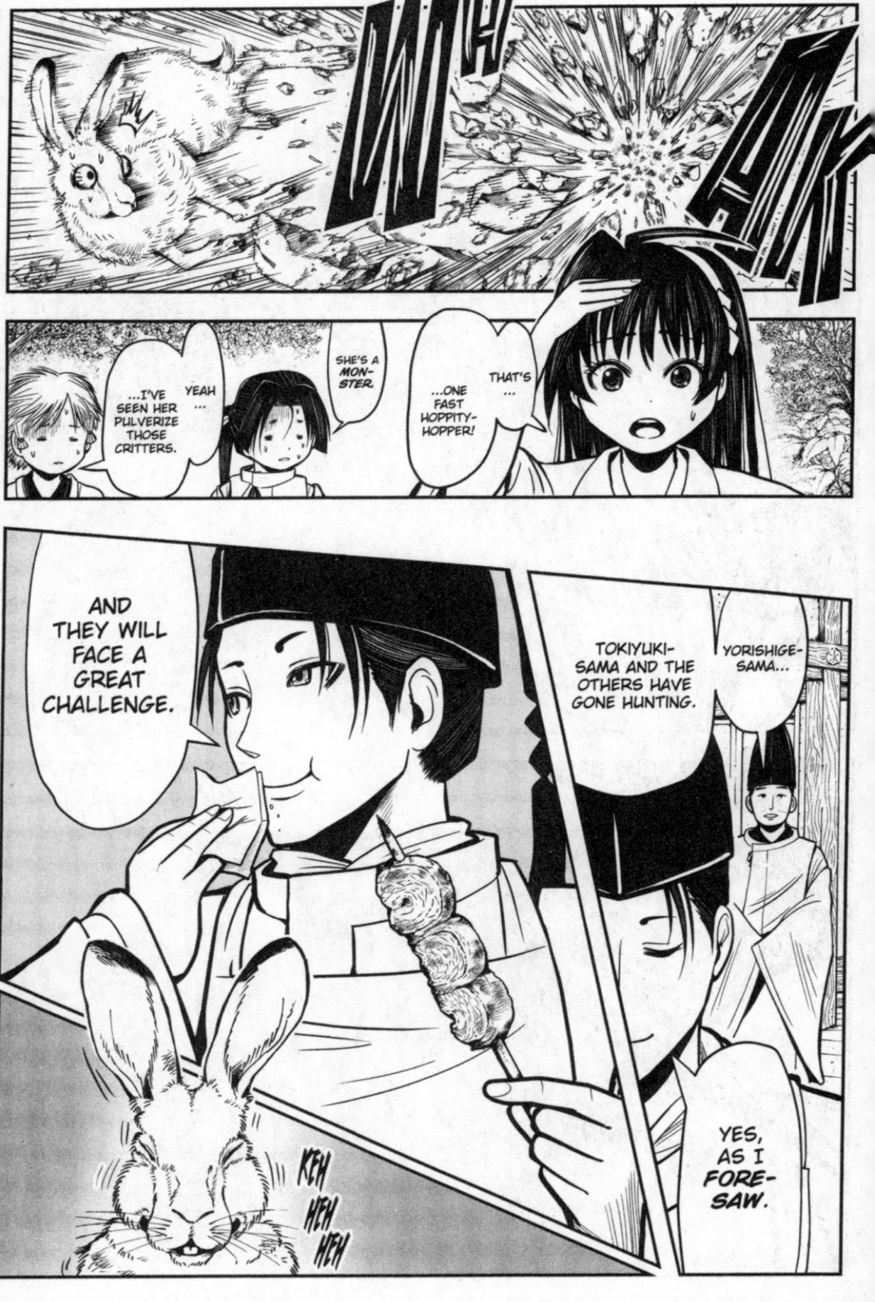
THAT'S ...
...ONE FAST HOPPITY-HOPPER!
SHE'S A MONSTER.
YEAH ...
...I'VE SEEN HER PULVERIZE THOSE CRITTERS.
YORISHIGE-SAMA...
TOKIYUKI-SAMA AND THE OTHERS HAVE GONE HUNTING.
YES, AS I FORESAW.
AND THEY WILL FACE A GREAT CHALLENGE.
KEH HEH HEH

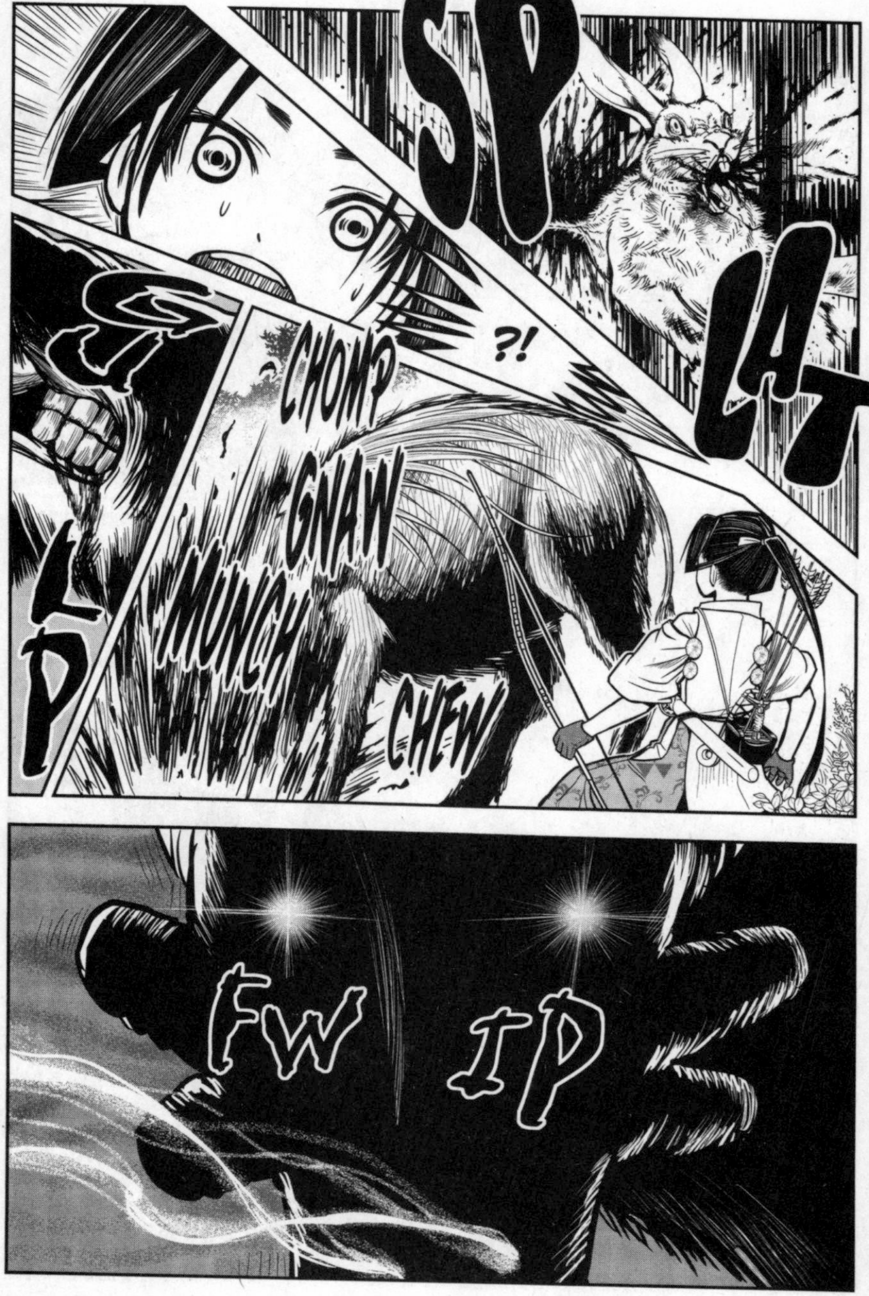
SPLAT
?!
GULP
CHOMP GNAW MUNCH
CHEW
FWIP

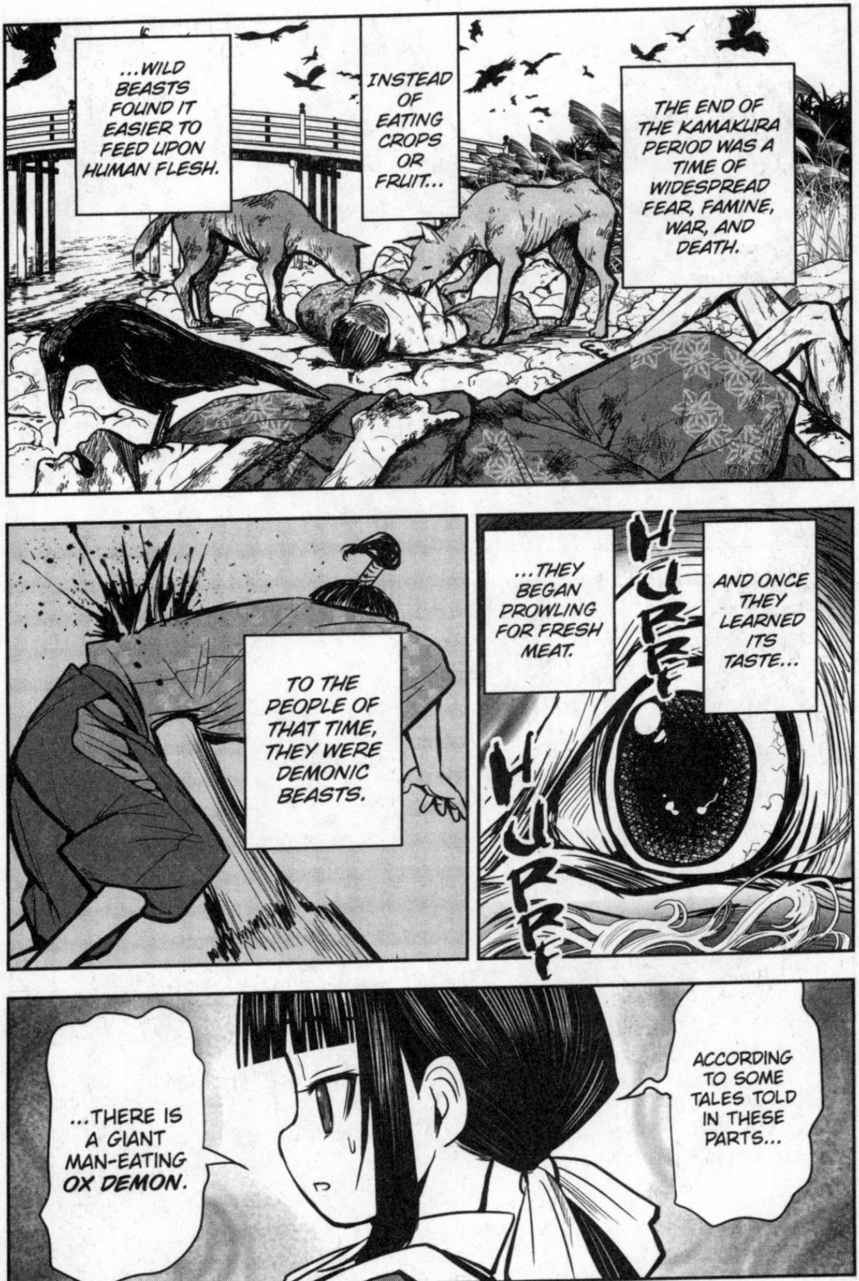
THE END OF THE KAMAKURA PERIOD WAS A TIME OF WIDESPREAD FEAR, FAMINE, WAR, AND DEATH.
INSTEAD OF EATING CROPS OR FRUIT...
...WILD BEASTS FOUND IT EASIER TO FEED UPON HUMAN FLESH.
AND ONCE THEY LEARNED ITS TASTE...
...THEY BEGAN PROWLING FOR FRESH MEAT.
HURRR
HURRR
TO THE PEOPLE OF THAT TIME, THEY WERE DEMONIC BEASTS.
ACCORDING TO SOME TALES TOLD IN THESE PARTS...
...THERE IS A GIANT MAN-EATING OX DEMON.

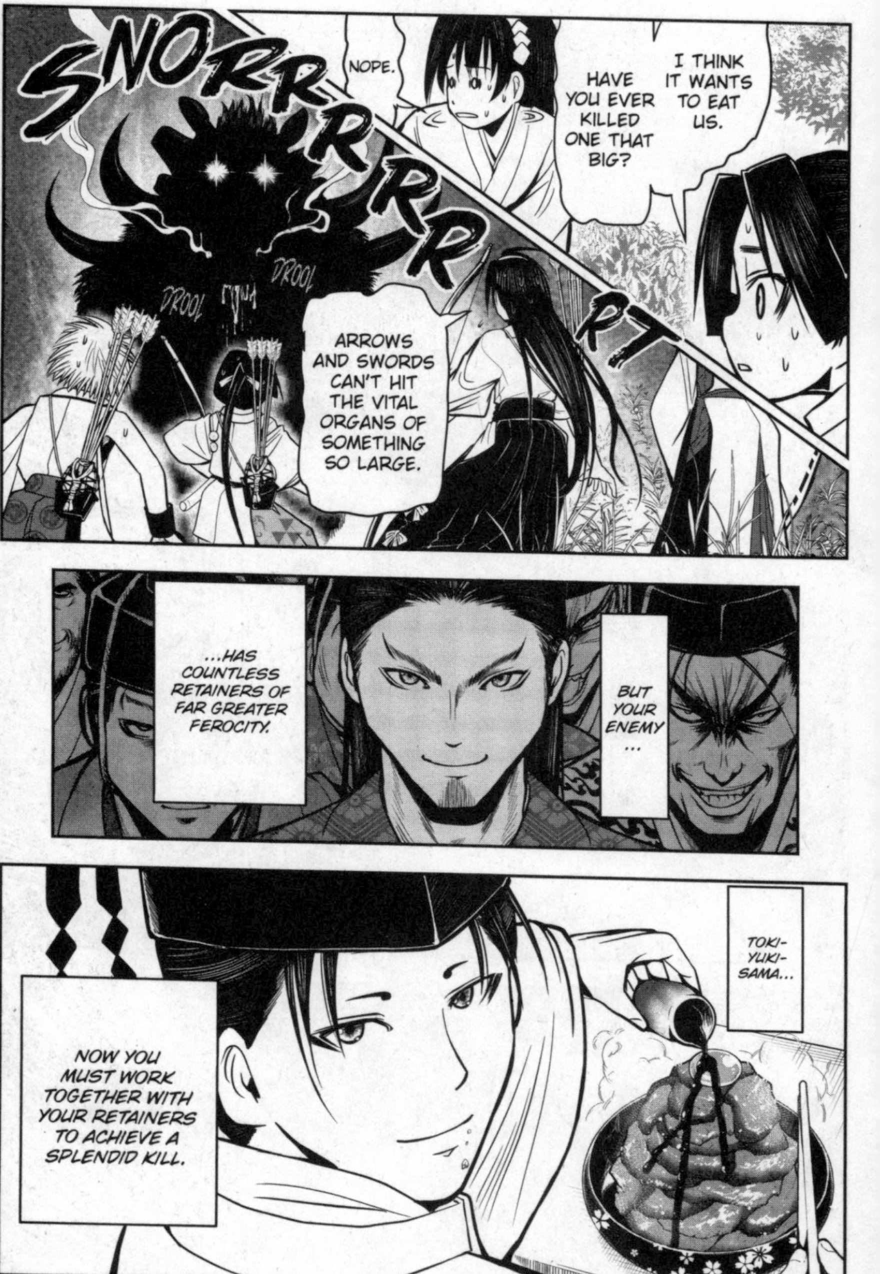
I THINK IT WANTS TO EAT US.
HAVE YOU EVER KILLED ONE THAT BIG?
NOPE.
SNORRRRRRRT
DROOL
DROOL
ARROWS AND SWORDS CAN'T HIT THE VITAL ORGANS OF SOMETHING SO LARGE.
BUT YOUR ENEMY ...
...HAS COUNTLESS RETAINERS OF FAR GREATER FEROCITY.
TOKI-YUKI-SAMA...
NOW YOU MUST WORK TOGETHER WITH YOUR RETAINERS TO ACHIEVE A SPLENDID KILL.

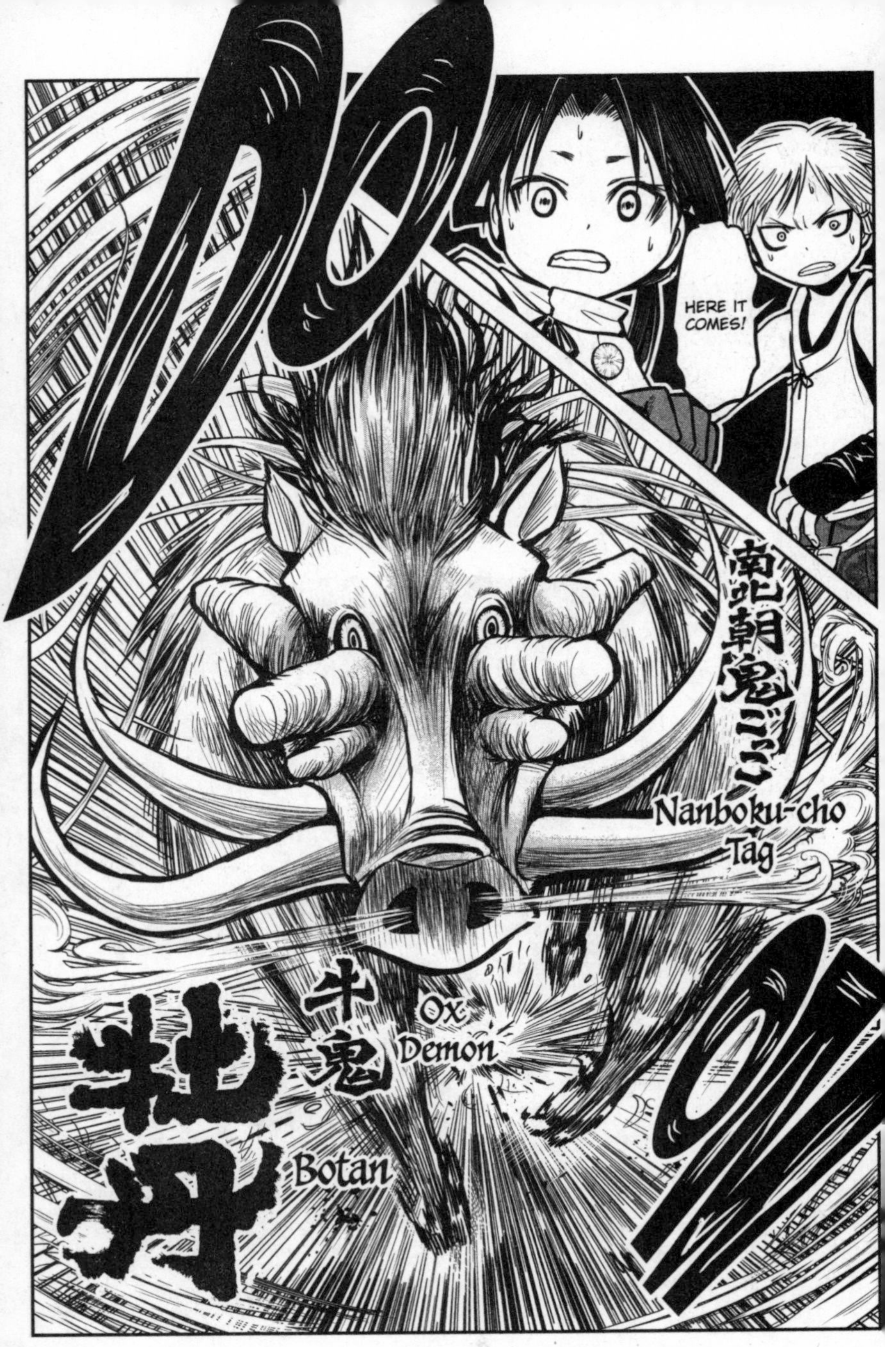
HERE IT COMES!
南北朝鬼ごっこ
Nanboku-cho Tag
牛鬼
Ox Demon
牡丹
Botan

YORISHIGE'S FUTURE LIFE 1

ROAST DEER OVER RICE

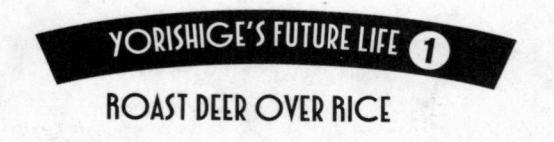

SOMETIMES HE CATCHES GLIMPSES OF FOOD FROM THE FUTURE, SO HE IMMEDIATELY MAKES WHATEVER HE SEES AND TRIES IT. BUT HE SOON FORGETS HOW TO MAKE IT. HE OFTEN KEEPS SUCH FUTURE DELIGHTS TO HIMSELF.

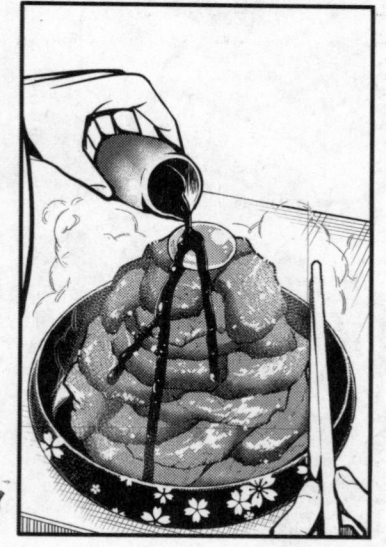

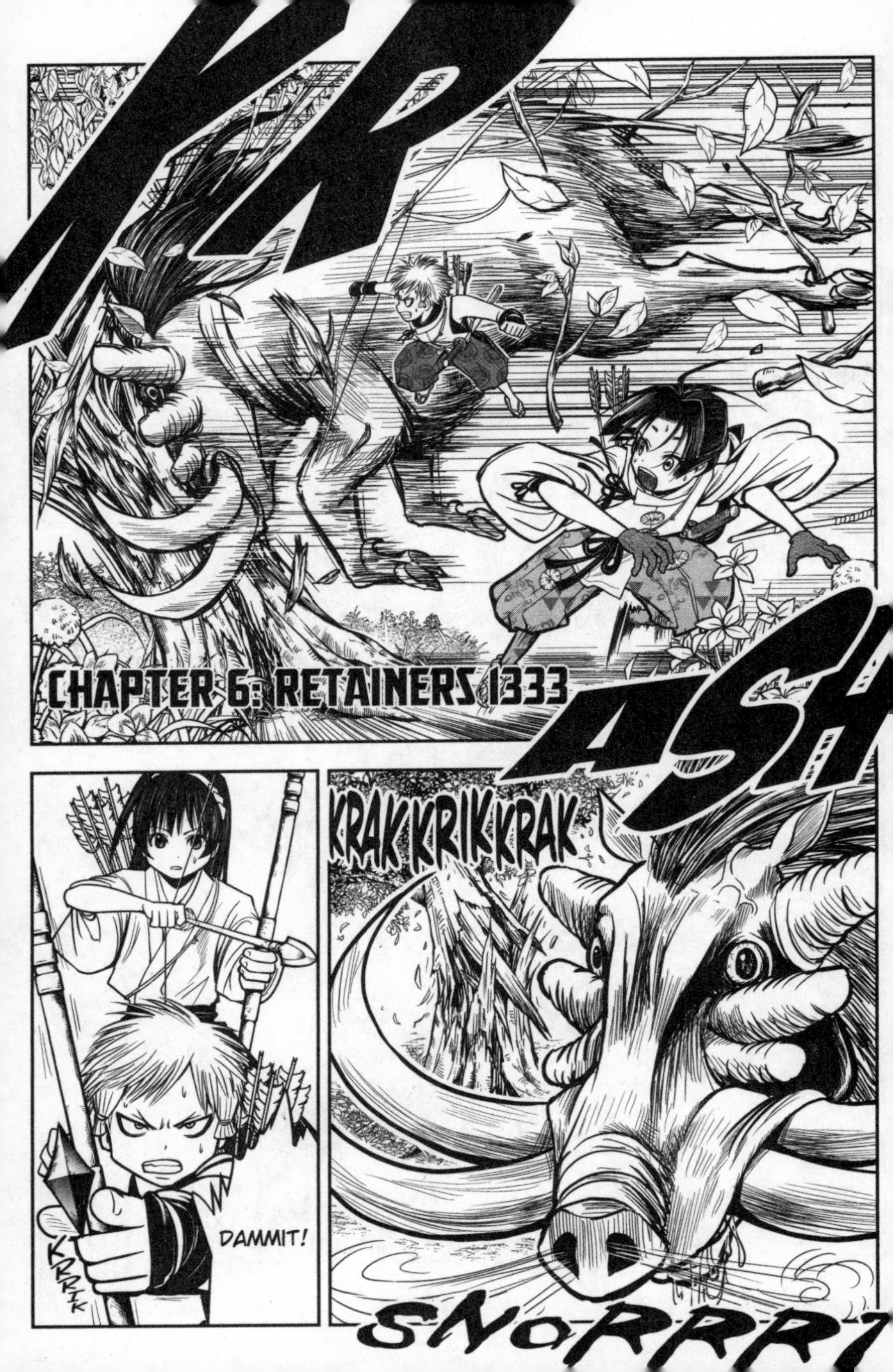
CHAPTER 6: RETAINERS 1333
KRAK KRIK KRAK
SNORRRT!
DAMMIT!
KRRRIK

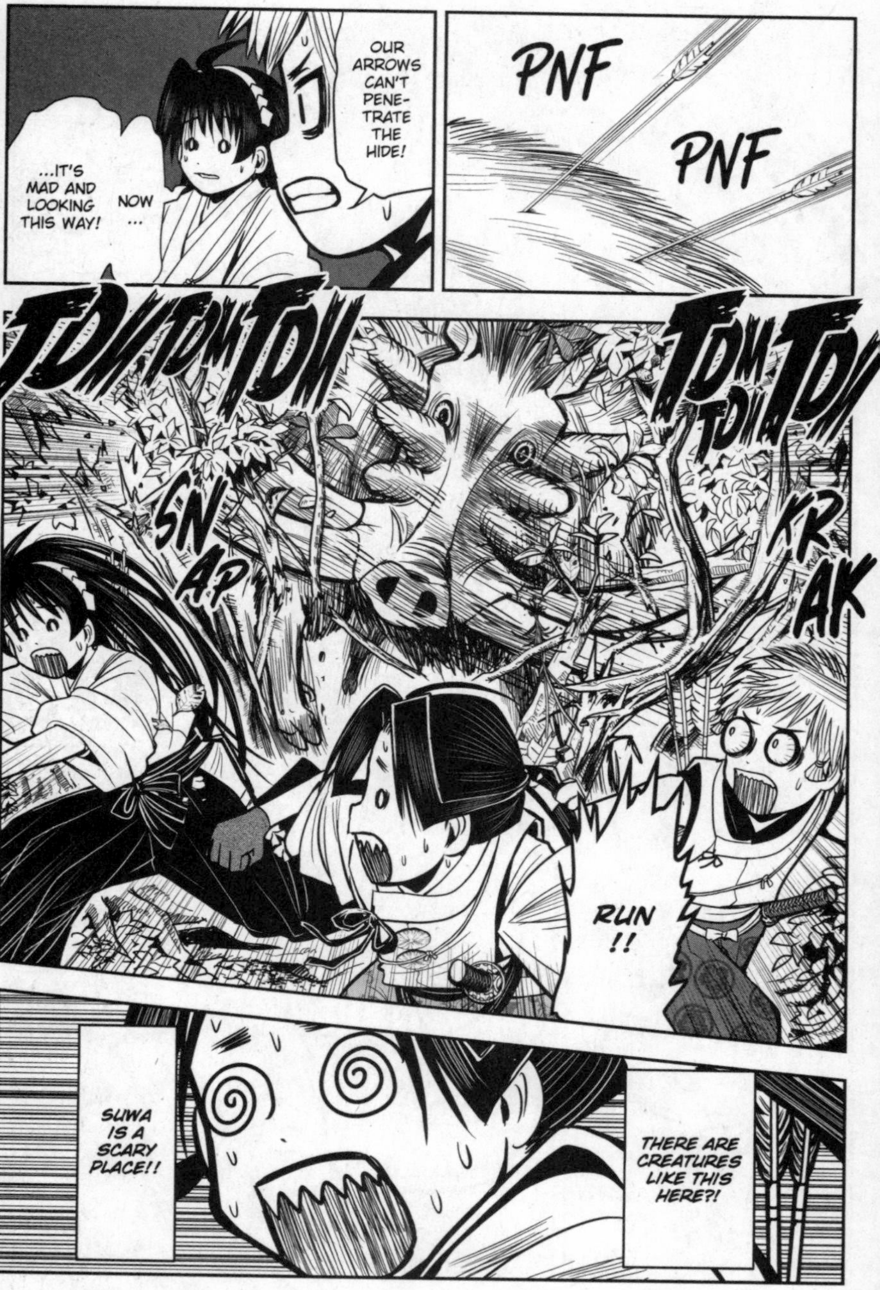
PNF
PNF
OUR ARROWS CAN'T PENE-TRATE THE HIDE!
NOW ...
...IT'S MAD AND LOOKING THIS WAY!
KRAK
SNAP
RUN !!
THERE ARE CREATURES LIKE THIS HERE?!
SUWA IS A SCARY PLACE!!

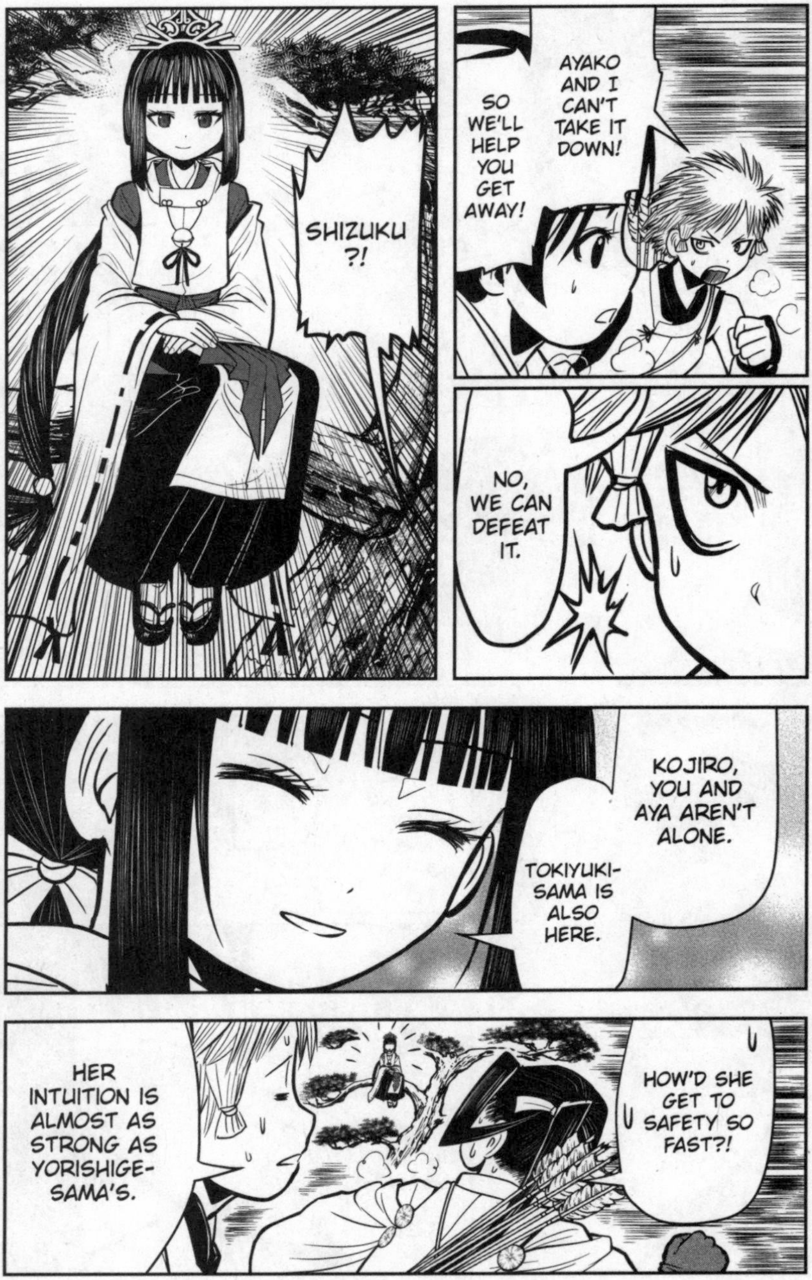
AYAKO AND I CAN'T TAKE IT DOWN!
SO WE'LL HELP YOU GET AWAY!
NO, WE CAN DEFEAT IT.
SHIZUKU ?!
KOJIRO, YOU AND AYA AREN'T ALONE.
TOKIYUKI-SAMA IS ALSO HERE.
HOW'D SHE GET TO SAFETY SO FAST?!
HER INTUITION IS ALMOST AS STRONG AS YORISHIGE-SAMA'S.

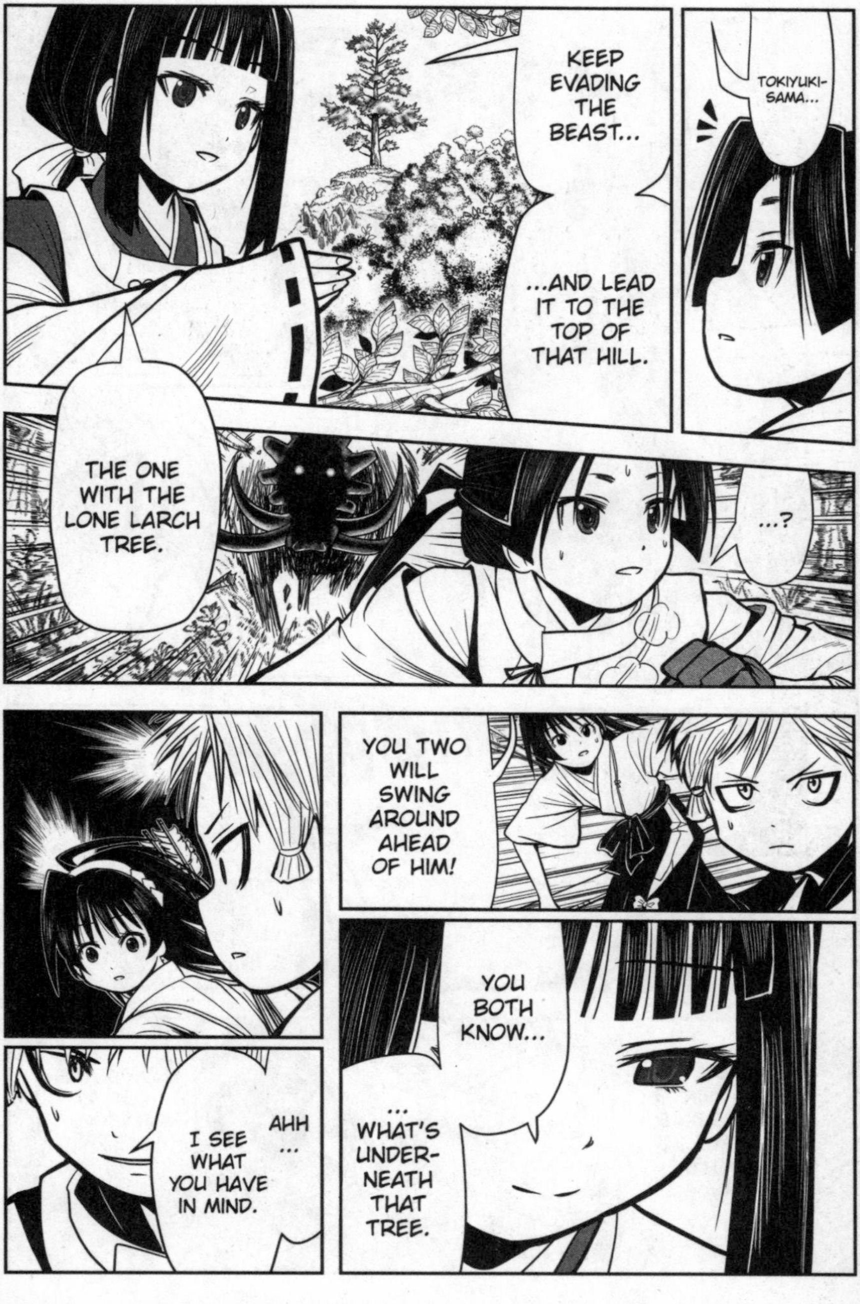
TOKIYUKI-SAMA...
KEEP EVADING THE BEAST...
...AND LEAD IT TO THE TOP OF THAT HILL.
THE ONE WITH THE LONE LARCH TREE.
...?
YOU TWO WILL SWING AROUND AHEAD OF HIM!
YOU BOTH KNOW...
... WHAT'S UNDERNEATH THAT TREE.
AHH ...
I SEE WHAT YOU HAVE IN MIND.

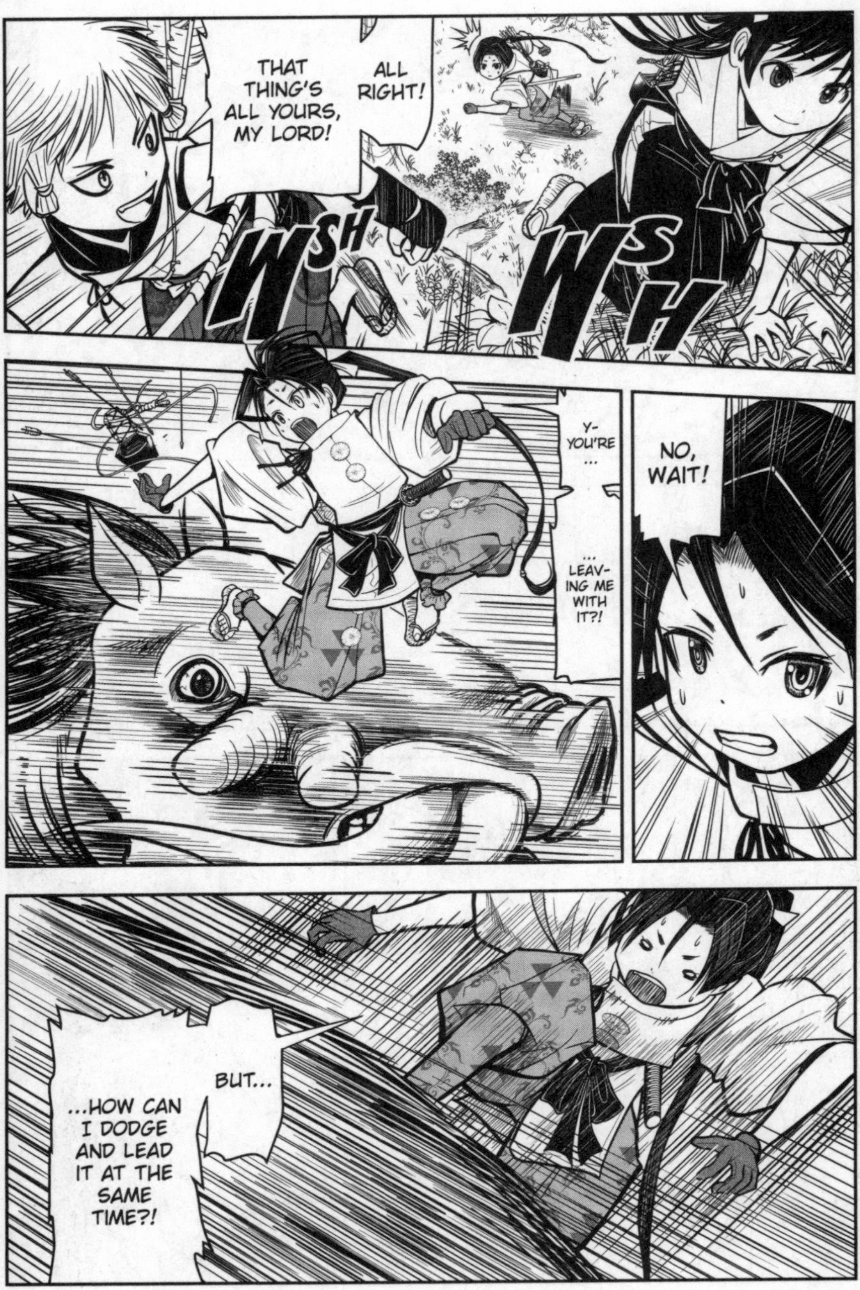
ALL RIGHT!
THAT THING'S ALL YOURS, MY LORD!
WSH
WSH
NO, WAIT!
Y-YOU'RE ...
... LEAVING ME WITH IT?!
BUT...
...HOW CAN I DODGE AND LEAD IT AT THE SAME TIME?!

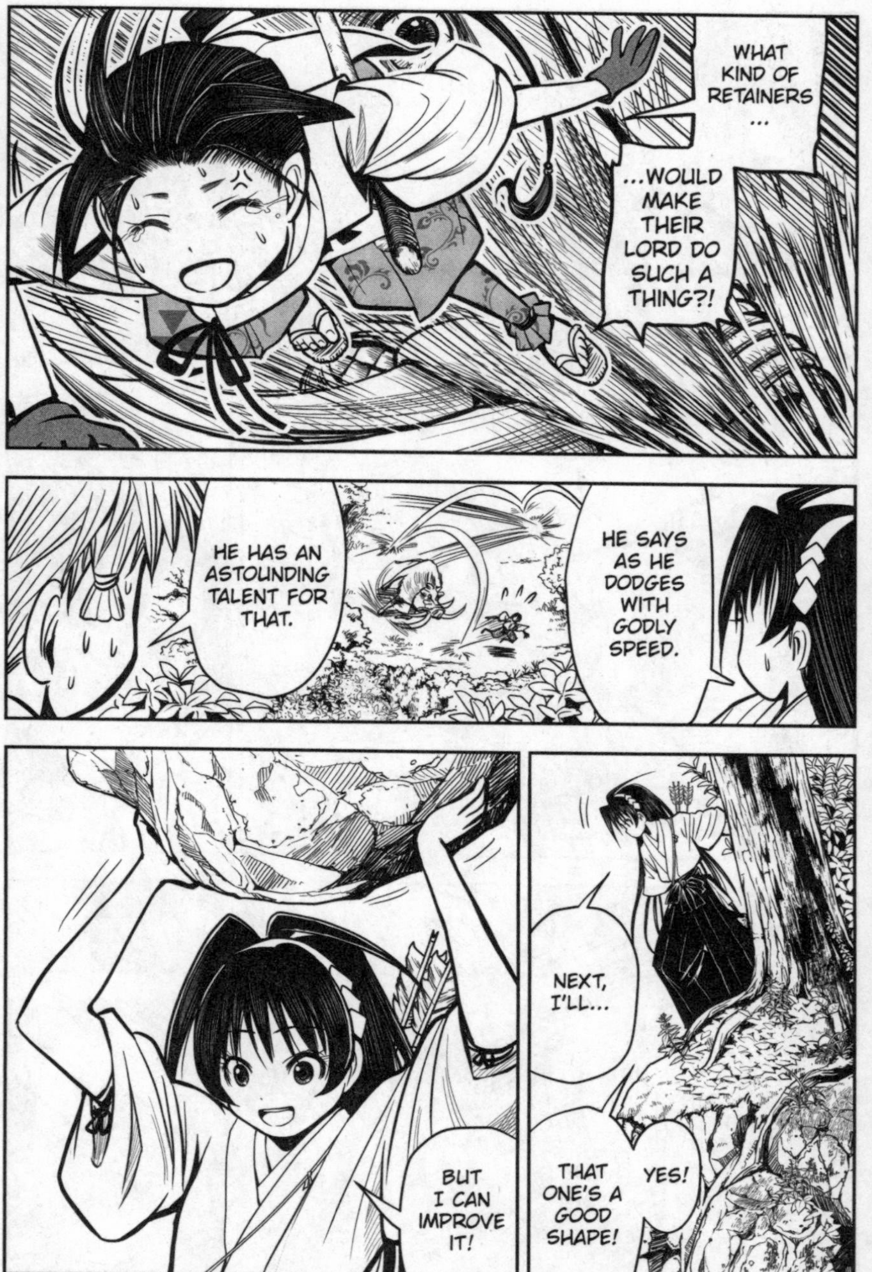
WHAT KIND OF RETAINERS ...
...WOULD MAKE THEIR LORD DO SUCH A THING?!
HE SAYS AS HE DODGES WITH GODLY SPEED.
HE HAS AN ASTOUNDING TALENT FOR THAT.
NEXT, I'LL...
YES!
THAT ONE'S A GOOD SHAPE!
BUT I CAN IMPROVE IT!

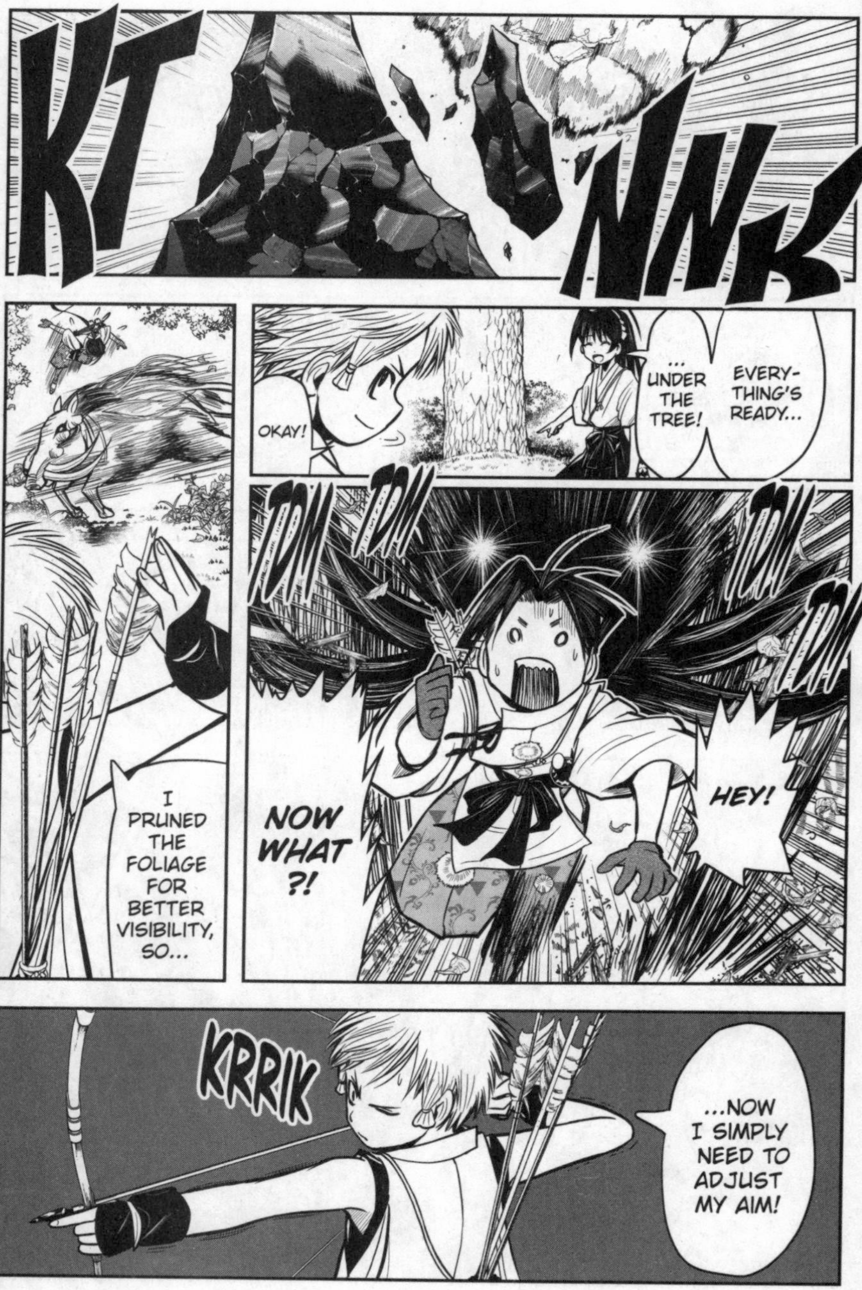
KT
NNK
EVERY-THING'S READY...
...UNDER THE TREE!
OKAY!
HEY!
NOW WHAT?!
I PRUNED THE FOLIAGE FOR BETTER VISIBILITY, SO...
KRRIK
...NOW I SIMPLY NEED TO ADJUST MY AIM!

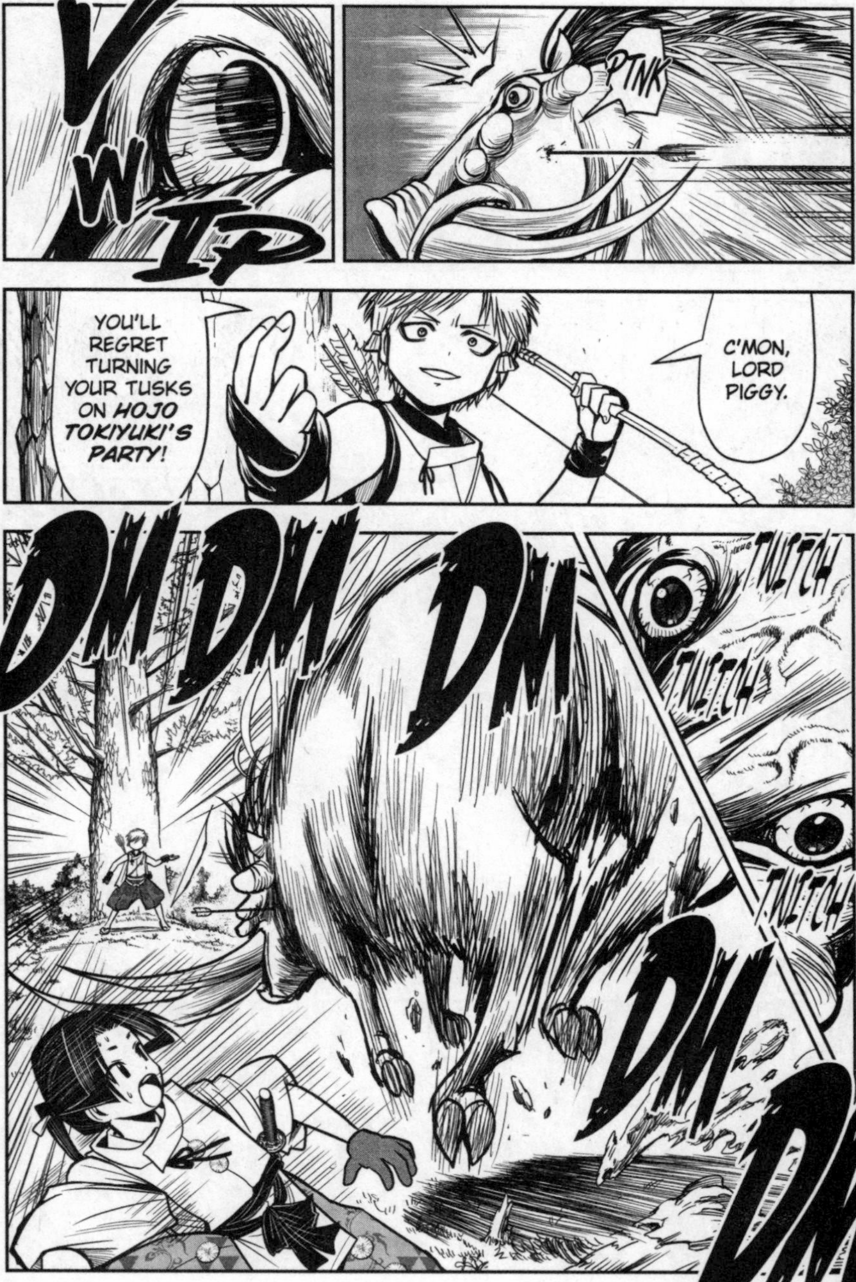
PTNK
VWIP
C'MON, LORD PIGGY.
YOU'LL REGRET TURNING YOUR TUSKS ON *HOJO TOKIYUKI*'S PARTY!
TWITCH
TWITCH
TWITCH
DM DM DM DM DM DM

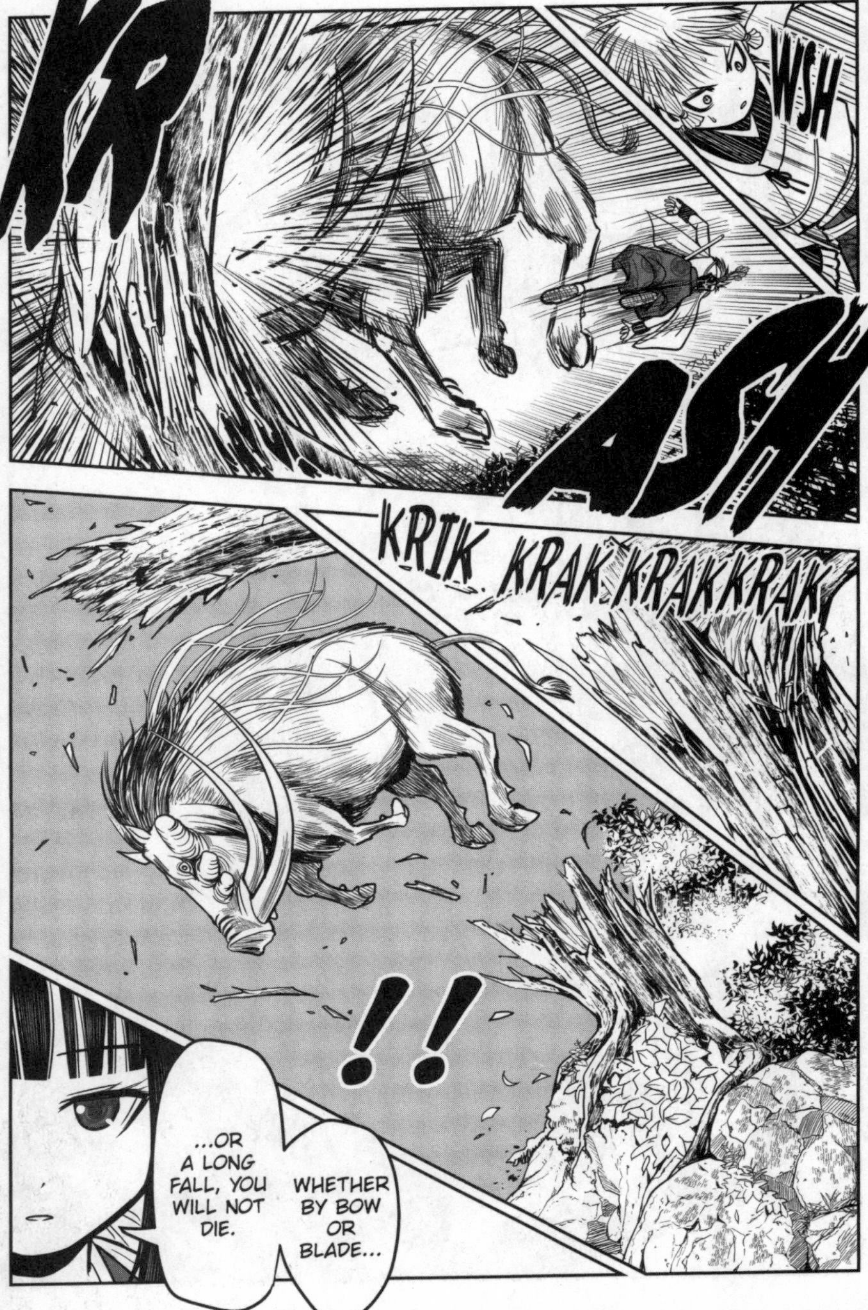
WSH
KRASH
KRIK KRAK KRAKKRAK
!!
WHETHER BY BOW OR BLADE...
...OR A LONG FALL, YOU WILL NOT DIE.

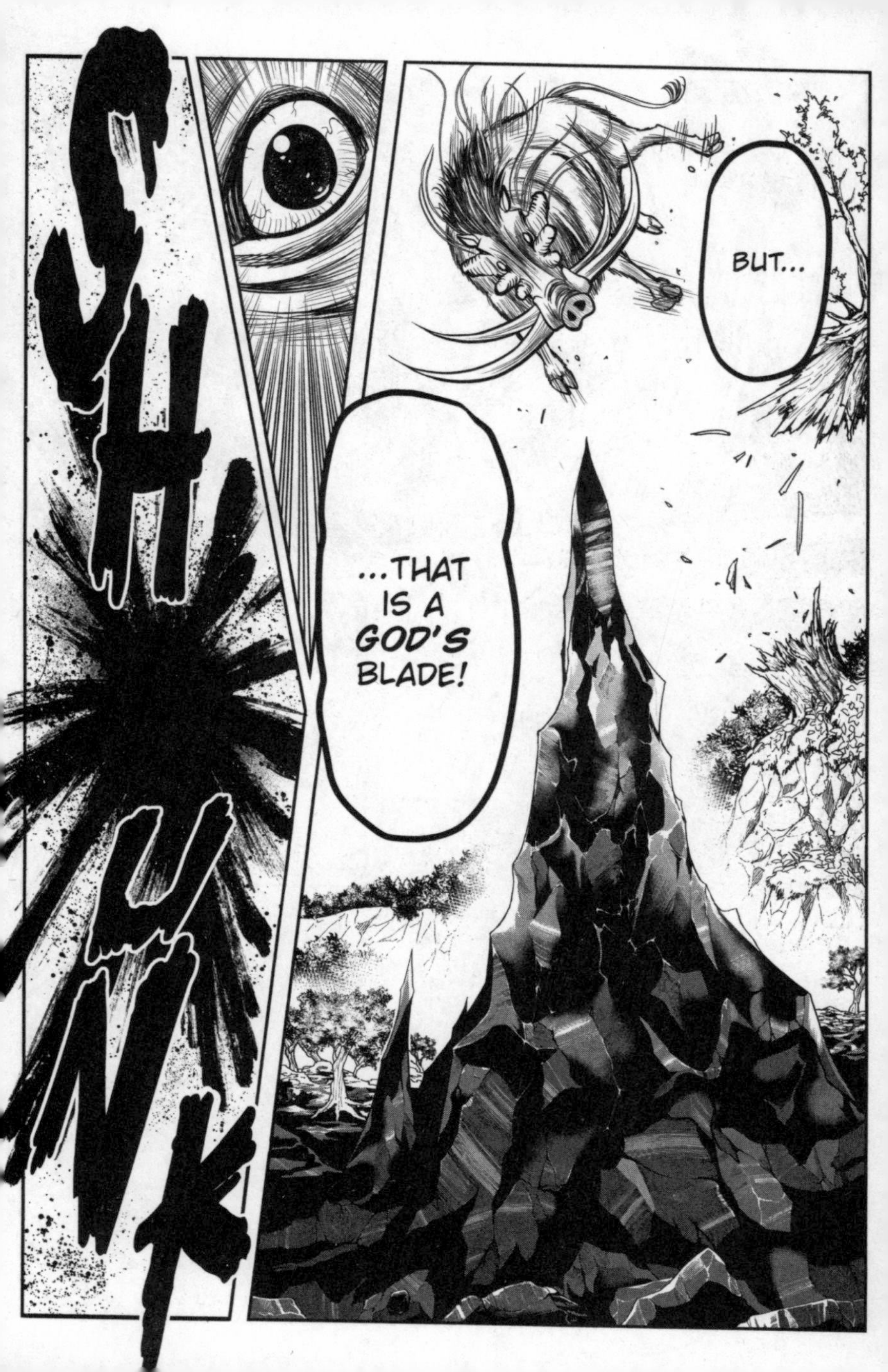
BUT...
...THAT IS A GOD'S BLADE!
SHUNK

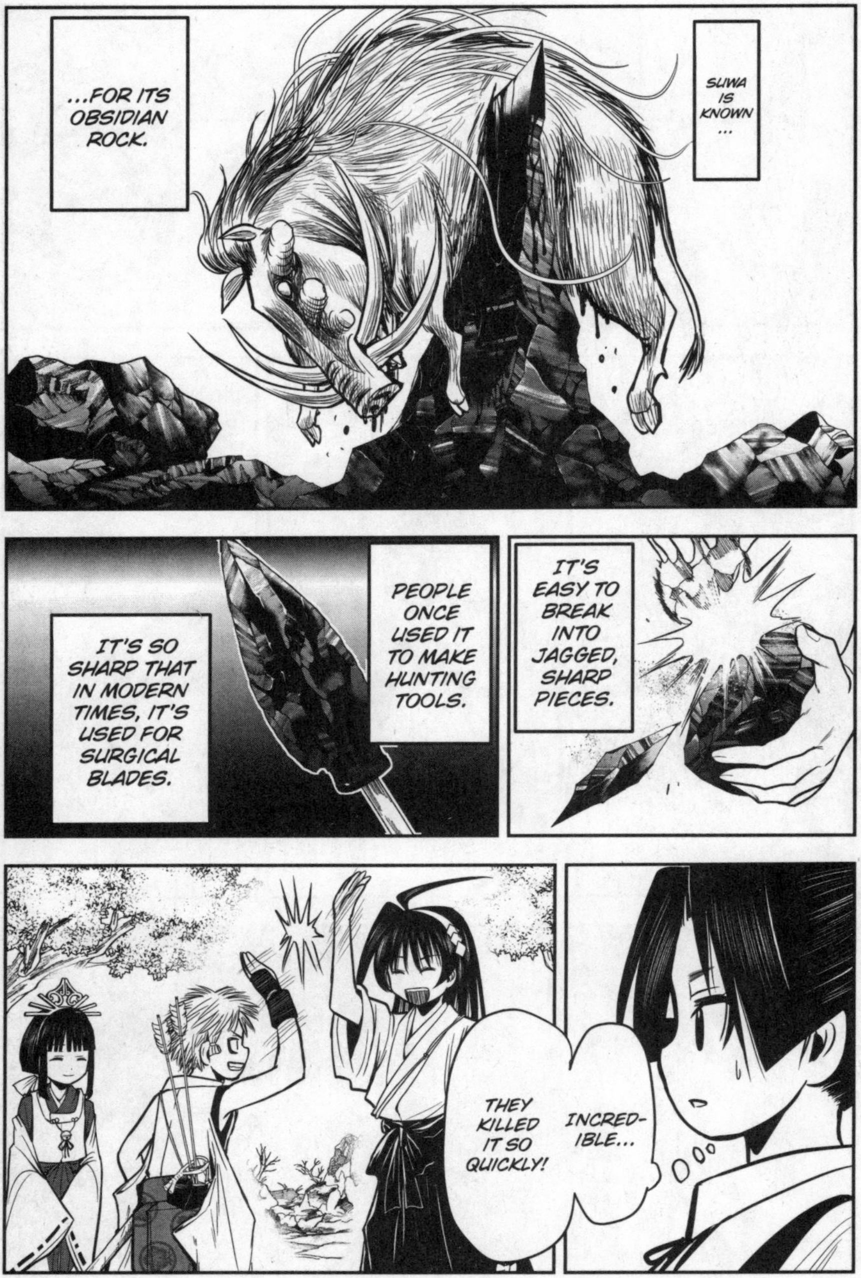
SUWA IS KNOWN ...
...FOR ITS OBSIDIAN ROCK.
IT'S EASY TO BREAK INTO JAGGED, SHARP PIECES.
PEOPLE ONCE USED IT TO MAKE HUNTING TOOLS.
IT'S SO SHARP THAT IN MODERN TIMES, IT'S USED FOR SURGICAL BLADES.
INCREDIBLE...
THEY KILLED IT SO QUICKLY!

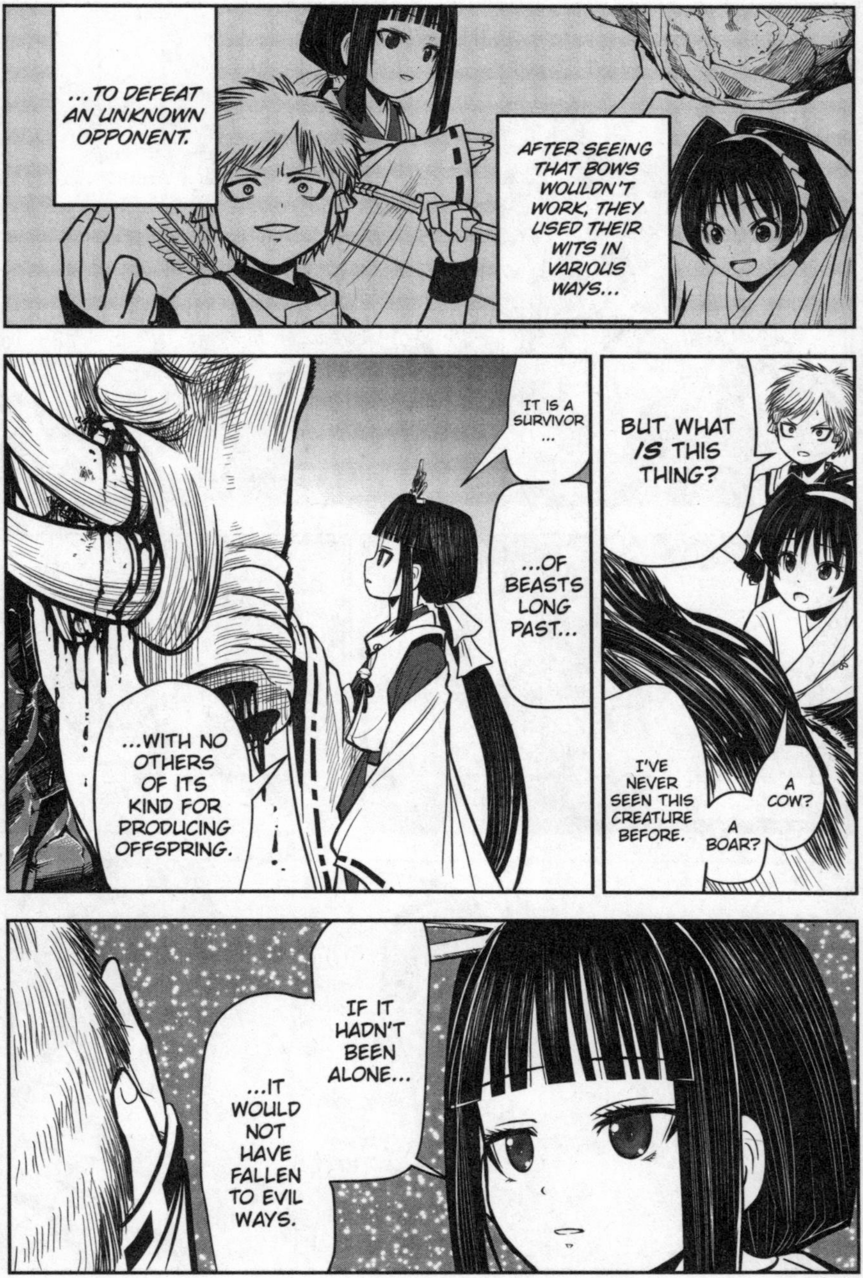
AFTER SEEING THAT BOWS WOULDN'T WORK, THEY USED THEIR WITS IN VARIOUS WAYS...
...TO DEFEAT AN UNKNOWN OPPONENT.
BUT WHAT IS THIS THING?
I'VE NEVER SEEN THIS CREATURE BEFORE.
A COW? A BOAR?
IT IS A SURVIVOR ...
...OF BEASTS LONG PAST...
...WITH NO OTHERS OF ITS KIND FOR PRODUCING OFFSPRING.
IF IT HADN'T BEEN ALONE...
...IT WOULD NOT HAVE FALLEN TO EVIL WAYS.

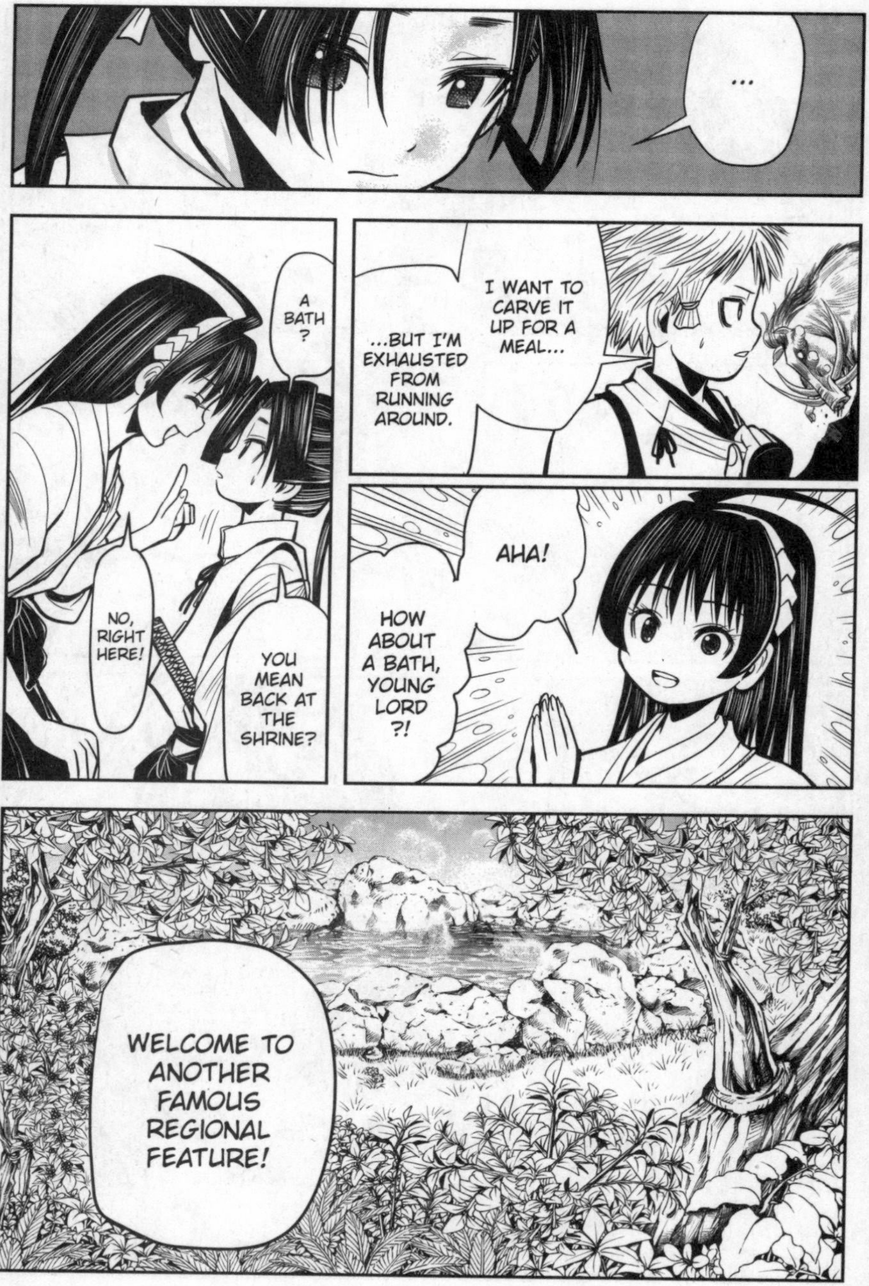
...
I WANT TO CARVE IT UP FOR A MEAL...
...BUT I'M EXHAUSTED FROM RUNNING AROUND.
AHA!
HOW ABOUT A BATH, YOUNG LORD ?!
A BATH ?
YOU MEAN BACK AT THE SHRINE?
NO, RIGHT HERE!
WELCOME TO ANOTHER FAMOUS REGIONAL FEATURE!

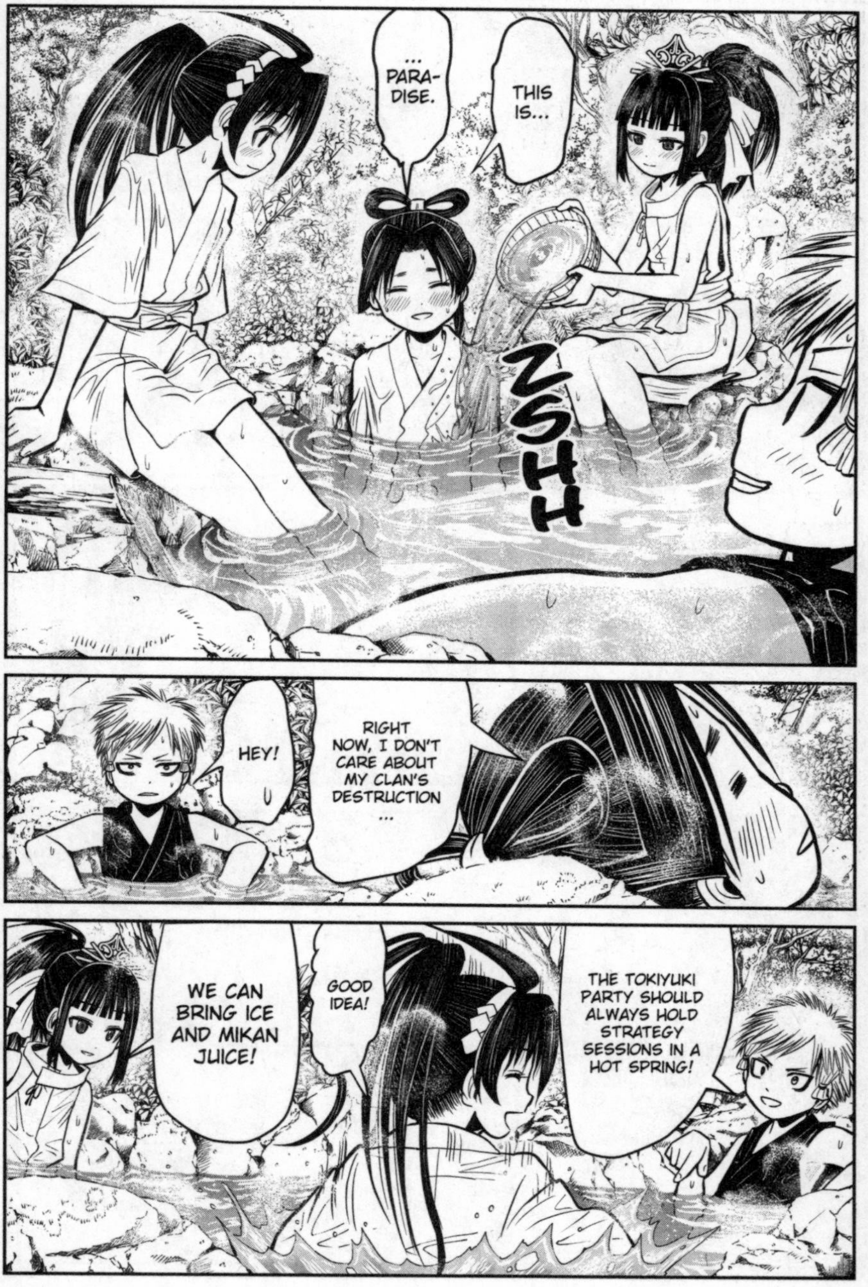
THIS IS...
... PARA-DISE.
ZSHH
RIGHT NOW, I DON'T CARE ABOUT MY CLAN'S DESTRUCTION ...
HEY!
THE TOKIYUKI PARTY SHOULD ALWAYS HOLD STRATEGY SESSIONS IN A HOT SPRING!
GOOD IDEA!
WE CAN BRING ICE AND MIKAN JUICE!

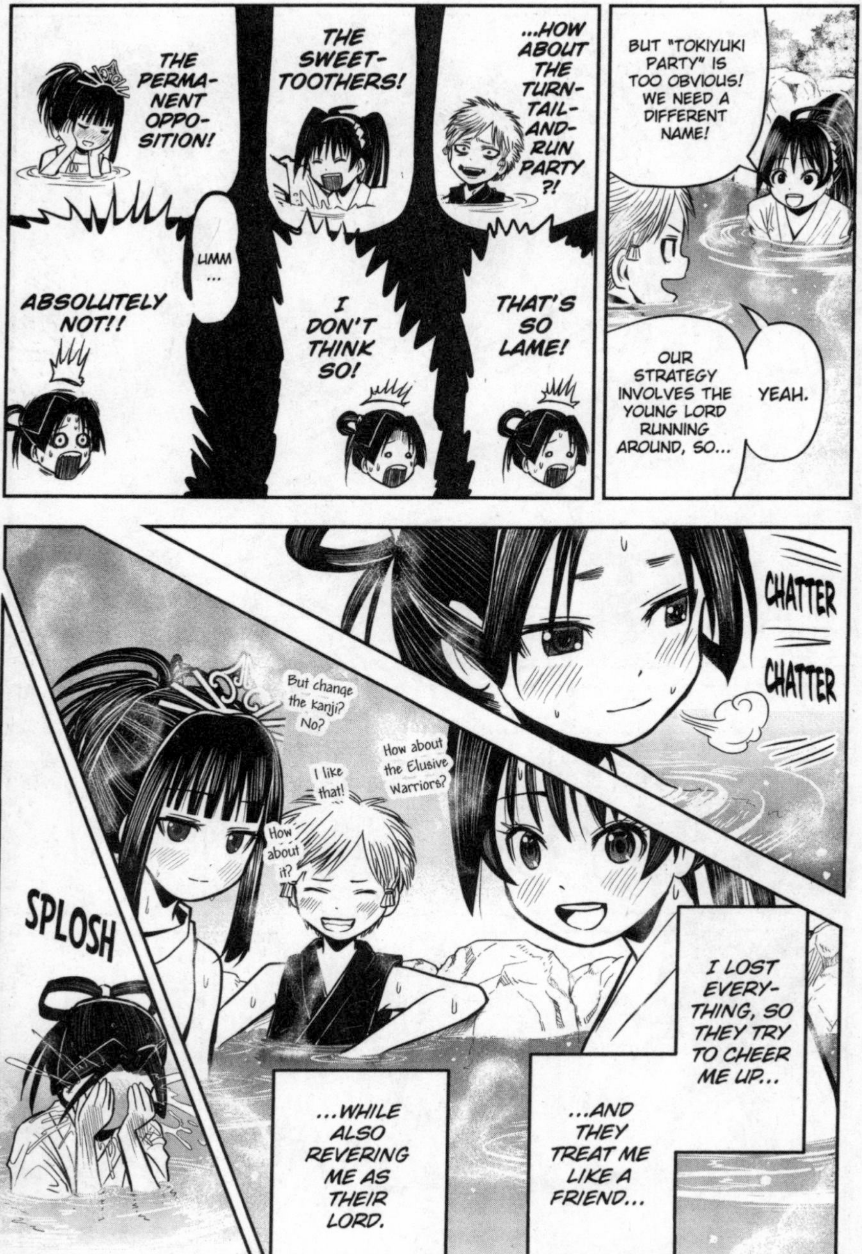
BUT "TOKIYUKI PARTY" IS TOO OBVIOUS! WE NEED A DIFFERENT NAME!
OUR STRATEGY INVOLVES THE YOUNG LORD RUNNING AROUND, SO...
YEAH.
...HOW ABOUT THE TURN-TAIL-AND-RUN PARTY?!
THE SWEET-TOOTHERS!
THE PERMA-NENT OPPO-SITION!
THAT'S SO LAME!
I DON'T THINK SO!
UMM ...
ABSOLUTELY NOT!!
CHATTER
CHATTER
I LOST EVERY-THING, SO THEY TRY TO CHEER ME UP...
...AND THEY TREAT ME LIKE A FRIEND...
How about the Elusive Warriors?
I like that!
How about it?
But change the kanji? No?
...WHILE ALSO REVERING ME AS THEIR LORD.
SPLOSH

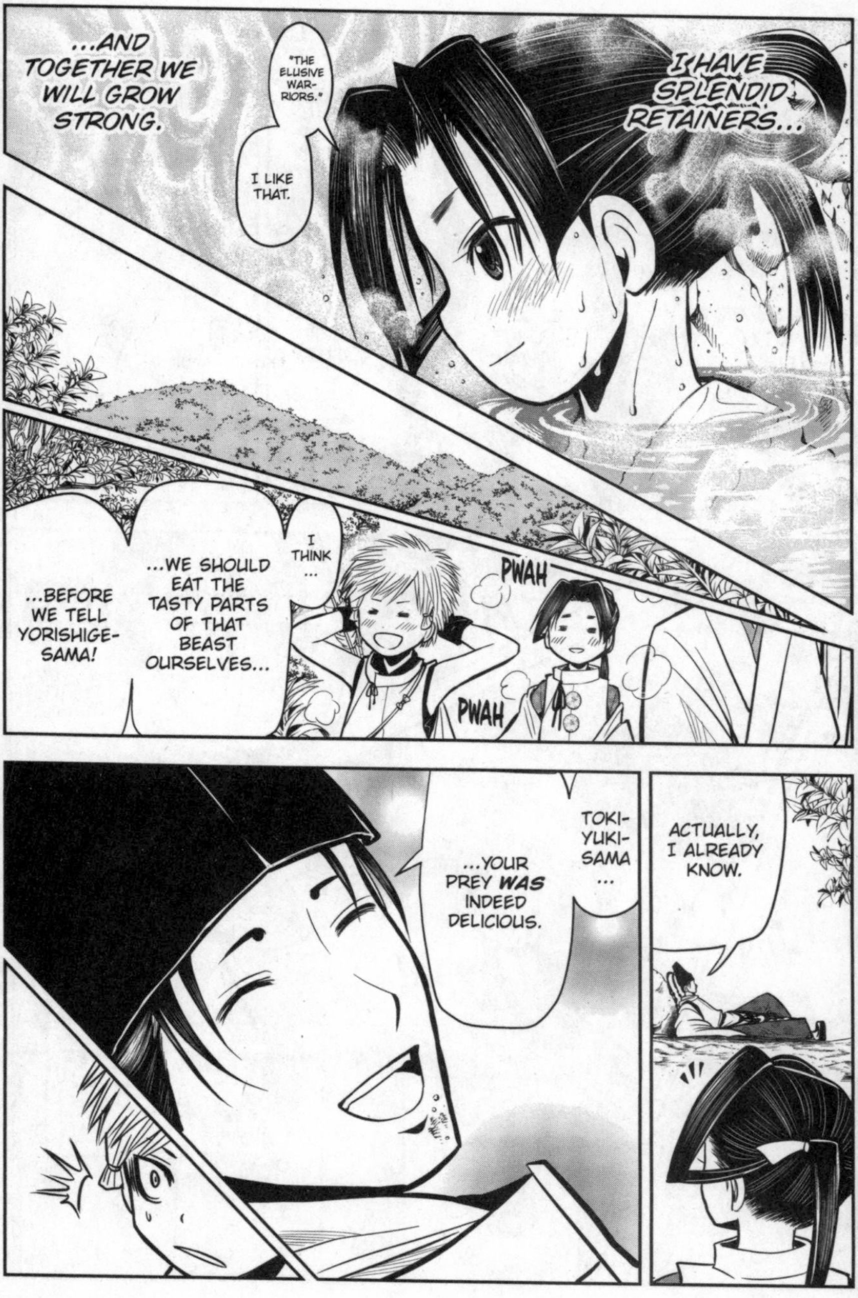
I HAVE SPLENDID RETAINERS...
"THE ELUSIVE WAR-RIORS."
I LIKE THAT.
...AND TOGETHER WE WILL GROW STRONG.
PWAH
PWAH
I THINK ...
...WE SHOULD EAT THE TASTY PARTS OF THAT BEAST OURSELVES...
...BEFORE WE TELL YORISHIGE-SAMA!
ACTUALLY, I ALREADY KNOW.
TOKI-YUKI-SAMA ...
...YOUR PREY WAS INDEED DELICIOUS.

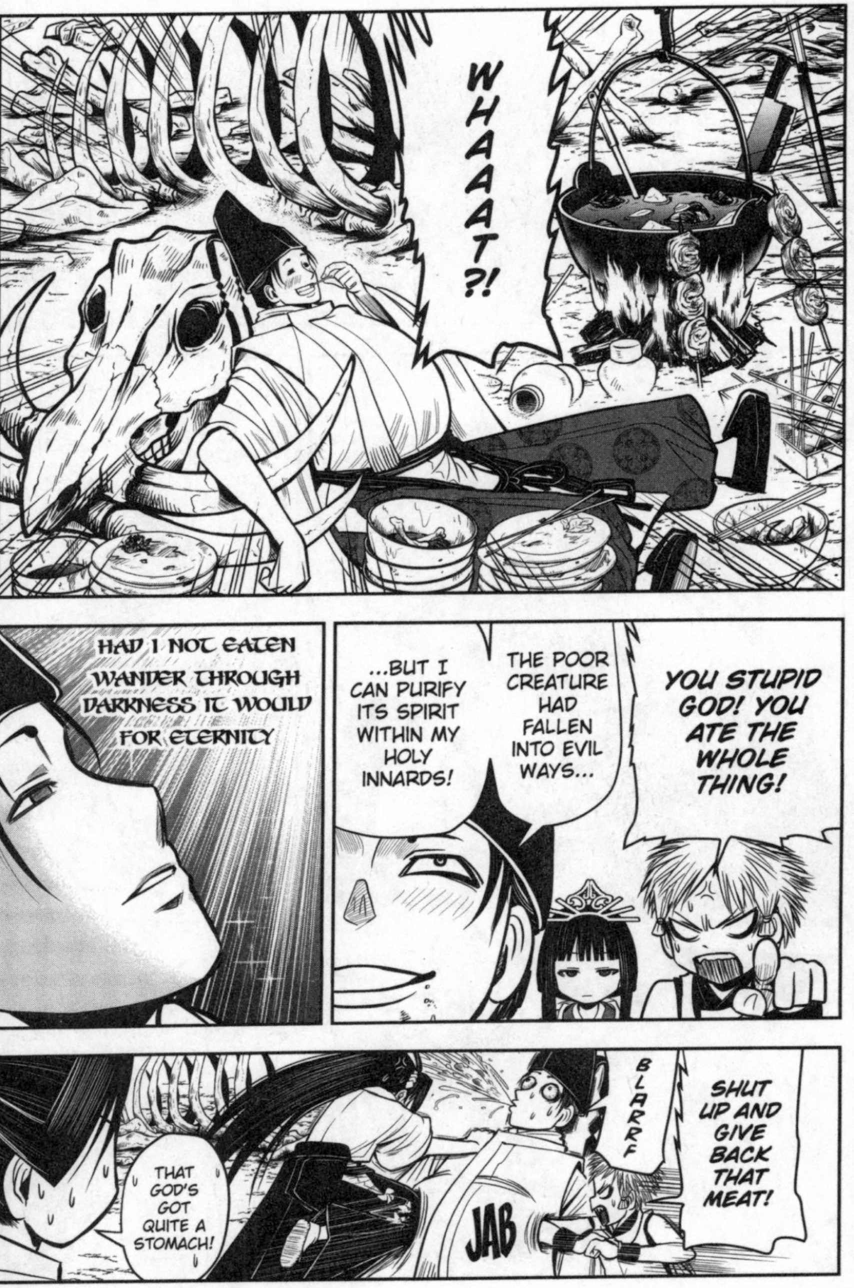
WHAAAAT?!
YOU STUPID GOD! YOU ATE THE WHOLE THING!
THE POOR CREATURE HAD FALLEN INTO EVIL WAYS...
...BUT I CAN PURIFY ITS SPIRIT WITHIN MY HOLY INNARDS!
HAD I NOT EATEN
WANDER THROUGH DARKNESS IT WOULD FOR ETERNITY
SHUT UP AND GIVE BACK THAT MEAT!
BLARRF
JAB
THAT GOD'S GOT QUITE A STOMACH!

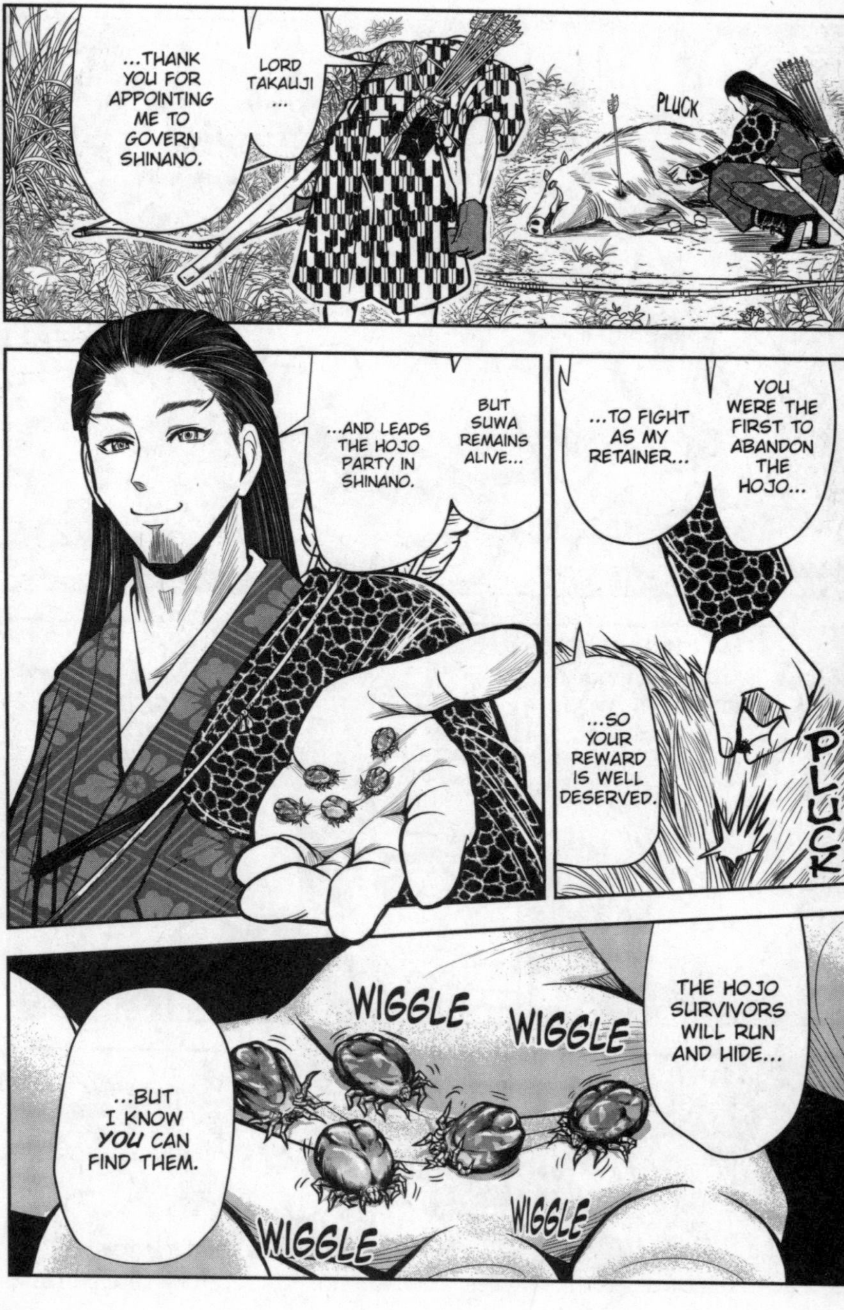
PLUCK
LORD TAKAUJI ...
...THANK YOU FOR APPOINTING ME TO GOVERN SHINANO.
YOU WERE THE FIRST TO ABANDON THE HOJO...
...TO FIGHT AS MY RETAINER...
PLUCK
...SO YOUR REWARD IS WELL DESERVED.
BUT SUWA REMAINS ALIVE...
...AND LEADS THE HOJO PARTY IN SHINANO.
THE HOJO SURVIVORS WILL RUN AND HIDE...
WIGGLE
WIGGLE
WIGGLE
WIGGLE
...BUT I KNOW YOU CAN FIND THEM.

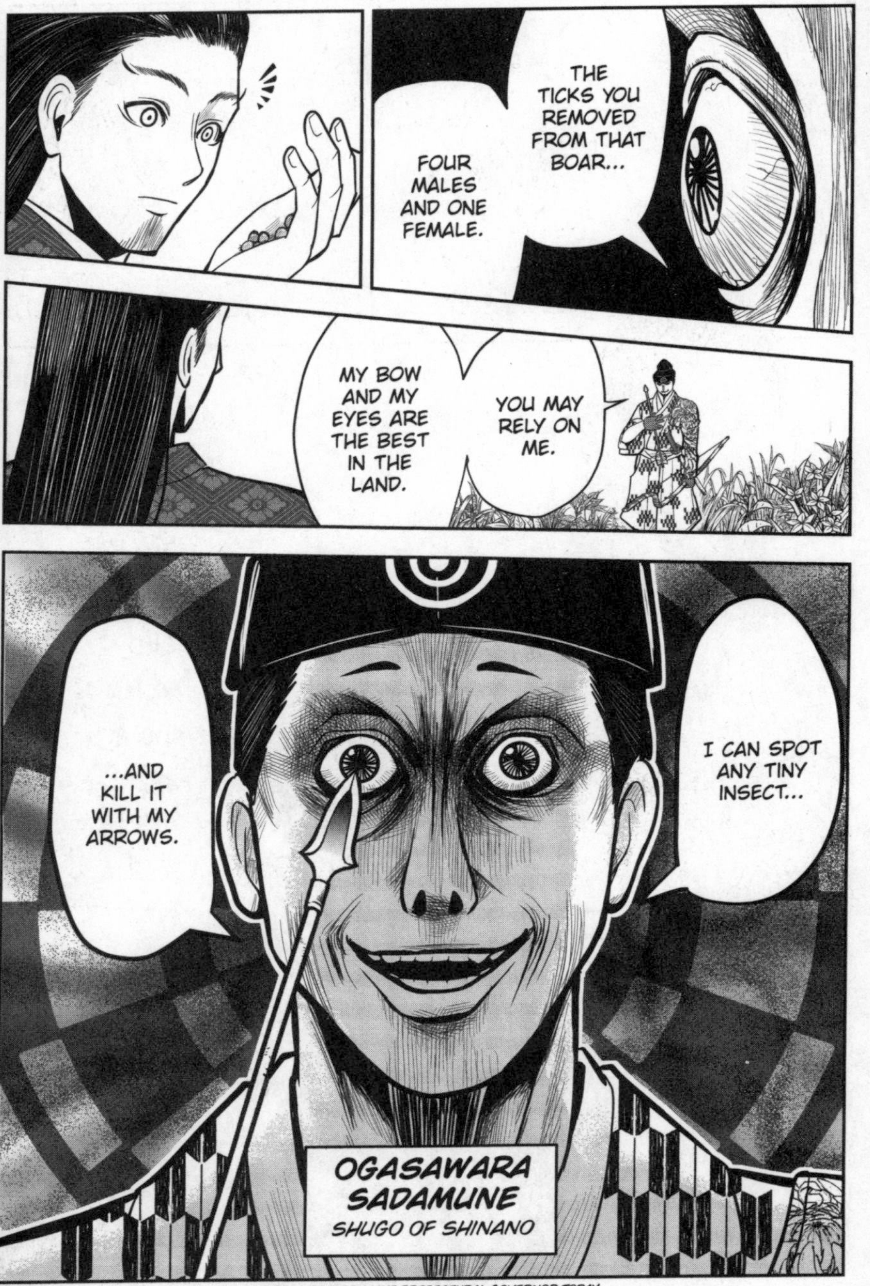
THE TICKS YOU REMOVED FROM THAT BOAR...
FOUR MALES AND ONE FEMALE.
YOU MAY RELY ON ME.
MY BOW AND MY EYES ARE THE BEST IN THE LAND.
I CAN SPOT ANY TINY INSECT...
...AND KILL IT WITH MY ARROWS.
OGASAWARA SADAMUNE
SHUGO OF SHINANO

*SHUGO: A POSITION LIKE PREFECTURAL GOVERNOR TODAY

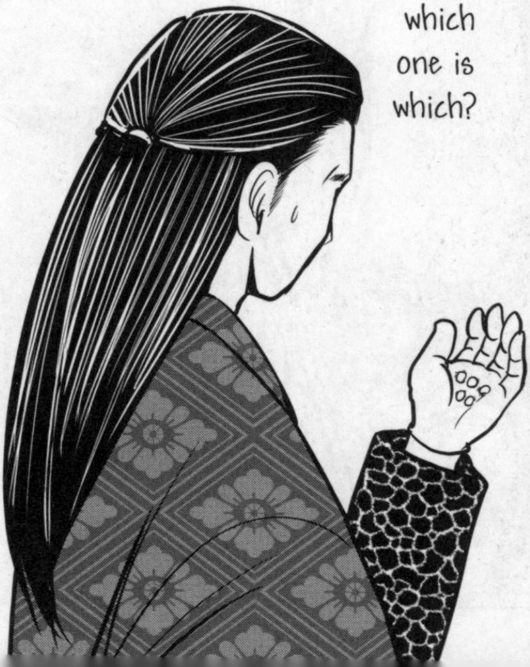
Um, which one is which?

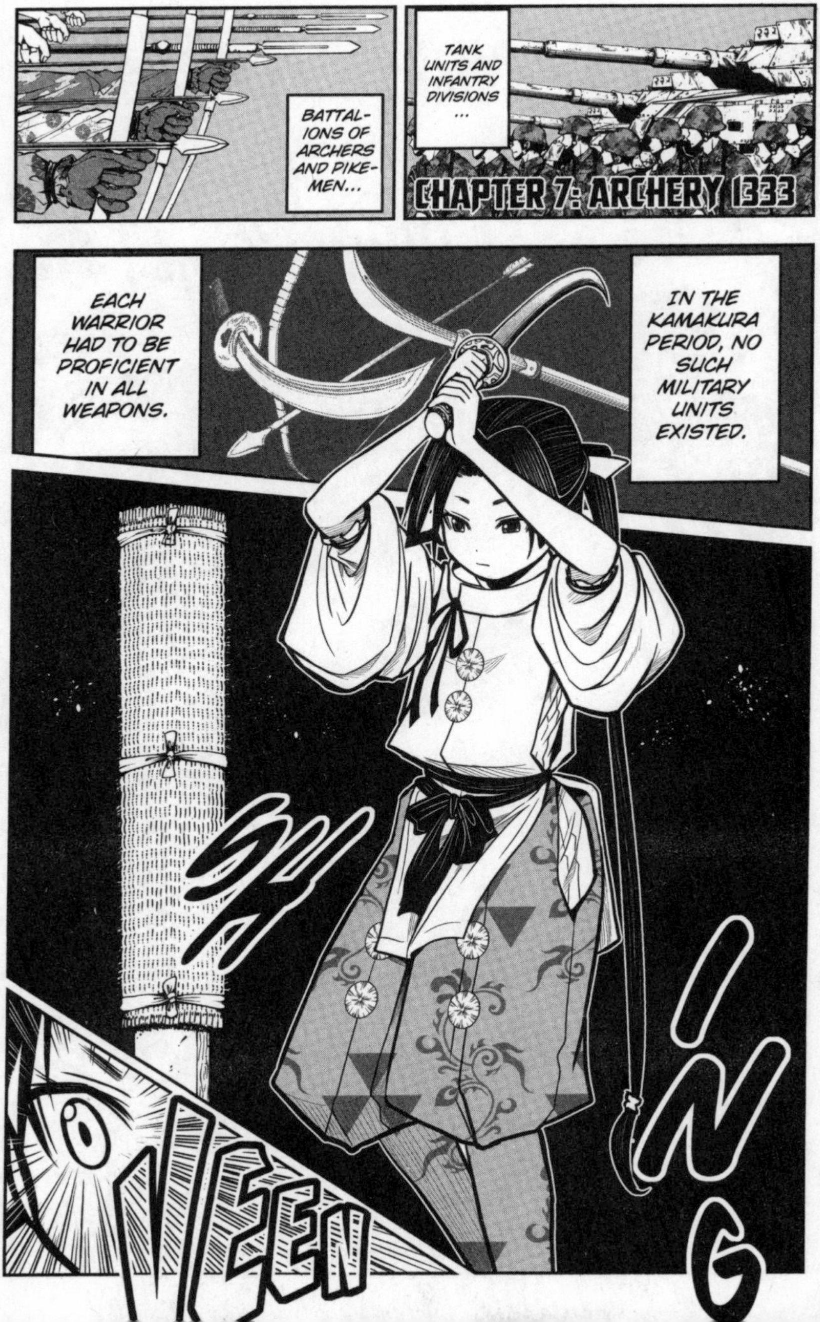
TANK UNITS AND INFANTRY DIVISIONS ...
CHAPTER 7: ARCHERY 1333
BATTALIONS OF ARCHERS AND PIKEMEN...
IN THE KAMAKURA PERIOD, NO SUCH MILITARY UNITS EXISTED.
EACH WARRIOR HAD TO BE PROFICIENT IN ALL WEAPONS.
SHING
WEEN

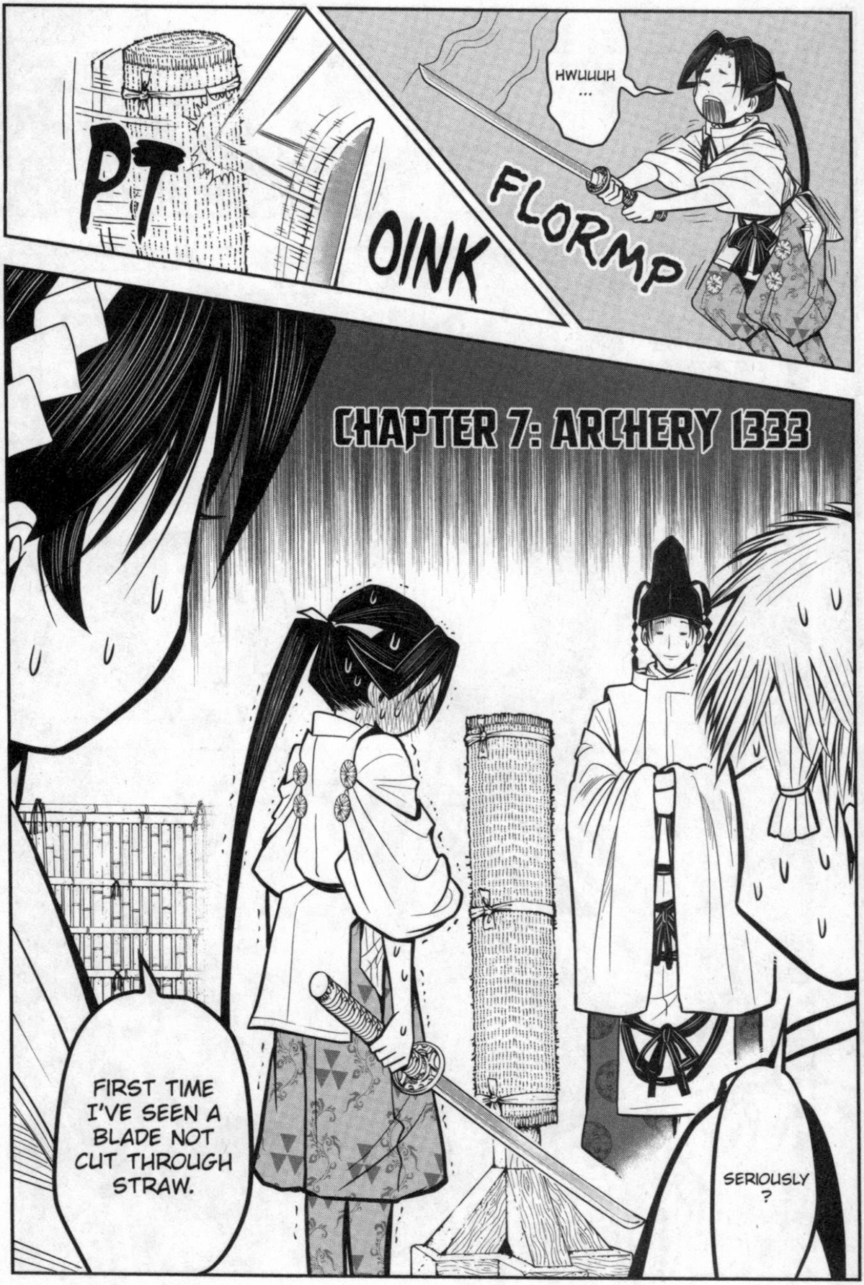
HWUUUH ...
FLORMP
PT
OINK
CHAPTER 7: ARCHERY 1333
FIRST TIME I'VE SEEN A BLADE NOT CUT THROUGH STRAW.
SERIOUSLY?

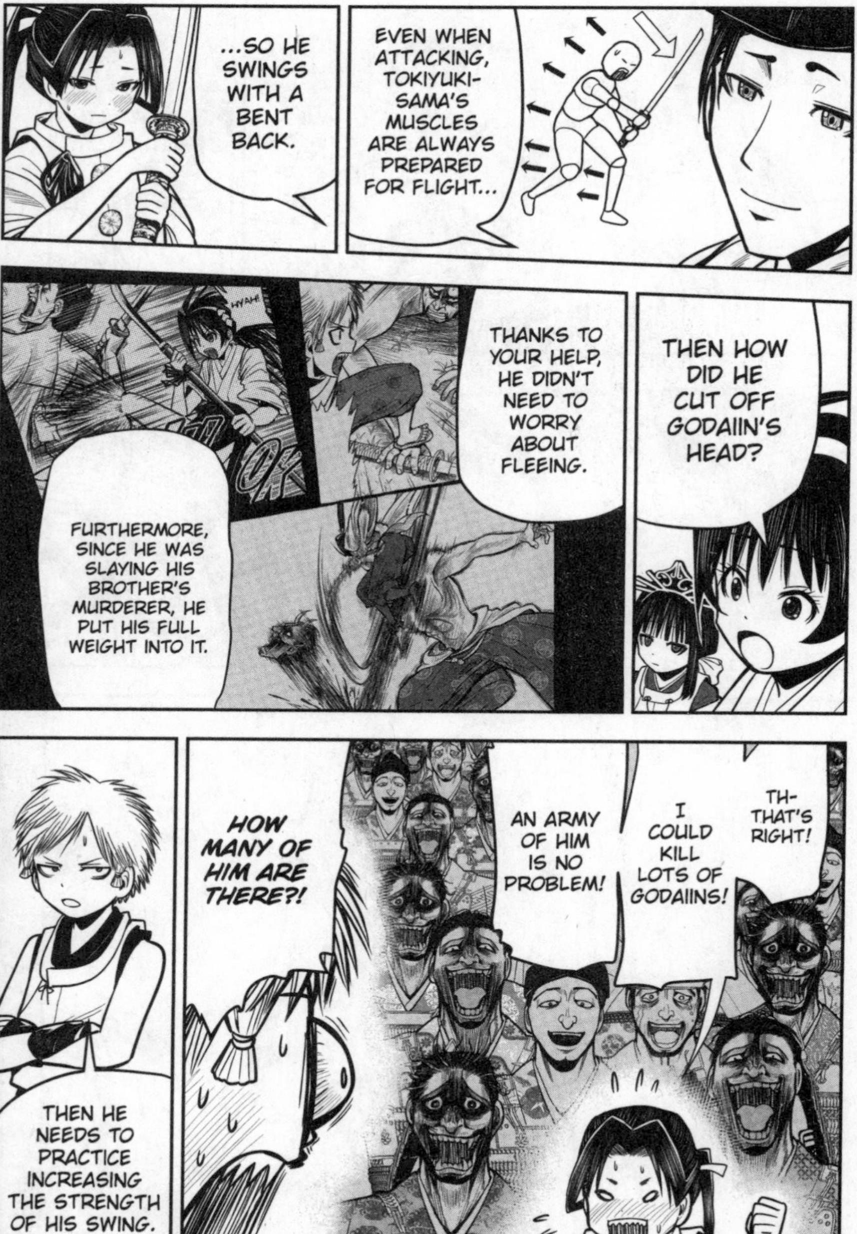
EVEN WHEN ATTACKING, TOKIYUKI-SAMA'S MUSCLES ARE ALWAYS PREPARED FOR FLIGHT...
...SO HE SWINGS WITH A BENT BACK.
THEN HOW DID HE CUT OFF GODAIIN'S HEAD?
THANKS TO YOUR HELP, HE DIDN'T NEED TO WORRY ABOUT FLEEING.
HYAH!
FURTHERMORE, SINCE HE WAS SLAYING HIS BROTHER'S MURDERER, HE PUT HIS FULL WEIGHT INTO IT.
TH- THAT'S RIGHT!
I COULD KILL LOTS OF GODAIINS!
AN ARMY OF HIM IS NO PROBLEM!
HOW MANY OF HIM ARE THERE?!
THEN HE NEEDS TO PRACTICE INCREASING THE STRENGTH OF HIS SWING.

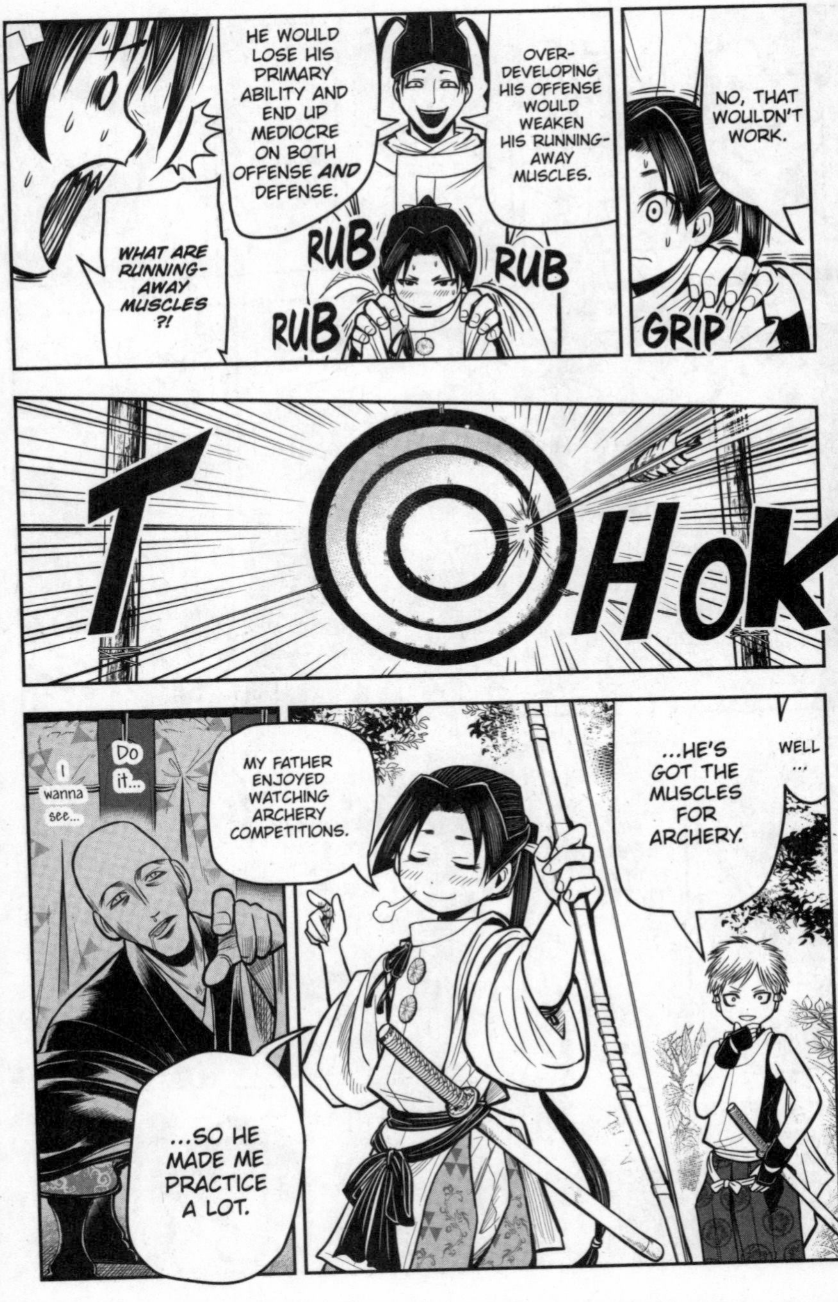
NO, THAT WOULDN'T WORK.
GRIP
OVER-DEVELOPING HIS OFFENSE WOULD WEAKEN HIS RUNNING-AWAY MUSCLES.
RUB
RUB
RUB
HE WOULD LOSE HIS PRIMARY ABILITY AND END UP MEDIOCRE ON BOTH OFFENSE AND DEFENSE.
WHAT ARE RUNNING-AWAY MUSCLES ?!
THOK
WELL ...
...HE'S GOT THE MUSCLES FOR ARCHERY.
MY FATHER ENJOYED WATCHING ARCHERY COMPETITIONS.
...SO HE MADE ME PRACTICE A LOT.
Do it...
I wanna see...

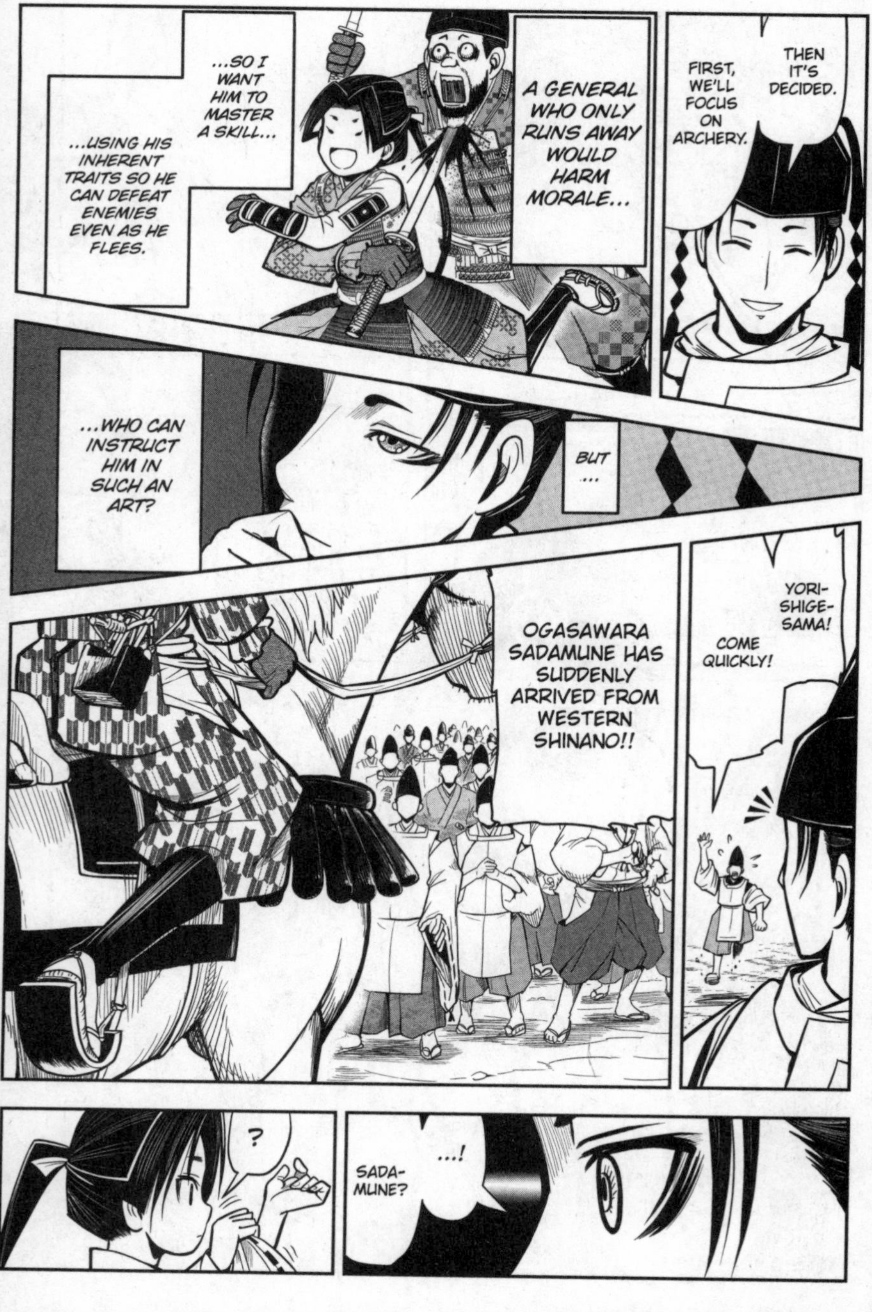
THEN IT'S DECIDED.
FIRST, WE'LL FOCUS ON ARCHERY.
A GENERAL WHO ONLY RUNS AWAY WOULD HARM MORALE...
...SO I WANT HIM TO MASTER A SKILL...
...USING HIS INHERENT TRAITS SO HE CAN DEFEAT ENEMIES EVEN AS HE FLEES.
BUT ...
...WHO CAN INSTRUCT HIM IN SUCH AN ART?
YORI-SHIGE-SAMA!
COME QUICKLY!
OGASAWARA SADAMUNE HAS SUDDENLY ARRIVED FROM WESTERN SHINANO!!
...!
SADA-MUNE?
?

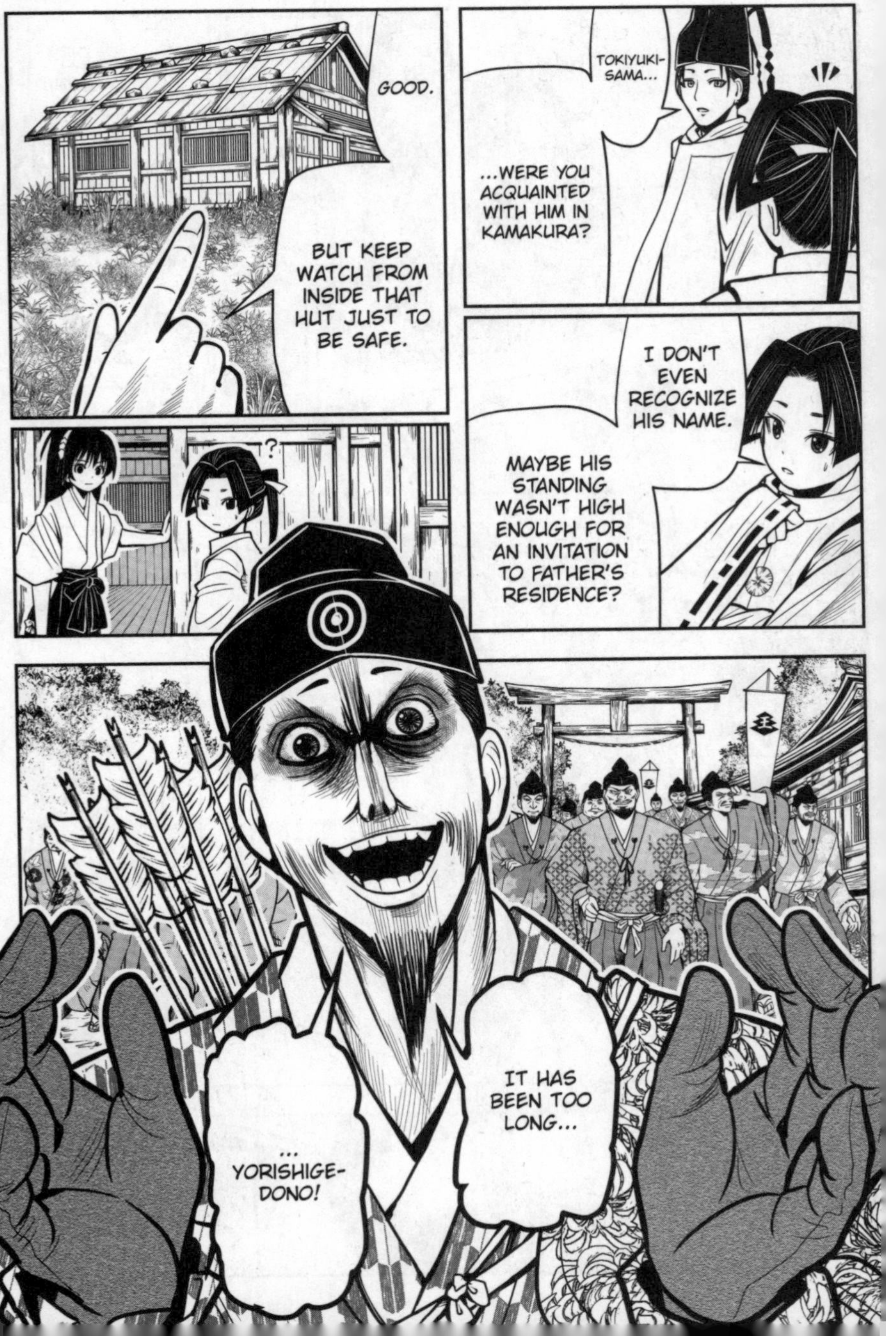
TOKIYUKI-SAMA...
...WERE YOU ACQUAINTED WITH HIM IN KAMAKURA?
GOOD.
BUT KEEP WATCH FROM INSIDE THAT HUT JUST TO BE SAFE.
I DON'T EVEN RECOGNIZE HIS NAME.
MAYBE HIS STANDING WASN'T HIGH ENOUGH FOR AN INVITATION TO FATHER'S RESIDENCE?
?
IT HAS BEEN TOO LONG...
... YORISHIGE-DONO!

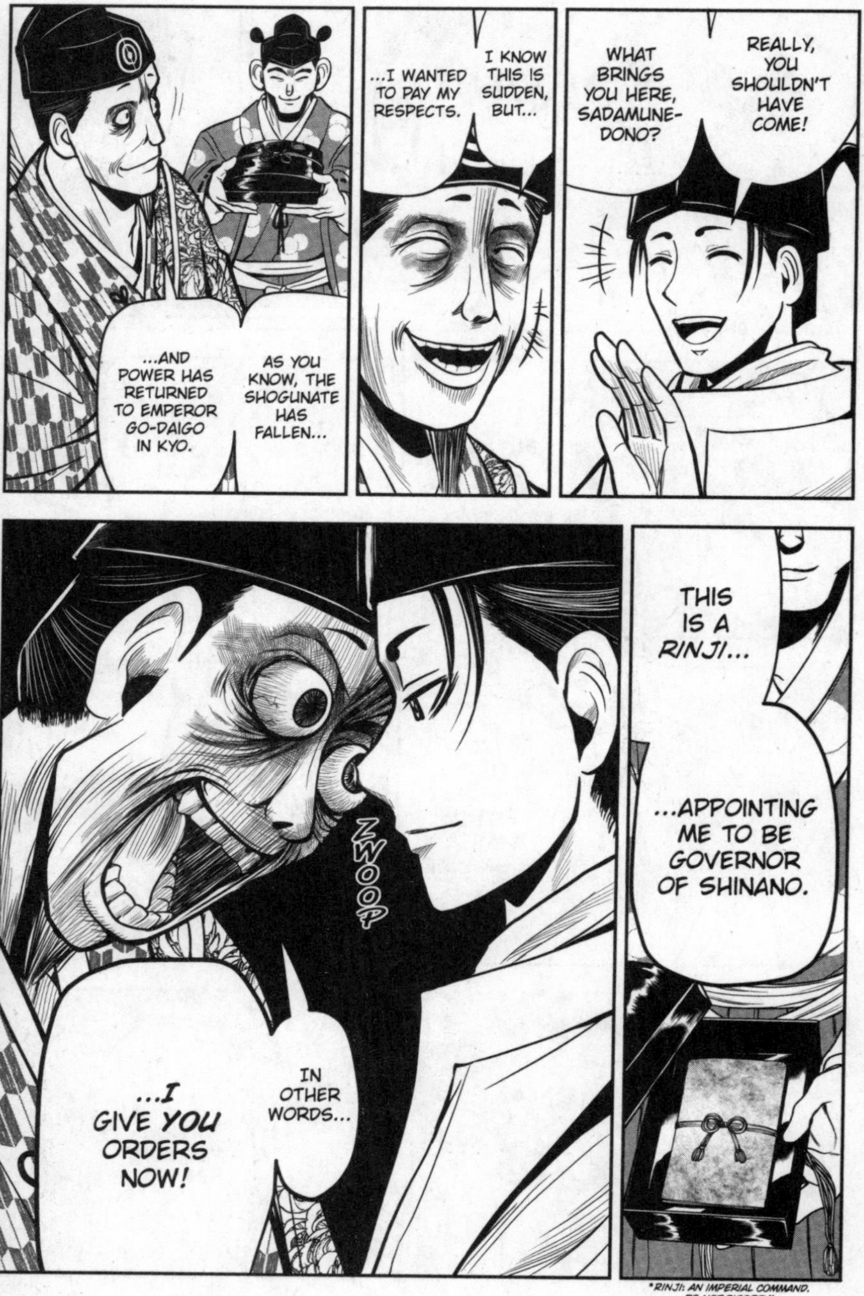
REALLY, YOU SHOULDN'T HAVE COME!
WHAT BRINGS YOU HERE, SADAMUNE-DONO?
I KNOW THIS IS SUDDEN, BUT...
...I WANTED TO PAY MY RESPECTS.
AS YOU KNOW, THE SHOGUNATE HAS FALLEN...
...AND POWER HAS RETURNED TO EMPEROR GO-DAIGO IN KYO.
THIS IS A *RINJI*...
...APPOINTING ME TO BE GOVERNOR OF SHINANO.
ZWOOP
IN OTHER WORDS...
...*I* GIVE *YOU* ORDERS NOW!

RINJI: AN IMPERIAL COMMAND. DO NOT DISOBEY!

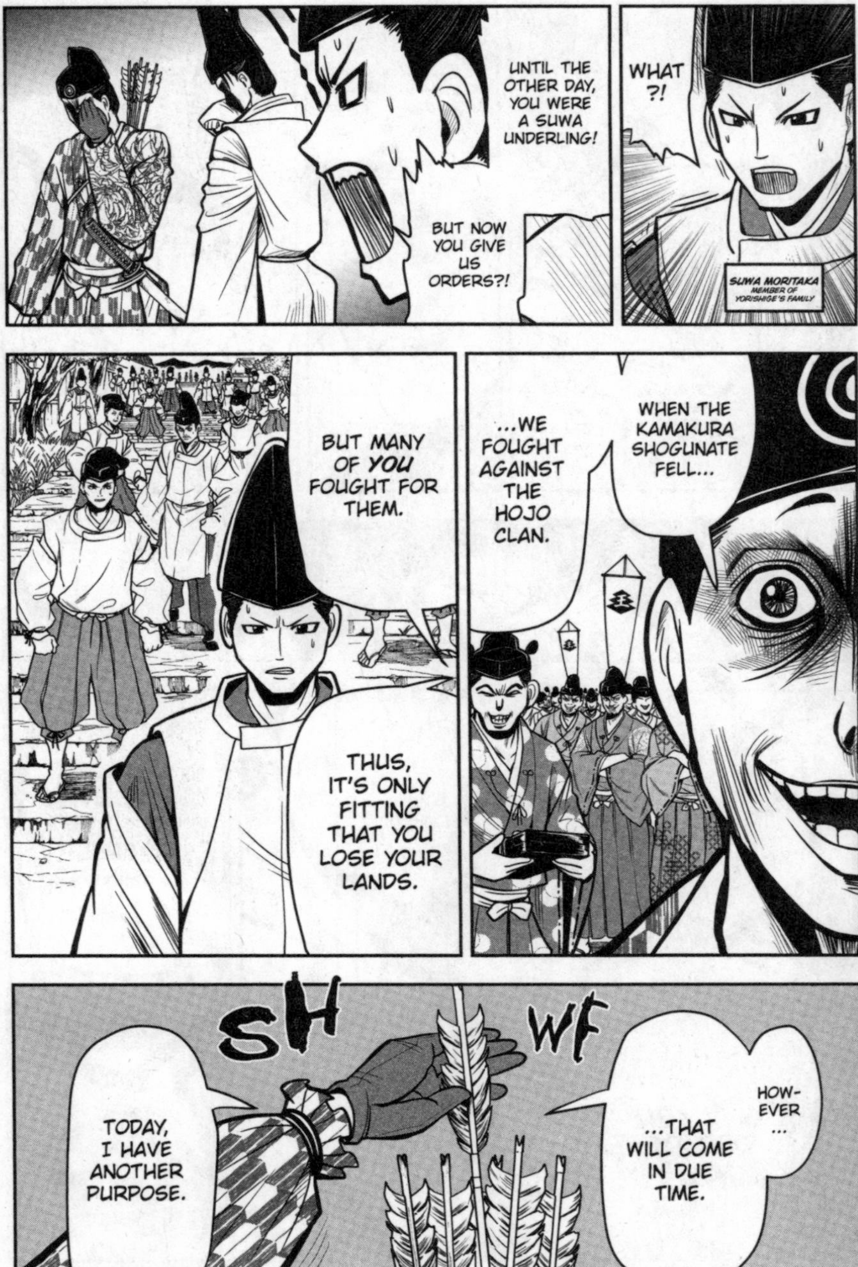
WHAT ?!
SUWA MORITAKA MEMBER OF YORISHIGE'S FAMILY
UNTIL THE OTHER DAY, YOU WERE A SUWA UNDERLING!
BUT NOW YOU GIVE US ORDERS?!
WHEN THE KAMAKURA SHOGUNATE FELL...
...WE FOUGHT AGAINST THE HOJO CLAN.
BUT MANY OF YOU FOUGHT FOR THEM.
THUS, IT'S ONLY FITTING THAT YOU LOSE YOUR LANDS.
HOW-EVER ...
...THAT WILL COME IN DUE TIME.
SH WF
TODAY, I HAVE ANOTHER PURPOSE.

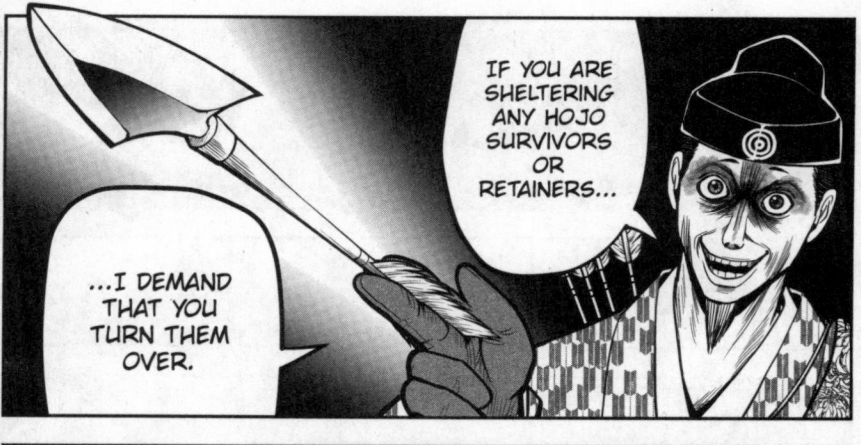

IF YOU ARE SHELTERING ANY HOJO SURVIVORS OR RETAINERS...
...I DEMAND THAT YOU TURN THEM OVER.
!!
ME? SHELTER FUGITIVES ?
I CANNOT GIVE YOU WHAT I HAVEN'T EVEN SEEN!
OH...
...YOU HAVEN'T SEEN ANY, EH?
TH
MP
HMM...

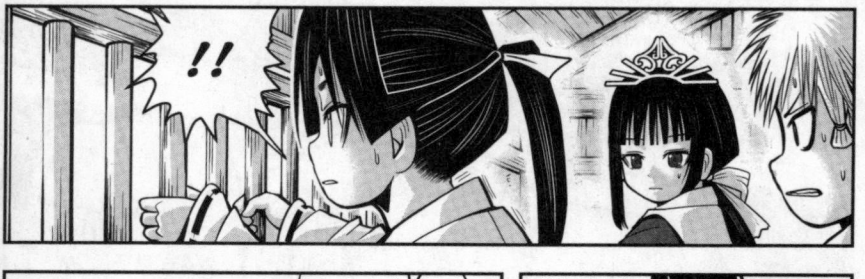

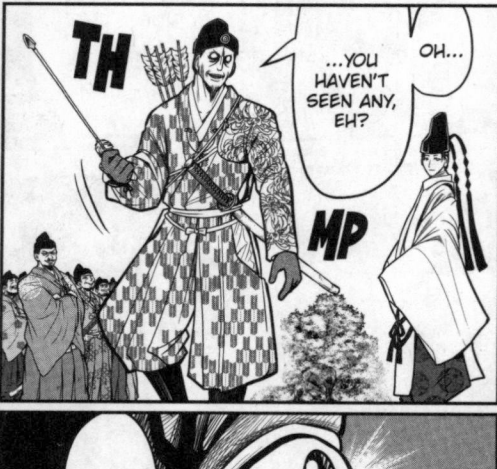

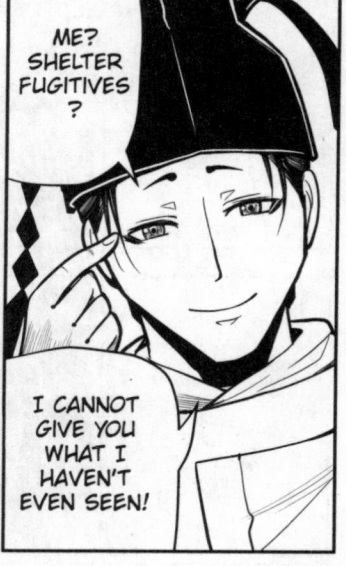

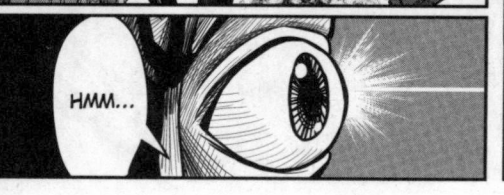

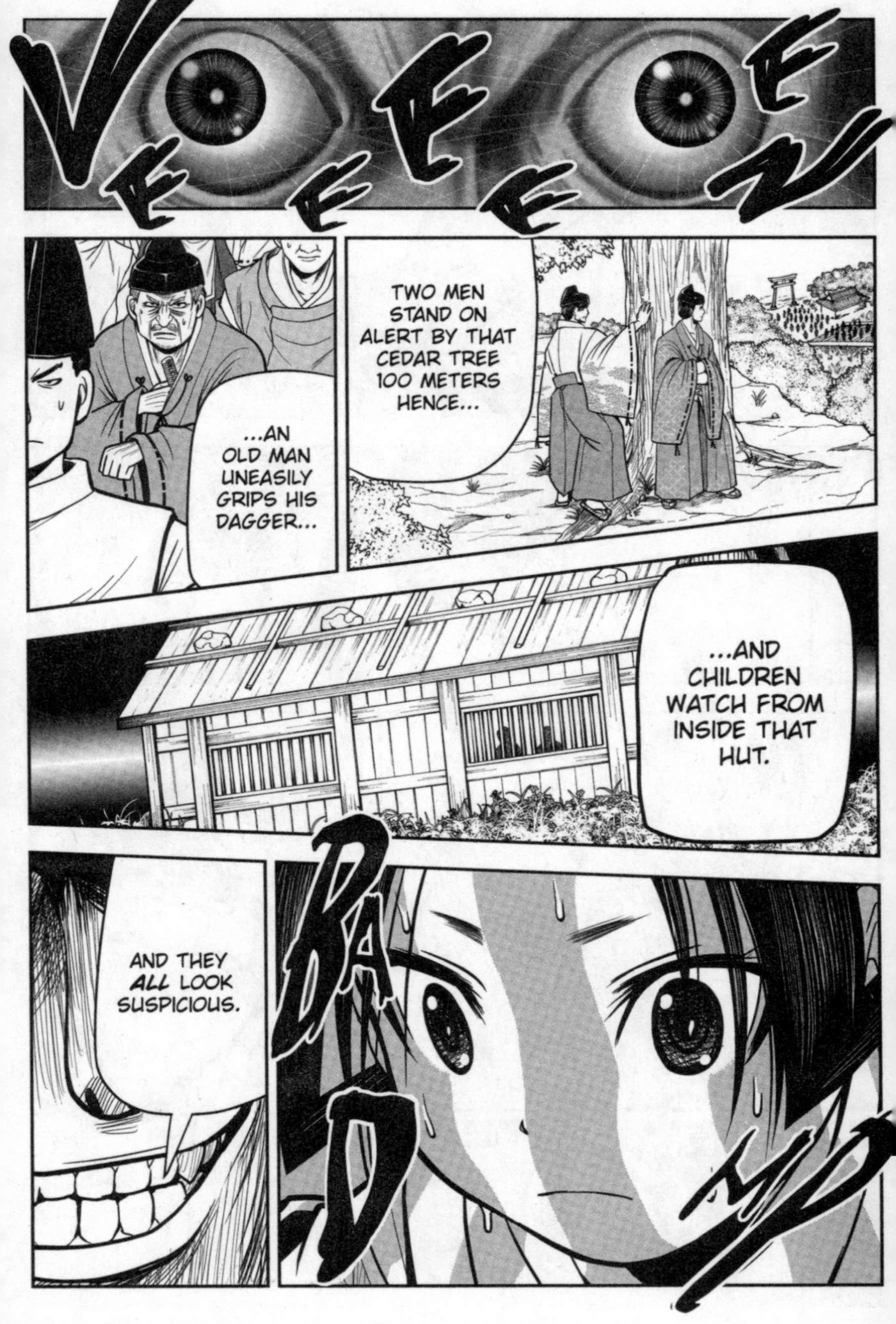
TWO MEN STAND ON ALERT BY THAT CEDAR TREE 100 METERS HENCE...
...AN OLD MAN UNEASILY GRIPS HIS DAGGER...
...AND CHILDREN WATCH FROM INSIDE THAT HUT.
AND THEY ALL LOOK SUSPICIOUS.

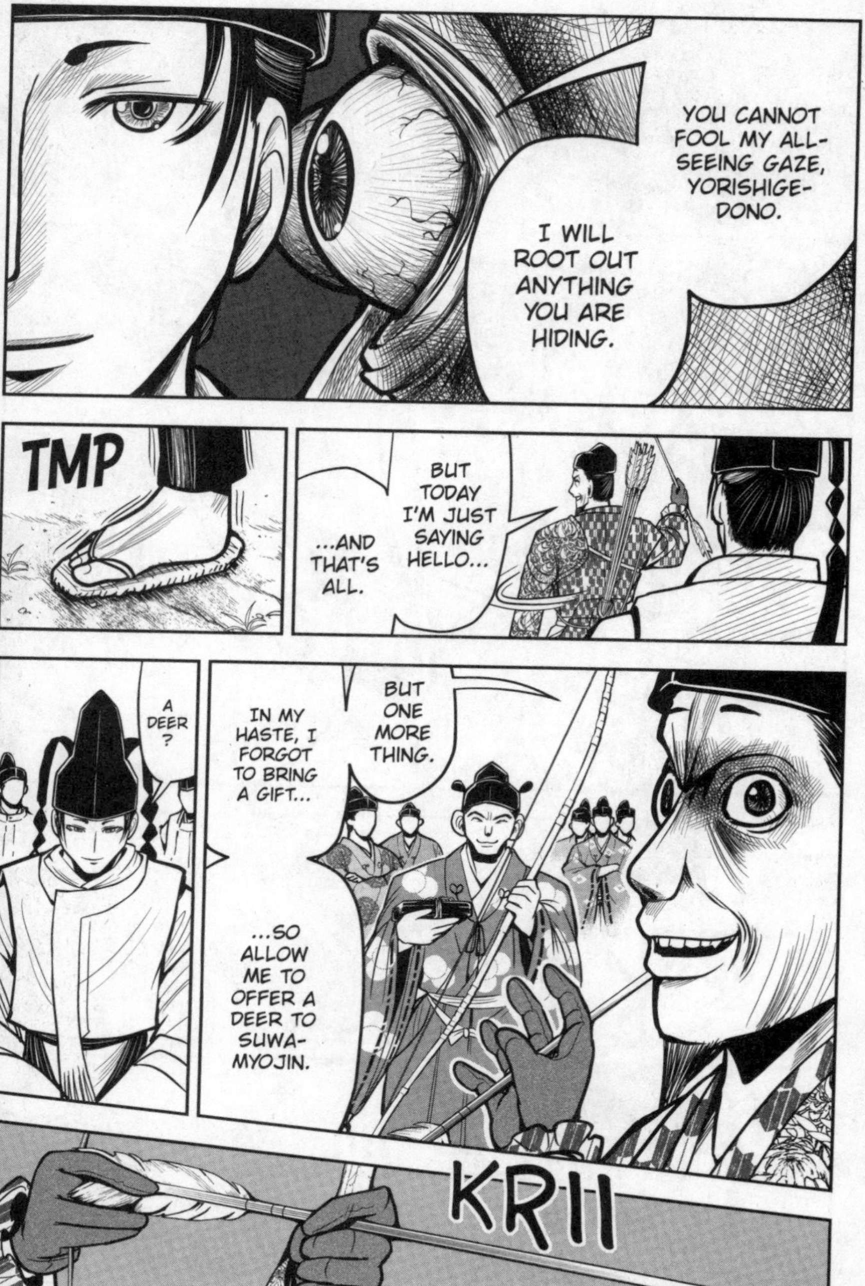
YOU CANNOT FOOL MY ALL-SEEING GAZE, YORISHIGE-DONO.
I WILL ROOT OUT ANYTHING YOU ARE HIDING.
BUT TODAY I'M JUST SAYING HELLO...
...AND THAT'S ALL.
TMP
BUT ONE MORE THING.
IN MY HASTE, I FORGOT TO BRING A GIFT...
...SO ALLOW ME TO OFFER A DEER TO SUWA-MYOJIN.
A DEER?
KRII

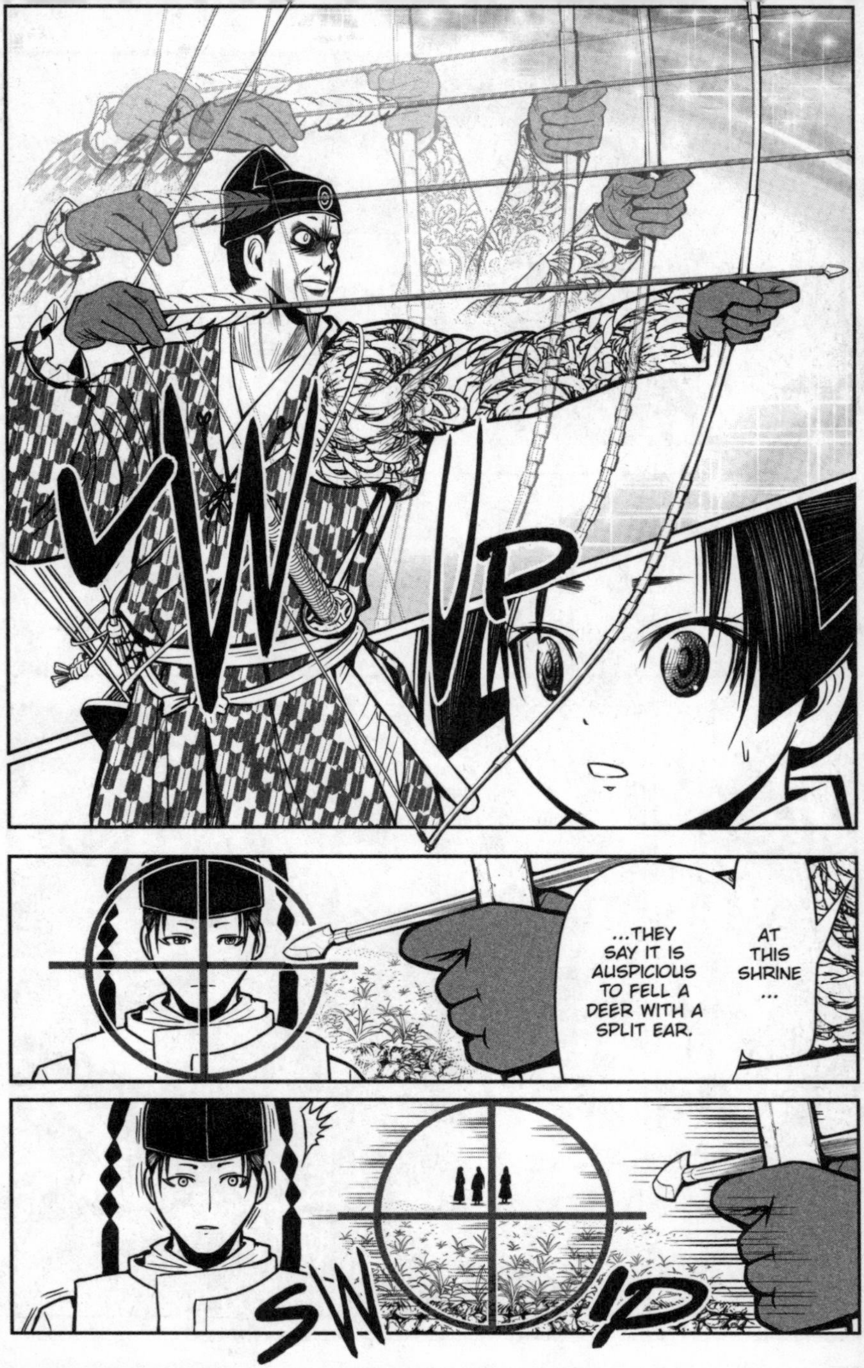
VWIP
AT THIS SHRINE ...
...THEY SAY IT IS AUSPICIOUS TO FELL A DEER WITH A SPLIT EAR.
SWIP

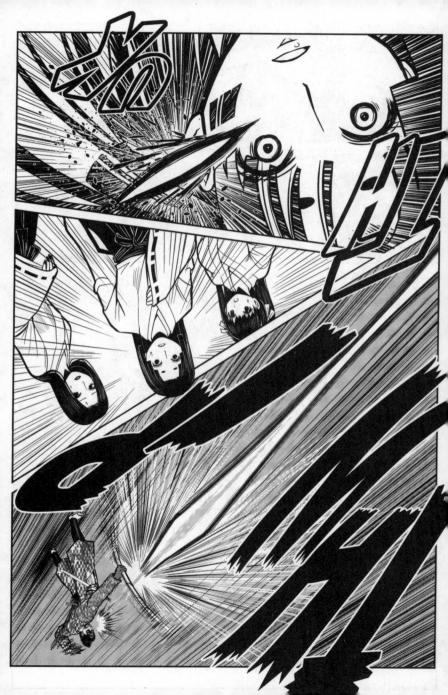

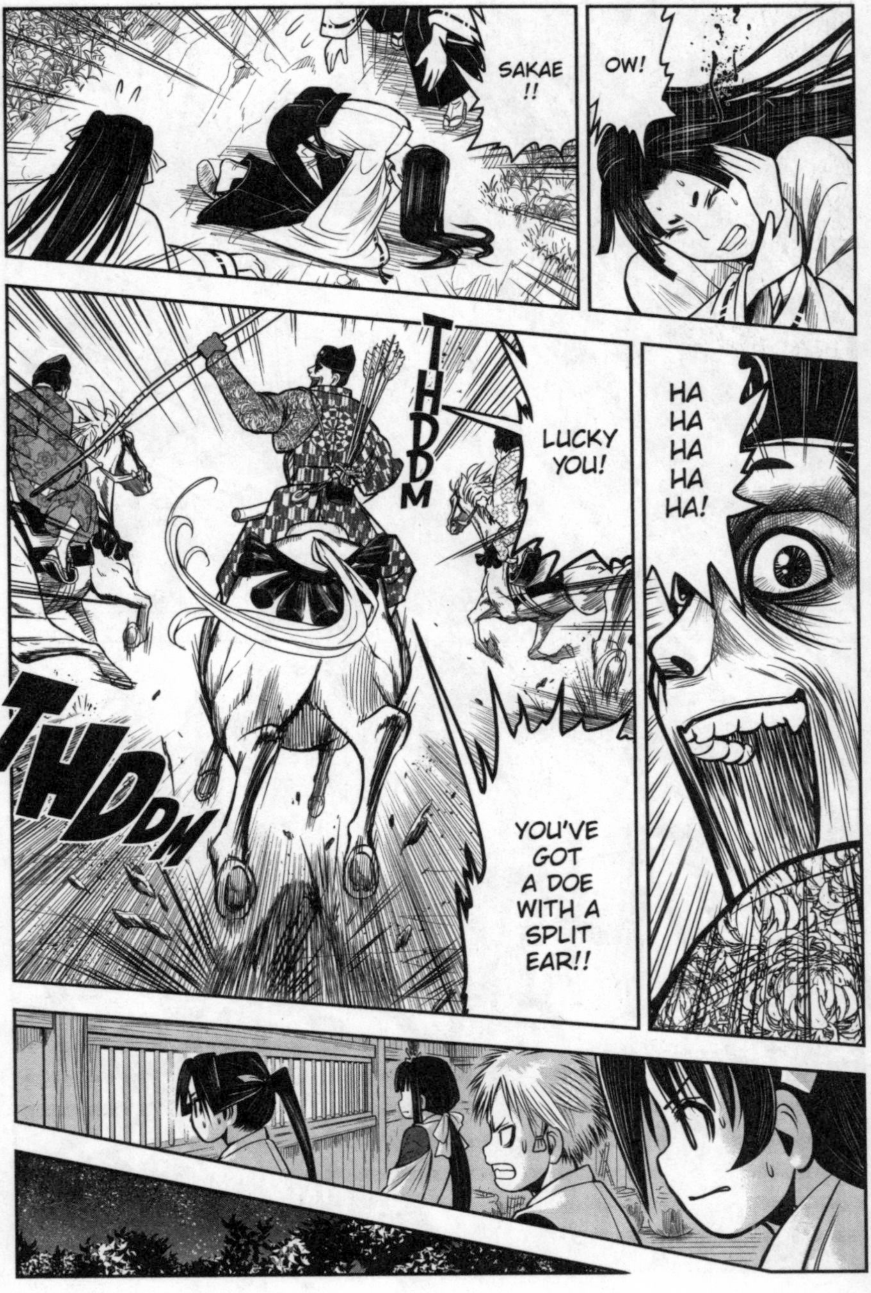
OW!
SAKAE !!
HA HA HA HA HA!
THDDM
LUCKY YOU!
THDDM
YOU'VE GOT A DOE WITH A SPLIT EAR!!

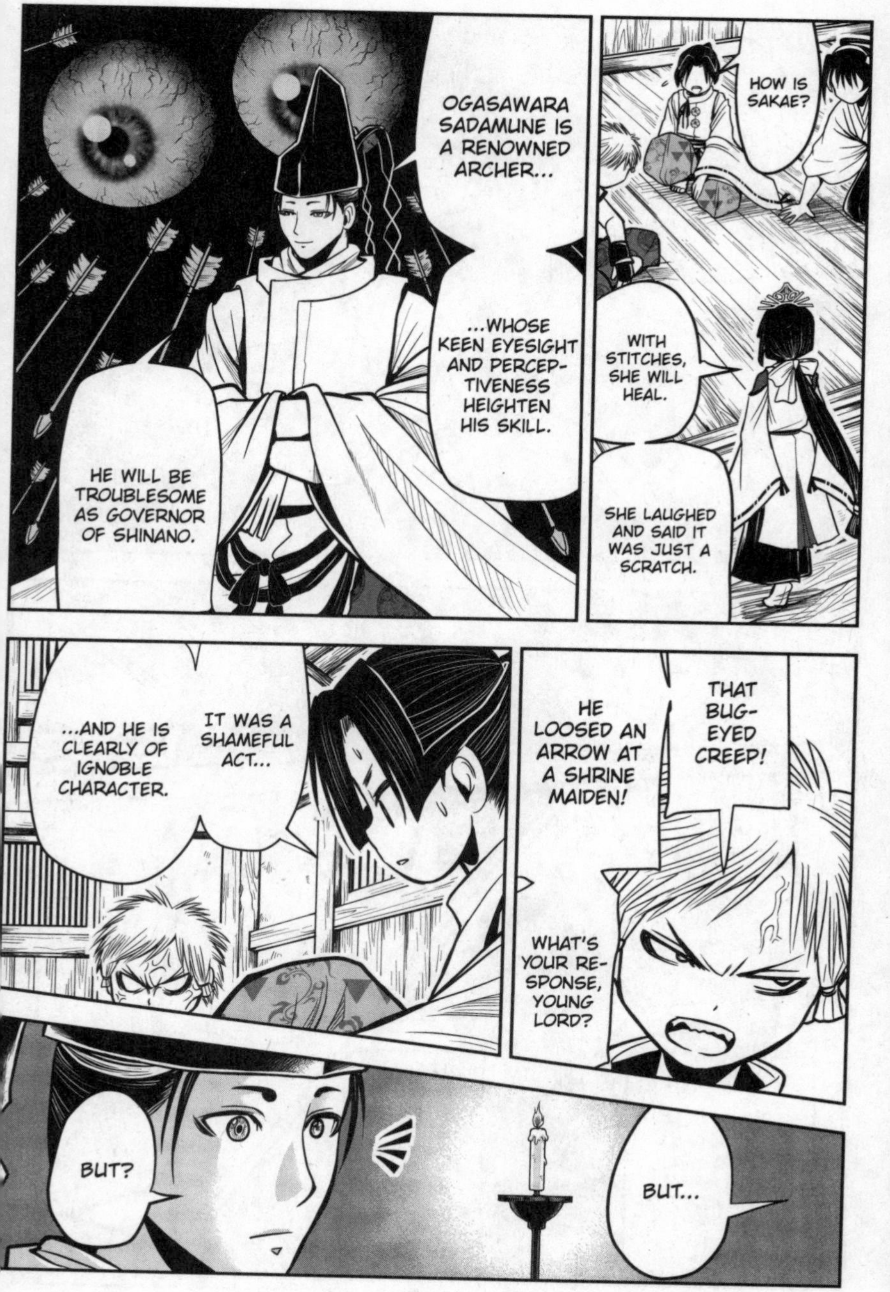
HOW IS SAKAE?
WITH STITCHES, SHE WILL HEAL.
SHE LAUGHED AND SAID IT WAS JUST A SCRATCH.
OGASAWARA SADAMUNE IS A RENOWNED ARCHER...
...WHOSE KEEN EYESIGHT AND PERCEP-TIVENESS HEIGHTEN HIS SKILL.
HE WILL BE TROUBLESOME AS GOVERNOR OF SHINANO.
THAT BUG-EYED CREEP!
HE LOOSED AN ARROW AT A SHRINE MAIDEN!
WHAT'S YOUR RE-SPONSE, YOUNG LORD?
IT WAS A SHAMEFUL ACT...
...AND HE IS CLEARLY OF IGNOBLE CHARACTER.
BUT...
BUT?

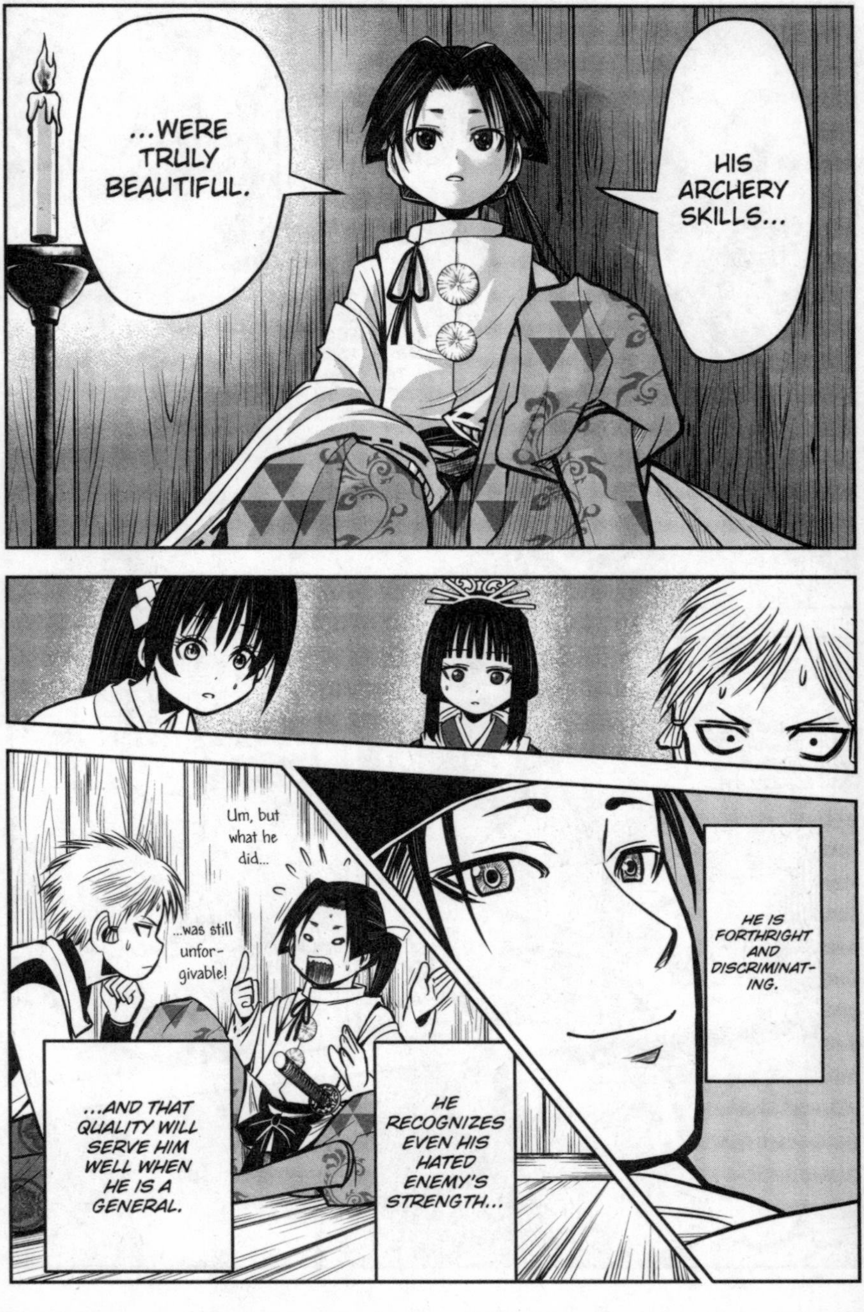
HIS ARCHERY SKILLS...
...WERE TRULY BEAUTIFUL.
HE IS FORTHRIGHT AND DISCRIMINAT-ING.
HE RECOGNIZES EVEN HIS HATED ENEMY'S STRENGTH...
...AND THAT QUALITY WILL SERVE HIM WELL WHEN HE IS A GENERAL.
Um, but what he did...
...was still unfor-givable!

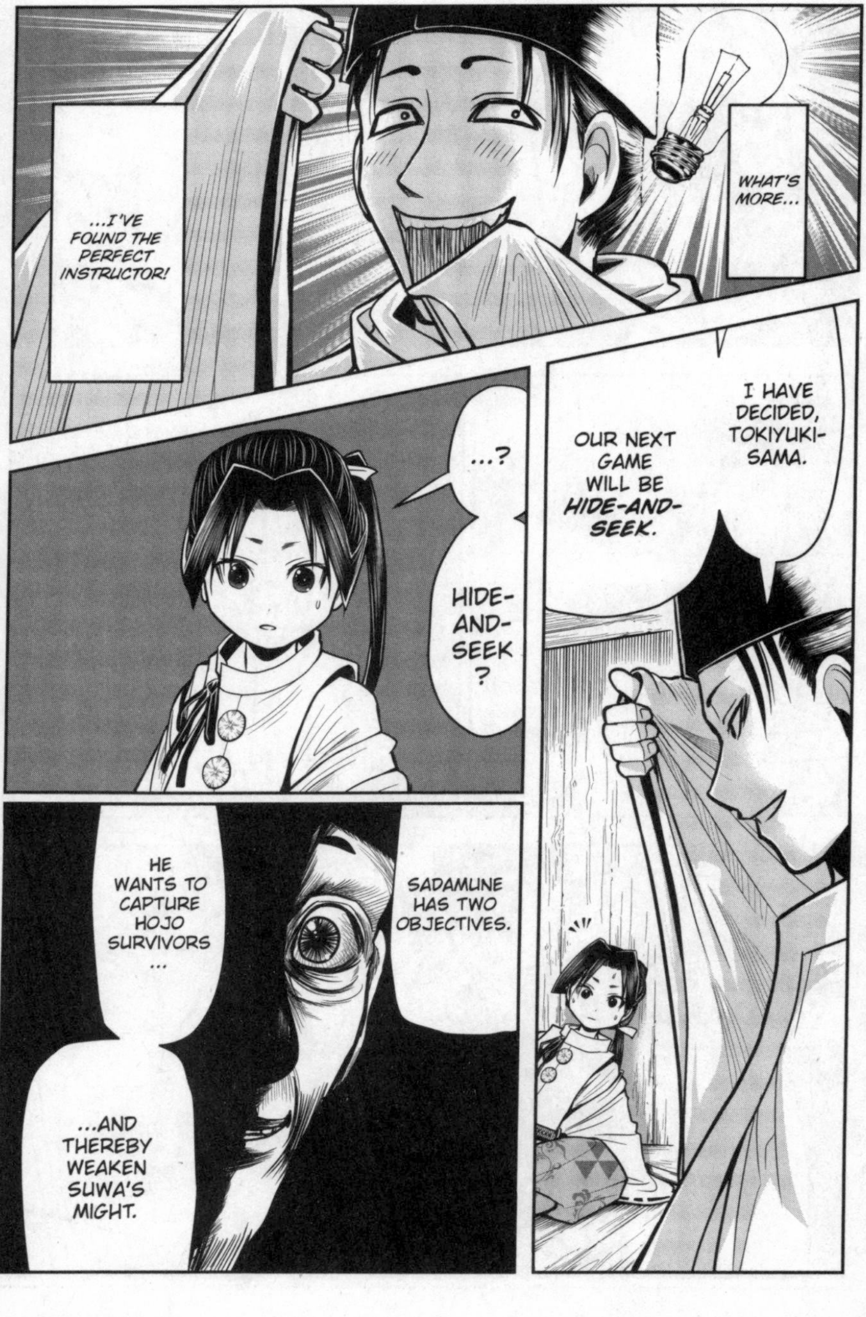
WHAT'S MORE...
...I'VE FOUND THE PERFECT INSTRUCTOR!
I HAVE DECIDED, TOKIYUKI-SAMA.
OUR NEXT GAME WILL BE *HIDE-AND-SEEK.*
...?
HIDE-AND-SEEK?
SADAMUNE HAS TWO OBJECTIVES.
HE WANTS TO CAPTURE HOJO SURVIVORS...
...AND THEREBY WEAKEN SUWA'S MIGHT.

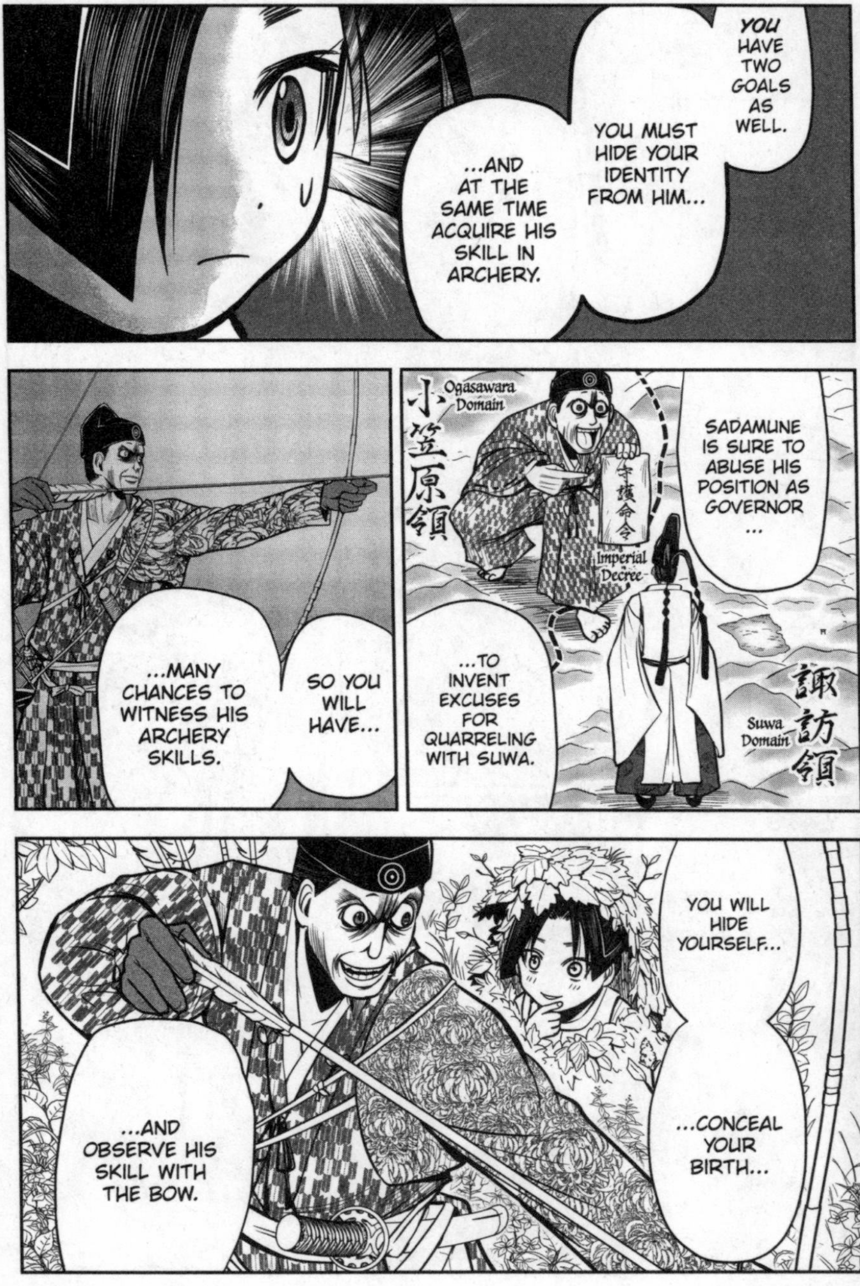
YOU HAVE TWO GOALS AS WELL.
YOU MUST HIDE YOUR IDENTITY FROM HIM...
...AND AT THE SAME TIME ACQUIRE HIS SKILL IN ARCHERY.
SADAMUNE IS SURE TO ABUSE HIS POSITION AS GOVERNOR...
諏訪領
Suwa Domain
小笠原領
Ogasawara Domain
守護命令
Imperial Decree
...TO INVENT EXCUSES FOR QUARRELING WITH SUWA.
SO YOU WILL HAVE...
...MANY CHANCES TO WITNESS HIS ARCHERY SKILLS.
YOU WILL HIDE YOURSELF...
...CONCEAL YOUR BIRTH...
...AND OBSERVE HIS SKILL WITH THE BOW.

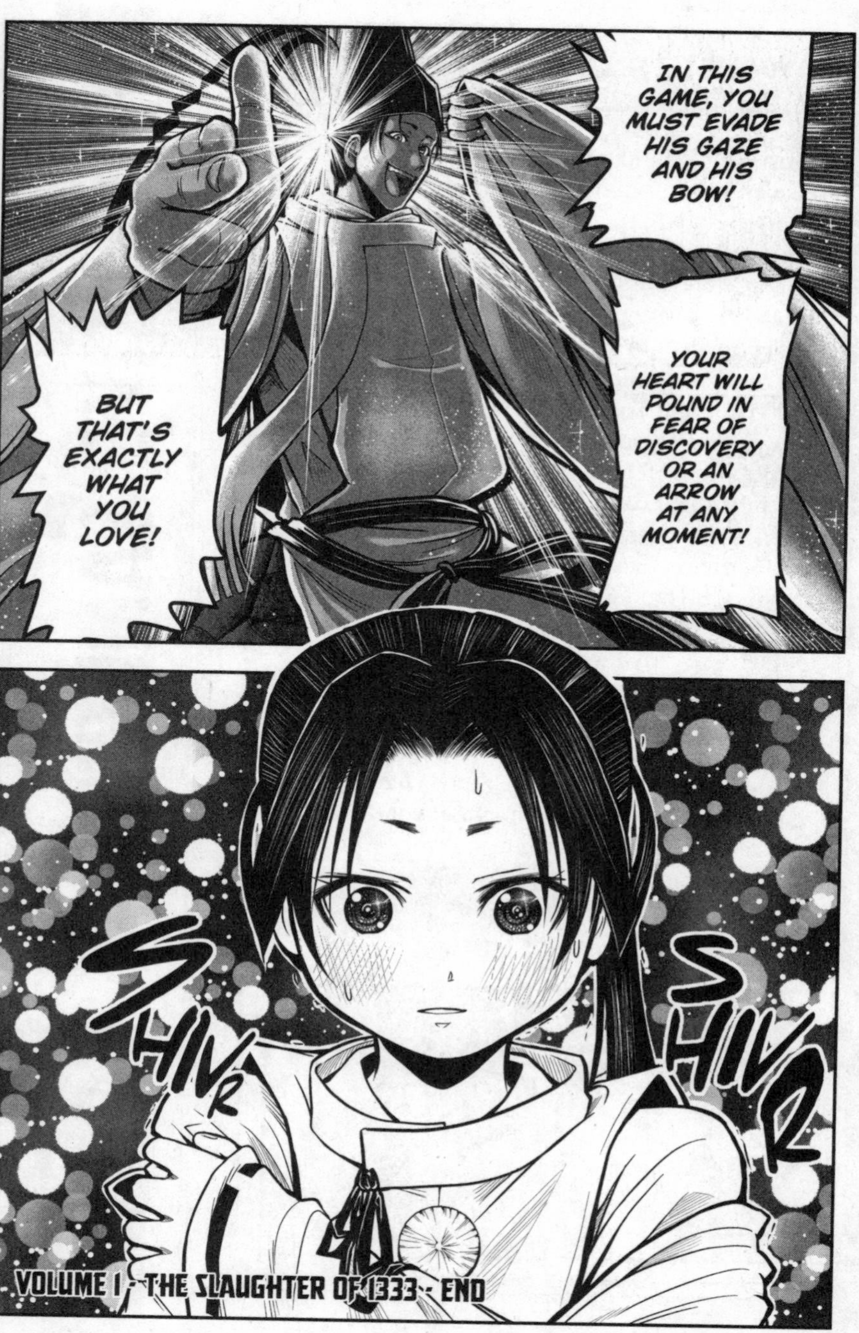
IN THIS GAME, YOU MUST EVADE HIS GAZE AND HIS BOW!
YOUR HEART WILL POUND IN FEAR OF DISCOVERY OR AN ARROW AT ANY MOMENT!
BUT THAT'S EXACTLY WHAT YOU LOVE!
SHIVR
SHIVR
VOLUME 1 - THE SLAUGHTER OF 1333 - END

THE ELUSIVE SAMURAI

INCREASE YOUR ENJOYMENT OF THIS MANGA BY LEARNING THE REAL HISTORY BEHIND IT!!

ANALYSIS
KAZUTO HONGO

HOW DID THE SHOGUNATE ORIGINALLY FORM?

Most people think of the Heian period as a peaceful time without war, but that's completely wrong. At the time, the Kanto region was a rural area ruled by the law of the jungle. Land bosses known as *zaichi ryōshu* ruled land averaging roughly 100 *chō* (100 *ha*, equivalent to the area of 20 Tokyo Domes) in size. The strong ones had over 500 *chō* (500 ha, or 50 Tokyo Domes). They didn't completely possess this land. The Kyoto nobility as well as temples and shrines levied considerable taxes.

Furthermore, they had to protect their own territory, so the land bosses surrounding them wouldn't steal their land (and there were no police)! So they mounted horses and took up arms. That was the birth of the *bushi* warrior class. The bushi looked to Minamoto no Yoritomo as their liege lord, giving rise to the title of *shogun*. The shogun represented their interests and resisted the imperial court. As vassals to the shogun, the bushi were known as *gokenin*, so a land boss was a warrior and a vassal. Thus, the shogunate was government by the shogun and his vassals.

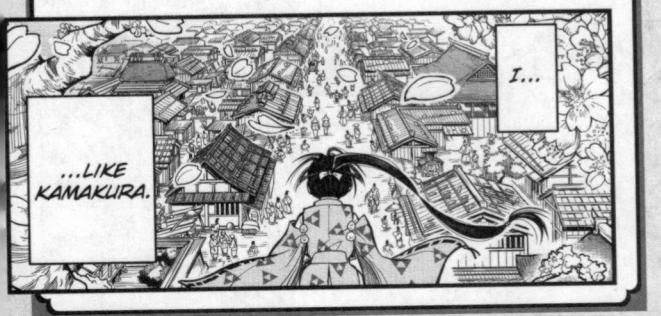

I...
...LIKE KAMAKURA.

*Adapted from material appearing in *Weekly Shonen Jump* issues 10-14

WHAT WERE THE REGENT'S RESPONSIBILITIES?

A distinguishing feature of Japanese history is that the top figures in an organization didn't do any kind of work. As times progressed, however, people like Minamoto no Yoritomo and Tokugawa Ieyasu were at the top working like crazy and creating new organizations and new rules. Thanks to their activities, society stabilized so the people at the top didn't need to do anything, and the common people welcomed this. For example, the 11th shogun, Tokugawa Ienari, was popular even though all he did was father 50 children. The shogun was merely a figurehead. That meant one of his subordinates had to handle military and governmental affairs. In the Kamakura period, that was the regent—a position dominated by members of the Hojo clan. As this situation of the regent being the true top authority continued into the late Kamakura period, the regent position also became merely ceremonial and was simply passed from one Hojo to the next. The main line of the Hojo clan held the reins of the regency, and the post came to be known as the *tokusō*.

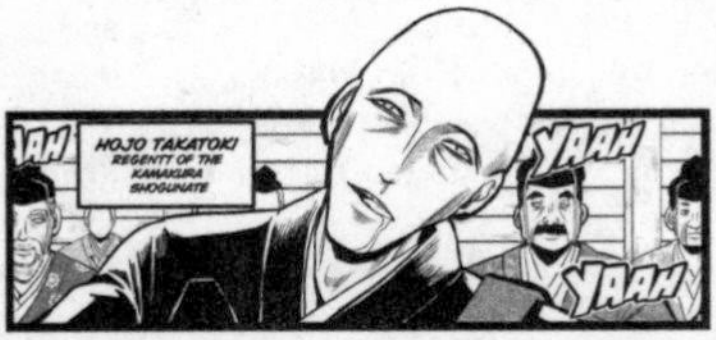
YAAH
YAAH
HOJO TAKATOKI
REGENTT OF THE
KAMAKURA
SHOGUNATE

WHAT KIND OF PERSON 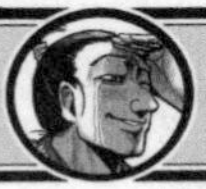 WAS GODAIIN MUNESHIGE?

The family name Godaiin is rare. In Japanese history, it appears only in the late Kamakura period. The main line of the Hojo clan was the *tokusō* family, and the Godaiin clan served the tokusō family as bushi for generations. Muneshige's younger sister became Hojo Takatoki's concubine and gave birth to his eldest son, Kunitoki. That means Muneshige was Kunitoki's uncle. Muneshige was Takatoki's blood relation and trusted vassal, so before Takatoki killed himself, he asked him to help Kunitoki escape.

Muneshige wanted a reward, though, so even though Kunitoki was his lord and nephew, he betrayed him and turned him over to Nitta Yoshisada, who had attacked Kamakura. Kunitoki was a survivor of the tokusō family, so they beheaded the poor boy. But even his enemy Nitta was disgusted by Muneshige's deed, so he scorned and refused to reward him. Scholars believe that what actually happened is that Muneshige was shunned by everyone around him and eventually starved to death.

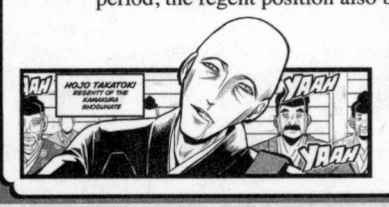

TOKIYUKI 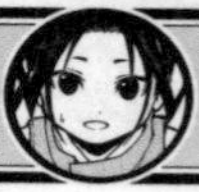 AND KUNITOKI 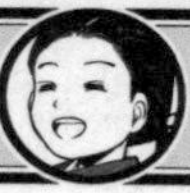

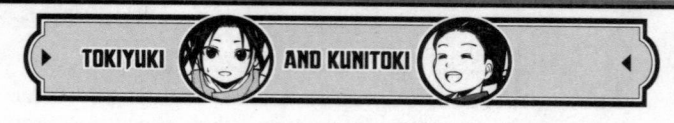

Hojo Takatoki's legal wife was from the Adachi clan. His concubine was Muneshige's younger sister. Tokiyuki was the child of his legal wife, and Kunitoki was the child of his concubine. The *Taiheiki*, a historical record from that time, refers to Kunitoki as the son and heir, but this may be a mistake. That's because society back then valued the child of a woman in a respectable family more. So while Tokiyuki may have been the younger brother, he should have been the heir.

The Adachis were among the most influential vassals of the shogunate and became as big as the Hojos. When Minamoto no Yoritomo, founder of the Kamakura shogunate, was living as an outlaw, the only bushi serving Yoritomo as a vassal was Adachi Morinaga.

Yoritomo wrote a love letter to a beautiful and renowned daughter of the Hojo clan and sent Morinaga to deliver it. Morinaga thought, "This is for the younger daughter of the Hojo, but the elder daughter is of better character and more appropriate to be Yoritomo-sama's wife," and gave the letter to the elder daughter. The elder sister was, of course, Hojo Masako. That led to the Adachi clan marrying its daughters into the Hojo clan, which was the tokusō family. The tokusō family continued as in the time line below. Tokiyori, Sadatoki, and Takatoki's mothers were all from the Adachi clan.

BUSHIDO = THE WAY OF THE WARRIOR

The Kamakura bushi obeyed a code of ethics known as " the way of the warrior." For example, they wouldn't lie, wouldn't engage in cowardly behavior, and would value their parents, siblings, and other family members. They would also value their allies and would place more importance on honor than wealth. Above all, they would not betray their lord. These practices became the basis for Bushido in later times.

For example, consider this story from the battle of Hoji in 1247, when Hojo Tokiyori fought and defeated Miura Yasumura, the foremost bushi in Kanagawa and a member of the Miura clan.

Mori Suemitsu ruled the area around what is now Moridai in Atsugi City, Kanagawa Prefecture.

- TOKIYORI — 5TH SHOGUN
- TOKIMUNE — 8TH SHOGUN
- SADATOKI — 9TH SHOGUN
- TAKATOKI — 14TH SHOGUN

Judging from this, since Tokiyuki's mother was from the Adachi family, it is likely that he was the rightful heir.

His father was Oe Hiromoto, who supported Minamoto no Yoritomo as director of the Mandokoro administration (the top position in governmental and financial affairs). Hiromoto was a low-ranking noble who was recruited and brought to Kamakura. That means Suemitsu wasn't born a bushi. He could have become a bureaucrat, yet he chose to become a bushi and tried to live an exceptional life as a warrior.

Suemitsu realized the Miura clan could not overcome the Hojo clan, so he intended to leave his house to join the Hojo camp. But then his wife asked him to help her older brother. That's right—Suemitsu's wife was the younger sister of Miura Yasumura.

At his wife's words, Suemitsu changed his mind. He was a bushi, so he had to value his family, and honor outweighed life. He knew he would lose, but he fought alongside the Miura clan and thus he died. In addition to the loss of Suemitsu, the Mori clan lost its land in Kanagawa Prefecture. Nonetheless, a young child survived and obtained new land in Hiroshima. One of that child's descendants was the warlord Mori Motonari, whose descendants ruled the Chōshū Domain during the Tokugawa shogunate.

In those times, everyone considered a man like Godaiin Muneshige, who didn't value his family and betrayed his lord, to be a scoundrel.

WAS CHANGING NAMES COMMON AT THAT TIME?

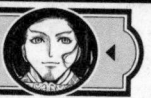

Kamakura bushi did not receive much education, so most couldn't read or write kanji characters. For that reason, not many were interested in choosing uncommon names. That's why a lot of people from that time have similar names. Furthermore, there was something called *tōriji*, which was a character that many people in the same clan would share. For the Hojo clan, it was 時 (toki). For the Ashikaga clan, it was 氏 (uji). And for the Chiba clan, the strongest clan on the Boso Peninsula, it was 胤 (tane).

Sometimes, a lord would bestow a character from his name upon a vassal. This was a great honor, so recipients would express their gratefulness for the blessing

YOU MAY NOW...
...WRITE YOUR NAME USING THE KANJI FOR *EXALTED*.
I AM HONORED, YOUR HIGHNESS.

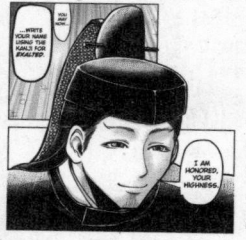

and change their name. When Ashikaga Takauji came of age, he received the character 高 (taka) from Takatoki of the Hojo main line and combined it with the traditional Ashikaga character to form the name 高氏 (Takauji). After toppling the Kamakura shogunate, he received the character 尊 (taka) from Takaharu, which was Emperor Go-Daigo's former name, thereby becoming 尊氏 (Takauji). He may be the only person to ever receive a character from the emperor.

WHAT WAS THE IMPERIAL COURT LIKE BACK THEN?

The imperial court had been around for a long time, but it began to weaken with the establishment of the Kamakura shogunate. During the Jōkyū War in 1221, former emperor Go-Toba raised an army to destroy the Kamakura shogunate, but he lost and was exiled to the Oki Islands. The shogunate then stripped the imperial court of its military capacity. While the shogunate was unmatched in warfare, it was inexperienced in administration and cultural matters. It also didn't have a good understanding of economics and had a lot to learn about government from the imperial court. So the two coexisted, with the shogunate in the east and the imperial court in the west. At this time, the imperial court realized it could not beat the shogunate militarily, so it polished its expertise in administrative and judicial affairs with the emperor at the forefront. That's why the emperors of the late Kamakura period include many notable rulers. Such was the state of things when Emperor Go-Daigo rose to power.

HOW TALL WERE JAPANESE PEOPLE?

Today, the average height of Japanese men is about 170 centimeters. What about long ago? From the study of physical remains, we know that people during the Kofun period were relatively tall, with an average male height of 163 centimeters. However, the numbers drop from then on. At the beginning of the Heian period, it was 161 centimeters, and toward the end it was 157 centimeters. In the Edo period, it was 155 centimeters. Then, the trend reversed in the Meiji period and has continued that way to this day.

Why is that? Researchers believe it is connected to intake of animal proteins. Buddhism came to Japan in the sixth century CE, and according to its teachings, the killing of living things is a sin and therefore forbidden. This idea was called *sasshō kindan*. For that reason, eating meat became taboo in Japan (although eating birds was allowed). And since Japanese uses the same kanji character to count rabbits as it does birds, they treated them like birds. However, they didn't eat wild boar, deer, cows, horses, and dogs. Thus, people didn't get much protein and decreased in height.

That all makes sense, but something doesn't add up. For one thing, when people get hungry, they'll eat anything, right? For example, irregular weather might result in a poor rice harvest. During the Edo period, many people died of starvation. In such hard times, there are even stories of cannibalism, so it's hard to imagine people wouldn't eat animals. We could explain an exception to the rule by making a distinction between normal times and times of emergency. But weren't bushi and hunting inseparable? Yes, they were. And this presents a problem.

WHAT WERE *BUSHI* [WARRIORS]?

Bushi arose in the Heian period, and they had to protect their lives and their property. That's why they armed themselves. That's what bushi were. Does that mean you could become a bushi just by putting on armor and donning a helmet? It wasn't that easy. You couldn't become a bushi without participating in a big hunt.

At the time, the officials who governed the provinces (today's prefectures) were *kokushi* (governors) who came from Kyoto (the top kokushi was like a prefectural governor today). They held four-year terms. Once during their tenure, the kokushi had to offer thanks to the local god, so they held a grand hunt. The kokushi hosted what was called an *ōgari* (great hunt), and those allowed to participate in this ceremony were bushi. Thus, bushi needed to be able to hunt. They had to be able to ride horses and wield a bow. Furthermore, they had to offer the game they felled during a hunt—wild boar and deer—to the gods.

This contributed to the formation of the bushi class. Bushi had to be able to hold hunts on their own land, so they polished their hunting skills—which means they were hunting wild boar and deer. But wouldn't they eat what they'd hunted? Would they just throw it away and let it rot? What a waste! So you'd think they ate it, right? The only seasoning would be salt, so they'd grill or boil it and eat it with salt. That would be delicious in a different way from fish. So wouldn't they go hunting about once a month, kill some boar or deer, salt the meat, and throw it on the dinner table? They didn't do it a lot, mind you... because they weren't very tall, remember? Yet there's no documentation attesting to meat on the dinner tables of the bushi, so there's no record of meat being a staple food. Why is that? Because they strictly obeyed the prohibition against taking life? That remains a mystery. We simply don't have an answer.

THE UNUSUAL PERSONALITY OF SUWA'S GOD

Many remains from the Jōmon period exist in the Suwa region. It has Lake Suwa and abundant forests, so there's plenty of fresh drinking water and fuel for starting fires. People have settled there for centuries. That's what Suwa was like. There'll be another occasion to explain Suwa Grand Shrine later, so I won't go into detail now, but the god of Suwa Grand Shrine and this region, where signs of a hunting culture remain, exhibited a trait unseen elsewhere. He received offerings of meat.

Long ago, the distinction between Buddhas and kami (Shinto gods) was unclear, so the Buddhist prohibition of killing also influenced shrines. People were reluctant to kill on shrine grounds. Thus, while they offered fish to the gods as creatures of the sea, they did not include wild boars and deer among their offerings of things from the mountain. In a special practice, the god of Suwa did recognize such sacrifices, however.

In light of that, it makes sense for Tokiyuki to fight the giant boar named Botan. When they successfully defeated Botan, maybe they all enjoyed wild boar hot pot. Yorishige is a priest, but now you know why he smacks his lips at wild boar meat. Let's eat!

HOW POWERFUL WAS THE *SHUGO* (GOVERNOR)?

Until recently, textbooks taught that the Kamakura shogunate began in 1192 with the appointment of Minamoto no Yoritomo as shogun. Scholars now think that the shogunate began with the placement of the *shugo* and *jitō* (manor lords) in 1185, so textbooks are changing. That's how important it was that each province had its own shugo.

At first, the shugo was merely a government official. He prosecuted serious crimes such as murder and enforced the practice of *ōbanyaku* (where the bushi take turns going to Kyoto to defend the emperor). Thus, the shugo was a sort of leader of the bushi, like a big brother. However, the shugo gradually came to hold the bushi in his service. He became the boss. That process resulted in the feudal-lord-like status of the shugo daimyo in the Muromachi period. This manga occurs during the transition of shugo from big brother to boss, perhaps with a slight emphasis on the latter.

WERE *RINJI* (IMPERIAL COMMANDS) IMPORTANT?

There's a Japanese expression, "The emperor's words are like sweat," that means that what the emperor says is incredibly important, so it cannot be undone later, just as sweat cannot be taken back. The emperor's words are called *ringen*, and written commands are called *rinji*. The written commands of former emperors are called *inzen*.

Official written commands of the imperial court were called *daijō kanpu*, but drafting one took some effort. So, in the Heian period, they issued something called *kansenji* instead. Drafting this document required the involvement of the emperor, one high-ranking noble, two mid-ranking nobles, and one low-ranking noble. But even that was a hassle. That's when rinji and inzen showed up. If the emperor held the real power, he issued a rinji. In the case of a former emperor, he issued an inzen. The emperor (or former emperor) could easily draft one of these with one mid-ranking noble. Rinji and inzen conveyed the will of the imperial court and were incredibly important documents. Emperor Go-Daigo insisted that rinji were all-powerful and were of the utmost importance. Bushi wore rinji in pouches hanging around their necks. Illustrations show bushi keeping them on their person at all times.

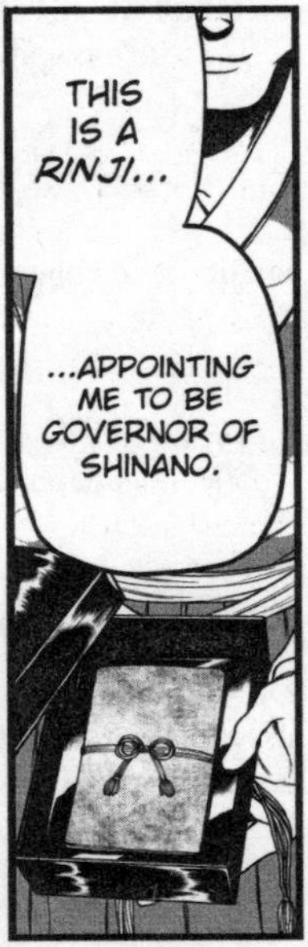
THIS IS A *RINJI*...
...APPOINTING ME TO BE GOVERNOR OF SHINANO.

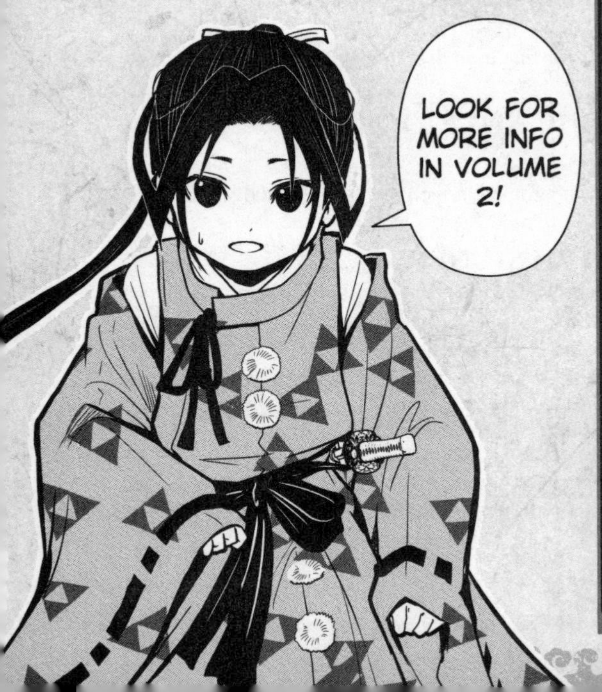
LOOK FOR MORE INFO IN VOLUME 2!

SPECIAL THANKS

I borrow a lot of people's talents for *The Elusive Samurai*.

PRODUCTION STAFF

Tei Ashigaki

Yuuki Imada

*His series *MINI4KING* begins in *CoroCoro Comic*
in August 2021!

Daisuke Enoshima

Sakuju Koizumi

Wahare Koyoi

They help me create the art. They're my Kamakura warriors
who're almighty in drawing what I want.

EDITOR

Riki Azuma

He's an editor for *Weekly Shonen Jump*. He's from a high-class upbringing,
so he's got a taste for fine food despite being so young.

GRAPHIC NOVEL EDITOR

Satoshi Watanabe

He handles stuff related to the graphic novel, and he's got really thin legs.

DESIGNER

Yuki Matsumoto (Banana Grove Studio)

She's in charge of the logo and design for the graphic novel.
She's a licensed art curator.

JAPANESE-STYLE ARTIST

Takafumi Asakura

I asked him to take care of the background and patterns for the graphic novel cover.
He has so much skill and dignity that it's hard to believe we're the same age.

CALLIGRAPHY
Kamari Maeda
I ask him to letter the scenes introducing the demons.
A person of many talents, he's got a lot of energy and excellent presentation skills.

ADVISER AND ARTICLE WRITER
Kazuto Hongo
I call upon him to supervise the historical details in the series and to write the pages
of historical analysis. Anything that departs from history is the author's own creation
or personal interpretation.

PERSONAL SYMBOL DESIGNER
Marika Matsumoto (& CAT)
She designs patterns for some of the characters' kimonos.
She's very service oriented, so she proposes numerous patterns.

WATER AND INK ARTIST
Tokuro Kitamura
He does the water and ink art in the manga. I think it would
be great if he contributed his wonderful work to creators in various genres.

3D CG MODELING
Melta Kabushiki Gaisha
They do 3D modeling for things like armor, helmets, and swords that aren't for sale
commercially. The biggest element for this time period, about which there aren't
many manga, is armor. And that's a real pain, so I'm thankful to them and their
digital-age skills for solving that problem.

SUWA RESEARCH COOPERATION
Michiho Ishino
She helped me with research about Suwa. She's had all kinds of various experiences
and has a lot of curiousity, so she knows everything, not just about Suwa.

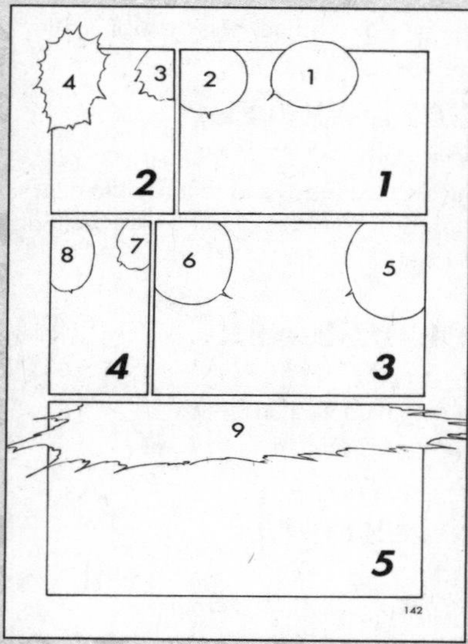
1
2
3
4
5
6
7
8
9
142

YOU'RE READING THE WRONG WAY!

THE ELUSIVE SAMURAI reads from right to left, starting in the upper-right corner. Japanese is read from right to left, meaning that action, sound effects, and word-balloon order are completely reversed from English order.

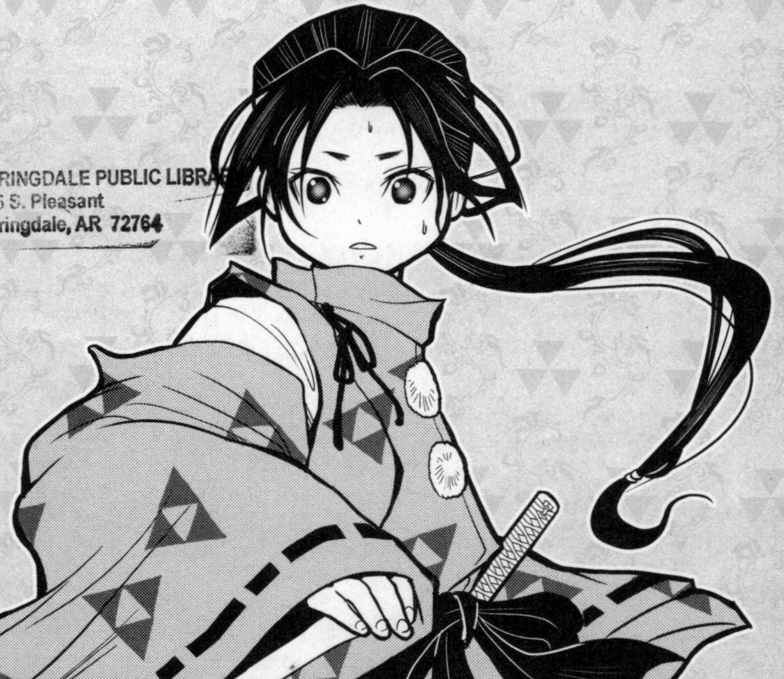